THE
CONSERVATIVE
RESURGENCE
in the Southern Baptist Convention

JAMES CARL HEFLEY, PH.D.

HANNIBAL BOOKS
921 Center, Suite A
Hannibal, MO 63401
Use coupon in back of book to order this and other helpful books

Dedicated to the Southern Baptist "people in the pews," who faithfully support the Southern Baptist Convention with their gifts, prayers and unheralded service.

Table of Contents

FOREWORD

History will no doubt record that the most definitive, objective and exhaustive account of the Southern Baptist Convention "Inerrancy Controversy" is the series of volumes penned by James C. Hefley. No work produced on the current issues in Southern Baptist life examines all the dynamics with the depth that Hefley does. Moreover, each book is quite objective as Hefley strives to present the issues from the "moderate" and "conservative" perspective alike. He has achieved his goal in a quite remarkable fashion. This is an accomplishment in itself and thus all factions can profit by it.

Now comes what he says will be the last book. Although Hefley vowed to make the 1990 volume his last, we can be grateful he has chosen to give us one more final appraisal of this current controversy, for it is still current. Although the New Orleans Southern Baptist Convention meeting of 1990 was a watershed and many felt the battle was over, much still needs to be said and understood regarding the fallout of the New Orleans Convention. This Hefley has undertaken to do and he does it in his usual able style. It has been a dramatic year and cries to be recorded.

Each chapter of the final Volume, The Conservative Resurgence in the Southern Baptist Convention makes its own unique contribution. Helpful are such chapters as: "Decades of Frustration" and "Eight Years of Resurgence" and "The Twelfth Win." These subjects present insights to aspects of the continuing controversy.

Further, the historical background of different phases of the inerrancy issue are most helpful, e.g. chapter sixteen, where a short but interesting historical sketch of Baylor University in Waco, Texas is outlined.

Most to be appreciated is Hefley's insight to the real dynamics of the various issues as they manifest themselves in all areas of Southern Baptist life. As a measure of the focus shifts away from national level concerns and more on local states, Hefley gives much help. Especially is this true concerning the controversy as it relates to state Baptist colleges.

Each chapter is well documented and no "loose ends" are left dangling. The book is very well researched and speaks of very able scholarship.

Therefore, it is without reservation I recommend this latest contribution of James C. Hefley to our understanding of Southern Baptists and the "Inerrancy Crisis." The prophetic element of the volume is such that it helps us to not only grasp what has taken place recently, but it aids us in seeing what may well take place in the future as Southern Baptists continue their struggle. This book will take its place along with the other five fine volumes and thus make its significant contribution.

Lewis A. Drummond, President
Southeastern Baptist Theological Seminary

PROLOGUE

"Harbingers From the Past"

In the year 1845 Baptists in 11 states broke away from the national Triennial Baptist Convention to establish their own convention. In the intervening 146 years, the Southern Baptist Convention has grown from 351,951 to over 15 million members in all 50 states. During this time the denomination survived a number of controversies, but none so far-reaching as the present one. Past controversies dealt with issues secondary to the authority of Scripture. Today's conflict centers on the nature and extent of Biblical truth and it is not exclusive to the SBC.

The division among American Baptists in 1845 did not come suddenly or by surprise. For over ten years some Baptist leaders in the South and West had talked of separation. Many western Baptist leaders resented the air of educational and moral superiority that they perceived among Eastern Baptists. In 1833 a western Baptist convention was convened. No fund-raising mechanism was established and the effort fizzled.

Southerners also thought their Northern brethren snobbish and neglectful of mission needs in the South. The national Home Mission Society finally sent James Huckins and William Tryon to plant churches in Texas. Both were warmly welcomed. Then a great fuss developed when eastern Baptist abolitionists learned that Huckins had purchased a slave, while Tryon had married a woman who owned slaves. The angry abolitionists organized their own mission society in the East to insure that their money did not go to support missionaries who owned slaves.

Some in the national Home Mission Society sought to assure the restive Southerners of their neutrality on the slave-owning issue. Georgia Baptists were not satisfied and submitted 51-year-old James E. Reeve, a slave-owning preacher, as a test for appointment by the Society. A beloved Georgia pastor, Reeve prayed and read Scripture to his slaves on a regular basis. Except for being a slave owner, he was as respected a test candidate as could be found. [1]

The national Executive Board met in Boston and turned Reeve down. His rejection triggered immediate plans to form a new denomination. The Alabama Baptist Convention, in November,

1844, called on the national convention to declare that slaveholders were as eligible as non-slaveholders for missionary appointment. The national board responded, "We can never be a party to any arrangement which would imply approbation of slavery."[2]

The Virginia Baptist Foreign Mission Society then called for a convention to meet "on Thursday before the 2nd Lord's day in May next" in Augusta, GA. Declared the Virginians: "From the Boston Board we separate, not because we reside [in] the South, but because they have adopted an unconstitutional and unscriptural principle . . . that holding slaves is, under all circumstances, incompatible with the office of the Christian ministry. . . . [We invite] all our brethren, North and South, East and West, who are aggrieved by the recent decision of the Board in Boston, and believe that their usefulness may be increased by cooperating with us, to attend the proposed meeting."[3]

The Virginia call suggested that other subjects besides missions could be discussed. Dr. W.B. Johnson, president of the South Carolina Convention, was convinced that an entirely new denominational structure was needed. Johnson had participated in the organization of the national convention in 1814 and had served as the convention president. He disliked the loose national structure, which allowed for the virtual independence of the mission societies from the national convention.

The South Carolina convention met the week before Augusta. Johnson "invited" fellow Baptists in the South to choose between two plans: one in which mission societies would be "separate and independent" of the larger body, or one which embodied "the whole Denomination together with separate and distinct Boards for each object of benevolent enterprise, located at different places, and all amenable to the Convention."[4]

Separation fever raged across the South. The only disagreement was on how far to go in breaking away from the national body. R.B.C. Howell of Nashville urged delay. Secession in May, he said, would give too much attention to rejection of Reeve by the Home Mission Society Board. It would be disrespectful to Northerners who thought the decision had been wrong.

Howell's argument did not prevail. According to SBC historian W.W. Barnes, 293 of 378 church-elected messengers, from 11 states, met at Augusta, May 8, 1945. Barnes says 34 messengers represented two or more constituencies and there are other names so closely alike that they may be the same person, suggesting other multiple representation.[5] The convention elected a committee, chaired by W.B. Johnson, which recommended the name, "Southern Baptist Convention." The messengers so voted.

This was no splinter, but a major split About half of all the Baptists in America were represented in the new Southern denomination. Although the leadership hoped that it would not be sectional, it turned out to be just that.

The issues in 1845 were sectionalism (despite the disclaimer by some leaders), insensitivity of denominational leaders to needs in the South, relationships of institutions to the national body, slavery and politics. The core issue was slavery, "pure and simple," as former SBC president Louie Newton told me in an interview before he died.[6]

The "primary source of today's controversy," according to our official 22-member Peace Committee, is "theological differences," with political causes as well. Denominational moderates say politics is the principal cause. This argument is weakened by the fact that well-known moderates signed, along with conservatives and "centrists," the Peace Committee report as accepted by the full Convention in 1987.

The theological issue, said the Peace Committee, is "more specifically, the ways in which the Bible is viewed." The Committee found "significant diversity in the understanding" of Article I "On Scripture" of the Baptist Faith and Message statements of 1925 and 1963. The Committee saw at least two separate and distinct interpretations of the article." One holds that 'truth without any mixture of error for its matter,' means all areas—historical, scientific, theological and philosophical. The other sees 'truth' as relating " 'only to matters of faith and practice.' "

The Committee cited four illustrations of this diversity, which "are intended to be illustrative but not exhaustive:

"(1) Some accept and affirm the direct creation and historicity of Adam and Eve while others view them instead as representative of the human race in its creation and fall.

"(2) Some understand the historicity of every event in Scripture as reported by the original source while others hold that the historicity can be clarified and revised by the findings of modern historical scholarship.

"(3) Some hold to the stated authorship of every book in the Bible while others hold that in some cases such attribution may not refer to the final author or may be pseudonymous.

"(4) Some hold that every miracle in the Bible is intended to be taken as an historical event while others hold that some miracles are intended to be taken as parabolic."

The Committee "found that most Southern Baptists see 'truth without any mixture of error for its matter' as meaning" the first statement in each example.[7]

However, the critical difference in the SBC today is not so simple as pitting errantists against inerrantists. There are many who espouse the latter belief—notably, Daniel Vestal—who have allied themselves with theological moderates. They would extend the parameters for denominational office to include those who say that while the text of the Bible has many historical and scientific errors, the Bible is true in "faith and practice." Conservatives say this will result only in a resumption of a debilitating liberal drift that was stopped by the resurgence of recent years. They argue: "How can the Bible be true in faith and practice, if it is not true in the text?"

In the chapters to follow we will attempt to trace this controversy from its roots to the present impasse, and hopefully provide a better perception for the future of the members, churches, associations, state conventions, agencies and institutions which make up America's largest evangelical denomination.

References

1 Biographical Sketches of Prominent Baptists, pp. 441-442. In death Reeve was "gathered, as a shock of corn fully ripe, into the garner of the Lord." His grave is a few miles west of Atlanta near the Pleasant Grove Baptist Church which he pastored from 1850-60.

2 Quoted by Robert A. Baker: The Southern Baptist Convention and Its People, 1607-1972, Broadman Press, Nashville, 1974, p. 159.

3 Quoted from the Religious Herald, April 10, 1845, p. 2 by W.W. Barnes: The Southern Baptist Convention, 1845-1953, Broadman Press, Nashville, 1954, p. 26.

4 Cited from the minutes of the special session and Johnson's address as printed in the Edgefield Advertiser, May 7, 1845, by Barnes, p. 27.

5 Barnes, op. cit., p. 29

6 The interview took place in 1976 at Newton's home in Atlanta. With the passing of Newton went much denominational history.

7 From the report of the Peace Committee as presented to and accepted by the Southern Baptist Convention, St. Louis, June 16-18, 1987.

Chapter 1

"The Roots of Today's Theological Conflict"

Diverse views on the nature of Biblical truth, comparable to that of today, scarcely existed, if at all, among Baptists when the SBC was founded. The inerrancy of Scripture was never questioned by the SBC founders, as is indicated by a sampling of views:

Jeremiah B. Jeter, first president of the Foreign Mission Board: "The manner of inspiration. . ,. is such as to preclude the possibility of error in the Scriptures."[1]

J.M. Frost, founder and first executive of the Sunday School Board: "Inspiration . . . is God's special work in the writer to guarantee the writing in making the record which God would have written.[2]

B.H. Carroll, founder of Southwestern Seminary: "The inspiration of the Bible does not mean that God said and did all that is said and done in the Bible" but "that the record of what is said and done is correct."[3]

Founders of other institutions and professors in seminaries for most of the first century of the Southern Baptist Convention believed much the same, with the notable exception of Crawford H. Toy, Professor of Old Testament Interpretation at Southern Seminary. Toy thought the flood-story in Genesis, for example, was "borrowed from the Assyrians or Babylonians, during or shortly before the exile. . . " He thought it "possible that in the serpent of Genesis 3, we have a survival of the dragon of Babylonian myth . . . woven into the general body of Jewish beliefs."[4] Toy lost both his position and his fiancee, the now celebrated Lottie Moon, because of his stated belief that the Bible was errant and in part mythical, although the Encyclopedia of Southern Baptists says only that he "resigned because of advanced views of biblical criticism which had become acceptable."[5] He moved to Harvard, which had long since fallen away from Christian orthodoxy and died a Unitarian.

Toy taught at Southern Seminary from 1869-79. For more than a century Western rationalism had been undermining trust in the historicity of Scripture, divine miracles and Biblical morality.

The 18th and 19th century rationalists assumed the Bible to be as errant as other ancient writings. They divided the creation account in Genesis, denied the unity and Mosaic authorship of the first five books of the Bible, split Isaiah into two books, post-dated prophecies until after their proclaimed fulfillment and attributed Biblical miracles to natural events that had been cloaked in a supernatural aura by simple-minded believers.

Darwin's new theory that life was evolving upward by the survival of the fittest served to further undermine confidence in the historical veracity of the Bible further. By Crawford Toy's time this new "scientific" way of thinking and studying the Bible was capturing the mind of many American theologians. With foundations undermined, Presbyterian, Methodist, Lutheran, Northern Baptist and many other denominational schools fell to heterodox ideas like dominoes. Southern Baptists, however, remained sheltered in the South and out of the rationalistic main stream. They hung on to orthodoxy, with Toy being the great exception.

"Fundamentals" and "Fundamentalists"

By 1910 the northern denominations were confused and dispirited. Many theologians not only denied the inerrancy of the Bible, but also the virgin birth and the deity of Christ. Seeking to bring Protestants back to orthodoxy, brothers Lyman and Molton Stewart financed the publication of a series of 12 small volumes, entitled, The Fundamentals: A Testimony of the Truth. The books were written and edited by leading conservative scholars and proclaimed "fundamental doctrines": the virgin birth and the deity of Christ, the bodily resurrection of Christ, the inerrancy and infallibility of Scripture, the substitutionary theory of the atonement and the imminent, physical second coming of Christ. Those who subscribed to these "fundamentals" became known as fundamentalists. Years later the term fundamentalist would take on a narrow, sectarian tone, but in the early 20th century, the label referred only to one who held to the fundamental doctrines presented in the 12 little books. The Fundamentals became, next to the Bible, the doctrinal guide of the "fundamentalist" bodies which split away from the Northern Baptists, Presbyterians, Methodists and Disciples of Christ denominations in the 1920's and '30's.

One of the scholars who helped prepare The Fundamentals was Edgar Y. Mullins, then President and Professor of Theology at Southern Baptist Seminary. Mullins is still considered by many as Southern Baptists' most important theologian. Yet his participation in The Fundamentals is not mentioned in Barnes' and Baker's histories of the SBC, nor in the article on him by Gaines S. Dobbins in the Encyclopedia of Southern Baptists. These writers may not have considered his involvement important. Or they may simply have decided that it was best readers not know.

It was inevitable that the liberal assumptions concerning the errancy of Scripture would filter into SBC institutions. No seminary professor, of course, dared deny the virgin birth and deity of Jesus, for calls would have come for dismissal immediately.

Evolution at Baylor

What some SBC teachers did was adopt the methodology of "higher criticism" and attempt to reconcile the theory of evolution with the creation account in Genesis. That could only be done by mythologizing parts of the Biblical record, as Toy did. They began presenting their new beliefs in the classroom and, inevitably, this became known.

The first big protest erupted at Baylor University, founded in the year of the SBC's birth by Judge Robert Baylor and the two missionaries, James Huckins and William Tryon, who had been sent from the east to appease complaints of neglect by Baptists in the south.[6] Around 1920 reports began coming that Grove S. Dow, a sociology professor, was using a textbook in his class that implied man evolved from the apes. To the fore came John Franklyn Norris, himself a Baylor graduate, a former editor of the Texas Baptist Standard and then pastor of First Baptist Church, Fort Worth where he once used a monkey in the pulpit in a sermon against evolution.

Norris charged in his church paper, The Searchlight, that Baylor President Samuel Palmer Brooks knew about Dow's evolutionary textbook, but still permitted him to use it in the classroom. Norris accused both Brooks and the state convention leaders of refusing to recognize the "longstanding infidelity" at Baylor.

Dow eventually resigned. The noisy Norris and his church were expelled from the state convention and the Tarrant County Baptist Association in 1922.[7]

Crowley vs. Texas Ecclesiasticism

The following year, a 22-year-old ministerial student named Dale Crowley, was "startled and bewildered" as he watched history professor C.S. Fothergill draw a diagram of man's "family tree," showing that man had evolved from a primordial germ cell.[8]

Crowley, who is still living today, asked Fothergill, "But, Professor, how does this theory square with the Genesis account of creation." According to Crowley, Fothergill replied that "Genesis tells the story of creation, but the way to interpret it is another thing. Modern scholarship believes that the method of creation is evolution."

Other students jumped into the argument. The class, by Crowley's remembrance, ended in confusion.

Crowley and two other ministerial students went to the professor "to keep the record straight." Fothergill, Crowley recalls, became angry and declared a "number of things in Genesis . . . could never have happened," including the story of Noah and the ark.

"By now," Crowley says, "we knew . . . we were dealing with an infidel. We asked, 'Professor, since you do not believe the Bible, do you think it is honorable to teach on the Baylor faculty, receiving your salary from people who do believe the Bible?' "

Fothergill, Crowley says, "looked on us with disdain and an air of contempt. 'What do I care about what you students think of my beliefs,' he angrily countered and walked away in a rage."

Crowley and his friends took their case to President Brooks who "defend[ed] the evolutionary hypothesis," but said he would talk to the professor. The three informed the student ministerial association which voted 43-6 to commend their actions.

Norris heard of what the students had done and sent a representative to interview Crowley who "respectfully refused to discuss the matter with him and sent word to Dr. Norris that I was determined to let the matter be handled through regular and proper channels."

Months dragged by. Crowley talked to Lee Scarborough, president of Southwestern Seminary. As the "shocking facts were presented to him," Crowley recalls, "Dr. Scarborough would shake his head and say, 'It doesn't look good to me. Something must be done about it.' " At Scarborough's request, Crowley wrote up the details for George W. Truett, a Baylor trustee and the renowned pastor of First Baptist Church, Dallas.

In the meantime, President Brooks declared in the Baylor Bulletin, "Creation is a process and evolution may be defined as that process. Evolution is all right if the Bible is rightly interpreted."

The Tarrant County Association then went on record as "disapproving" Brooks' statement and passed a resolution urging the state convention to investigate all Baptist schools to determine whether evolution was being taught.

The Baptist Standard commended the association and said that evolutionism, if found, should be "extirpated root and branch."

The Baylor trustees investigated and found not "a vestige of truth in the charge . . . that there is evolution in Baylor."

Crowley now "realiz[ed] for the first time that there was something even worse than evolutionism; and that was an ecclesiasticism that would cover it up, protect it and defend it! It was difficult for me to understand it, but I now realized that [on this] issue Frank Norris was right and the [denominational] leaders were wrong."

Crowley then went to Norris who published the story under large red letter headlines in his Searchlight. A thousand copies were sent to the Baylor campus and, according to Crowley, "pandemonium broke out."

President Brooks, Crowley says, "whipped up the student body into white heat. Streamer headlines appeared in the Lariat, the campus paper, such as, 'Seniors Ask Misled Students to Get Out.' " Crowley was "branded as a traitor and as he walked across the campus heard cat calls.

Crowley was warned that if he didn't leave Baylor, he would be expelled. President Brooks told the Baylor faculty that certain students of Baylor had been paid by Norris for spying on the school. Crowley denied this, saying he held "no personal grievances" against Brooks and the faculty. "I believe Baylor University is the greatest school in our land — but Baylor is not free from evolution, the rankest form of infidelity. And this I can prove and will."

The faculty passed a resolution, calling Crowley a "disloyal" student. An hour later the dean notified him that he was "suspended ... "

Crowley sent a letter to Brooks, dated October 23, 1924, "request[ing] the honor and right of appearing before the Baylor faculty, in open session [to] defend every statement that I have made."

Brooks, according to Crowley, said the "issue" was "closed."

After Brooks did not reply to his second request to speak to the faculty, Crowley packed his bags and left. The First Baptist Church of Texas City called him as pastor.

Pastors and laymen brought pressure to bear on President Brooks. Professor Fothergill was forced to resign, "on the grounds," to Crowley recalls, "not of his evolutionary teachings, but because he was responsible for the controversy."

Fothergill published a statement in the Waco News-Tribune on October 19, declaring, according to Crowley, "his disbelief in the creation story and the record of Noah's ark" and asking for reinstatement.

Crowley appealed for the lifting of his suspension on the basis of the professor's statement. His appeal was rejected.

He wrote twice to Governor Pat Neff, then chairman of Baylor's trustees and asked for a hearing before the board. Neff did not respond, Crowley says. Crowley then announced through the press that he intended to appeal his expulsion to the state convention which met at the First Baptist Church of Dallas a few weeks later with over 4,000 messengers.

The Baylor controversy was the main topic of discussion in the hallways and indeed, the reason many had come, but the leadership ignored the issue until Crowley walked to the rostrum and called out, "Mr. Moderator!"

The moderator asked for what purpose he had addressed the chair.

Crowley, who was "never so scared in all my life," identified himself as "the student suspended by the Baylor faculty for exposing the evolution of Professor C.S. Fothergill. "Mr. Moderator, I appealed to the faculty for a hearing and it was denied me; and I subsequently appealed to the Trustees for a hearing, but the same has not been granted. I now appeal to this Convention that I be given a hearing in this matter."

Governor Neff was already on his feet. "Mr. Moderator, as Chairman of the Board of Trustees of Baylor University, I rise to promise the speaker and to promise the Convention that we will give him a hearing in due time."

Shortly thereafter, Crowley was invited to appear before a called meeting of the Board in Waco and bring a paper stating the details in connection with his request for readmittance to Baylor.

Only the five local members of the full board of 21 trustees were present. Crowley says he "knew instinctively that I could not trust my case with those men, because they had often made it known they were for Dr. Brooks, right or wrong, so I objected: 'Gentlemen, I was promised by Governor Neff . . . that I would be given a fair hearing by the Board of Trustees. This is not the Board of Trustees and therefore I decline to present my appeal. . .'"

Crowley wrote Neff, explaining why he had left the meeting. Several months later, the Board Secretary notified him of a hearing, again at Waco. Crowley brought a court reporter to this meeting.

Neff was there to preside, but only nine other trustees were present, one short of a quorum. Neff asked Crowley if he was willing to go ahead. Crowley read his appeal, then asked if there were any questions.

According to Crowley's record, one of the trustees then moved that "we . . . not consider [this matter] until we can go into executive session with a full quorum present." The motion was seconded and quickly adopted. Governor Neff told Crowley, "If we need you, we will call for you." Crowley objected in vain to the procedure.

The trustees later met in executive session with a full quorum and denied Crowley's request for reinstatement. Crowley later heard that the principal argument against his appeal was that reinstatement would be a victory for J. Frank Norris. Crowley says he was also told that President Brooks had threatened to resign, if he was reinstated.

Crowley then announced that he would appeal again to the next state convention. Publicity in the newspapers and in Norris' paper brought a flood of supportive mail. Many who had dismissed Norris' charges of evolution at Baylor before, now believed he had been telling the truth.

At the 1925 convention, Crowley was granted time to make his statement. Crowley noted that he had not been given a fair hearing by the trustees. He asked for a "different kind of hearing," that the Convention name a special 25-member committee to "make a full investigation of my suspension from Baylor University." Crowley pledged that he would be "happy to abide" by the decision of such a committee.

The revered George Truett rose and raised the point of order that the matter was within the province of the trustees and that it was their responsibility alone. The moderator referred the matter to the Executive Committee.

Crowley now felt his only remaining recourse was to take his appeal to messengers in an outside meeting. Norris quickly had handbills printed that announced he and Crowley would speak at four p.m. at a nearby vacant lot. The crowd jammed the area to hear the two men.

The trustees met that night and the next day Governor Neff went to Crowley's hotel to tell him that he had been reinstated.

Crowley never went back to Baylor. It was the middle of the term, he says. His church had grown so large that he felt it would be unfair to them and he did not want to return to the unfriendly climate at Baylor.

Nevertheless, Crowley's persistence gave him hero status in the minds of many Texas Baptists. His marriage the following year was performed by J.B. Leavell, pastor of First Church, Houston. Later he joined up with Fundamental Baptists and moved to Washington, D.C. where he developed the nationally known "Bible Quizmaster" radio program and where he also helped establish the National Prayer Breakfast.

At 90 he continues a daily broadcast, publishes a paper called Capital Voice, sells books and tapes and speaks as he has strength.

Dale Crowley is not mentioned in the articles on Baylor and J. Frank Norris in the Encyclopedia of Southern Baptists. Nor does his name appear in the W. W. Barnes and Robert A. Baker histories of the SBC. One of his sons happens to be Robert Crowley, pastor of Montrose Baptist Church in Rockville, Maryland, the largest SBC church in the Maryland-Delaware Convention. The younger Crowley served as chairman of trustees at Southeastern Seminary during the period when SBC conservatives wrested control of the seminary from moderate trustees and their president, Randall Lolley.

The Widening Conflict

Protests against the teaching of evolution in Baptist schools in the 1920's spread far beyond Texas as Norris' Searchlight and other papers spread the story. Pastors and laity in other state conventions demanded that their schools be watched to prevent such instruction.

President E.Y. Mullins told the 1922 Southern Baptist Convention: "First, we will not tolerate in our denominational schools any departure from the great fundamentals of the faith in the name of science falsely so-called. Second, we will not be unjust to our teachers, nor curtail unduly their God-given right to investigate truth in the realm of science. Firm faith and free research is our noble Baptist ideal. Third, we will be loyal to every fact which is established in any realm of research, just as we are loyal to the supreme fact of Christ, His virgin birth, His sinless life, His atoning death, His resurrection and present reign."[9] Mullins received thunderous applause.

An alarmed committee of Baptist educators, apparently trying to head off a purge of faculties, asked professors "not to use the textbooks in their curriculum which are calculated to undermine the faith of the students in the Bible. If, in certain departments of the curriculum, textbooks cannot be found which are not, in their teaching, destructive of the faith of the students in the inspiration and inerrancy of the Bible, the teachers . . . ought to be of such pronounced faith in the Bible and of such learning. . . as to be able to so explain the defects of the textbooks as to magnify the message of the Bible rather than to discredit it . . . "

The educators quoted from the SBC Education Board in recommending that "if a faculty member of a Baptist college be charged with heretical or immoral conduct, let an attempt or several attempts be made to settle the point at issue by taking it up either with the accused party or with the president or with the trustees and, failing with these three, separately or combined, then publicity may be given it. Our schools should not be pampered nor treated as if they were yet in swaddling clothes."[10]

The 1922 convention passed a recommendation that a joint committee of nine Southern Baptists and nine Northern Baptists be appointed at the 1923 conventions of both bodies "with the duty of preparing a statement of faith and polity briefly embodying the basic and fundamental principles and beliefs of Baptists."[11]

At the 1923 convention, President Mullins again decried attacks upon the Bible and the supernatural because of alleged discoveries in science and the teaching of hypotheses as though they were facts. That convention adopted Mullins' statement as its own views.[12]

The Northern convention failed to adopt a confession of faith. With pressures mounting the SBC appointed a committee, with Mullins as chairman, to report to the 1925 annual meeting in Memphis.

This was the year of the famous Scopes trial in Dayton, TN. The evolution question boiled over into the Memphis convention. Still fearful of a crackdown, the Baptist Educators' Association urged schools to "avoid alliance with either Fundamentalism or Modernism." The educators also declared that the "Bible cannot be taken literally and never was meant to be."[13]

The educators' statement stirred up a furor. T.T. Martin from Mississippi, a leading critic of "liberalism" in the schools proposed that the SBC divide: "Let all who endorse . . . this stand taken by the Southern Baptist Educational Association go into one convention; let all who reject and repudiate this action go into the other convention." Martin warned of "fearful division and strife" if this were not done.[14]

Defining Inspiration

A possible split was averted by adopting the Baptist Faith and Message statement as presented by the Mullins committee. The document included a revision of the 1833 Confession of Baptists in New Hampshire, covering major doctrines historically held by Baptists and a short section on science and religion taken from Mullins' address at the 1923 convention.

The New Hampshire article on the Bible was included with the statements that the Bible has "truth, without mixture of error, for its matter" and that it is the "supreme standard of Christian union . . . " A statement was added to the preface that the Confession was "not to be used to hamper freedom of thought or investigation in [non-religious] realms of life."

Some thought that a sentence in the section on science and religion did not go far enough against evolution: "Man was created by the special act of God as recorded in Scripture." Committee member C.P. Stealey sought to add, "This creative activity was separate and distinct from any other work of God and was not conditioned upon antecedent changes in previously created forms of life."

Stealey's amendment was defeated and the Confession adopted. But the next year, SBC President George MacDaniel declared, "This Convention accepts Genesis as teaching that man was the special creation of God and rejects every theory, evolution or other, which teaches that man originated in, or came by way of, a lower animal ancestry."

Then a motion by M.E. Dodd of Louisiana passed, calling for MacDaniels' statement to be adopted as the sentiment of the convention and the creation-evolution issue be dropped from further discussion.[15]

The passage of the new Baptist Faith and Message statement, along with Dodd's motion, brought great relief. It was hoped that the actions would serve two purposes: (1) fend off attacks from Norris and other "independent Baptists" on the right and (2) put teachers in denominational schools on notice that they could be fired for teaching that the Bible was in error.

Thus the protests that started at Baylor University led directly to the adoption of the Baptist Faith and Message and to the convention taking strong stands against the teaching of evolution and Biblical errancy in Baptist schools. However, the problems did not go away. Indeed they have been magnified in the denominational struggle of recent years.

This is the same Baylor University which by majority vote of trustees voted September 21, 1990 to break away from the Baptist General Convention of Texas to ensure academic freedom and to "distanc[e] ourselves from a group of extremists," according to President Herbert Reynolds.[16] Educator Jim Parker, voicing the feelings of many conservatives, called the Baylor breakaway a "Machiavellian move . . . reminiscent of Adolf Hitler's seizure of the Sudetenland or Japan's surprise attack on Pearl Harbor."[17] This new Baylor crisis will be considered in detail in a later chapter. In immediate chapters to follow, we will continue with the march of events leading to the crisis of this present hour.

References

1 J.B. Jeter: "The Inspiration of the Scriptures," in Baptist Doctrines, Edited by Charles A. Jenkens, St. Louis, Chancy R. Barns, 1881, pp. 49, 62, 68, 69.

2 J.M. Frost: Our Church Life, Nashville, Sunday School Board, 1899, pp. 159, 160.

3 B.H. Carroll: Inspiration of the Bible, Compiled and Edited by J.B. Cranfill, Fleming H. Revell, New York, 1930, pp. 20, 32.

4 Crawford H. Toy: Judaism and Christianity, Little, Brown and Company, Boston, 1890, pp. 194-195.

5 Article on Toy by Gaines S. Dobbins in Encyclopedia of Southern Baptists, Volume 2, Broadman Press, Nashville, 1958, p. 1423.

6 C.E. Bryant, "Baylor University," Article in Encyclopedia of Southern Baptists, Volume 1, Broadman Press, Nashville, 1958, p. 150.

7 Wilburn S. Taylor: "John Franklyn Norris," Article in Encyclopedia of Southern Baptists, Volume 2, Broadman Press, Nashville, 1958, p. 983. Also Douglas Wong: "History of BU's Battle With Fundamentalists Begins in 1920s," Waco Tribune Herald, November 11, 1990, p. 11A.

8 Except when otherwise noted, the information relating to Dale Crowley and the controversy at Baylor in the 1920's is taken from Crowley's biography, My Life a Miracle, National Bible Knowledge Association, Washington, D.C., 1971, pp. 27-52; Dale Crowley: "Battle for the Bible In SBC — When It Actually Began," March 1, April 1 and June 1, 1990 issues of Capital Voice. The authenticity of Crowley's material is supported by verbatim reports, including a stenographer's record of one meeting with trustees, a petition supporting Crowley by Baylor ministerial students, statements by Crowley, a letter from Crowley to President Brooks and Brooks' reply in which the president refused to

consider Crowley's request for reinstatement. The Baylor controversy of the 1920s deserves more complete study by researchers who have the wherewithal to comb through old issues of the Texas convention's Baptist Standard, J. Frank Norris' Searchlight, convention minutes and news articles in Texas papers.

9 Southern Baptist Convention Annual, 1922, pp. 35, 36.

10 Southern Baptist Convention Annual, 1922, p. 34.

11 Southern Baptist Convention Annual, 1922, p. 21.

12 Southern Baptist Convention Annual, 1923, p. 19. As cited by Baker, op. cit., p. 398.

13 Walter Shurden: Not a Silent People, Broadman Press, Nashville, 1972, p. 96.

14 Op. cit., p. 97.

15 Southern Baptist Convention Annual, 1925.

16 "Conversation With the President," The Baylor Line, November, 1990, p. 8.

17 "Extremists Seize Baylor: Day of Infamy, Conservative Texas Baptist Report, October, 1990, p. 1.

Chapter 2

"Decades of Frustration"

Fifty-four years of frustration for conservatives stretched between 1925 and 1979, the year when the conservative resurgence really took hold.

The Baptist Faith and Message confession didn't end the concern about the teaching of evolution. As the 1926 convention approached, it became obvious that some messengers were still not convinced the matter had been settled. Fearing that the fuss could go on for years, convention president George W. McDaniel, pastor of the First Baptist Church of Richmond and a trustee of Richmond College, declared in his presidential sermon:

"This Convention accepts Genesis as teaching that man was the special creation of God, and rejects every theory, evolution or other, which teaches that man originated in, or came by way of, a lower animal ancestry."[1]

By pre-arrangement, M.E. Dodd moved that McDaniel's statement become the sentiment of the Convention, "and that from this point on no further consideration be given to this subject, and that the Convention go forward with the . . . main kingdom causes to which God has set our hearts and hands."[2] The Convention then called on all Convention institutions, boards and missionaries to affirm McDaniel's statement. That resolution was adopted.

When it became evident that some faculties were dragging their feet on evolution, the Baptist General Convention of Oklahoma voted to withhold undesignated funds of the newly established Cooperative Program from SBC seminaries whose faculties refused to sign the McDaniel statement. When the faculties still did not comply, the Oklahoma convention extended the embargo at their 1928 convention. The funds were finally released that year.

Many truly believed that the adoption of the Baptist Faith and Message Confession would stop the perceived drift toward the kind of liberalism that was undermining other mainline denominations. They failed to realize that a statement of faith was only as good as its application in Convention institutions. That could not occur if institutional staff and teachers did not subscribe to the BFM, as was the case at seminaries where faculty signed the Abstract of

Principles which called the Bible "infallible in purpose." Many
teachers did not take this to mean textual inerrancy. An errant
Bible could still be without error in the faith doctrines which were
taught, even though the Abstract author, Basily Manly, Jr. wrote
in The Bible Doctrine of Inspiration Explained and Vindicated that
"an uninspired Bible . . . . would furnish no infallible standard of
truth. It would leave us liable to all the mistakes incident to failure
of the writers, to their errors in judgment, or their defective
expressions of correct thought."[3]

Still, SBC membership more than doubled in the next 15 years.
The Northern convention, which had declined to adopt a statement
of faith and embraced liberalism in some institutions, lost
hundreds of churches to the General Association of Regular
Baptists (1932), the Conservative Baptist Association (1947) and
the independent Fundamentalist Baptist movement. The SBC
suffered few defections during this time.

John Birch Versus Mercer

When a doctrinal protest did occur in the south, the blame was
usually laid on J. Frank Norris. That was the case at Georgia's
Mercer University in 1939 where young John Birch, the top
student scholar, led a group of ministerial students in charging
that Bible professor John D. Freeman and four other teachers were
teaching heresy. Freeman, they alleged, believed that Adam and
Eve were mythical, Christ's death was not essential for salvation
and the Biblical writings were tangled in the superstitions of the
time and pocked with contradictions.

The Georgia Baptist editor refused to print the charges of Birch
and his friends. Mercer president Spright Dowell thought Norris
was behind the complaints. However, the uproar became so great
that Mercer trustees and Dowell held a "committee of inquiry" in
the college chapel at which both the students and professors spoke.
When the "inquiry" ended, the student "prosecutors" walked
outside to face an angry crowd who supported the professors. The
police had to be called to keep the peace.

The committee exonerated all the professors but Dr. Freeman,
who said only that he had made "some mistakes." Freeman soon
resigned and slipped quietly away.

Dowell sought to expel Birch, then backed down when a trustee
worried that Birch might sue. After graduation, Birch felt
estranged from Southern Baptists and enrolled at Norris'
"seminary" in Fort Worth before going to China as a missionary
that fall. Norris, however, had played no part in stirring up the
Mercer conflict.

The 1939 fracas at Mercer was reported in the New York
Times, but was given little play in SBC denominational papers
which tended to shun internal controversy.

Birch achieved hero status as an American intelligence officer in China during World War II. Shortly after the war ended, he was brutally murdered. Pro-Communists in the U.S. government suppressed a military report showing Birch had been killed by Chinese Communists, perhaps because he knew too much about their post-war plans. When the cover-up was finally disclosed years later, it set off a furor in the U.S. Congress. Robert Welch heard about the disclosure and, in 1958, named his new "anti-Communist" society after Birch.

The Rise of Neo-Orthodoxy

The liberalism which had riddled northern denominations proved to be impotent. Neo-orthodoxy became the avant-garde theology of the 1940's and '50's. Barthianism, as it was also called, said God had revealed Himself in an imperfect Bible in mighty "acts," culminating in the Incarnation. Yet the new theology assumed, as liberals did, that the Biblical writers were shackled to the superstitions and errors of their times. Some Southern Baptist teachers brought back Barthian ideas from their studies in other graduate schools. They began using textbooks by neo-orthodox writers. They saw the new theology as allowing belief in supernatural acts without holding to an inerrant Bible. Thus came the theology and critical methodology which would ultimately lead to a rising up by SBC conservatives.

The Baptist Faith and Message declared the Bible to have "truth, without mixture of error for its matter." Neo-orthodox SBC teachers affirmed that publicly, while privately believing that only faith truth, as interpreted by the Holy Spirit to each individual, was authoritative. Thus a Biblical event — such as Jonah being swallowed by a "great fish" — could be interpreted as a story, with the "teaching" applied as truth.

Retired Kentucky editor C.R. Daley spilled the "beans" in a taped lecture to a Southern Seminary class in 1984: "Doctrinally or inerrancy wise, the poison [conservatives] claim [today] is Biblical criticism. That's what they are after . . . When the seminaries started teaching Biblical criticism and started talking about documentary hypothesis and other conclusions, that's when the poison started. When I came to [Southern] Seminary [in the 1940], I can remember only one professor who stood up strongly for the Mosaic authorship of the [first five books of the Bible]. . . The seminaries have been moving in that direction. . ."[4]

How the SBC was "Managed"

Convention leaders who functioned as an informal, unofficial control group believed that administrators could keep the new theology within manageable bounds They feared most a reaction from the right. To hold down the right, they had to elect "cooperative, conservative" Convention officers who would reassure the people that "all Southern Baptist teachers believe the Bible."

During the decades before the conservative resurgence began, the far-reaching powers of the elected SBC president were not widely known. It was he who appointed the Committee on Committees, which nominated the Committee on Boards (now Nominations), which nominated new trustees to replace those rotating off the agency boards each year, which elected administrators and set policies in agencies.

The control group was made up of key administrators and a few influential pastors of large churches. The president made his appointments from names submitted by these people and other cooperative denominational "servants." Elected trustees served more for the honor of the office and, in effect, rubber-stamped most executive decisions. The executives, for their part, were able to keep down in-house controversies by controlling the flow of news to denominational papers. Thus a very few people, in a time when denominational leaders were revered, could manage the vast Southern Baptist Convention.

Informal control groups in the states networked with the national leadership. The state people held the keys to career advancement for pastors. A pastorless church, committed to the denominational heritage, usually checked with the state convention executive and/or the associational director of missions before calling a new shepherd. If the executive, or one of his staff, labeled a candidate non-cooperative, the preacher was not considered. Short of building a big church from scratch, a blacklisted preacher could only depend on the Lord and a small circle of friends. The only exceptions were the conservative pastors of the super churches whose careers could not be managed. That, according to W.A. Criswell, is why only a few "big preachers" took stands in the early years of the conservative movement. "The little preachers knew they'd be blackballed," Criswell said.[5]

The state control groups managed their conventions much as the national groups kept electing the "right" people in the larger denomination. "Cooperative" pastors, supportive state "headquarters" staff which included the influential editor, and administrators of colleges affiliated with the state convention worked together to keep their constituency on the "unity amidst diversity" path. There was nothing innately evil in this; it was a way by which democratic organizations were directed.

The national "managers" communicated by letter and phone and met informally in hotels during the annual convention and when they came to Nashville for meetings of the Executive Committee.

Old letters, discovered in the archives of Oklahoma Baptist University, disclose how the control group elected their man as president in 1960.[6] The correspondents included five prominent pastors — J.D. Grey, Ramsey Pollard, Carl Bates, Wayne Dehoney, Herschel Hobbs and Mrs. R.L. Mathis, president of the WMU. Grey, noted for his jocularity, was a former SBC president. Pollard was concluding his second term as president. Dehoney and Bates would later be elected. Most of the letters are addressed to Hobbs, or are copies sent to him of mail sent to other persons that make reference to others in the informal group.

November 18, 1960, Pollard wrote Hobbs that he was the group's choice to succeed Pollard as president in 1961. As the incumbent, Pollard didn't think he should nominate Hobbs. The group would meet, he said, and decide on the right person.

January 7, 1961, Dehoney wrote Bates that there had been a meeting and the consensus was that Dehoney should nominate Hobbs. Dehoney noted that Roy McClain, pastor of First Church, Atlanta was going to be nominated. Dehoney did not favor McClain.

More letters flew back and forth. March 29, Grey assured his "pal" Hobbs that his election was "in the bag."

Bates agreed to nominate Hobbs. Harold Seever would second the nomination. Marie Mathis asked to speak also, but it was decided that this might not be best since some might think she was taking advantage of her position as president of the WMU.

Further correspondence shows growing support for Hobbs, including backing from Winfred Moore, pastor of First Church, Amarillo, TX.

May 17, Grey sent Bates some suggestions for the nominating speech. That same day, Grey wrote Hobbs, "Field Marshall 'Master Bates' and a few of his lieutenants and sergeants like me continue to be busy."

The convention was held in St. Louis, May 23-26. Hobbs, McClain and W.O. Vaught, Jr. of Arkansas were nominated. McClain withdrew and Hobbs then defeated Vaught.

The Elliott Controversy

Hobbs' first term in office was overshadowed by protests against Midwestern Seminary professor Ralph H. Elliott's The Message of Genesis, published by the Sunday School Board's Broadman Press. Elliott classified as non-historical and error-prone the stories of Adam and Eve, Cain and Abel, Noah and the Flood, the Tower of Babel and some events in the life of Abraham. Elliott, in typical neo-orthodox fashion, maintained that error in the literary vehicle didn't necessarily mean that the faith message or the purpose of God in the message was in error.[7]

Broadman editors apparently assumed that the book would be

acceptable as part of the theological diversity among Southern Baptists. If so, they assumed incorrectly. K. Owen White, the influential pastor of First Church, Houston, called the book "death in the pot . . . liberalism, pure and simple, a sort of rationalistic criticism [which] can lead [us] only to . . . disintegration as a great New Testament denomination."[8] Sixteen of the 28 SBC state editors joined White and other pastors in criticizing the book.[9]

Nevertheless, BSSB trustees urged Broadman to continue publishing a diversity of theological views. The Midwestern Seminary Board declared Elliott a "loyal servant of Southern Baptists. . ."[10]

The 1962 convention in San Francisco, where Hobbs was re-elected,was the 1920's all over again. It was dominated by criticisms of the Elliott book. Messengers unanimously supported a motion by K. Owen White, reaffirming "faith in the entire Bible as the authoritative, authentic, infallible Word of God." A second White motion passed by a large majority, expressing "abiding and unchanging objection to the dissemination of theological views in any of our seminaries which would undermine such faith in the historical accuracy and doctrinal integrity of the Bible. . . " The motion called on trustees to "remedy at once those situations where such views now threaten our historic position."[11]

Motions were defeated instructing the Sunday School Board to stop selling the Elliott book. The Board stopped anyway. Midwestern trustees asked Elliott to ease up on teaching higher criticism and not give his Genesis book to another publisher. Elliott re-published the book and was fired. He took a church in the Northern convention. C.R. Daley later slammed the trustees for the firing action. If Elliott is "a heretic," Daley said, "then he is one of many . . . . Professors in all our seminaries know that Elliott is in the same stream of thinking with most of them, and is more in the center than some of them."[12]

A "New" Confession of Faith

The anger over Broadman's publication of Elliott's neo-orthodox commentary was so great that President Hobbs and Porter Routh, Executive Secretary-Treasurer of the Executive Committee, feared a split if trust was not restored. Routh suggested that a committee be appointed, chaired by Hobbs and with state convention presidents serving as members, to draw up a new confession of faith for presentation at the 1963 convention in Kansas City. Again, this was a replay of the mid-1920's.

The committee inserted verbatim the phrase, "The Bible has . . . truth, without any mixture of error," from the 1925 BFM and the 1833 New Hampshire confession. Then, in a tip of the hat to neo-orthodoxy, they added, "The criterion by which the Bible is to be interpreted is Jesus Christ." And they stated in the preamble,

"Confessions are only guides in interpretation."[13] Most conservatives went along, not realizing how loosely some denominational employees took the phrase, "truth, without any mixture of error."

Hobbs' reputation as a conservative helped prevent wide-scale defections from fellow conservatives. As the consensus candidate for the "control group," he maintained the "unity amidst diversity" that the control group felt was necessary to keep the denomination together. Hobbs, now 93, says that his generation sought to steer the SBC between "extremes."[14]

The 1963 statement, like the 1925 confession, did not provide the house cleaning conservatives wanted. The same leadership picked the presidential candidates and promoted them informally to other influential persons across the Convention. The presidents appointed the people whom the consensus group wanted. The Committee on Boards nominated trustees who would not challenge institutional policies.

In the 1960's, as now, Baptist institutions tended to be more liberal in the east than in the west. Consequently, Gerald C. Primm, M.O. Owens, Jr. and a few others in North Carolina were more concerned about doctrinal integrity than, say, conservatives in Texas. When The Sword and the Trowel, founded by Charles H. Spurgeon, discontinued publication in England, Primm took the name for a new independent publication. Spurgeon had fought valiantly to maintain a commitment to Biblical inerrancy among English Baptists. Primm said in his first issue in January, 1969, "The Trowel will be used [in the SBC] just as zealously to build Zion's walls."[15]

The first article in the new Trowel was "The Evangelical Imperative" by Clark H. Pinnock, a young professor at New Orleans Seminary, who said, "[The SBC is] facing the greatest crisis in all her history. . . . Not the Virgin Birth or the Creation, but the very existence of divine truth [is being questioned]."[16]

Young Paige Patterson, then a student at New Orleans and the son of the Executive Director of the Texas Convention, resonated with Pinnock. Before coming to the seminary, Patterson had been shocked by teachings in Baptist-owned Hardin Simmons University in Abilene where he ran into professors who "not only doubted what I had been taught at home, but ridiculed it."

Paige Patterson says he was astonished that some professors depicted the Genesis account of creation as a myth and that other Bible stories might be more fable than history. "I'd stand up and ask for equal time," he recalls. "The professor would say sarcastically, 'Let's listen to the 13th century version. Go ahead, Paige.'"[17]

His father had told him how great Christian-founded universities such as Yale, Brown and Harvard lost their Christian orthodoxy. Paige saw SBC institutions drifting in the same direction.

He had heard his father, W.A. Criswell and others preach against creeping liberalism with no results. The bureaucracy that controlled Southern Baptist organizations seemed not to care. Indeed, as Patterson became more vocal in expressing his concern, he was blacklisted as a Norrisite by some organization men.

Patterson Meets Pressler

He completed his Bachelor of Divinity and was admitted to graduate study in New Orleans. Late one evening in March, 1967 he answered a knock. The callers introduced themselves as Paul and Nancy Pressler from Houston. They were at the seminary to attend a laymen's conference. A mutual friend had suggested to Pressler that he should "get together" with young Paige Patterson because "you two see things alike."

Patterson picks up the story: "It was about ten o'clock, I was tired of studying, so I said, 'Let's go down to the Cafe du Monde and have beignets and cafe au lait.' So we went with our wives to the French Quarter. We were down there until after midnight discussing things we were concerned about. And the judge asked me one question: 'Who is going to do something about [the liberal drift]?' And I said, 'Well, God will raise up somebody.' And he said, 'Why not you?' I said, 'I'm just a student.' He said, 'Somebody needs to devote themselves across a period of months,' which ended up being a period of years, to understand thoroughly how the whole Convention works and what the processes are [to bring about change]. I said, 'Well, the main reason it's never happened is that every time somebody attempted to do it, they were doing it as a Lone Ranger, and as a result they got ruined.' He said, 'That's where I come in. If you're willing to work with me, maybe with my organizational background and your knowledge of Southern Baptists, maybe together we can do something.' And so we agreed that night that what we would do is to make contacts across the Convention with those who held our same concerns and that we would thoroughly study the Constitution and Bylaws of the Convention to understand how it worked. It ended up being a ten-year track, locating the people of like mind and studying the Constitution and Bylaws."[18]

Pressler, a Sunday school teacher in Second Baptist Church, Houston, knew something about the decadent effects of liberal theology. As a student at Phillips Exeter, an Ivy League prep school, he had seen "a church there . . . that was on its last leg because [of] theological liberalism." Pressler "came on down to Princeton . . . and saw a university that, again, had been founded by believers to train people in the Word of God, which was then completely secular and humanistic and was undermining the basic truths of the gospel."[19]

Pressler saw the "acuteness of the problem" among Southern Baptists when some of his Houston Bible class students went to Baylor University and "being very much confused, . . . asked that I come to Waco and meet with them, . . . and see their textbooks, and listen to what had been going on in Baylor."

In 1977 Pressler went to Baylor and read a textbook that "talk[ed] about the errors in Daniel [and] the historical inaccuracies." The book had been co-authored, Pressler says, "by the one who would soon become chairman of the Baylor Religion Department, and who was teaching the same thing . . . in the class, according to the students. I felt that I was not going to sit around any longer, and help finance the destruction of the faith of my young people. Something had to be done."[20]

Criswell Versus the Professors

W.A. Criswell was elected president at the 1969 convention in New Orleans. Criswell made appointments from a list provided by Porter Routh, Executive Secretary-Treasurer of the SBC Executive Committee. "I regret now," Criswell said in 1985, "that I was unwittingly a part of the process that permitted our Convention to reach the place where we have men in our seminaries who deny the truth of parts of the Bible."[21]

Criswell was not popular with the SBC's left wing. Nor was Broadman Press in their good graces, for Broadman had published in 1969 Criswell's Why I Preach That the Bible Is Literally True. Criswell wrote: "There is no contradiction in the Bible to any fact of science," adding that "no small part of our problem [in seeing errors] lies in our stupidity."[22]

Criswell slammed neo-orthodox theology: "Many of those who are paid to stand in our pulpits and defend the truth of God are now the very ones . . . destroying the faith of those to whom they minister."[23]

The Association of Baptist Professors (ABPR) took Criswell's book and its heavy promotion by Broadman as an attack on academic freedom. At their 1970 meeting the ABPR adopted a resolution brought by Robert Alley and W.C. Smith of the [Virginia Baptist] University of Richmond critical of the publicity given the book. At this same meeting Professor T.C. Smith of Furman University urged that the books in the Biblical canon be reconsidered in the light of modern scholarship. Several years later Alley would go on record as saying that Jesus did not believe himself to be divine and that the virgin birth was a myth.

The professors were not comforted by the conservative spirit of the New Orleans convention where a motion passed stating: "That this convention call [the BFM] to the attention . . . of agencies and vigorously urge the elected trustees . . . to be diligent in seeing that the programs assigned to them by the convention be carried out in a manner consistent with and not contrary to the convention's aforesaid statement of faith."[24]

The Broadman Commentary Controversy

Broadman Press and the Sunday School Board were not unaware of the clamor from denominational moderates. Planning for a new 12-volume Broadman Commentary series had been going for 12 years. The first volume was to encompass Genesis and Exodus. Bob Mowery, a member of the planning committee had objected when Board editorial secretary Clifton J. Allen announced that G. Henton Davies was to author the Genesis section. Noting that Davies was known to be more liberal than the average Southern Baptist, Parker recalls saying, "Dr. Allen, Southern Baptists went through the trauma of the Elliott controversy. Why do you want to take us through the same thing again with a liberal commentary on Genesis?" According to Parker, Allen replied, "Southern Baptists have come a long way since the Elliott controversy." Parker says that Landrum Leavell, another member of the planning committee and now president of New Orleans Seminary, then spoke up: " 'Dr. Allen, if you think Southern Baptists are going to swallow a liberal line on the Bible, you don't know Southern Baptists.' "[25]

Allen and his editors apparently didn't "know" Southern Baptists. Davies took the non-historical approach to the first eleven chapters of Genesis. He even said that Abraham had been mistaken about hearing God's command to sacrifice his son, Isaac. "The idea," Davis said, came as "the climax of the psychology of [Abraham's life]."[26]

Conservatives raised their voices again. Missouri editor W. Ross Edwards wondered "why some theologians do not emphasize the truths of the Bible without raising doubts . . . . Southern Baptists cannot grow spiritually on a diet like Dr. Davies offers. I'm not prepared to 'eat it.' "[27]

J. Wash Watts, revered head of the Old Testament department at New Orleans seminary, said Davies' writings "casts dark doubt on the word of the Bible."[28]

But Kentucky editor C.R. Daley argued that Davies hadn't denied divine inspiration. Harking back to the fuss over the Elliott book, Daley said it was "the same old story of literalism versus nonliteralism."[29]

Joe Odle and other aroused conservatives set up an "Affirming the Bible Conference" for May 30, 1970 to precede the convention that year in Denver. Odle, a major speaker, was alarmed over Sunday School Board materials "which are raising questions in the minds of a large segment of Southern Baptists." The "rumbling" is not going to "be silenced . . . as long as objectionable materials continue to appear. . . . Have we become so weak doctrinally, that we cannot even say this is what Baptists believe. . . . . "

Arguing that distinctive doctrines were the lifeline of the SBC, he recalled that a conservative pastor in another denomination had told an SBC evangelism meeting in Nashville: "I should like to take each of you by the nape of the neck and shake you, and say . . . , Act while you have the votes. Get rid of liberalism while you can. If you do not, the day will come when the situation will be like it is in my denomination. There the liberals can vote the conservatives out any day they want.' "[30]

Following up on the Bible conference, Gwin T. Turner of California presented a motion at the Denver convention calling for the withdrawal of the first volume of the commentary, because it is "out of keeping with the beliefs of the vast majority of Southern Baptist[s]," and that it "be rewritten with due consideration of the conservative viewpoint."[31] Despite objections from Sunday School Board head James L. Sullivan and Clifton J. Allen, the motion passed by almost a three-fourths majority.

The rewrite was not satisfactory. At the next convention conservatives pushed through a motion instructing the Sunday School Board to replace Davies with another writer. Clyde Francisco of Southern Seminary was secured, although Francisco said he did not reject the work of Davies.

The Convention continued unsettled. Two independent schools had recently been started, Criswell Center for Biblical Studies in 1971 (later to become Criswell College) and Mid-America Baptist Seminary in 1972. These, along with Luther Rice Seminary, were enrolling many conservative ministerial students. There was also talk that some churches would withdraw from the SBC if a turnaround did not happen soon. Alarmed by the perceived liberalism in some denominational institutions and fearful that many conservatives might pull out, conservative leaders decided to start a national publication that would expose liberal views and voice their concerns.

A New Conservative Paper

They met in the First Baptist Church of Atlanta in 1973 and organized as the Baptist Faith and Message Fellowship. They named their publication the Southern Baptist Journal and elected William A. Powell as editor.

Southern Baptist conservatives were encouraged by happenings among Missouri Synod Lutherans. At their 1973 annual meeting, church representatives adopted a resolution declaring that there was heresy at Concordia Seminary. The Lutherans called for the seminary's board of controls to take action against Concordia's president, John Tietjen. They also accepted a "State of Scriptural and Confessional Principles" from conservative theologian Robert Preus that established doctrinal parameters for the denomination. Tietjen was suspended. A substantial number of faculty and students went on strike, then split away to organize their own Seminary in Exile.

Powell printed every quotation he could find which he felt showed liberal influences in SBC agencies and seminaries. He wrote professors and administrators, asking if they believed Adam and Eve, Cain and Abel, Noah and Jonah to be historical persons and if they thought Biblical miracles actually happened "just as they are recorded in Scripture. Please answer yes or no," he always requested, "so Southern Baptists will know where you stand." Then he printed both his letters and the replies in the Journal. If the person didn't answer, he noted that also.

Powell's reporting, which occasionally dipped into scandal-mongering, gave agency administrators fits as conservatives began following up on the paper's allegations. The Journal also helped motivate conservative activists to make plans for changing the boards of agencies.

Powell flew his own plane. On one trip he told his passenger, Larry Lewis, that a conservative resurgence could only come by "elect[ing] trustees who will follow the will of the Convention and not be rubber stamps for agency heads. It's a two-year process," Powell noted, that "starts when we elect a Convention president." It is the president who appoints the Committee on Committees, Powell explained, which nominates the Committee on Boards, which nominates the trustees. A string of action-minded presidents would have to be elected, Powell told Lewis, "because only a percentage of board seats are open each year."

Lewis, who would later be elected president of the Home Mission Board, didn't believe it could be done. The Convention had been electing conservative presidents for years and the agencies had not changed.[32]

The Baptist Faith and Message Fellowship group continued meeting. In 1977 at least one conservative pastor from every major state convention came to Atlanta for a planning meeting. Paul Pressler had studied the SBC Constitution and come to the same conclusion as Powell. Pressler told the group that the first step was to elect a president who would not allow his appointments to be controlled by the denominational bureaucracy.

Organizing to Win

Patterson had completed his doctorate and had been appointed president of the new Criswell school in Dallas. Pressler was now a judge. By 1978 they, and a number of other conservatives, had come to feel that the movement must be broadened beyond the Baptist Faith and Message Fellowship. Publicizing "liberalism" in the SBC wasn't enough. They had to start changing the organizational machinery.

The founding board members of the BFM Fellowship were known. The attenders at the 1977 and 1978 meetings in Atlanta were not disclosed because of fear that they might be ostracized and their ministerial careers blunted by denominational leaders. Pressler and Patterson agreed to become targets for an anticipated barrage of criticism. Pressler was a layman and had no ministerial ambitions. Patterson was president of an independent school. With direction from Pressler, the strategist, the anonymous pastors went back to their states and began quietly explaining to other conservatives how they could work through the system to change the Convention. Patterson and Pressler were invited to speak to conservatives in various states.

Most denominational leaders initially regarded Bill Powell, Patterson, Pressler and a few other outspoken activists as only troublesome pests. They were blissfully unaware of the depth of conservative convictions in the SBC and the growth of the movement. C.R. Daley and a few others were concerned. Daley foresaw what could happen and pegged Memphis pastor Adrian Rogers as "the most brilliant of this group, the one who poses the gravest threat" to the SBC.[33] To head off a groundswell for Rogers in 1976, Daley and several other editors promoted James Sullivan in editorials.

Daley, the dean of the denominational editors, explained how this was done. ". . . With my mind on him, . . . I described in [editorials] paragraph after paragraph, the kind of leader we needed for the convention. This was done by other [editors]. Dr. Sullivan was nominated. He was elected. He was used by some of us to head off Adrian Rogers."[34]

They then worked for Jimmy Allen, who in 1977 went from state to state, telling influential people, in effect, "It's Adrian or me." Allen was elected, defeating conservative Jerry Vines in a runoff after an untrue rumor was spread that Vines' church did not give to the Cooperative Program or use Sunday School Board curriculum.

The re-election of the president for a second one-year term was a tradition in the SBC. Conceding Allen's re-election in 1978, conservatives set their sights on 1979 with Pressler and Patterson speaking to conservative "rallies" in 15 states. They did not endorse anyone, but it was understood that Adrian Rogers would be their best candidate. Rogers, a classmate of Patterson's at New Orleans, had succeeded Ramsey Pollard as pastor of the second largest church in the Convention. He was now president of the pre-convention Pastors' Conference.

Pressler and Patterson focused on two concerns: (1) A liberal drift in theology centered on departure from the faith of the founders of the convention in an inerrant Bible. To make this point, the two Texans simply read from the writings and speeches of alleged "liberals." (2) A plan to reverse this drift by sending messengers to the convention who would vote for a president who would appoint people of action. They explained how the president's appointive powers led to the election of trustees, noting that only trustees could change denominational agencies.

The two Texans made no apologies for their pre-convention campaign swing. "We have to communicate," said Pressler. "The Baptist press has constantly misrepresented . . . . what we have been doing. . . . We have to have a method . . . to let people know what is actually going on."[35]

The meetings were denounced as "political," even though Jimmy Allen had done substantially the same only two years before. Oklahoma editor Jack L. Gritz called them "an insult to the intelligence and ability" of the church messengers coming to Houston for the June convention."[36]

Rogers, however, arrived at the convention still not convinced that he should be the candidate to start the resurgence. The Memphis pastor told Patterson Monday evening at six that God hadn't told him to be a candidate. The election would be at 2:30 the next afternoon.

Later that night, Bertha Smith, a much beloved retired missionary, told Rogers that God had impressed her he should run. His wife, Joyce, who had opposed his candidacy, said God was changing her heart. About 11:30 p.m. Rogers went downstairs in the hotel to walk and pray about the decision. He ran into Jerry Vines and Paige Patterson. The three returned to Rogers' room and prayed for an hour. Rogers sensed a "clear direction" to run and later told reporters, "God came down in tears of joy as I was praying with two friends."[37]

The Resurgence Begins

The convention opened with a sense of foreboding among some. William M. Pinson, Jr., then president of Golden Gate Seminary, said it could "mark the most serious crisis" in the SBC "since the financial crisis of the Depression. Our vital signs are weak. Our institutions are under attack from within. It troubles me in my gut."[38]

Rogers and five other men were nominated. Opponents of Rogers hoped he could be forced into a runoff and be defeated by a coalition of denominational loyalists. When Rogers won handily on the first ballot, there were gasps from stunned opponents and whoops of joy from supporters. Conservative leaders sitting in "sky boxes" — executive suites loaned by friends of Judge Pressler — embraced one another in joy.

Rumors circulated that the election might have been stolen. One pastor claimed he had seen a man voting eleven ballots.

Conservative leaders denied impropriety, while saying privately that some messengers might not have followed all the rules because they had never attended a convention before. A later investigation showed no "massive" wrongdoing.

The 1979 convention did not completely belong to conservatives. The Sunday School Board, which controlled the bookstore exhibit, refused to stock Harold Lindsell's <u>The Bible in the Balance</u>. In a chapter on the SBC, Lindsell, editor emeritus of <u>Christianity Today</u>, included results of a thesis survey at Southern Seminary indicating a decline in orthodoxy as students progressed through studies there.[39] The 1976 thesis, by Noel Wesley Hollyfield, was titled "A Sociological Analysis of the Degrees of 'Christian Orthodoxy' Among Selected Students in the Southern Baptist Theological Seminary," 1976. It had been copied and sold by Bill Powell without permission of the author.

A second incident centered on the failure of Baptist Press to report an explosive "doctrinal" integrity resolution on the Bible. Presented by Larry Lewis, the resolution was patterned after one passed at the Missouri Baptist Convention the year before for that state's convention's agencies. The Houston resolution called for SBC agencies and institutions to employ only teachers "who believe in the inerrancy of the original [Bible] manuscripts, the existence of a personal devil and a literal Hell, the actual existence of a primeval couple named Adam and Eve, the literal occurrence of the miracles as recorded in the Bible, the virgin birth and bodily resurrection and the personal return of the Lord Jesus."[40]

Before Lewis' resolution was to be voted upon, Wayne Dehoney, a former SBC president, introduced a motion reaffirming the Bible to be "truth, without any mixture of error." President-elect Rogers asked that Dehoney be "more specific. . . . If he means the truth of the Bible is true, that's nonsensical. The truth of everything is true."[41] Dehoney conferred privately with Rogers, then told the messengers, "My interpretation and Adrian's is that in the original autographs God's revelation was perfect and without error — doctrinally, historically, scientifically and philosophically. . . . I bring that and ask you to support it."[42] Lewis "cheerfully" withdrew his resolution.

Herschel Hobbs affirmed the motion, noting that he had received many letters asking what the Baptist Faith and Message Committee had meant in 1963 "by the Bible 'is truth, without any mixture of error' — if that included the entire Bible or just the part that is truth." Hobbs said the "Committee understood and so recommended to this convention [in 1963] and the convention adopted it understanding it to include the whole Bible."[43]

With this explanation, Dehoney's motion was accepted by a sizable majority.

However, Dehoney's and Hobb's interpretations of the motion

were not noted in the Baptist Press story made available to the press. Larry Lewis later brought a tape to the press room and played it for a skeptical reporter. The reporter asked BP news director Dan Martin why it had not been included in the BP convention report for the press. Martin said the man assigned to cover Dehoney's motion had been pulled off to do another story. "The guy who covered for him didn't get all the details."

"Well, you've got the details now," the reporter said.

"I think we'll let it pass. The folks in the churches don't care about such detail."

"You'd better believe they care," the reporter countered. "I suggest you put it in the next report."

Martin still declined.[44]

When Adrian Rogers met with the press, he left no doubt about his view of the importance of the Bible issue. He pledged to "support an investigation by a fair and balanced committee" of denominational institutions. He was "in favor of any [seminary professor] being replaced when it is proven by his admission that he doesn't believe the Bible to be the Word of God."[45]

Adrian Rogers' election marked the end of an era in which the Convention and its elected presidents had been managed behind the scenes by a group who were more concerned about keeping the denominational machinery running smoothly and Cooperative Program money coming in, than with doctrinal purity. Although most Southern Baptists didn't realize it yet, a new leadership was already inside the gates. They would not have a majority of trustees on denominational boards and committees for several years, but they were headed in that direction. In the forefront was Adrian Rogers. By his side were Paige Patterson, the theologian of the movement and Paul Pressler, the strategist. Others coming up fast, included future SBC presidents Bailey Smith, Jimmy Draper, Charles Stanley, Jerry Vines and Morris Chapman. All were committed to realizing in the next decade what countless resolutions, motions and sermons had been unable to accomplish during the past half century.

Why did it happen in 1979? Looking back, a number of factors can be seen for the defeat of the old control group. The nation and evangelical Christians had changed. The placid fifties turned into the turbulent sixties when institutional leadership and traditions in every segment of society were challenged. School prayer and Bible reading were declared unconstitutional. The entertainment industry pushed back moral fences which had held for centuries. A raging secularism and atheism sought to shove Christians out of the public arena. Amidst this turbulence, conservative Christians began calling for a shoring up of moral and theological foundations in their institutions.

Southern Baptists changed. New ideas, liberal and

conservative, gushed into the South. The SBC went national. Thousands of ministerial students entered seminary from public colleges and universities where they had been more influenced by Campus Crusade for Christ and InterVarsity Christian Fellowship than the Baptist Student Union. Nancy Ammerman, in her epochal work, Baptist Battles, notes that Southern Baptist graduates of secular schools were less likely to become liberal than Southern Baptists who attended denominational schools.[46]

Sydnor Stealey, the first president of Southeastern Seminary, warned in 1961 that the SBC is "in the process of being taken over by the dominant fundamentalist elements in the Southwestern and Western states." He begged his "Baptist brothers to slow down the admission of new state conventions until more maturity and less divisiveness is evident... I tell you even today they are plotting to take over... SBC institutions and boards."[47]

It was during this time of ferment that the Sunday School Board, in Herschel Hobbs' words, "let the old Baptist Training Union die" where "our people studied our Southern Baptist heritage and faith."[48] During the Training Union era an establishment figure like Hobbs could cap an eruption at a convention with the promise that the problem would be addressed. It often wasn't. Southern Baptists of the late 1970's were not schooled in Training Union and did not stand in holy awe of the knighted denominational leadership which had allowed the leftward drift.

Beyond all of this was the get-out-the-vote effort that brought thousands of church "messengers" to Houston to vote for a conservative president who would seek to make a difference. The old "control group" simply couldn't match this new coalition in votes.

In 1979 little analysis was made of the reasons for and the consequences of the election of Adrian Rogers. Many moderates and agency executives were not greatly concerned as they began leaving the hotels. "Oh, it'll pass; it's the same old Norris stuff," some were reassuring themselves in one lobby. Suddenly a young church history professor from Southern Seminary began shouting, "Fire! Fire!"

One of the old heads tried to reassure him. "Walter [Shurden], you just aren't old enough to remember; we've seen it before; we'll see it again; don't get too excited about it."[49]

What the old heads had seen before would not be comparable to what they would see in the years ahead as a conservative resurgence swept into every institution and agency.

References

1 Southern Baptist Convention Annual, 1926, p. 18.

2 Ibid, p. 98

3 Published privately in Louisville, KY, n.d., pp. 15, 16.

4 C.R. Daley: Lecture and discussion on denominational ethics in the class on Ministerial Ethics. The lecture was also videotaped for the Southern Seminary library.

5 Personal Interview, Hannibal, MO, May, 1985.

6 The letters are cited in more detail on pp. 18-21 of Volume 5 of The Truth in Crisis.

7 Nashville, 1961, p. 15.

8 Walter B. Shurden: Not a Silent People, Broadman Press, Nashville, 1972, p. 106.

9 Ibid, pp. 107, 108.

10 Ibid, p. 106.

11 Southern Baptist Convention Annual, 1962, pp. 65, 68.

12 James C. Hefley: "The Historic Shift in America's Largest Protestant Denomination," Christianity Today, August 5, 1983, pp. 38-41.

13 Baptist Faith and Message Statement, 1963. Printed by the Baptist Sunday School Board.

14 Herschel H. Hobbs: "The Status Quo: An Analysis, The Christian Index, January 24, 1991, pp. 6, 13.

15 Editorial by Primm, p. 10.

16 Op. cit., p. 4.

17 Glenna Whitley: "Baptist Holy War," D Magazine, January, 1991, pp. 60-68.

18 Telephone interview with Patterson, March, 1991.

19 "An Interview With Judge Paul Pressler," in "The Controversy in the Southern Baptist Convention," a special issue of The Theological Educator. Published by the Faculty of New Orleans Baptist Theological Seminary, 1985, pp. 15-24.

20 Op. cit., pp. 17,18. Pressler also recalled these experiences in interviews with me.

21 Personal Interview, Hannibal, MO, May, 1985.

22 P. 47.

23 Op. cit., p. 78.

24 Southern Baptist Convention Annual, 1969.

25 Bob Mowery: "The Current Controversy Among Southern Baptists — Power Politics or Theological Division?" The Sword of the Lord, May 17, 1985, p. 3.

26 G. Henton Davies: "Genesis," Vol. 1, The Broadman Bible Commentary, Broadman Press, Nashville, TN 1969, p. 198.

27 "Witnessing to the Truth," Editorial, Word and Way, January 8, 1970, p. 2.

28 Op. cit. Shurden: Not a Silent People, pp. 113, 114.

29 Ibid, p. 114.

30 Odle's entire address is printed in William A. Powell's The SBC Issue & ?, Baptist Missionary Service, Buchanan, GA, n.d. pp. 158-173.

31 Southern Baptist Convention Annual, 1970, p. 63.

32 Personal interview with Larry Lewis, Hannibal, MO, 1985.

33 Op. cit., Daley lecture to Southern Seminary class.

34 Ibid.

35 Op. cit. "Interview With Judge Paul Pressler," The Theological Educator, p. 18.

36 James C. Hefley: "Southern Baptists Turn Toward Inerrancy," Moody Monthly, September, 1979, pp. 126-134.

37 This story has been told many times by Rogers, Patterson and Vines.

38 Op. cit. James C. Hefley: "Southern Baptists Turn Toward Inerrancy."

39 Zondervan Publishing House, Grand Rapids, MI, p. 173.

40 From a tape recording of the proceedings.

41 Ibid.

42 Ibid.

43 Ibid.

44 I was the reporter who urged Martin to include the interpretation in the Baptist Press story of the Houston convention.

45 Press Conference, Southern Baptist Convention, Houston, TX, June, 1979.

46 Rutgers University Press, New Brunswick and London, 1990, p. 140. Dr. Ammerman's study is must reading for those who wish to understand the sociological and cultural factors affecting the controversy.

47 "Voice from the Past," The Enquiry, student publication of Southeastern Baptist Theological Seminary, October, 1987, p. 3.

48 "The Status Quo: An Analysis," The Christian Index, January 24, 1991.

49 Walter B. Shurden: "The Erosion of Denominationalism: The Current State of the Southern Baptist Convention." Address given to the South Carolina Baptist Historical Society, November 12, 1984.

Chapter 3

"Eight Years of Resurgence: 1980-1988"

The conservatives' big card was their proclaimed belief that every word of the Bible is true. As moderate scholar Nancy Ammerman noted: Most Baptists "could say 'yes' to . . . the fundamentalist call for the ouster of professors and writers who do not believe the Bible. The moderate rhetoric of freedom and cooperation was simply not powerful enough to overcome the fundamentalist rhetoric based on unquestioning belief in the Bible. By claiming the Bible as their chief symbol, fundamentalists . . . gained the initiative in defining the rest of the agenda for the conflict. They wanted [denominational] employees who believed the Bible and agencies that would run by biblical rules."[1]

This the conservatives proclaimed in evangelism rallies, revivals, and the pre-convention Pastors Conference. The defenders of the status quo—some of whom were inerrantists themselves—called the Bible "authoritative," "inspired" and "trustworthy." The challengers used these same words, but went further by declaring that the Bible was historically, scientifically and philosophically without error.

The old guard was not unduly alarmed at Adrian Rogers' election in 1979. Most did not recognize the readiness of so many pastors and laity to jump on the conservative bandwagon. The managers were simply out of touch with the grassroots. They did not realize how "conservative" Southern Baptists really were.

They felt it safe to give Rogers the traditional second one-year term. In two years he couldn't possibly put a majority of trustees on any board. So they looked ahead two years to Los Angeles in 1981. As a denominational editor noted at Houston in 1979: "The inerrantists cannot afford to bring as many supporters to L.A. Institutional people are on expense accounts and will be there in force."

A Defeat in Georgia

Adrian Rogers' election in 1979 gave conservatives hope that the theological trend in the Convention could be reversed. This encouraged any pastors who had been thinking of leaving the SBC to stay put.

Some wanted to open other "fronts" in state conventions. Pressler and Patterson urged that energies and attention be concentrated on electing trustees on the national level who would do the job. Pressler kept reminding, "Let's first stop the flooding [of the SBC with neo-orthodox theology]. Then we can begin to clean up the inside of the house."

Bill Powell disregarded Pressler's advice and began an effort to oust Jack Harwell, the popular state denominational editor in Georgia. Five years before a friend of Powell's had written to ask Harwell if he believed all the Bible to be true and if Adam and Eve were people "just like us." Harwell replied that in his opinion the Bible had "all types of contradictions." The Baptist Faith and Message, Harwell said, did "not say that the Bible is not mixed with error." Harwell saw Adam and Eve as representative of "mankind and womankind."

Without Harwell's permission, Powell used the five-year-old letter in a campaign to have Harwell dismissed at the upcoming Georgia Baptist Convention. Learning of Powell's intention, Harwell met with his board before the convention and reaffirmed the Baptist Faith and Message. The board voted that he "continue his services as editor" and reported this to the state convention a few days later. The convention approved a motion by a four-to-one vote, expressing "our full confidence in the personal and professional integrity of the Editor."[2]

The Pressler-Patterson "information" campaign was getting more attention across the Convention. Southern Seminary President Duke McCall warned that a triumph by the inerrantist group would spell the end of free elections in the Convention and cause many churches in the east to withdraw Cooperative Program support. McCall said this could be avoided by having members of the Committee on Committees appointed by state conventions, instead of by the SBC president.[3] Critics called this connectionalism and a violation of the SBC constitution.

Going from state to state, Patterson and Pressler kept asking the same questions Powell was printing in his paper: "Do you believe the Bible to be totally and completely true? If you do, then do you believe that denominational staff and teachers should believe that?" Patterson and Pressler were convinced, as Patterson told Toby Druin of the Baptist Standard, that "a very large contingency in significant denominational posts" did, in fact, no longer believe all of the Bible to be true."

Dodging the Bible issue, denominational people responded with charges of improper politics. Retorted Patterson: "We are concerned Baptists, and if that is politics, then what state paper editors do when they write is also politics."[4]

The denominational editors sought to keep the heat on Patterson and Pressler. They tended to ignore the concerns of other conservatives. Dan Vestal, for example, was a solid establishment Texas pastor who would later oppose the conservative "takeover." His First Baptist Church in Midland, TX was a leader in Cooperative Program giving. Vestal, who held two graduate degrees from Baylor University, delivered a sermon May 14, 1980, on "The Danger of Error" in which he recalled a personal crisis that "came after I had graduated from college and was doing graduate study in religion [at Baylor]. I suddenly realized that what I had always believed, been taught, and even preached was drastically different from what I was now hearing . . . . I had always believed Adam and Eve were the first man and woman created in a literal garden. Now I was told to question that and not by atheists, but by trained people smarter than I. I had always believed the children of Israel had left Egypt because the Red Sea opened. Now I was told to question that. The story of Jonah, Abraham's offering of Isaac, Sodom and Gomorrah, were all questioned. The nature miracles of the New Testament were suspect; the demoniac possessions were only psychological. And the early church created oral tradition which gave us a fallible New Testament. If it hadn't been for some godly professors and strong parents and Christian friends, I could have fallen into error."[5]

Rogers Declines a Second Term

A month before the 1980 St. Louis Convention, Rogers asked not to be nominated, pleading that he needed more time with his church and family. His withdrawal threw moderates off guard. If conservatives elected another man at St. Louis, he could serve two years.

The conservative nominee was Bailey Smith, pastor of a 14,000 member church in Oklahoma. Smith had name recognition — he was a past president of the Pastors Conference. He had averaged baptizing over 1,000 for the past several years. He was an inerrantist who believed, for example, that "Jonah was a literal person swallowed by a literal fish and was in a literal mess."[6]

Even though his church gave only two percent to the Cooperative Program, Smith won a clear majority over five opponents, including Richard Jackson who was initially favored by many conservatives. Jackson was also an inerrantist. He had a baptismal record that compared favorably to Smith's. Unlike Smith's congregation, his church gave liberally to the Cooperative Program. Jackson might have taken Smith into a runoff, had not a story swept the hotels that he had made a deal with the establishment to maintain the status quo.

Statesman Hobbs Strikes Out

Conservatives had been frustrated over the refusal by Baptist Press to put Herschel Hobbs' and Wayne Dehoney's 1979 interpretation of "truth, without any mixture of error" on the record. In 1980 they spelled out inerrancy in an even stronger resolution, calling on denominational institutions to "only employ, and continue the employment of faculty ... and ... staff who believe in the ... infallibility of the original manuscripts, and that the Bible is truth without any error."[7]

Hobbs asked that the resolution be softened. On a hand vote, Hobbs' amendment failed decisively, with the 40-odd denominational agency heads and state editors sitting at tables voting in a bloc for it. The vote indicated that the time had passed when a denominational "statesman" like Hobbs could bend the Convention his way on the Bible issue.

Then another resolution passed which called for "a constitutional amendment prohibiting abortion except to save the life of the mother." This was a solid rebuke to the Christian Life Commission on abortion, which sided with religious liberals in favor of abortion on demand.

The establishment was shaken by these and other losses. Clearly, the agency heads and editors had not commanded this convention as they had shaped convention agendas before 1979.

"The tide is now moving our way," declared Judge Pressler. "But we have to continue electing presidents who will, by their appointments, follow the will of the majority of Southern Baptists."[8]

Moderates Fight Back

Pressler hit the speaking circuit again. In Virginia, he said, "The lifeblood" of the SBC "is the trustees. We need to go for the jugular—we need to go for trustees."

The statement was picked up and printed by Baptist Press. Pressler was unable to get denominational editors to print his explanation: "I was not referring to an actual, literal jugular vein of anybody or anything. . . . I was only trying to show the source of strength and power, where the lifeblood of Southern Baptists lies."[9]

"Going for the jugular" became a code phrase in branding Pressler as an evil villain, out to destroy the SBC. It would be cited thousands of times in derogatory articles and speeches against the conservative movement.

The remark triggered the first organized meeting of self-proclaimed "denominational loyalists" to counter the conservative movement. Led by brothers Cecil and Bill Sherman and Kenneth Chafin, a score of pastors met in Gatlinburg, TN to plot strategy. They called on agency heads to unite with them in opposing the "take-over" group. Only Duke McCall of Southern Seminary and Grady Cothen, president of the Sunday School Board, responded, and they did not mount a campaign.

Continuing to dodge the Bible issue, moderates, as they were now labeled, sought to broaden the political charge by identifying conservatives with the "religious right" in the U.S. They saw a golden opportunity when Bailey Smith hit the front pages for telling a Dallas rally for "traditional values" that God "doesn't hear the prayers of Jews" or anyone else who doesn't accept Jesus as Messiah. Moderates immediately branded Smith "intolerant."

Paige Patterson, however, used the publicity over the remark to set up a dialogue between Smith and the Jewish Anti-Defamation League in Dallas. The well-publicized talks resulted in the first of a number of trips to Israel by Southern Baptist conservative leaders and American Jews.

Patterson Debates Moderates

Conservatives continued to pound on the Bible issue which moderates didn't want applied to denominational employees. Then, in February, 1981, Paige Patterson and Cecil Sherman squared off before a pastors' conference in North Carolina. Patterson maintained that the Bible was historically and scientifically true in the original writings, a position held by all the SBC founders. Sherman acknowledged the "authority" of Scripture, but said this did not prevent the "human" writers from making errors. Sherman said he was "concerned with the message of the Bible, not the inerrancy."[9a]

Patterson debated Kenneth Chafin before the Religious Newswriters Association on the day before the Los Angeles convention began. Patterson affirmed and Chafin argued against the proposition: "Belief in Biblical inerrancy is crucial for the survival for Southern Baptists as an evangelistic force." Patterson stuck to the issue while Chafin denounced the "monumental ignorance" of those who claimed SBC agencies were harboring liberals. Chafin characterized the conservative effort as "a naked, ruthless reach for personal power that acts in ways that say any means are justified."

The Third Year in a Row

Chafin's attacks did not help the failed moderate effort to elect Abner McCall, then president of Baylor University, on a "center field" ticket. Incumbent Bailey Smith won by a 60-40 majority, despite charges that he was the candidate of the "take-over" party of the "ultra-conservative right."

It had been two years since conservatives elected their first president. Adrian Rogers' appointed Committee on Committees had nominated a Committee on Nominations who presented trustee nominees for over 100 board vacancies in Los Angeles. Moderates presented substitute nominees and succeeding in knocking ten from the roster. Conservatives established a solid trustee "toe-hold" on every board.

Adrian Rogers Returns

After a few months of quiet, the controversy heated up again when Baptist Press printed excerpts from the tape of a speech given by Adrian Rogers in Georgia. Rogers said the SBC had started "with a moderately narrow theology," then in 1925 adopted the unified Cooperative Program budget plan. In the years since, Rogers noted, the theology had broadened while the program had remained narrow. The SBC, he said, now "has many professors who do not believe the Bible is historically, philosophically and scientifically true," while "some within the denomination would like to put a steel band around our dollar. They say you do not have room to wiggle program-wise, but we've got plenty of room on the other side to wiggle theologically. . . . I say, what is sauce for the goose is sauce for the gander."

Rogers thought the "best solution" would be to "go back and narrow our theology again," but "I sincerely doubt that will ever happen. . . . The Cooperative Program has become a sacred cow."

The "next best thing," Rogers proposed, "is to allow both freedom of belief and freedom to support or decline to support various agencies and programs in the denomination."[10]

The fur flew over Rogers' characterization of the CP as a sacred cow. Rogers and his fellow conservatives were flailed as "disloyal," "independent" and "uncooperative" for not supporting the denominational budget plan. Rogers then said he didn't "believe the Cooperative Program in itself [to be] a sacred cow, [but] we have made of it a sacred cow."[11]

1982: Conservatives Win in New Orleans

Bailey Smith kept the heat on in his convention sermon, a month later in New Orleans. It is "inexcusable," he said, "to teach evolution and deny Genesis as historical fact . . . in our schools."[12] At that convention, conservative Jimmy Draper, whose church gave strong support to the Cooperative Program, took 56.97 percent of the vote in a runoff against Duke McCall. W.A. Criswell, who had been amazed when conservatives kept winning, was euphoric. "Lad, it's a miracle," he told Paige Patterson. "It's like the crossing of the Red Sea."[13]

New Orleans brought the second slate of conservative trustees. Moderates, by substitutions, managed to replace only three.

Conservatives raised moderate ire by passing resolutions backing "voluntary" school prayer and the teaching of "scientific creationism" in public schools. James Dunn, Executive Director of the Baptist Joint Committee on Public Affairs (BJCPA) declared that his agency, composed of representatives from nine Baptist bodies but more than 90 percent supported by Southern Baptists, would fight any efforts to restore school prayer. Dunn called President Reagan's effort on a prayer amendment, "despicable demagoguery" and "playing politics with prayer."[13a] A motion to censure Dunn was withdrawn, but from this time on it became clear that Dunn and the BJCPA were in trouble with SBC conservatives.

Jimmy Draper pledged to "get Southern Baptists talking to each other, instead of about each other." He asked leading moderates for help in finding "common ground." They suggested that he make appointments to the Committee on Committees from a pool of names provided by state convention executives. Draper promised only to consult with the SBC vice presidents.

Draper invited major agency heads and moderate and conservative leaders to a "summit" in Irving, TX. Moderate Don Harbuck said "the judgmental spirit and exclusivistic posture of fundamentalism" was tearing the denomination apart. Paige Patterson disagreed and urged the agency executives to (1) give conservatives parity with moderates in employment, (2) have employees who will not use the term "inerrancy" to state "publicly, clearly, and unamibigiously" what they believe about the Bible and other essential doctrines, (3) keep students holding to inerrancy from being ridiculed in classrooms, (4) support restructure of the Cooperative Program so that churches can support only agencies whose ministries they can in "good conscience" approve. The denominational leaders did not respond.

1983: Draper Wins Again, Proposes Doctrinal Parameters

Moderates did not oppose Draper's re-election at the 1983 Pittsburgh convention where the Texas pastor proposed an "irreducible minimum theology that a person must subscribe to in order to be acceptable as a professor, . . . or as a worker, writer, or policymaker in one of our agencies": the "undiminished diety and the genuine humanity" of Jesus Christ, the "substitutionary atonement," the "literal, bodily" resurrection of Jesus, a "literal" bodily ascension into heaven, and "justification by God's grace through faith."[14]

At Pittsburgh, Paul Pressler explained how conservatives had been successful thus far: "We sought to work within the system instead of tearing down. We followed a definite plan that would get conservative trustees nominated and elected who would change the system. We did not make frontal attacks on the integrity of those we felt were liberals. We merely read [in meetings] what they had written and published and asked our constituency whether that was what they wanted taught in their schools."[15]

Pittsburgh brought a slackening in harsh rhetoric. However, two divisive portents for the future were revealed in the steel city. Nine hundred persons attended a moderate "fellowship." Leaders said there would probably be a program in 1984, in Kansas City. "Women in Ministry" held their inaugural pre-convention meeting in Pittsburgh and reported 175 ordained "clergywomen" in the denomination. Partly as a result of this organizing, women's ordination led all other controversies in the fall state conventions.

1984—Agency Heads Join the Controversy

The moderates held their first Forum in Kansas City as expected. Their presidential candidate was Grady Cothen, who had recently retired (because of ill health, he said) from the presidency of the Sunday School Board. Three years before, the Board had lost a nasty court suit brought by a former personnel administrator who had exposed a scandal among some Board executives. Trustees had not even been provided a trial transcript.

Conservative Jerry Vines nominated Charles Stanley, pastor of FBC, Atlanta. The church didn't give much to the Cooperative Program, but it was heavily involved in its own mission ministries. Stanley proclaimed the Bible to be inerrant and he was well known through his television ministry. Stanley defeated Cothen and a third candidate, "centrist" John Sullivan, on the first ballot with a 52.18 percent majority.

Moderates also lost in efforts to replace conservative nominees for new trustees. The closest vote came on the nomination of Judge Paul Pressler to the Executive Committee. A motion by Winfred Moore that Bruce McIver replace Pressler was unsuccessful. Moore would be heard from again.

To this time, no sitting agency heads had taken sides in the conflict. At Kansas City, Southwestern Seminary president Russell Dilday came out swinging in his convention sermon against an "emerging, . . . incipient Orwellian mentality" in the SBC. Dilday clearly meant the conservative movement.[16]

Two months later, Southern Seminary president Roy Honeycutt, in his fall convocation address, declared "holy war" against the "unholy forces" who are "seeking to hijack" the denomination and "take control" of agencies.[17] Honeycutt refused Paige Patterson's challenge to "debate on a public platform and let people ask questions, instead of making unfounded charges and personal attacks" on those who oppose "liberal trends."[18]

Southeastern Seminary president Randall Lolley followed Honeycutt, comparing SBC conservatives to the Moonies and cult leader Jim Jones. Paige Patterson urged Lolley and Dilday to join him in a public debate. They also refused.

Baylor University president Herbert Reynolds then jumped into the fray, declaring that "a priestly and self-anointed ... college of cardinals was out to 'clone' the SBC educational system."[19]

1985—Advent of the Peace Committee

Shortly before convention time in Dallas, Foreign Mission Board president Keith Parks announced that he could not support Stanley for a second term. He urged missionaries who would be messengers to "choose officers of the convention and trustees of agencies who are unquestionably committed both to the Bible and to our convention approach to missions."[20] The opposition to Stanley's re-election by the agency heads created a backlash that brought thousands of conservative messengers to Dallas who might otherwise not have taken the trouble to come. What sealed Stanley's election to a second term was a news story on the night before the vote that Billy Graham had endorsed Stanley. With a record 45,404 messengers registered, conservatives gave Stanley 55.3 percent of the vote. Then in a gesture of conciliation they helped elect the moderate candidate, Winfred Moore, as first vice president.

The first vice president could do little more than hold press conferences, which Moore did. Unappeased moderates moved at Dallas to replace the entire Committee on Boards with the presidents of state conventions and WMUs. In the parliamentary confusion that followed, Stanley first ruled that the substitutes would have to be voted on one by one, then later declared both motions out of order. The convention finally voted to accept the original slate. An expensive lawsuit was subsequently filed by moderates against the SBC and its Executive Committee in which plaintiffs charged they had been "irreparably harmed" by Stanley's "erroneous rulings." The unsuccessful suit cost the SBC Cooperative Program over $200,000 in legal fees.

Dallas also brought the election of a 22-member Peace Committee with representatives from both sides and the perceived middle. Charles Fuller, who called himself "a 'non-union' conservative," was named chairman of the committee.

The division deepened in 1985. The conservative plan to gain control of trustee boards advanced. Moderates—having realized they could not beat conservatives on the Bible question—could only attack conservatives in terms of politics and subsidiary matters. Some of their accusations appeared patently absurd, as when moderate Bill Self warned at Dallas that the Annuity Board might lose its almost $2 billion in assets if the "political" takeover was not prevented.[21]

1986—Rogers Returns as President

In February, the Peace Committee dropped a bombshell in announcing that investigatory committees, sent to the six seminaries and five other agencies, had found "significant theological diversity" on the historicity of Adam and Eve and various events in Scripture, authorship of various books in the Bible, and whether miracles were to be taken as historical happenings.[22] This proved that conservative charges of liberal drift were not unfounded.

In May, the Peace Committee reported that it had found both sides to be guilty of political activities and of using "intemperate, inflammatory and unguarded language." Both groups, the committee added, had shown prejudice in "autonomous independent journals," and some "denominational papers had" shown "prejudice against the conservative political activists."[23]

The 1986 Atlanta convention, at which over 40,000 messengers registered, marked the eighth straight conservative win. Adrian Rogers took almost 55 percent of the votes to defeat Winfred Moore, who had been nominated by Richard Jackson, once a conservative favorite. Moderates and many denominational executives were dismayed. Southern Seminary president Roy Honeycutt told an alumni luncheon, "We may have to do as they did in Rome, when they survived the Dark Ages, by creating pockets of civility, intelligence, and morality." Honeycutt then inducted Moore—not a seminary graduate—as the first honorary alumnus in Southern's 127-year history.[24]

Both sides were now anxiously counting trustees. Estimates showed the makeup of most agency boards to be about 40 percent conservatives, 20 percent moderates, with the balance classified as "swing" votes.[25] A minority of trustees elected during the conservative resurgence had not measured up to expectation.

Moderates were worried about the Home Mission Board where a search committee, dominated by moderates, was then looking for a new president. Concern increased when HMB trustees met in September and elected conservative Clark Hutchinson as board chairman. Hutchinson and other conservatives then marshalled a 40-36 majority to secure the resignation of the moderate search committee and the appointment of a new committee "representative of the constituency of the Home Mission Board."[26] Several staff resignations followed.

Back in April, long-time Christian Life Commission executive Foy Valentine, then 63, had announced his "approaching retirement" because of a "heart condition" and asked the board to begin looking for his replacement.[27] Conservatives were caught off-guard by the announcement. They had been looking forward to Valentine's retirement, principally because of his pro-choice position on abortion. His unexpected announcement gave the moderate majority on the CLC board the opportunity to elect the search committee that would nominate Valentine's successor.

The committee reportedly had difficulty finding a suitable candidate willing to take the job, perhaps because he knew he might be dismissed after conservatives attained a board majority.

Back in 1980 the convention had taken a strong pro-life position. The 1985 convention voted, over moderate opposition, to observe a Sanctity of Life Day in January on the anniversary of the Roe v. Wade Supreme Court decision permitting abortion on demand. In 1986, a conservative board member moved that the agency for moral concerns attune its literature on abortion to pro-life convention resolutions and to "vigorously" oppose "abortion on demand." The motion failed by a 14-13 vote. An attempt by conservatives to elect their candidate, Coy Privette, as board chairman lost 15-13. Moderates held out hope of electing a new executive director of their choice.

Pressure on the seminaries had been increasing all year. Before the Atlanta convention, conservative pastor Jimmy Stroud of Knoxville, TN cited a published statement by Southern Seminary professor Glenn Hinson that "undoubtedly some embellishments did occur . . . with regard to the healing and miracle narratives" of Jesus. Moderates claimed that this and other citations by Stroud had been taken out of context.[28]

In October, Midwestern Seminary was shaken by a trustee inquiry into the beliefs of Professor Temp Sparkman. Though the board voted 21-11 to affirm Sparkman's writings as being "within the context of the seminary articles of faith," the affair increased the pressure on the theological schools.[29]

The Peace Committee had already reported a faculty "imbalance" against conservatives at Southern and Southeastern seminaries. Seminary presidents Dilday, Lolley and Honeycutt were continuing to receive flak for taking sides in the partisan conflict. For these and other reasons the six seminary presidents met in October and affirmed "the Bible to be fully inspired" and "not errant in any area of reality." They confessed that conservatives had not been given "a fair shake" in the seminaries and promised to "enforce compliance" of "seminary confessional statements, . . . foster theological balance in classrooms," be more fair in selecting future faculty and special speakers and "hold three national conferences on biblical inerrancy." However, upon arriving home, Honeycutt and Lolley quickly qualified their views on inerrancy.

1987—A Very Big Year, Power Politics at the CLC

In January, the CLC's moderate search committee, at a specially called board meeting, nominated Larry Baker of

Midwestern Seminary to succeed Foy Valentine. Conservative trustees had been unable to question Baker before the meeting and were allowed only one question each before voting. Though Baker differed with many trustees on abortion, capital punishment and ordination of women, he pledged to be a "team player" with the divided board. Baker was elected by a 16-13 secret ballot vote.[30] Then in a move that would be widely criticized, the moderate board majority rehired Valentine to serve as executive officer of development until he reached 65. His salary and expenses for the next 13 months were set at $116,829.24. Conservative trustee James Wood called the retirement of Valentine, the hiring of Baker and the rehiring of Valentine, "the most flagrant example of power politics I've ever witnessed."[31]

New President of the Home Mission Board

In April the realigned Home Mission Board search committee nominated Larry Lewis, president of Hannibal-LaGrange College in Missouri, for the presidency of the HMB. Lewis, a leading figure in the conservative movement, was fiercely assailed by some moderates. Still he was elected by a surprising 52-15 margin. Many moderates apparently voted for him because of his experience in starting new churches and his evangelism record while pastor of a large St. Louis church before entering academic life.

Lewis quickly came under fire for new HMB polices on refusing financial support to women pastors and restrictions on appointments of divorced persons and those who spoke in charismatic tongues. Lewis noted that he had not originated the policy changes, but the criticism continued.

The Inerrancy Conference

The first seminary-sponsored Inerrancy Conference was held May 4-7 at the Ridgecrest Conference Center. Six well known inerrantist scholars from outside the SBC spoke in plenary sessions. After each address, an SBC moderate and a conservative or a centrist and a conservative responded. The conference apparently didn't change many minds. Some conservatives saw the conference as an attempt by the seminaries to show that differences over the nature of Scripture were not as serious as they had been made out to be. The seminary presidents probably also hoped to keep the Peace Committee from coming down too hard when the committee reported at the upcoming June convention in St. Louis. Roy Honeycutt "worried that in 45 days we will adopt an interpretation for a creed that tells people how to interpret the Bible."[32]

The Peace Committee Report

The eagerly awaited Peace Committee report was not released until the morning of the second day of the St. Louis convention. It was as bad as many moderates feared and better than many conservatives dared hope. It repeated previous findings that the "primary source" of the controversy "is theological," but "there are political causes as well." The core difference is over "the extent and nature of [Biblical] authority," the committee said.

The report affirmed "the narratives of Scripture [to be] historically and factually accurate.... Most Southern Baptists see 'truth, without any mixture of error, for its matter,' as meaning that Adam and Eve were directly created as real persons," that "the named authors did indeed write the biblical books attributed to them by those books," that "the miracles described in Scripture did indeed occur as supernatural events in history" and that "the historical narratives ... are indeed accurate and reliable..." The Peace Committee called "upon Southern Baptist institutions to recognize the great number of Southern Baptists who believe this interpretation of our confessional statement and, in the future, to build their professional staffs and faculties from those who clearly reflect such dominant convictions and beliefs held by Southern Baptists at large."[33]

Rogers Defeats Jackson

An estimated 96 percent of the 25,607 registered messengers voted at St. Louis to adopt the document as the Report of the Convention. Adrian Rogers defeated moderate candidate Richard Jackson for the presidency with 59.97 percent of the vote. Jerry Vines, rumored to be the conservative candidate for 1988, gave the convention sermon, calling the school of higher criticism of the Bible a "crafty old thief." [34] Moderates left St. Louis in deep discouragement.

Tenery's Seminar on Trustee Power

In addition to the Southern Baptist Journal, conservatives now had the Southern Baptist Advocate. The new tabloid was edited by Bob Tenery, a new trustee of the Sunday School Board, who had succeeded Russell Kaemmerling, Paige Patterson's brother-in-law. The Advocate charged no subscription price and appeared irregularly because of funding limitations. When it did appear, moderates saw red, especially when they read Tenery's scalding editorials. Blunt and plain-spoken, he read new trustees their board rights and responsibility to the Convention.

At St. Louis, in 1987, Tenery held an informal strategy seminar for conservative board members. Agency employees, he reminded, are "subject to control and direction of" their board. The conservative majority didn't elect trustees to rubber stamp bureaucratic decisions, Tenery said. Don't be "stampede[d]" into making decisions. He recalled that the nomination of Lloyd Elder for the presidency of the Sunday School Board had been announced to the press before trustees "ever had an opportunity to talk with him. Insist upon complete information well in advance of your meetings so that you can be well versed on the issues that are to come before [your] board."

Tenery explained how moderates had been using committee assignments to "shut" conservatives "out of any real participation in the decison making processes of the board." They place conservatives on "innocuous committees" and pack "the important committees which make the strategic decisions" with moderates. Conservatives should demand that their majority "be well represented on all of the major committees." Don't be intimidated from "voicing" your feelings, he warned. "You are in charge. . . . . Never allow bureaucrats" to take the "authority" the Convention "has placed in your hands."[34a]

Movement in Seminaries

The conservative influence was now plain to see in seminaries. William Crews was inaugurated as the new president at Golden Gate. Crews had not been a conservative activist, but he had the full confidence of leaders in the resurgency movement. Crews saw no difficulties in Golden Gate's adapting to the Peace Committee report. The seminary, he pledged, would "remain committted" to the belief that "the Bible has truth without any mixture of error, for its matter."[35]

The big seminary story in 1987 came at Southeastern where a clear conservative trustee majority after St. Louis had been anticipated by President Lolley and the faculty. In March the faculty had formed a chapter of the American Association of University Professors (AAUP) to help protect them from feared trustee actions and to assist in a public relations program. Lolley laid down the gauntlet to the new trustees by declaring that he "would not give one millibar of his energy" to producing the kind of school which he knew the new trustee majority wanted.

Defiant student demonstrators confronted trustees as they arrived for their October 12-14 board meeting. The new board majority heard themselves denounced by moderate Bill Self at a campus alumni rally. At a called press conference, faculty spokesman Richard Hester thundered that the faculty would not sign the Baptist Faith and Message.

Undaunted, the board majority voted to put the hiring of new faculty under the president, who was directly answerable to the trustees. The faculty had previously played the major role in the selection process. President Lolley said he could "live with" the policy change if the president was allowed to "consult" with faculty.[36] Lolley also agreed to meet with the trustee executive committee on how the Peace Committee Report could be implemented at the seminary.

To the surprise of many, Lolley stepped down the following week, just in time to nominate moderate Leon Smith for president of the North Carolina convention. Dean Morris Ashcraft and three other administrators resigned from the seminary on November 17. Two days later the recently organized Southern Baptist Alliance established a task force to look into the feasibility of starting a new seminary for moderates.

Movement in Other Agencies

Conservative pressure was being felt in other agencies. In 1985 conservatives had persuaded a reluctant Sunday School Board and its president Lloyd Elder to publish a new multi-volume "inerrantist" commentary. That year protests had erupted over a Sunday School Board lesson in which the writer had said the "satan" of Job was not the "devil of the New Testament," but a "kind of heavenly inspector" for sin.[37] The trustees called for Board administrators to "exercise special care in determining the doctrinal and biblical commitment of writers" in the future.[38]

The 1987 convention at St. Louis gave conservatives a sufficient trustee majority to pass a motion that required the BSSB to incorporate "sanctity of human life and opposition to abortion" into Board curriculum. Another successful trustee motion, introduced by Southern Baptist Advocate editor Bob Tenery, called on the BSSB to "operate . . . in compliance with the spirit and letter of the Peace Committee Report."[39]

To this time, no attempt had been made to replace sitting agency heads. However, the Christian Life Commission was considered a special case because of the manner in which Larry Baker had been elected. St. Louis gave conservatives a small majority on the CLC board, but a motion to dismiss Baker failed by a 15-15 tie vote.

Conservatives had a working majority in the powerful Executive Committee (EC) where, at the September meeting, a policy was adopted requiring EC staff to "demonstrate strong commitment to the Bible" and accept "without reservation, the entirety of the Baptist Faith and Message statement with the illustrations (including belief in Adam and Eve as actual persons and Biblical miracles as actually happening) given in the Peace Committee report of the prevailing views of Southern Baptists."[40]

Confrontations Over Public Affairs

The stormiest meetings in 1987 centered on disputes between

the Baptist Joint Committee on Public Affairs (BJCPA) and the SBC-elected Public Affairs Committee (PAC) which still held only a third of the votes, while providing most of the budget for the BJCPA. In a meeting of the PAC in Nashville, Chairman Sam Currin charged that the PAC majority, which did not have program money, had been "shut out of the decision making processes of the Joint Committee."[41] Currin and other conservative members of the PAC proposed that the PAC should control the funds going from the SBC to the BJCPA.

Many members in the PAC were also angry with James Dunn for his past involvement with the liberal People for the American Way (PAW). They demanded that the PAC withdraw from circulation a PAW fund-raising tape "highly critical of Southern Baptist leaders" and on which Dunn appeared, and that the BJCPA "cease and desist from any further association with [PAW]. . . "[42] At this same meeting a PAC majority voted to support the nomination of Robert Bork to the Supreme Court, an action which aroused the ire of SBC moderates and provoked James Dunn to write U.S. senators a letter stating that the BJCPA, which "serves . . . the Southern Baptist Convention," had "taken no action" on Bork's nomination.[43]

The PAC asked the SBC Executive Committee to clarify the relationships between the SBC, the PAC, and the BJCPA. The EC appointed a sub-committee to study the questions.

The PAC elected a sub-committee of its own to evaluate staff of the BJCPA. Information on staff expense accounts and correspondence which the PAC thought essential to the evaluation was refused by the BJCPA in a raucous October session. The BJCPA also refused the Public Affairs Committee's request to reprimand Dunn for writing the "clarification" letter to the senators, and the BJCPA declined to rescind a 1980 BJCPA position paper which spoke about monitoring the "Religious Right." The BJCPA did request the PAW to withdraw the objectionable videotape fund raiser.

The PAC then met after the close of the BJCPA meeting and voted to ask the SBC to "dissolve its institutional and financial ties" with the BJCPA and "allocate" funds specified for the BJCPA ($485,100) to funding the PAC.

Struggles in the State Conventions

The conservative resurgence was causing waves in many state conventions where conservatives had been sounding the alarm about secularism, heresy and loss of convention control of some colleges. The most heated battle took place in Georgia where conservatives had been elected to Georgia Baptist Convention (GBC) offices in November, 1986.

The media focused on coeds posing for Playboy and alleged

lewd and licentious behavior on campus, but the real dispute was over ownership, control, philosophy and teaching at a Baptist university. Mercer's charter, revised in 1929, permitted a virtual self-perpetuating board of trustees. The state convention could only approve trustees from suggested nominations.

Mercer's Playboy problems had helped elect conservative Clark Hutchinson to the presidency of the GBC in 1986. In August, 1987, conservatives asked Mercer trustees to permit the GBC to control future trustee nominations. This request was refused.

Conservative Lee Roberts then mailed a 16-page "open letter" on the Mercer situation to all Georgia Baptist pastors and other influential persons, alleging the toleration of immorality and heresy. Roberts included quotes from a lecture given by President Kirby Godsey in which Godsey said, "Jesus did not come to tell you and me how to be saved but to let us know that we live in the arms of grace."[44]

Mercer mounted an expensive public relations campaign which put the spotlight on Roberts' business problems and brought hundreds of supportive moderates to the 1987 state convention at which conservative Clark Hutchinson was denied a second presidential term by 51 votes. The conservative tide was—at least temporarily—turned back in Georgia. However, conservatives took courage in the resignation of controversial state editor Jack Harwell.

The fireworks at Southeastern Seminary, capped by the resignation of Randall Lolley, resulted in a large moderate "sympathy" vote turnout in North Carolina for Lolley who nominated Leon Smith for president. Conservative candidate Ned Matthews received enough votes to win in an ordinary year, but 1987 was not a typical year.

Moderates also won in Virginia after condemning a computerized mailout by conservative T. C. Pinckney, giving resumes of preachers to churches without pastors. Virginia and other state convention offices had been providing the same kind of service, on a much more sophisticated level, for years.

Florida conservatives elected Bobby Welch as president of their state convention. Moderates won in Louisiana, by 44 votes, after raising a furor over a letter mailed to pastors by conservative Jim Richards, urging messenger turnout for the election of conservative Fred Lowery as president. Acclaimed middle-of-the road personal conservatives were elected as presidents in a number of other state conventions.

Despite the state convention victories, the future of moderates in the SBC looked gloomy at the end of 1987. Larry Baker's tenure at the CLC appeared limited. Conservatives had their man, Larry Lewis, at the HMB. The Inerrancy Conference had not increased any great measure of confidence in the seminaries, particularly in

Southern and Southeastern. The St. Louis convention had turned out to be a disaster for moderates. Conservatives had the presidency for another year. The Peace Committee report was worse than had been expected. Lolley was out as president at Southeastern. The Sunday School Board had made concessions to conservative trustees. Aggressive actions by the PAC had the BJCPA on the defensive. All in all, 1987 had been the darkest year for moderates since the conservative resurgency began.

Still, moderates took courage from their wins in Georgia and North Carolina. Indiana editor, David Simpson, a staunch conservative, conceded that the SBC might even be seeing a "moderate resurgence."

The year ended with conservatives under attack from the secular media. The most notable example was a special public television report by former Southern Baptist Bill Moyers on the controversy in his former denomination. Moyers, by skillful editing, inserting new questions before answers previously given and selective interviewing, painted SBC conservatives as narrow-minded, ultra-right, extremist and anti-democratic. SBC moderates hailed the PBS special and vowed to reverse the nine-year string of conservative victories in 1988 at San Antonio.

References

1 Nancy T. Ammerman: Baptist Battles, Rutgers University Press, New Brunswick and London, p. 179.

2 "Georgia Committee Affirms Harwell as Index Editor, Baptist and Reflector," December 26, 1979.

3 James Lee Young: "McCall Voices Concern Over Stability of SBC,": Baptist and Reflector, May 7, 1980, p. 3.

4 Toby Druin: "Patterson-Pressler Group Seeks SBC Control," as reported for the Baptist Standard and reprinted in the Baptist and Reflector, April 30, 1980, pp. 4, 5.)

5 From a printed copy of the sermon as reported by Conservative Texas Baptist Report, Vl. 2, No. 3, October, 1990.

6 Gayle White: "Bible 'Infallible,' " The Atlanta Constitution, June 12, 1980, pp. 6A.

7 James C. Hefley: "Conservative Tidal Wave Sweeps SBC," Moody Monthly, September, 1980,pp. 122-125.

8 Personal Interview, St. Louis, June, 1980.

9 Personal Interview, Los Angeles, June, 1981.

9A Quotes from a tape recording of the debate.

10 Dan Martin: "Doctrinal Unity, Program Unity Rise, Fall Together, Rogers Says' Baptist Press, May 14, 1982.

11 Ibid.

12 Baptist Press, June 16, 1982.

13 Related by Glenna Whitley: "Baptist Holy War," D Magazine, January 1991, p. 65.

13a Dunn made these remarks to reporters in New Orleans.

14 Draper later placed his "minimums" in a book: Authority: The Critical Issue for Southern Baptists, Fleming H. Revell, Co., Old Tappan, N.J., 1984, pp. 105, 106.

15 Presidential Press Conference, Pittsburgh, June, 1983.

16 Interview, Pittsburgh, June, 1983.

17 Russell H. Dilday, Jr.: "On Higher Ground," Convention Address, June 13, 1984, p. 9.

18 From printed copy of his 1984 convocation address supplied by Southern Seminary News Department.

19 Mark Kelly: "'Concerned' Arkansas Pastors Condemn 'Liberal Drift,'" Arkansas Baptist Newsmagazine, March 14, 1985, pp. 10, 11.

20 Parks' statement was released to the press April 19, 1985 and sent to missionaries on May 2 under a cover letter by Charles W. Bryan, Senior Vice President for Overseas Operations. Bryan asked only for prayer for the Board and the Convention and noted that "persons with widely differing viewpoints are seeking God's leadership."

21 Craig Bird: "Baylor President Denounces SBC 'College of Cardinals,'" Baptist and Reflector, October 17, 1984, pp. 1, 2.

22 Baptist Press, Convention Reports, Dallas, 1985.

23 Dan Martin: "Peace Panel Adopts Statement on Diversity," Baptist Standard, March 5, 1986.

24 "Political Activities Statement is Issued," Baptist Press, May 16, 1986.

25 Baptist Press Report, Atlanta, June, 1986.

26 See Gustav Niebuhr: "Fundamentalists Controlling Boards," SBC Today, October, 1986, pp. 1,2.

27 From a copy of the letter.

28 Jim Newton: "New HMB Search Committee Appointed to Seek President," Home Missions News Service, Baptist Standard, September 17, 1986, p. 5.

29 Jim Stroud: "Opposes Hinson's Teaching," Baptist and Reflector, February 5, 1986, p. 5.

30 For a fuller account of the Sparkman inquiry see Volume 2 of The Truth in Crisis, pp. 113-117.

31 David Wilkinson: "Baker Elected," Light, February, 1987, p. 1, 3, 4.

32 Marv Knox: "Seminary Presidents Discuss Inerrancy," Baptist Press, May 6, 1987.

33 Marv Knox: "Seminary Presidents Discuss Inerrancy," Baptist Press, May 6, 1987.

34 Quoted from the Peace Committee report, Released at the St. Louis

convention, June, 1987.

34a I happened to wander uninvited into the meeting and was invited to stay. Quotes are from a paper and other comments presented by Tenery.

35 Quoted from Vines' manuscript.

36 "Crews Affirms Bible, Ministry to West," Indiana Baptist, June 30, 1987, p. 3.

37 From my tape of Lolley's remarks.

38 Linda Lawson: "Sunday School Board Acknowledges Errors," Baptist and Reflector, July 17, 1985, pp. 1, 2.

39 "Trustees Adopt Response to Job Lesson Errors," Arkansas Baptist Newsmagazine, August 15, 1985, p. 13.

40 From minutes of the BSSB trustees' meeting, August, 1987.

41 Toby Druin: "PAC Funds, Non-SBC Exhibit Studies Ordered," Baptist Standard, September 30, 1987, p. 3.

42 Personal Interview, Washington, D.C., October, 1987.

43 Taken from the official minutes of the PAC meeting and a BP article by Dan Martin and Mark Kelly: "Dispute Over Funding Highlights Meeting," Indiana Baptist, September 19, 1987, p. 7.

44 Quoted from Dunn's letter which was released to the media.

Chapter 4

"The 'Second' Battle of the Alamo"

A fter nine straight losses, moderates were grimly determined to win in San Antonio. Every board, except Southern Seminary's, now had a clear conservative majority, and the results were showing:

— A conservative now occupied the president's office at Southeastern Seminary. Elected at the March board meeting, Lewis Drummond, who had served as the Billy Graham Professor of Evangelism at Southern, struck an irenic tone while pledging to lead the seminary to "fulfill the intent of the seminary's Abstract of Principles and the Baptist Faith and Message . . ."[1] Southeastern's faculty, still protesting the new trustee hiring policy for teachers, put a chill on relations by announcing that the school's two accrediting agencies would be coming to the campus shortly to look into the changes at Southeastern.

— At Southern Seminary rumors had abounded that the thin moderate board majority might vote at their spring meeting not to seat new conservative trustees elected at the 1987 convention. Southern's charter seemed to make this legally possible. But the effort failed in the board's executive committee — a clear defeat for the more militant moderates. Later the full board unanimously accepted President Honeycutt's recommendation to add conservative professor David Dockery to the faculty. Honeycutt's recommendation that tenure be granted to controversial theology professor Molly Marshall-Green was opposed by seven trustees.

— Conservatives elected North Carolina pastor Mark Corts as board chairman at the spring meeting of the Foreign Mission Board. FMB president Keith Parks, who had stayed out of convention politics since opposing Stanley in 1985, was in no danger, but the conservative board majority was clearly in charge.

— At the Home Mission Board, newly elected conservative president Larry Lewis was exercising strong leadership. Lewis asked the regional director of the HMB's interfaith witness department to accept a transfer to another department, after the employee stated he did not believe Jews should be evangelized. The employee declined the transfer and resigned.

Battling in the Media

Angry moderates kept protesting through the media, accusing conservatives of power plays and violations of academic freedom. The Wall Street Journal ran a front-page story announcing, "Fundamentalists Fight to Capture the Soul of Southern Baptists. Purges and Censorship Grow as Zealots Try to Finish Takeover from Liberals."[2] Rachel Richardson Smith, a part-time professor of Bible at Meredith (Baptist) College in Raleigh, NC wrote in Newsweek that the issue was whether Baptist schools would offer "indoctrination" or "quality education." Smith said that Biblical "stories like the Creation, the Tower of Babel, Noah and the Flood, seemed to fit into the category of theological myth."[3]

Tired of taking a beating in the media, three conservative SBC presidents called a press conference following the February Executive Committee meeting in Nashville. They declared the central issue in the controversy to be the nature of Biblical truth, not "New Right secular politics" and "some particular interpretation of Scripture." Baptists, they said, have a "right to set [theological] parameters for the institutions and agencies which they support."

HMB president Larry Lewis "agree[d] with everything said" by the presidents. Southwestern Seminary president Russell Dilday called the statement "another defense of the takeover strategies of the past ten years." BSSB president Lloyd Elder didn't "take much issue" with the presidents' statement, but disagreed with "the thrust and implications" of their "political methodology."

Strategies for San Antonio

It was now virtually certain that Jerry Vines and Richard Jackson would be the presidential candidates at the upcoming San Antonio convention. Both were inerrantists with outstanding records in evangelism. At one time Jackson had been considered a part of the conservative resurgence. Now he was the candidate of the moderate-"centrist" coalition.

Jackson insisted that he was beholden to no one, yet he had appeared back in February with moderates Randall Lolley and Leon Smith at a news conference in North Carolina. A story circulated that Lolley would be Jackson's vice presidential running mate. Lolley, now pastor of FBC, Raleigh, NC, then said that he would not support "Jerry Vines' type of leadership if I can have anything to do with it as a pastor of a local church. And if I have any influence in North Carolina, I'm going to see to it that the [North Carolina Convention] doesn't do it either."[4] When it became evident that his beligerent stance was hurting Jackson's chances for the presidency, Lolley withdrew his name for nomination as first vice president.

The strategy of moderates for electing Jackson in 1988 was now clear. In the more liberal east he was being portrayed as "the turnaround candidate;" in the more conservative west, he was the "conservative peace candidate."

Conservatives were seeking to build a broader base among their theological kin. Their emphasis continued pretty much the same: Keep the Bible issue in the forefront. Show people evidence of the liberal drift. Urge conservative pastors to bring their church's maximum number of messengers to San Antonio.

The colorful Bill Powell was now seriously ill and off the scene. The hard-hitting Southern Baptist Advocate, with Bob Tenery as editor, was now going monthly to every Southern Baptist church and pastor. On the moderate side, the Advocate's counterpart was SBC Today, a subscription paper going to a much smaller readership, with Jack Harwell as editor.

Pre-convention Warmup

Paul Pressler and Paige Patterson had long been the chief targets of moderate "mud." A few weeks before San Antonio, moderates sent a mailout, under "centrist" Winfred Moore's name, to every SBC pastor, charging that Patterson and Pressler had ties to "the frightening cultic Reconstructionist Movement which wants to do away with the United States Constitution and base our society on Old Testament law, enforce the death penalty for at least 15 crimes including adultery and blasphemy, [and] enforce the death penalty for a rebellious child...."[5] The accusations were so patently ridiculous that the mailout angered many readers. One pastor later counted at least 50 votes that the pamphlet lost for Jackson in the Dallas-Fort Worth area alone.

Houston's John Bisagno, a professed neutral, called for a "candidate of unity" who would oppose both "the neo-orthodoxy of the Left and the excesses of the Right."[6] Bisagno said he would be delighted to nominate such a person, but no one ever surfaced. As convention time neared, Herschel Hobbs pleaded for an end to the controversy [in which we are] like wild animals devouring one another."[7]

The Bill Moyers special on Southern Baptists, which had infuriated SBC conservatives several months before, was re-run on several stations in North Carolina before San Antonio. The program was then aired in San Antonio on the Saturday night before the convention.

Speakers at pre-convention meetings of Women in Ministry and The Forum blasted the conservative effort. Forum speaker Libby Bellinger, for example, compared conservative leaders to bad "wizards" who have led us into a "growing Nothingness that is . . . like a cancer slowly spreading out its ugly fingers."[8]

All while conservatives at the Pastors Conference kept insisting that the problem in the SBC was a departure from Bible truth.

Bailey Smith: "I don't like anything that puts a question mark over the Word of God. Do you know why? Because watered-down penicillin never cured anybody."[9]

Richard Lee: "Let's put the blame where it belongs [for the drop in baptisms]. It's puny preaching from powerless pulpits by men who don't believe the Word of God."[10]

W. A. Criswell: "It is very apparent why the decline [of membership] in other denominations. The curse of liberalism has sapped the strength of their message. . . . Liberals today call themselves moderates. However, a skunk by any other name still stinks."[11]

Moderates held their noses, but not in amusement, when they read Criswell's remarks in the local papers on Tuesday morning. During the opening session of the convention several moderates quacked from a balcony in mockery of Adrian Rogers who was presiding.

Rogers' presidential sermon on legalists and liberals brought conservatives to their feet in applause while moderates sat grumpily waiting for the presidential vote.

Conservatives Win Again

Ralph Smith, a former president of the Texas convention, nominated Jerry Vines as "the kind you and I will be proud to have as president of this great convention." George Harris touted Richard Jackson's Cooperative Program and evangelism record. He believes in "an error-free Bible," declared Harris.

The difference again was not in the theology of the candidates, but in perceptions of their philosophy of leadership. Vines, it was felt, would keep the resurgence going. Jackson would start a comeback that would restore moderates to the board rooms.

When the vote tallies were announced, conservatives whooped in delight. Vines had won by a thin 50.53 percent margin. Some moderates threw their ballot cards down in disgust. Others walked out of the hall with tears in their eyes.

Both Vines and Jackson held press conferences afterward. The mild-mannered Vines hoped "[we can now] eliminate hurts and get on about the business of winning people to Christ. . . . . My purpose is not to exclude, but . . . to reach out to all our brothers and sisters in Christ."[12]

Jackson, who differed with Vines only "in philosophy," was encouraged by Dr. Vines' statement that he's "going to be fair and include everybody [in his appointments] who is a committed

Southern Baptist." Jackson said he "probably . . . would not be nominated [for president] again."[13]

It was hard for moderates to pick a fight with Vines. The big outcry at San Antonio came over a Wednesday resolution on the priesthood of the believer that affirmed "belief" in the doctrine, while stating that it "in no way gives license to misinterpret, explain away, demythologize, or extrapolate out elements of the supernatural from the Bible." The resolution further stated "that the doctrine . . . in no way contradicts the biblical . . . authority of the pastor" in the local church. The resolution passed, despite spirited objections from moderates, especially against the statement about pastoral authority.

That afternoon Randall Lolley led about 200 protesters to the registration counter. After turning in their ballot books, the group then marched to the nearby Alamo fort where Lolley held up a copy of the resolution before TV cameras and declared it "the most non-Baptistic, heretical" statement "ever made since we've been in existence since 1845!" Backed by loud Amens from the crowd, he ripped the paper in pieces — "thus making it the junk it ought to be."[14]

San Antonio was probably the most acrimonious convention in SBC history. Except for the mission board reports, the convention sermon by Joel Gregory was the only message which drew Amens from both sides. The Fort Worth pastor and then president of the Baptist General Convention of Texas told of a group of Irish workmen who tore down a castle to get materials for building the wall to protect the castle. "This is a parable of our beloved, historic" convention, Gregory said. "We must not build the wall [of orthodoxy] and tear down the castle [of the denomination by attacks on one another]."[15]

Conservatives won the presidency for the 10th year in a row by a 692 vote margin at San Antonio. They won with an attractive, non-abrasive candidate who would be hard to beat as an incumbent at the next convention in Las Vegas. Until they could turn the convention back to the old order, the moderate-"centrist" coalition could only try to slow more changes by conservatives in agencies.

Baker Out, Land In at the CLC

To this time, conservatives had elected agency heads only where there were vacancies: at Golden Gate Seminary (where Bill Crews was the consensus choice of almost everyone), at Southeastern Seminary and at the Home Mission Board after dismissing a moderate dominated search committee and electing a new committee representative of the full board. An attempt to dismiss Larry Baker at the CLC had failed by virtue of a tie vote.

Baker was clearly uncomfortable with conservative policy changes at the CLC. He was unhappy with a proposal by some trustees that the CLC merge with the Public Affairs Committee. Shortly before the San Antonio convention Baker agreed to resign on July 15 on condition of receiving $41,835 in severance pay and a car.

Richard Land was elected as the new CLC executive in September. Land came from the vice presidency of academic affairs at Criswell College and held a doctorate from Oxford University. He was strongly opposed to abortion on demand and also more in tune with other moral convictions of the board majority than Baker had been. Land took office on October 24 and was subsequently installed during a CLC seminar on the sanctity of life. Right-to-lifers, who had chafed under pro-choice Valentine and been disappointed by Baker, took heart.

The seminary situation was mixed after San Antonio. Golden Gate and New Orleans, both with conservative presidents, had been little touched by the controversy. Midwestern's president and trustees appeared to be working together. President Roy Honeycutt of Southern had stopped talking "holy war."

Southwestern's Russell Dilday had not stopped talking about the conflict. At San Antonio, Dilday had called Adrian Roger's convention sermon, which conservatives had cheered, "steamroller demagoguery." He admitted that his board had made "very clear" that he was not to speak out on the controversy, but said he intended to keep voicing his convictions. Dilday blamed Patterson and Pressler for using "fear words" and "intimidation."[16] A showdown seemed inevitable between Dilday and the conservative majority on his board.

More Troubles at Southeastern

The most troubled school continued to be Southeastern. At the seminary alumni luncheon in San Antonio, unkind remarks were made from the platform about President Drummond and board chairman Robert Crowley. Some trustees walked out.[17] Former president Randall Lolley was continuing to make life difficult for the new administration. Some financial supporters had stopped giving — due to influence from Lolley, it was thought. The faculty remained adamantly opposed to the new trustee policy that took hiring of additional faculty from their control. The faculty was further aroused when the board met in executive session and declined to rehire Janice and Mahan Siler as adjunct professors — reportedly because of articles Mahan Siler had written that some interpreted as advocating homosexual life styles.

The Association of Theological Schools (ATS), in an 18-page report issued after the San Antonio convention, called Southeastern "troubled" and "divided."[18] The ATS did not say when or what action it might take on the report with regard to accreditation. A special fact finding committee sent by the other accrediting agency, the Southern Association of Colleges and Schools [SACS], reported in December that the seminary was "not functioning effectively as a scholarly community." In responding to the SACS report, trustee chairman Robert Crowley said, "We desperately want peace . . . on the campus of SEBTS with the teachers and students, but not, of course at the cost of [refusing] to honor [the seminary's] commitment" to the "owner" and "supporter" of the school, the SBC.[19]

Squabbling continued between the Baptist Joint Committee and the SBC Public Affairs Committee over actions by the BJCPA staff. BJCPA Associate Director Stan Hastey resigned to become executive director of the moderate Southern Baptist Alliance which was opening an office in Washington. Another BJCPA staffer left to be Hastey's assistant. The switches confirmed to many SBC conservatives that the BJCPA had not been representative of Southern Baptists.

The State Convention Scene

Rejoicing by moderates over winning the presidency back in Georgia proved short-lived. The November, 1988 convention elected conservative Ike Reighard as president. Georgia moderates were further set back by the disclosure of a $14 million deficit at Mercer University, the resignation of the school's chief financial officer and a call for the resignation of President Kirby Godsey by some faculty. It was also disclosed that Godsey was receiving $120,000 in salary, plus perks which included a $900,000 annuity payable on his retirement.

The situation in other state conventions continued to vary from state to state. Moderates remained strongly in control in Virginia and North Carolina. Virginia moderates kept pressing for an agreement that would, in effect, allow their state convention to name the Virginia members of the national Committee on Committees. In North Carolina the changeover at Southeastern Seminary and political activities by Randall Lolley kept tensions high. Throughout 1988 the conflict continued on the national level, with conservatives increasing in strength on boards of agencies. After ten straight years of conservative advance, the future looked bleak for those who would stretch diversity to include seminary teachers and other denominational employees who could not accept the truth of the whole Bible.

Still, moderates were unwilling to accept defeat. At Las Vegas in 1989 they would try again to start a reversal of the tide that was sweeping across the denomination and affecting every agency.

References

1 Liz Lambert: "Drummond-Crowley Press Conference," The Inquiry, April, 1988.

2 March 7, 1988, pp. 1-15.

3 Rachel Richardson Smith: "Swordplay in Sunday School," December 21, 1987, p. 9.

4 Baptist Press, April 24, 1988.

5 Quoted from the mailout.

6 Marv Knox: "Both Sides at Fault, Bisagno Says of SBC," Baptist Press Report, May 10, 1988.

7 "Herschel Hobbs Compares Current SBC to 'Wild Animals Devouring One Another,'" Word & Way, May 26, 1988, p. 6.

8 Libby Bellinger: "Going Home By a Different Way," Folio, Winter, 1988, pp. 6, 7. J. Michael Parker: "Moderate Pastor: Baptist Power Struggle Similar to 'Wizard of Oz,'" San Antonio Express News, June 14, 1988, pp. 1A, 11A.

9 Addresses, Pastors Conference, 1988, pp. 1, 2.

10 Pastors Conference Roundup, Baptist Press, San Antonio, June, 1988.

11 From a tape of Criswell's address and "Monday Night Pastors Conference," Baptist Press, San Antonio, June, 1988.

12 From my tape.

13 From my tape.

14 Ginger Hall: "Moderates Protest Resolution, Stage Alamo March in Outrage," San Antonio Express News, June 16, 1988, p. 16A.

15 Anita Bowden: "Gregory Convention Sermon," Baptist Press Report, June 15, 1989. J. Michael Parker: "Minster Warns Southern Baptists to Stop Spewing Venom," San Antonio Express-News, June 16, 1988, pp. 1, 17A.

16 Remarks in the Convention Press Room at San Antonio.

17 From my taped notes at the luncheon.

18 From the ATS Report released August, 1988.

19 R.G. Puckett: "Accrediting Committee Cites Problems at Southeastern," Biblical Recorder, March 4, 1989, p. 3.

Chapter 5

"From Nashville to Las Vegas"

Next to the annual convention, the 77-member SBC Executive Committee is the most important entity in the SBC. The EC meets in February and September in Nashville and at the annual convention site in June.

This powerful committee has its own staff and "act[s] for the Convention *ad interim* in all matters not otherwise provided for."[1] Many motions presented at the annual convention are referred to the EC for consideration and to report back to the next convention.

A referral to the EC is typically assigned to a sub-committee or special study committee which examines the matter and makes a recommendation to the full EC meeting in plenary session. During much of 1988 a special study committee had been looking at into the tangled web of Southern Baptist representation Washington . In January, 1989, this committee announced that it would recommend to the EC February meeting that a new Religious Liberty Commission (RLC) agency be formed "as the sole office" in Washington "through which" the SBC would maintain "contact with the federal government." The study suggested that a budgeted amount be allocated to the RLC which would then decide on the portion to be given to the Baptist Joint Committee on Public Affairs. The study committee further proposed that additional funds be provided for the Christian Life Commission's Washington office and for operations of the SBC Public Affairs Committee.

"Centrist" Press Conference

On Monday evening, an hour before the EC was to open its February meeting, seven self-labeled "centrists," calling themselves "Baptists Committed to the Southern Baptist Convention," held a press conference in a Nashville hotel to announce opposition to the new agency and to consider the "integrity crisis" in the new leadership of the SBC. The group included Winfred Moore, Richard Jackson, Daniel Vestal, James Slatton, John Baugh, Steve Tondera and George McCotter, plus two paid staff. In a joint press handout, they said "the most serious crisis in [SBC] history" had arisen because "a relatively small group of fundamentalists has captured the presidency . . . since 1979, by means of a highly organized political machine."

Moore said the RLC would "further divide Southern Baptists when we [already] have representation [the BJCPA] in Washington." Jackson "denounce[d] the influence of Baptist Independents with a capital 'I', saying he had come to champion the identity of true Southern Baptists." Vestal was "deeply concerned about the future of Southern Baptists." There was a time, he admitted, when "some . . . . theological problems . . . posed a threat to this convention" but these "problems pale in insignificance in comparison to the threat of this present situation . . ."

Richard Jackson's Perspective

A reporter asked Jackson, "Do you intend to allow [yourself] to be nominated for president of the SBC in Las Vegas and have you been contacted by any individual asking for permission to nominate [you]?"

Jackson replied forcefully, "As for the last question, NO, I have not been contacted by any individual asking to nominate me. Answer to the second question, has anybody talked to me about it? NO. I think they've had enough of me. Answer to the first question, do I intend to allow my name to be presented? If I had to answer that question today, No, but never is a long, long time."[2] After the meeting, Jackson said in an interview that the principal problem was that conservatives had been too exclusive in their nominations and appointments. Asked where he would like to serve, Jackson declared, "I don't want a crust of bread. I want the whole loaf. I want to be chairman of the Committee on [Nominations]."[3]

EC member Fred Wolfe happened to attend the press conference. In a later EC session, Wolfe demanded a "public apology from this centrist group for sowing seeds of discord and mistrust of our present leadership." No apology was given.[4]

The Business and Finance Sub-committee discussed the proposed new RLC agency the next day. When Richard Jackson, a non-member, was given permission to speak to the group, he directed a sarcastic comment at member Paul Pressler. The committee chairman suggested the two talk outside the committee room.

Jackson walked out grumbling to reporters about Pressler "thinking he controls it all." When Pressler emerged a few moments later, Jackson charged him with "dealing with everything in Southern Baptist life."

Pressler responded, "Richard, my brother, I have wanted to just sit down with you. I have — "

Jackson interrupted. Pressler repeated his desire to talk with Jackson. Jackson interrupted again, charging Pressler with making contradictory statements, controlling votes, misrepresenting him (Jackson) and being dishonest.

Pressler asked for an apology, which Jackson refused to give. Jackson continued attacking Pressler, accused him of running rough shod over the rights of Jackson and others in denominational affairs. Pressler denied this and was cut off again in mid sentence.

The exchange, which was more of a monologue by Jackson than a dialogue with Pressler, was overheard by 50 or more reporters, editors and others with tape recorders running. It continued until a man stepped between them.[5]

A New Agency Recommended

The full Executive Committee debated the proposed new Religious Liberty Commission that evening. EC member Ed Drake, an attorney from Dallas, said the RLC would widen SBC effort in Washington, because "there is the perception that the Baptist Joint Committee speaks for the liberal element."

Foreign Mission Board president Keith Parks was granted permission to speak. Parks said he opposed the new agency because it "will have a negative impact on foreign missions and be viewed as a political move [and] divisive."

After lengthy debate, the EC voted 42-27 to recommend the RLC for approval by the convention in Las Vegas.

The EC then considered a proposal to cut funds for the BJCPA from $400,000 in 1989-90 to $50,000, with the balance going to the PAC and the CLC. EC member Frank Lady moved an amendment that BJCPA funding be the same as originally proposed. Pressler offered a substitute motion, asking that the BJCPA be given $241,000. Pressler's substitute was defeated 35-34. Lady's amendment passed 39-30.

Pressler also introduced a resolution expressing "concern about the biased content of the Bill Moyers special series" and the "use of federal tax dollars to support one faction in the [SBC] through the use of the Public Broadcasting System." This resolution passed 40-14.

In another controversial action, the EC received a "memorial" [message] from the Virginia convention asking, among other things, that the SBC President appoint to the SBC Committee on Committees "persons proposed by the Virginia convention." The EC did not act on the request because it would be a step toward establishing a connectional church. The memorial was referred to a special committee for study and report back to the EC.

Conservative Press Conference

Charges by the Baptists Committed group and other opponents of the conservative movement were widely reported in the press. A few days later the five conservative presidents — Rogers, Smith, Draper, Stanley and Vines — met with several other conservative leaders in a hotel near Atlanta for "prayer" and "reflection" on "the state of our churches and denomination." They noted that President Vines had not received a single invitation to speak at a state convention evangelism conference during the past year, while Jackson, who was widely expected to oppose a second term for Vines, had received more than he could accept.[6]

This was followed by a larger meeting of about 100 conservatives at FBC, Atlanta. When asked why conservatives were meeting, Adrian Rogers said "it was because of the shenanigans of the [Southern Baptist] Alliance compounded by the intentions of the erstwhile group now calling themselves 'centrists,' and seeing they might be trying to unseat Jerry Vines."

The presidents and others at the Atlanta meeting issued a long press release exhorting conservatives, among other things, to "devote renewed energy to support" SBC "agencies in the missionary enterprise" through the Cooperative Program and to proclaim "the Bible [as] the infallible and inerrant Word of God."[7]

While conservatives were meeting in Atlanta, members of the Southern Baptist Alliance met in Greenville, SC. After bewailing the "loss of academic freedom" at Southeastern Seminary, where 10 days later the conservative board majority would elect conservative theologian Russ Bush as dean, the SBA voted to start their own seminary as a cooperative venture with theological schools of several other denominations in Richmond. The SBA also voted to adopt a non-Baptist form of government, with delegates elected by state and regional chapters to vote on proposals presented by a board of directors.[8]

Tapes of the Pressler-Jackson exchange in Nashville were now circulating across the convention.[9] Jackson then hurt himself further by saying that he was considering the "independent route." He was not intending to withdraw from the SBC, but he didn't "know if" he could "continue to ask" his church to give sacrificially to the Cooperative Program.[10]

Vestal Launches His Campaign

With prospects of Jackson's candidacy fading, Daniel Vestal, pastor of Dunwoody Church in an Atlanta suburb, announced on April 16 that he would permit his nomination as president. Vestal had been at the church only six months, after coming from FBC Midland, Texas where that church had led the SBC in Cooperative Program giving for a number of years. Vestal's announcement meant that the moderate-"centrist" coalition would again be breaking tradition in opposing an incumbent president for a second term.

Vestal termed himself an inerrantist who counted among his friends "some" of those who had begun the conservative movement back in 1979. Vestal had served as Chairman of the Committee on Boards in 1983 and later on the Peace Committee. "Theologically and doctrinally," he said, "I was very much identified with [the conservative] perspective." But the movement became too tightly controlled, he lamented. He "hoped for a theological and denominational renewal and ultimately, a spiritual renewal" through the movement. When that did not come, he said, he joined in the February press conference with other members of Baptist Committed.

After returning to Georgia from Nashville, he began receiving "phone calls literally from across the country" asking if he would consider being a presidential candidate. He was now offering himself as a "responsible reconciler, a bridge to call our people back together."[11]

The moderate-"centrist" coalition paid $26,000 to have Vestal's statement and a tape mailed to every pastor in the SBC.

Conservatives who shared Vestal's theological orthodoxy believed he was naive or had been misled about the extent of liberalism in SBC institutions. David Baker of Missouri talked to Vestal about "men who denied the historical, literal resurrection of Jesus, questioned the virgin birth, denied the absolute truth of Scripture and espoused a form of universalism." Baker reported that Vestal listened but did not acknowledge "that real problems do exist. . . He felt the approach of conservative leaders was wrong and inappropriate," Baker said, "so I asked him what approach he would suggest as an alternative. Essentially, he . . . did not know how to approach these problems, he just felt we had become too political." Baker found it "ironic that Dan Vestal is now a part of an obviously political effort to stop the conservative shift in Southern Baptist life."[12]

Vestal, who had once derided denominational politics as sinful, launched a whirlwind campaign for his candidacy up to the very day of the election of officers at the Las Vegas convention. At a May "symposium" (actually more of a get-out-the-vote rally) in Nashville sponsored by Baptists Committed, he complained that "the pattern [of presidential appointments] for the last 10 years has been basically a philosophy of winner-take-all. My philosophy would be that winner shares all" and "include all Southern Baptists — even the present leadership" in appointments. Vestal also pledged, if elected, to seek a limitation on presidential appointive powers and emphasize Southern Baptist missions and evangelism."[13]

Vines Talks Soul Winning

Late in April, Vines announced his committee appointments. "My appointments," he said, "have been made on the basis of recommendations received from state executive [directors], pastors, directors of missions, church staff members and members of local churches. These appointments reflect my commitment to appoint the best Southern Baptists I could find. They are Bible-believing people who love the Lord, believe the Bible and are committed to the Southern Baptist Convention. I have consulted with my vice presidents [Darrell Robinson and Rudy Hernandez]. We have gone over these appointments together. They issue these appointments jointly with me."

Vines noted that "the overwhelming majority of these appointees have never served on any committee in the Southern Baptist Convention. . . . I am confident these Bible-believing Southern Baptists will carry out their assignments with the desire that God's will be done in our SBC and without any personal hostilities or private agendas."[14]

Since his election the past June, Vines had said little about the controversy, choosing instead to preach on personal soul winning in appearances around the Convention. In particular, he kept talking up the door-to-door pre-convention witnessing campaign planned by the Home Mission Board to reach every home in Las Vegas.

No site for a convention had ever been so controversial. Objectors saw Las Vegas as "Sin City," noting that it had legalized liquor, gambling and prostitution, all strongly opposed by most Southern Baptists. Others argued that if Southern Baptists could send missionaries to Las Vegas, why couldn't the convention be held there? As the debate continued, fear was expressed that the reputation of the city might keep many conservatives away, while many moderates might make a special effort to go and vote their opposition to the proposed Religious Liberty Commission.

Vines Reduces Tension

After the February EC meeting, Vines became aware that the proposed RLC was not being received well in many quarters. The mission board presidents, Keith Parks and Larry Lewis, were opposed to it on grounds that any new entity would take from mission dollars needed for missions. Vines decided to write EC chairman Charles Sullivan and ask that discussion of the RLC be deferred to another time. "Whatever the merits of the recommendation to begin" the new agency, Vines said, "the focus in Las Vegas must be on missions and evangelism." Sullivan said he would present Vines' request to the EC Monday meeting at Las Vegas before the convention began.[15]

Distribution of Vines letter to Sullivan brought widespread praise. North Carolina editor R. G. Puckett said, "Vines may have defused the most controversial item on the agenda" at Las Vegas. "Some think Vines is concerned that the RLC proposal will attract many people to Las Vegas to vote against it and they just might vote against him in his bid for a second term as president. For whatever reasons he may have, we support the SBC President in his request and hope that the issue is buried forever. We don't need a Religious Liberty Commission, now or ever." A number of other denominational editors felt the same way.[16]

As convention time approached, Vines made no effort to match Vestal in political activities. However, about 70 "Young Conservatives" held a rally in FBC, Euless, Texas "to encourage people to attend the Southern Baptist Convention in Las Vegas," according to rally organizer Rick Scarborough. Although Scarborough said that conservatives should promote peace and healing, one speaker, Kerry Peacock, noted, "The rats and skunks are still inside the wall [of the SBC]. Are we just going to leave them there?"[17]

The Vestal campaign rolled on. The candidate's backers announced in Raleigh, NC on June 1 that a half-hour of TV time had been purchased on a Las Vegas TV station at 10:30 p.m. on the Sunday before the convention, when many messengers would be in their hotels. Baptist Press observed that "never before has a presidential candidate purchased [broadcast] time to pitch his case to messengers."[18]

On another front the Moyers' TV documentary about the SBC controversy was re-run on all public TV stations in North Carolina. The North Carolina **Biblical Recorder** announced that the telecast would "feature new introductions and conclusions by Moyers which will address the efforts by Paul Pressler, Houston, to discredit the program since its original showing." The denominational paper quoted Moyers as charging Pressler and his fellow "fundamentalists" with "moving to establish in Washington a committee [the Religious Liberty Commission] that will lobby for the agenda of the Religious Right."[19]

Nearing the end of his year in office, Jerry Vines spoke optimistically about the future of the SBC. "To my view, we have settled the debate over the nature of Scripture. . . . The theological renewal in our convention is underway. I am confident that our administrations and the boards of trustees of our institutions will lovingly monitor its progress until resolution."[20]

Witnessing in Vegas

Revivals in 90 of Nevada's 120 SBC churches preceded the convention. On Saturday before the convention, 2,025 persons, including SBC President Jerry Vines, contacted 120,000 households in Las Vegas. About 5,000 church prospects were found with over 470 making professions of faith. Names of new converts, along with prospects, were given to local Southern Baptist congregations for follow-up. While Vines and others were involved in the witnessing blitz, Dan Vestal spoke to reporters in the Religious Newswriters Association (RNA). Vestal bemoaned the loss of "authentic diversity" in the SBC. "Those in control say if you don't vote a certain way, you don't believe the Bible, you are a liberal." Vestal said that if elected he would work to "depoliticize the presidency" and "take away the control from the group in power."

Vestal Courts the Press

Vestal recognized there had "always been politics, but since 1979 we have had a different kind of politics, which arrived at theological control." Vestal conceded that the "inerrancy" movement had brought a "valid correction." He agreed with "interpretations" of the Peace Committee that most Southern Baptists believed "truth, without any mixture of error for its matter" to mean "that mankind was directly created and therefore . . . Adam and Eve were real persons, . . . the named authors did indeed write the biblical books attributed to them by those books, . . . miracles described in Scripture did indeed occur as supernatural events in history," and the Biblical "historical narratives . . . are indeed accurate and reliable as given by the authors."

"I don't know of a Southern Baptist professor," Vestal continued, "who would [not] believe the Bible [to be] historical in some ways, [although] they differ on interpretations. If [a professor] says there really wasn't a Noah, I would say he's wrong, but I want . . . to allow a greater divergence of interpretation. . . . The main difference between me and [the inerrancy group supporting Vines] is freedom. I want Southern Baptists to be free, not intimidated or controlled."[21]

Vestal and his key lieutenants made themselves available to reporters all week-end. On Monday, in the convention press room, he continued talking to reporters.

"I do hold to doctrinal parameters, [but] there is a difference between a creed and a statement of faith. My fear is that the Peace Committee interpretation of Article 1 [with the four examples — direct creation of mankind, Adam and Eve are real persons, etc.] is narrowing those parameters. . . . We need to allow freedom of interpretation of doctrine. . . .

"I do have theological concerns, but am also committed to openness and freedom. . . . There cannot be real unity in the SBC as long as you disenfranchise large groups of people. . . . If Jerry Vines had matched his public statement on the controversy with his appointments, I would be more amenable. . . .

"I don't want to make a threat, but if we don't see a significant change soon, the fragmentation which we have seen is just a harbinger of what you will see."

However, Vestal "intend[ed] to win tomorrow and if I win, I will win again in New Orleans."[22]

Falwell on the Scene

Despite all of his efforts to enlighten the press, Vestal was eclipsed in the media by Jerry Falwell who had been invited to be "roasted" by the RNA and to speak to the Southern Baptist Evangelists' meeting. Falwell used his appearance before the RNA to announce the dissolving of the Moral Majority. "We've accomplished everything we set out to do," he said. Then he set about dispelling some rumors that had circulated for years.

It wasn't true, he said, that "Adrian Rogers, W. A. Criswell, Charles Stanley, Jimmy Draper, Jerry Vines and Jerry Falwell all sat down and said, 'Let's take over the Southern Baptist Convention. There's never been such a meeting, [or] phone calls, [or] correspondence."

Nor did he have any intention of "joining the Southern Baptist Convention." His church, he said, "has its own school [and] own mission board to support. . . . The Southern Baptist Convention would be of no value to our ministry." Falwell later told the evangelists that he wanted to work alongside Southern Baptists toward world evangelization. "I don't believe any of us can do it alone."[23]

Pre-convention Preaching

Militant rhetoric was absent at the pre-convention Pastors' Conference, where Tom Elliff was elected president of the group without opposition, succeeding Ralph Smith. Several thousand preachers heard sermons on special challenges facing them and the need for spiritual renewal. Charles Stanley called on fellow pastors to maintain a personal quiet time with God. Joel Gregory urged proclamation of "pillars of truth about Heaven." John Click warned that "doctrinal stance has no impact if it is not baptized in agape love." Larry Lewis urged the pastors to make soul winning a top priority."[24]

Top attendance at the moderate-sponsored Forum was no more than 700. Carolyn Weatherford, outgoing executive director of the Woman's Missionary Union, received the Forum's "Denominational Statesperson Award."

Two Forum speakers took aim at the resolution on the priesthood of the believer passed in 1988 at San Antonio. Molly Marshall-Green of Southern Seminary, in reference to the part about pastoral authority, said, "Leadership does not require intimidation, but empowerment. All believers must share in the pastoral care of the flock." Clyde Fant of Stetson University said "pulpit popes," who see themselves as "infallible when speaking," are undermining the doctrine of the priesthood of the believer. "As with all ecclesiastical monarchies, there is no room for fresh interpretation in the study [of the Bible], no room for humanity in the pulpit. . . "[25]

While the Forum and Pastors Conference continued meeting on Monday, the Executive Committee voted to accept Jerry Vines' request that convention action on the proposed Religious Liberty Commission be deferred. The EC re-scheduled the vote for New Orleans.

The Moyers' Affair

At the EC's February meeting, Paul Pressler had presented a resolution critical of Bill Moyers' public television special on Southern Baptists. Moyers then asked to appear before the EC in June to discuss the matter with Pressler at the EC's pre-convention meeting in Las Vegas, June 12. Committee Chairman Charles Sullivan replied that he would ask the EC in June if they wished to hear Moyers, a former Southern Baptist, at the September meeting.

However, on June 11 Moyers sent a fax message to Sullivan in Las Vegas, with a copy going to Baptist Press, withdrawing his request and saying, "Forget it," noting that Pressler had declined his offer of free time on PBS to discuss the issue following the program re-run in May and attacking Pressler as a "secular politician who has infected this Christian fellowship with the partisan tactics of malice, manipulation and untruth. Under his thumb, you [the EC] do only his will."

Sullivan deleted from the EC agenda discussion of Moyers' request to appear. Pressler requested BP director Al Shackleford not to publish the text of Moyers' attack, calling the fax letter "ridiculous." BP went ahead and distributed a story with Moyers' accusations to the media. While admitting his unhappiness with BP for publishing Moyers' message, Pressler declined further comment, saying only that, "[Moyers' request to appear] has been deleted [from the EC agenda]."[26]

A knowledgeable source within the EC (not Pressler) said, "We saw that the media was planning to make this Moyers' thing a major event. We backed off in the interest of peace and harmony."[27] This, along with deferral of the Religious Liberty Commission proposal, appeared to clear the deck for a relatively peaceful convention.

Vines Wins Again

The convention drew 20,423 messengers, about 2,000 more than had been predicted. It happened that a championship prize fight was scheduled for the week-end before the convention. On the plane coming in, a man reportedly asked former SBC president Herschel Hobbs if he was "going to the fights." Hobbs replied, "Yeah." Except for an unexpected impassioned debate over funding to the Baptist Joint Committee, a big fight was avoided.

In keeping with his theme for the past year, Jerry Vines devoted his presidential sermon to personal evangelism. When elected president last year, he said, "God laid it upon my heart to recommit myself personally to lead people to faith in Jesus. I . . . started writing in a little red notebook. . . the names and the dates of people I led to faith in Jesus. And you know what, folks, something wonderful has happened to me this year. . . . It has been the sweetest, joy-filled year in all of my life." Personal soul winning "will put the joy back in the Southern Baptist Convention."[28]

Tom Elliff nominated Vines for a second term, saying "he has been a model to us as preacher, pastor and certainly as president." He has called Southern Baptists to be soul winners and "also called us to reaffirm our position on the authority and integrity of the Bible." Elliff further noted that missions giving had increased 257 percent since Vines had come as co-pastor of FBC, Jacksonville, Florida.

David Sapp, pastor of FBC, Chamblee, Georgia nominated Dan Vestal. Sapp lauded Vestal for leading churches he had pastored to give large percentages to the Cooperative Program. Vestal, he said, "has called us to come out from our trenches and be brothers and sisters again. . . . He seeks to share presidential appointments with all Southern Baptists committed to the healing process. . . ."[29]

When the vote tally was received, Registration Secretary Lee Porter spoke in his customary slow drawl as he reported 10,754 votes for Vines and 8,248 for Vestal, giving Vines the win by a 56.59 to 43.41 percent margin. Moderates took courage. Vestal had received a larger percentage running against a conservative incumbent than had the popular Richard Jackson two years before in St. Louis.

Only 68 percent of the total number voting for president cast ballots for first vice president. Similar dropoffs had been noticed in past conventions. Many people came, registered, voted for their presidential candidate and went home. At Las Vegas this apparently happened in both camps. Evangelist Junior Hill, the conservative favorite, received 54.25% of the 12,884 votes cast. The rest was divided among two well known moderates, Bill Poe (1,005 or 7.80%) and Brian Harbour (683 or 5.3%) and retiring WMU president, Carolyn Weatherford (1,005 or 32.65%).

Less divisiveness in business sessions had been widely predicted for Las Vegas. The Resolutions Committee, under the leadership of Mark Coppenger, purposefully reported out non-divisive resolutions. But no one could predict what messengers might do from the floor.

The Executive Committee's proposed Cooperative Program allotments for agencies and other recommendations sailed through without objection. It included $391,796 for the Baptist Joint Committee, down from the previous year by only 2.05 percent, the same reduction which most regular agencies were given. Then came time for the introduction of motions.

One called for the Las Vegas convention to censure the EC for allowing EC member Paul Pressler to become involved in the conflict with Bill Moyers over Moyers' controversial public television special on the SBC. Another asked that the San Antonio priesthood of the believer resolution be rescinded and rejected. The Committee on the Order of Business (COB) ruled both motions out of order.

Another motion asked that Dr. Curtis Caine be removed as trustee of the Christian Life Commission for alleged racist remarks he had made at a CLC board meeting. The COB postponed action to the New Orleans convention with the understanding that the EC would conduct an investigation and make a recommendation there.

A controversial motion to put an item on the agenda asked that the president's message and the convention sermon be scheduled after the election of president at future conventions. This motion had failed before and it failed again, but by a razor-thin margin of only 41 votes.

The Executive Committee had honored Jerry Vines' request and deferred action on their recommendation for a Religious Liberty Commission. This did not prevent individual messengers from proposing changes in religious liberty representation.

Diversion Debate

Virginia messenger Charlie Waller set off a buzz by moving "that $350,000 be diverted from the Baptist Joint Committee to the operating budget of Southeastern Baptist Theological Seminary."

Rudy Yakym, a board member of the Christian Life Commission, moved that the EC consider "foregoing its recommendation to establish a Religious Liberty Commission" and instead expand the program statement and budget of the CLC to include the proposed duties of the RLC and report its findings to the next convention in New Orleans.

Kenneth Barnett, an EC member from Colorado, moved that the previously approved budget for agencies be amended to provide "a more equitable distribution of funds" for missions, the PAC and the CLC. Barnett asked that $200,000 be deleted from the BJCPA budget and be reallocated with $60,000 going to the Foreign Mission Board, $50,000 to the Home Mission Board, $50,000 to the PAC and $40,000 to the CLC.

The Committee on Order of Business ruled Barnett's motion out of order, referred Yakym's motion to the Executive Committee and set Waller's motion for discussion and voting on Wednesday, the next day.

The Wednesday debate on Waller's motion, to the discomfiture of BJCPA supporters, came a few minutes after Sam Currin, chairman of the Public Affairs Committee, gave his report. Currin said the PAC was "unwaveringly committed to the preservation of our religious values and freedoms upon which America was founded." Currin noted that the PAC had been involved in "several key legislative issues impacting church and state relations." The PAC, he said, had "opposed congressional efforts to enact national child care legislation which would discriminate against Christian parents and churches, ... fought against passage of the so-called Civil Rights Restoration Act of 1988," and was "continu[ing] to work for . . . outright repeal or substantive amendment" of the act.

The PAC and the BJCPA, Currin said, "continue[d] to have unresolved differences regarding institutional and financial ties, as well as disagreement on issues. This ill serves our convention at the very time we need to be restoring our nation to biblical principles."[30]

The Waller motion called for reconsideration of the previously adopted SBC budget and diversion of $350,000 from the BJCPA to Southeastern Seminary. Adrian Rogers was recognized first to speak in favor of the motion. "We have marched around this mountain [funding for the BJCPA] so many times, the body now needs to speak and move on," Rogers said.

Debate came fast and furious. Examples:

Opposed to diversion from the BJCPA: "We have already spoken on the budget. We need now to go ahead and trust the Executive Committee and the Convention."

For diversion: "The Baptist Joint Committee has consistently opposed prayer in public schools and said nothing about the holocaust of abortion. We must reconsider distribution of funds."

Currin, a North Carolina Superior Court judge, was asked how much of the total BJCPA budget was being provided by the SBC. Currin said "almost 90 percent, . . . but we are getting reports . . . of anywhere from $100,000 to $200,000 being solicited outside the Cooperative Program from other Southern Baptist sources." Currin lamented that the PAC "is unable to get an accounting from the Baptist Joint Committee on something as basic as where their money is coming from and how it is spent."

When the time to vote arrived, Lee Porter intoned, "Pass your ballots to the right." Hearing chuckles, he said, "I'm trying to be neutral here. One time we go to the left, the next time to the right."

BJC executive director James Dunn had been itching to speak. He protested to Adrian Rogers that Currin's percentage of SBC support of the BJCPA was "not true. [It's] a factual error. . . . I'm not getting [a] chance to be heard."

Rogers huddled with two assistant parliamentarians, Jimmy Draper and John Sullivan. They talked with President Vines who ruled that Dunn could take three minutes.

Dunn charged that the BJCPA "has been maligned and misrepresented by the PAC report. We are fully accountable," he said. Every BJCPA member, "received a certified audit verifying the agency's income and expenditures." (Dunn later provided a copy of the 1988 BJCPA audit to Baptist editors that showed allocations of $499,625 from the nine Baptist bodies, including the SBC, that made up the BJCPA. Of that amount, the SBC had supplied $448,400, 89.7 percent, only a trifle less than Currin had stated. But the $448,400 from the SBC was 70 percent of the $638,210 BJCPA income for the year which included funds received from special projects. As for questions of accountability, Dunn had refused to turn over to the PAC certain financial records showing staff expenditures and staff correspondence from the BJCPA files.)

Dunn disputed Currin's figures. "Fifty three percent is coming [this year] from the SBC. The SBC gave 60 percent last year and 70 percent the year before. It is true that many [SBC] churches and state conventions have contributed [to the BJCPA, although] we have not conducted a campaign among Southern Baptists. We have stayed within the boundaries. . . . Thank you for allowing me to correct factual errors."

Southern Baptist Advocate editor Bob Tenery was standing nearby. "Figures do lie, but liars do figure," Tenery muttered. "That [90 percent] figure has been around for some time. I think Currin is on target. And they did refuse to open the books."

The convention had moved on to other business when Porter announced that Waller's motion to reconsider had failed by 53.75 percent to 46.28 percent. Later that evening, President Vines gave Currin time to respond to Dunn's statements. The PAC chairman stood firm on his declaration that the BJCPA was receiving 90 percent of its operating budget from Southern Baptists. According to the 1988 SBC Annual, he noted, $435,000 of the $476,000 BJCPA budget had come from Southern Baptist sources. Monies through the Cooperative Program would constitute 60%, the figure cited by Dunn.31

Dunn was visibly relieved at having escaped another attempt at defunding. When this was noted to Jerry Vines, the SBC president said, "He has no reason to feel good. The vote this morning was an affirmation of the Executive Committee and its budget procedure, not James Dunn and the Baptist Joint Committee. He's like the man who fell from the 40th floor who remarked as he was passing the 30th, 'I feel good.' "[32]

Vines made these remarks as he was on his way next door to the Las Vegas Hilton where the Executive Committee was holding its organizational meeting on Wednesday afternoon to receive new members and elect new officers. Enroute over, he passed a young security guard sitting by a gate in the 107 degree temperature and reading a gift New Testament provided by the Sunday School Board.

Pace and Pressler Elected

The large conference room in the Hilton was jammed with EC members, press and denominational dignitaries, with many persons standing in the back. The EC elected Sam Pace, a Director of Missions from Oklahoma, as their new chairman by a 53-15 vote and Paul Pressler as vice chairman by a 43-26 margin. In each instance, fervent Amens followed the announcement of the vote count. Some cynics in the room could not hold their tongues. "Well, Pace will resign in six or seven months and turn it over to the judge," said one. Another grimly predicted, "By September they'll be burning witches."

EC members quickly completed their business and hurried out. One fluffed off the snide remarks and declared, "Sam Pace is his own man. Anybody from Oklahoma will tell you that."

The Moyers' affair and even the rancorous debate over diverting funds from the Baptist Joint Committee ranked secondary to the Bible issue in the minds of conservatives at Las Vegas. That became evident in Morris Chapman's convention sermon and Jerry Vines' post-election press conference.

Chapman's Call

Chapman was pastor of FBC, Wichita Falls, Texas, former president of the Pastors Conference and one of the final three candidates considered for presidency of the Home Mission Board. He had also been talked about as a future prospect for the SBC presidency.

The Texas pastor brought applauding conservatives to their feet when he called for Baptist teachers "who believe in the inspired, infallible Word of God. Baptist schools," Chapman said, "need professors who believe in the inerrancy of Scripture and in the virgin birth, the atoning blood, the resurrection and the second coming of Christ."

Chapman pointed to Baptist history as justification for Southern Baptists to require that their professors believe in the fundamentals of the faith. It has always been part of our history and heritage, he said, to insist that our schools be true to the faith.[33]

Presidential Press Conference

Jerry Vines, in his presidential press conference, repeated his earlier contention that "the issue of the Bible is settled in Southern Baptist life. . . . Southern Baptists, every time they have had an opportunity to do so, have overwhelmingly affirmed we believe the Bible is without error. Those who say that there are errors in the Bible are in pronounced minority in Southern Baptist life. That has been settled."

This didn't mean that the controversy was over, Vines said, but "that the administrators of our institutions [and] the trustees . . . clearly understand the direction which Southern Baptists want to go. . . . The process of theological renewal is underway."

Dallas writer Helen Parmley asked Vines, "How many Baptist professors are there who do not believe in the virgin birth?" Vines declined to answer, saying, "We'll let the trustees and the administrations decide that for us."

Asked if he was part of a "fundamentalist faction," Vines replied that he had "always asked that I not be referred to as a fundamentalist. If you mean by fundamentalist that I'm one of those who believes in the fundamentals of the faith, yes. But if you mean that I would fall in the category of a legalist, an unloving person, an Ayatollah Khomeini or a Jim Jones, then the answer is no. I would like to be known as a Bible-believing Christian."

Vines promised to extend his emphasis on personal evangelism to promote the "building" of "great soul-winning churches." His appointments would be made by the same criteria as followed during the past year: "I will appoint the best Baptists I can find. I will not knowingly appoint anyone who believes there are errors in the Bible."[34]

Views of the Defeated Candidate

The defeated candidate, Dan Vestal, followed the tradition begun by unsuccessful candidate Richard Jackson at San Antonio by holding a press conference after the elected president's. Vestal reiterated that his greatest concern in the denomination was not the Bible, but freedom, whether the SBC would be non-creedal and not exclude a large number of Southern Baptists from denominational life. "The present power movement that's in control is doing exactly what they accuse others of doing before 1979 [of controlling the SBC elective processes]. . . . I want to return to a greater freedom and openness. . . . I want to see a return to shared power."

Vestal didn't think it "proper" for "some state convention to secede now." He didn't "want to be a prophet of doom or . . . make threats, [but] I do think we should face reality. The disenfranchised will not always support the Cooperative Program." His church was giving 12 percent to the Cooperative Program, he said and would remain "committed." Vestal was "disappointed" over losing to Vines. He couldn't make "a commitment today" on his availability for being nominated in New Orleans.[35] He told a group at a breakfast sponsored by "Baptists Committed . . . " that he wanted to "go home and pastor" before deciding to try again for the presidency.

Winfred Moore, spokesman for Baptist Committed drew applause at the breakfast when he addressed Vestal. "I know you need to talk to your people and as a pastor I appreciate that, but I want you to know that I sent a telegram to your deacons this morning." Moore quickly added, "And I signed your name to it."[36]

The editorials in most Baptist papers following Las Vegas tended to be upbeat. Indiana's Gary Ledbetter noted that "in the 11th year of the conservative resurgence . . . , the worst things predicted by those who disagree have not come to pass. Regardless of the campaign rhetoric of this year, no one has been fired, no one has lost his voice in our annual meeting and we have not split our denomination. The boards and committees we elect still reflect the diversity of our body, (when was the last time you read of a unanimous vote?) and there is no master plan to keep certain people from being a part of the process. Some of our agencies are stronger than ever before and evangelism has a new priority in our publications and planning. . . . We are seeing some good reasons to believe that we are presently on the right track as a body and have good, godly plans for the future."[37]

Missouri's Bob Terry, after lauding Jerry Vines for focusing on witnessing and evangelism, saw some "encouraging signs that trustee designations from the Committee on Nominations "may be more inclusive than in recent years."

Jackson Appointed

Terry didn't mention the nomination everyone was talking about.[38] It came about this way. Home Mission Board president Larry Lewis suggested to Jerry Vines that Richard Jackson be named to fill a trustee vacancy on the HMB. Vines talked to HMB trustee chairman, Ralph Smith, who also thought this was a good idea. The Committee on Nominations agreed and Jackson, who had made strong statements about representation on boards, was elected.

Vines called this "a wonderful move. I have a great love for Richard Jackson [his opponent for the presidency in 1988]. I want this to be a kinder, gentler Southern Baptist Convention."[39]

References

1 Bylaws of the SBC, SBC 1989 Annual, p. 12.

2 From my notes and tape recording of the press conference.

3 Personal Interview, Nashville, February 20, 1989.

4 News Conference Remarks Called Insulting," Religious Herald, March 9, 1989, p. 10.

5 From my tape of the exchange.

6 From news release issued following the meeting.

7 Quotes from the press statement.

8 Marv Knox: "New Seminary Approved at Alliance Annual Meeting," Biblical Recorder, March 18, 1989, pp. 1, 8.

9 I taped the exchange and provided copies to both Jackson and Pressler.

10 Toby Druin: "Jackson: SBC on Strange Road He Can't Travel," Baptist Standard, March 22, 1989, pp. 13, 14.

11 From Vestal's Statement, April 16, 1989.

12 David Baker: Southern Baptist Coalition for Biblical Inerrancy Newsletter, May 10, 1989, p. 1.

13 Marv Knox: "Vestal: Presidency Would be 'Winner-share-all, Baptist Standard, May 10, 1989, p. 4.

14 Jerry Vines: "Statement on Appointments," May, 1989.

15 Dan Martin: "Vines Asks New Commission Be Deferred," May 3, 1989, pp. 3, 5.

16 R.G. Puckett: "Puckett's Perspectives, Looking to 'Vegas," Biblical Recorder, May 13, 1989, p. 2.

17 "Political Activities Escalate as SBC Approaches," Word & Way, June 8, 1989, p. 9.

18 "Vestal Campaign Buys TV Time," Indiana Baptist, June 13, 1989, p. 1.

19 "Moyers Documentary Set May 23," Biblical Recorder, May 20, 1989, p. 9.

20 Dan Martin: "Southern Baptists Ready for New Era, Vines Says," Biblical Recorder, May 20, 1989, p. 7.

21 From my notes and tape recording of Vestal's remarks to the RNA group.

22 From my notes and tape recording of interviews with Vestal in the press room.

23 Baptist Press Convention News, June, 1989, Las Vegas. I also talked to Falwell and was at his press conference.

24 "Pastors' Conference Speakers Share Thoughts on Facing Ministry Challenges with Confidence," Word & Way, June 22, 1989, p. 10.

25 "Forum Wrap up," Baptist Press Convention News, Las Vegas, June, 1989. "Forum Speakers Emphasize Priesthood of the Believer," Word & Way, June 22, 1989, p. 14.

26 "Moyers Withdraws Request for Discussion," Religious Herald, June 22, 1989, p. 4; "Moyers Withdraws Request to Speak Before Executive Committee," Word & Way, June 22, 1989, p. 4.

27 Personal Interview, Las Vegas, June, 1989. The source asked not to be named.

28 SBC President's Address, "Going, Weeping; Sowing, Reaping," Word & Way, June 22, 1989, p. 6.

29 Messengers Re-elect Jerry Vines as SBC President," Word & Way, June 22, 1989, p. 3. Some information from my taped notes.

30 From the Report as printed in Southern Baptist Public Affairs, Convention Issue, Las Vegas, June, 1989, p. 1.

31 From my taped and written notes and "Effort to Reduce BJCPA Funding Fails Again." Some information from Religious Herald, June 22, 1989, p. 5 and Toby Druin: "Dunn Answers Questions on BJCPA Funds," Baptist Standard, July 19, 1989, p. 4.

32 Vines made this statement to me after the vote.

33 Jim Newton: "Convention Sermon," Baptist Press Convention News, Las Vegas, June, 1989.

34 From my notes at the press conference and "Vines Reiterates: Issue of the Bible 'Over,' " Baptist Standard, June 21, 1989, p. 8.

35 From my notes taken at the press conference and Toby Druin: "Vestal Won't Rule Out New SBC Bid in 1990," Baptist Standard, June 21, 1989, p. 9.

36 Roy Jones: "Baptist United Breakfast," Baptist Press Convention News, Las Vegas, June, 1989.

37 Gary Ledbetter: "Prognostication," Indiana Baptist, June 20, 1989, p. 4.

38 Bob Terry: "Encouraging Signs from the SBC," Word & Way, June 22, 1989.

39 From my notes of talking to Lewis and Vines and at Vines' press conference.

Chapter 6

"Tough Times in Denominational Agencies"

The usual after-convention breather didn't come after Las Vegas. The SBC sky quickly clouded and the storms began coming, starting with protests over actions by a trustee committee of the Foreign Mission Board.

Before this problem arose, the FMB had been moving ahead with little conflict. Conservative trustee Mark Corts had been reelected board chairman by acclamation at the past spring's board meeting. Moderates had run out of steam over the firing of missionary teacher Michael Willett for what FMB officials described as a lack of clarity in his views on God, miracles and the resurrection of Christ. Willett was now going to teach at the liberal United Methodist-related St. Paul School of Theology in Kansas City.

A compromise of sorts had been reached in a dispute between Paige Patterson and Keith Parks over the effort by Criswell College, owned by FBC of Dallas, to purchase a Belgian school for an outreach of the Dallas-based college.

FMB trustees adopted a resolution reaffirming the SBC's commitment to cooperative missions, while also recognizing the autonomy of Baptist churches to engage in their own mission endeavors.[1]

The Pennington Affair

All in all, things were going pretty well until protests erupted over a trustee sub-committee's 9-4 vote not to accept a staff recommendation for missionary appointment of an ordained Oklahoma couple, Greg and Katrina Pennington.

The committee maintained that women's ordination was not the primary issue. Two years before, they had approved two ordained women. In the Pennington situation, the trustees received a letter from the Director of Missions of Enon Baptist Association strongly opposing the appointment. Don Clark, the DOM, noted that the Penningtons had been "adamant in their pursuit of ordination" in spite of associational opposition. One month before their ordination service the association had voted to automatically remove from its membership any church ordaining women. "It is our conviction," Clark said, "that the ordination of Mrs. Pennington violated clear Bible teaching," as well as another Biblical principle that Christians should refrain from actions that might offend fellow Christians.

Harlan Spurgeon, FMB vice president for mission management and personnel, told Baptist Press that the trustee committee had rejected the Penningtons because "of the way [they] dealt with the issue of ordination in the climate of the local association." Committee chairman Paul Sanders said the Penningtons had placed the issue of Katrina's ordination above the fellowship and witness of their local church and the rest of the churches with whom they had formerly cooperated. . . . We must send [as missionaries] those we feel will not be divisive and [will be] able to work well with others."[2]

The Penningtons' case became another cause celebre for moderates. During the next two months the FMB received over 300 letters on the turndown, with most writers accusing the committee of overriding the autonomy of the local church which had ordained Katrina, violating the spirit and principle of cooperative missions and supporting one political viewpoint in the wider denominational controversy. Many letters, pro and con, were printed in denominational papers.

A Controversial Job Switch

The dust raised over the Penningtons' case was beginning to settle, when a protest arose among the trustees over an executive appointment by Keith Parks, the FMB president. The man in question was William R. O'Brien, husband of the new WMU executive director, Dellanna O'Brien. Mrs. O'Brien succeeded Carolyn Weatherford, who had resigned to marry a pastor in Ohio.

The WMU offices are in Birmingham. Upon his wife's election, William R. O'Brien asked to be relieved of his job as executive vice president for the Richmond-based Board. Several weeks later, Parks announced that he was appointing O'Brien as a top special assistant to the president, with his office in Birmingham.

Twenty-eight of the board's 89 trustees signed a letter protesting the arrangement on grounds that it had the "appearance of cronyism" and of "linkage" of two independent organizations, the FMB and the WMU. The letter said the move would not be cost effective, that it would be difficult for O'Brien to supervise employees from Alabama and would put a person with "open identification with the moderate faction" in the SBC in an objectionable role. In his lengthy reply, Parks said there would be no linkage between the FMB and the WMU and that they would "work carefully to demonstrate there is no conflict of interest." Birmingham, Parks said was "more central" to SBC agency constituency than Richmond. Budgetary concerns would be "carefully monitored." Problems of administrative supervision "is something . . . we will have to evaluate as to effectiveness." Parks felt "insulted" at the suggestion of cronyism. "This makes it appear that my integrity is being questioned."

The trustees accepted his explanations. Trustee Michael Goodwin, one of those who had signed the letter, said the exchange reflected "healthy tensions" between Parks and the board. "This is just part of the process of getting to know one another."[3]

Of greater concern was the downward trend in new missionaries. Appointments had topped 400 for the first time in 1982, reached an all-time high of 429 in 1985, then dropped back to 411 in 1986, 407 in 1987 and 358 in 1988. Trustee Betty Swadley called the slowed growth "distressful. I think part of the reason is because of the negative press the Foreign Mission Board has been getting." Swadley explained that more attention was sometimes given to problems and disagreements than to good things happening in foreign missions."[4]

The Holly Correspondence

Conflicts at the FMB were mild compared to the furor that resulted from an effort by some trustees to dismiss Sunday School Board president Lloyd Elder in August. The attempt failed because the conservative board majority divided over the appropriateness of the action.

A number of BSSB trustees were unhappy with Elder for a variety of reasons. Trustee Larry Holly, a pediatrician from Beaumont, Texas, put some of their concerns and his own in a letter to all trustees which he released to the press shortly before the August board meeting in Glorieta, New Mexico. Holly did not mail Elder a copy at that time.

One concern was the perception that Elder had been too involved in SBC politics, particularly in expressing himself in the on-going dispute between the SBC Public Affairs Committee and the Baptist Joint Committee on Public Affairs. By virtue of his agency position, Elder was a member of the PAC. Time and again, Elder had vocally disagreed with a majority of the PAC on the role of that committee in dealing with religious liberty issues and relationships between the PAC and the BJCPA. Stan Hastey, who had left the BJCPA staff to head the moderate Southern Baptist Alliance, termed Elder the most consistent defender of the BJCPA and "positions on separation of church and state."[5]

Back in February, 1989 the BSSB's Executive Committee had met and approved a $400,000 gift from the BSSB to assist the SBC Executive Committee in paying off the indebtedness of the Baptist

Building in Nashville. At that meeting, Holly said he didn't want
to see the contribution used to restore funds that might be cut from
the BJCPA. Elder replied that the money could be used for no other
purpose than to pay off the indebtedness.[6]

The SBC Executive Committee met a few days later and voted
to cut the BJCPA allotment for 1989-90 from $400,000 to $50,000.
Elder opposed this reduction. EC minutes reveal the involvement
of Elder in a floor discussion of the BSSB gift:

"It was Dr. Elder's opinion that if the allocation of the proposed
budget changed, as suggested during this [EC meeting in which a
cut in the BJCPA allotment was discussed], he would feel obligated
to give this new information to the trustees of the Sunday School
Board for their possible reconsideration. He stated that he did not
know whether they would withdraw the offer [of the $400,000 gift],
but he felt it would be his responsibility to advise the trustees of
the Sunday School Board regarding the Executive Committee
action in this meeting."[7]

After Elder and others made known their opposition to the
BJCPA cut, the EC reversed its earlier decision and voted to
restore almost all of the original allocation to the BJCPA. In a letter
to fellow EC members, Jerry Brown, a layman from Oklahoma,
saw Elder's statement as an effort to "manipulate . . . some [EC]
members into changing their vote on the BJCPA allocation. In
support of Brown's letter, EC member Fred Wolfe said, "This kind
of intimidation and pressure must stop."[8]

The following morning an EC member asked EC Executive
Director Harold Bennett if Elder had made a threat to withhold
money if the BJCPA funding was not restored. Bennett, according
to Elder in a statement to the BSSB trustees, said there had been
"no threat at all." Elder said he thought "the matter was closed."
Elder said he was "proceeding to do exactly what our board voted
to do about the $400,000 contribution."[9]

Holly was not satisfied with Elder's explanation. On July 10,
he wrote new BSSB trustees that "there are members of the [SBC]
Executive Committee who sincerely believe that Dr. Elder
attempted to use the $400,000 to influence funding for the Joint
Committee. Dr. Elder vigorously denies this."[10]

Holly was also dissatisfied with BSSB curriculum. He had
found the literature, "upon occasion, to contain accidental errors .
. . and what appeared . . . to be intentional inclusions which I would
judge to be heretical. But, most often I found the material not to
be so much wrong as to be insipid, vacuous, superficial and
bland."[11]

In his experience as a trustee, Holly said he had witnessed "a
great deal of effort [by the BSSB administration] . . . to 'manage'
the board of trustees." He "found . . . a sense among the trustees
that any differences with the administration's policy was disloyal

and divisive. . . . Anyone who questioned the accuracy of [administration] statements was labeled as a mean-spirited, non-team player, who was not to be trusted. . . . Such a person would be systematically excluded from significant participation in the Board's activities by being placed on relatively insignificant committees and having his correspondence answered in a perfunctory way. . . . The present administration," Holly said, had "adopt[ed] the last administration's management style, which was essentially autocratic, rigid and closed."[12]

Holly urged additional board meetings, a "re-evaluation of the priorities" of trustees, more "openness" by the administration and quicker response to trustee requests for material, appointment of trustees to "responsible positions without regard to their being 'safe' or 'loyal,' " a "demonstration project" for developing better curriculum and a survey of churches which "are using alternate literature to give us their candid comments on why they are not using Sunday School Board material."[13]

Holly said that "recent events at the Executive Committee" of the SBC "demonstrate the need for the review of Dr. Elder's presidency so that Southern Baptists can stay in charge of their own institutions."

Holly also included in his July mailout a 12-page "history of the presidency" of the BSSB for the past six years, with extensive documentation that he claimed would back up his citations. He cited,

— The BSSB administration's "management" of the Durham-Job mansucript in which the writer "stated that the Old Testament had no conception of the personification of evil in . . . a person named Satan."

— Elder's "discontent with the conservative resurgence" as expressed in a press release to the Nashville Tennessean, April, 1985 which "had the tone of opposing the re-election of [Charles Stanley], a sitting president" of the SBC. Holly noted that Winfred Moore had spoken at the BSSB chapel in the year he opposed Stanley for the presidency, that Richard Jackson was "prominently part of major" BSSB "activities" in the years that he ran for president of the Convention," and that Daniel Vestal had been "commissioned to write the doctrinal study for 1990," in the year "when he will run as the moderate-liberal candidate" for the SBC presidency.

— Board publication of a chapel address by past BSSB president James Sullivan which "amounted to a personal attack on the conservative resurgence . . . " In his address, Sullivan spoke of "inexperienced [SBC] leadership" in "this extreme rightist group" who "make glaring blunders."[14]

— Administrative disregard of a request by trustees that the BSSB president "not . . . be involved in Convention politics." Holly

noted from the Nashville Tennessean that in February, 1986 Elder
and Southwestern Seminary president, Russell Dilday, had been
in "a group that surrounded" three SBC [conservative] presidents
after the presidents had given a news conference "to refute some
of the trio's statements to the denominational and secular media."

— Using the results of a dubious poll to oppose the publication
of "a conservative commentary."

— Opposing the placement of "a Sanctity of Human Life lesson
in the dated curriculum of the Board."

— Difficulties experienced by trustees in obtaining "certain
information from the administration."

— Board publication in 1989 of an article by a seminary
professor stating that "little question apparently existed in the
minds of Joshua, David, or Elijah that other gods existed alongside
the God of Israel. . . "

— The opinion of several SBC EC members "that Dr. Elder
had attempted to manipulate the vote on the BJCPA." Holly said
that during the debate "over removing money from the BJCPA,"
Elder "went to the platform and motioned for Dr. Bennett to come
to the side." According to Holly, Bennett then "turned to the
secretary of the Executive Committee and said, 'We're this far
(holding his fingers a quarter of an inch apart) from losing the
$400,000 from the Sunday School Board.' The secretary of the
committee said to him, 'Do you mean if this motion passes?' Dr.
Bennett responded, 'That's exactly what I mean.' "

Holly concluded that if the BSSB president could "give his full
energies" to the BSSB and "whole-heartedly support the policies of
the trustees, without being distracted by Convention issues not
relevant to his responsibilities, then the trustees can continue to
work with him. Unfortunately," Holly said, "it seems that his
emotional and doctrinal wedding to the past prevents him from
cooperating with the Divine Spirit and the movement which is
sweeping the Convention."

Holly then requested "a special [trustee] discussion, perhaps
in executive session, to review the conduct and performance of the
President. . . "[15]

The full board meeting was set for August 7-9 at the Glorieta
Conference Center. Upon arrival Holly distributed to the press
copies of material previously sent to trustees.[16]

Administrative Committee Concerns

Holly and several other trustees, along with President Elder,
met with the Board's General Administration Committee (GAC)
on August 7, before the general board meeting was to begin. Holly
was given ten minutes to make a presentation of his concerns.
Several trustees then spoke. One was "aggrieved" that Elder had

"been denied due process" by Holly's "letter-writing campaign," Another trustee said he had felt manipulated by Holly's threat.[17]

Elder denied a "crisis of leadership" at the BSSB. "Dr. Holly has only made there appear to be one," he said The GAC then went into executive session for over four hours and discussed the problems alleged by Holly.[18] The committee drew up a five-point recommendation on questions about Elder which they presented as the first order of business when the general board meeting began.

1. The committee "regret[ted] Dr. Elder's judgment and timing" in making statements about the $400,000 gift from the BSSB for paying on the SBC Building debt, which "caused confusion" among the BSSB trustees "and gave the perception of political activity." However, the committee accept[ed] his explanation. "Without questioning his integrity, we instruct him to make every effort to avoid any activity which could reasonably be perceived as political."

2. The committee "request[ed]" Elder "to make a documented explanation, to the General Administrative Committee [and] the full trustee board."

3. The committee "instruct[ed]" Elder to "instruct all [BSSB] speakers, writers and authors . . . to refrain from agitating the political climate within the SBC," and "to seek a balance in such speakers, authors and writers."

4. The committee recommended that the GAC chairman "appoint a subcommittee to revise and/or develop an instrument for performance or evaluation" of the president.

5. The committee "encourage[d] trustees with grievance regarding the performance of the president to forward their concerns to the [GAC] for consideration in his annual performance evaluation."[19]

Elder's Defense

Elder then spoke in his defense. He gave a lengthy summary of the sequence of events related to the $400,000 gift for the Baptist Building debt. He cited Harold Bennett as saying there had been no threat of withdrawal of the gift. He said he had supported the EC's Special Study Committee on the BJCPA. For two years he had "plead[ed] for the continued participation and funding" of the BJCPA. He was grieved about published letters from EC members, containing "unfounded rumors, distortion and biased opinion about somebody else's motives or behavior." They never "talked to me about their strong opinions," he said.

Elder said he had "at no time discussed, with the SBC Executive Committee's Business and Finance Sub-committee, the gift in reference to the Baptist Joint Committee on Public Affairs." As an SBC member of the Public Affairs Committee he did have "some convictions" about the BJCPA, which he had expressed in PAC meetings.

Elder had been asked by the GAC to only explain his remarks about the BSSB gift to the SBC Executive Committee's debt. Unexpectedly he launched into a defense of himself against Larry Holly.

Elder said he had obtained a copy of Larry Holly's first mailing from a third party. Holly, Elder said, had declined to send him a copy at that time but did send him a later mailing. Trustee Holly's six-year history [of actions by the administration and other BSSB staff], Elder declared, was not fair to the BSSB or the record written by the trustees and himself. Elder said he would respond only to Holly's allegation that he had intentionally misled the trustees on the Durham Job manuscript. "I will never mislead you," Elder told the trustees.

Elder said he requested Holly to send additional information in reference to allegations that he [Elder] had tried to the influence the funding cut proposal for the BJCPA. "Larry . . . declined and said he would do so after the [Las Vegas] convention. I regret that very much. I operate a $170 million business and I just don't go around just waiting on letters from any single trustee, but I'm faithful to carry out the dictates of the trustees. So if holding in suspense [by Holly] is an effort to have undue influence on the president, [that] ought never to be tolerated by the trustees and it ought not to have undue influence on the president of the board."

Elder said Holly had sent other letters to trustees, about problem areas over a period of time, without sending him copies. "We ought to stand by the record," Elder said, "rather than by the private interpretations of one trustee [Holly]. I do not think it serves you well as a Board to form your opinions by what one person may select as the history of our board and the interpretations. . . . It is not fair to you and to Southern Baptists for a single trustee to try to rewrite the history of this Board."

Elder insisted that "we do not have a crisis of leadership among the trustees or the president. I believe the president is doing exceptionally well in the playing field he has to play on. These are difficult days. We owe it to our people, not to let someone lead us to an impasse."

During his almost-six-year tenure, Elder said he had "won the fellowship and in most cases the affection of 2,000 employees. Don't throw that away. I have . . . worked with 37 state executive directors, so that they believe and trust the BSSB. I plead with you, don't throw that away. I've tried to work with every [SBC] agency and serve [them] better. Don't damage the leadership you're allowing me to have."

Elder said he had to "the best" of his "ability carried out every action that has been voted on by the trustees." He had "voluntarily by discipline stayed out of politics." He had spoken only in his "exercise as president . . . in the midst of a denomination as we are right now." He had neither supported nor worked against any SBC presidential candidate, nor had he "spoken to the [SBC] Forum." He "understood and honored" who the Board of Trustees was. He was "excited about being president" of the BSSB and was "looking forward to years of fruitfulness."

Elder came back to Holly. "There is no answer to some of the perceptions and interpretations he has put on me. . . . When one trustee sends a letter to 90 trustees and says that the president intentionally misled the trustees, that ought not to be. I will never, never mislead you. You may question my judgment, my calling — I think we're doing some outstanding work, . . . and I do not want us to cast aside that which we're building together. And frankly I do not believe that you will." After 45 minutes of speaking, Elder sat down.

Trustees Respond to Elder

Elder's remarks had clearly upset a number of trustees. Trustee Gene Swinson declared that he was tired of the BSSB president and trustees "being maligned, sometimes unjustly, sometimes justly. I do not come to this trustee meeting with purpose of maligning Dr. Elder." Swinson then moved that the GAC report be amended to "remove the entire report that Dr. Elder just gave. And that we accept the report of the GAC.

"I can tell you my friends," Swinson continued, "Larry Holly is not the only one [who has been concerned]. He just happened to have the time and money to put words on paper that a lot of us don't have. I urge you to strike from the record the entire report Dr. Elder gave [as it] relates to Larry Holly."

After considerable discussion, pro and con on both Elder and Holly, Swinson's motion to strike from the record was defeated.

Several trustees questioned Elder about other matters. One asked what he had meant in a recent speech to student ministers: "I'm not going to let the discouragement of the last decade overcome 450 years of Baptist heritage." Elder said he was talking about discouragement with some churches withdrawing support from the Cooperative Program, not over SBC presidents.

Asked about the perception of many trustees that he had been involved in SBC politics, Elder stated it was difficult in the present environment for anyone to do something others might not perceive as political.

After more questions by trustees and responses from Elder, trustee Allen Harrod stated his concerns that Elder not participate in political action. Harrod expressed grief that Elder had attacked Holly. He did not think Holly was out to get Elder fired. Harrod had received the impression at trustee orientation that Elder was angry with the conservatives who had taken over. Harrod said Elder's statement to the student ministers was "foolish and needless."

A Motion to "Fire"

At this point, trustee Joe Knott asked if the board was discussing the report from the GAC dealing with the personnel matter; if so, he had a substitute motion for the board. Receiving an affirmative answer, Knott said, "Then I wish to make a motion to fire Dr. Elder and declare the presidency vacant." In making the motion, Knott said, "I have no rancor or anger toward Dr. Elder personally." It would later come out that neither Knott nor Holly had come to the meeting with any plans to fire Elder.

After a second, Knott spoke to his motion: "The trustees' responsibility is not to establish guidelines for the president's behavior; it is to make sure that we have the best man possible for the job. If we believe that there is a better person available for this job, then we are obligated to find him."

Another trustee said, "If we apply this logic then all of us would have to be replaced . . . "

Another board member said, "Dr. Holly spoke his piece; Dr. Elder has spoken his piece. Why not bless what [the GAC] has given on paper and be done."

Holly spoke for Knott's motion urging that the board give Elder adequate notice, provide a settlement package that would make the transition easdy for him, then move on.

Trustee Dan Collins was troubled that Elder had not recognized the consensus of 18 members of the GAC. Trustees, Collins said, were charged with having the BSSB president operate within the limits, but the limits had not been precisely set. Collins said that while he loved Larry Holly, he urged the body not to wreck the BSSB by passing Knott's motion to fire Elder.[20]

The Motion Withdrawn

Trustee Tommy French was sitting by Knotts. French had been surprised by Knott's motion. "I finally told Joe," he recalls, " 'You don't have the votes to pass this; withdraw your motion.' Finally, Joe acquiesced. When he did, Dr. Elder shot out of his chair, pointed his finger and said, 'You cannot withdraw that motion; it belongs to the body.'

"I said to Joe, 'We've been set up. This is why Elder attacked Holly; he wanted to precipatate this [motion to fire]. With 20 new trustees and the first order of business of their tenure, they would certainly not vote to fire you. It was a power play to destroy the influence of the conservative faction."[21]

After a number of other procedural moves, including a failed attempt to delay a vote on dismissal, Knott asked permission to withdraw his motion. Trustee Nolan Kennedy opposed withdrawal, saying the trustees owed Elder the decency to tell him what we think rather than running and hiding. Several trustees agreed with Kennedy.

Larry Holly then spoke in favor of withdrawal, but said, "No one is running and hiding. The will of the body is obvious. The motion to fire will fail, but if you think that all the men who are going to vote not to fire Dr. Elder are doing so in order to affirm [him], then you misunderstand their motive."

Trustee Gene Swinson opposed voting on Knott's motion to withdraw and asked to go on record that "there's a lot of us in this meeting who did not come with any intent" of firing the president.

Finally the vote was called and Knott's request for withdrawal passed by a substantial voice vote.

The original motion to adopt the GAC report was now back on the floor. Dan Collins moved that one more point be added to the five points given by the GAC: "In an effort to promote harmony, we instruct Dr. Elder to instruct all speakers, writers and authors enlisted by the [BSSB] to refrain from agitating the politcal climate of the SBC. Furthermore, we instruct the president to seek a balance in speakers, authors and writers for the Board. In order to give better evaluation of the president, we recommend that the chairman of the GAC revise or develop an instrument for performance of the evaluation and report in February, 1990 at the regular trustee meeting... In this context," Collins moved that "we support Dr. Elder as president of the Board and pledge our commitment to make him a success in operating this Board." Collins' amendment was accepted and the GAC's motion passed overwhelmingly.[22]

An "Alternate Approach" for the BSU

Wednesday morning, trustee Floyd Hughes moved that an addition be published to the student guidebook with Baptist Student Union (BSU) director Max Barnett of the University of Oklahoma serving as the managing editor for the material. Barnett had long been known for his aggressive evangelism and discipleship ministry on that campus. Hughes expressed concern that the BSSB's Student Ministry Department had not been as productive as parachurch groups, Campus Crusade for Christ, in particular.

Trustee Don Dilday offered a substitute motion, asking that voting on the addition with Barnett as editor be deferred until the February board meeting because "of the precedent it was setting" in allowing trustees to name a managing editor. The substitute lost and after more discussion an amendment was added to insert the words "consisting of the Barnett team approach." The new addition to the guidebook was approved with some opposition. The vote expressed the belief of many BSSB trustees that the BSSB's Student Ministries Department could stand to learn from the methods of Campus Crusade, an organization which a writer for the moderate tabloid, SBC Today, had called "simplistic" and right-wing extremist — "a group of young zealots with an aggressive style of 'witnessing' who won't take 'No' for an answer."[23]

Conservative trustees were also pleased with a report from a secular marketing company employed by the Board to project sales of the New American Commentary. The consultants said the commentary stood a good chance of being very successful because of its method and its premise that Scripture was inerrant. This report was welcomed because a previous BSSB study, which many trustees considered flawed, had projected gloomy sales. Following the new marketing forecast, one conservative trustee quipped, "In the words of Gomer Pyle, 'Surprise! Surprise! Surprise!' "

Elder Speaks to Employees

Elder spoke his personal feelings in his customary post-board meeting report to a meeting of about 1,000 BSSB employees: "After the motion [to fire the president] was withdrawn — which I consider the depth of cowardice on the part of the trustee who withdrew it — I felt as if I had been laid out on a table for surgery and cut wide open and left there to see if I would live. I have not felt so abandoned since our daughter died in an automobile accident."

Elder also told the employees, "No one of us is above accountability and I will not run from it."

The employees gave him a standing ovation. Many signed statements of written support.[24]

The Hultgren Letter

Holly wrote Elder his personal disappointment of the speech to employees. Holly's letter to Elder was passed on to Warren Hultgren, chairman of the BSSB trustees. Hultgren wrote Holly that he had acted out of place as an individual trustee in taking it upon himself to write Elder. Hultgren suggested that Holly might be censured by the Board if "you persist in your present course of conduct."

Trustee T. C. French Jr. then wrote Hultgren, with copies going to trustees, that he had exceeded his authority as trustee chairman. French said that Board officers had no bylaw-approved responsibilities between meetings of the Board. The board chairman, French said, could not direct a trustee "to do anything other than notifying him of an official action of the full board to convene a trial. . . " French suggested that Hultgren retract his letter to Holly before it is reported in the press. If it does reach the press, then you may have created a situation that will only be settled by Dr. Holly's removal as a trustee, by Dr. Elder's dismissal as president, or both."[25]

Opinions in the Press

The eventful August BSSB trustee meeting was front page news in Baptist papers. The various headlines placed over the Baptist Press story indicate the different perceptions of the state editors and perhaps their feelings about the meeting. The North Carolina Biblical Recorder declared, "Efforts to Fire SSB President Fail; Politics Discussed."[26] The Missouri Word & Way headed its report, "BSSB Trustees Reject Attempt to Fire President Elder"[27] The Indiana Baptist gave the story a different twist, "Lloyd Elder Rebuked for 'Political Activity.' SSB Trustees Resist Firing While Reviewing Criticisms."[28] The Nashville Tennessean headlined, "Baptist Board Chief Rebuked" with a subhead in smaller type, "Conservative Move to Fire Fails."[29]

Editorial comment in several state papers tended to portray Elder as the victim. Virginia editor Julian Pentecost saw a "strategy of intimidation. . . . The whole scenario of callous public censure of a long-term and effective denominational servant is indicative of the depths to which some trustees were willing to descend in order to advance their political takeover agenda."[30] Opinions appearing in the "Letters to the Editor" columns of state papers were more divided. Larry Toothaker, a BSSB trustee from Oklahoma, said "the overall tone of the [Baptist Press] news article reflects Lloyd Elder's perception that all of these problems are due to one trustee, Larry Holly. . . . There are many trustees who are unhappy with Elder's performance." Toothaker was "tired of having to apologize for our literature, mistakes and blandness, . . . and tired of warning friends to read our books carefully because they may contain doctrinal error."[31]

Bruce Irving, a Texas pastor termed Elder "as good a man as Baptists have! I am appalled at this absurd effort by some . . . trustees to fire him. I would like to move instead that the [SBC] ask Joseph T. Knott and Larry Holly to resign as trustees. . . . If they reflect the caliber of trustees we're electing these days, then we are in serious trouble."[32]

September Reports to the Executive Committee

Harold Bennett, the agency executive for the Executive Committee, was in no danger of being fired. The amiable Bennett was viewed by many as a strict neutral in denominational politics.

Bennett was past 65 and the only speculation about his future was over who would take his place upon retirement.

The EC met in September, in the modernistic Baptist building, with its talking elevators, just down the street from the Sunday School Board.

A major order of business for the September EC meeting is reports by agency heads, along with requests for budget allocations from the Cooperative Program during the coming fiscal year. Among those giving reports were —

— Lewis Drummond, who was now living under the shadow of colon cancer. Drummond spoke of "a great day at Southeastern [Seminary], with a new dean of faculty and a dean of students." Drummond drew heavy "Amens" when he said, "Instead of heavy metal in the student center, we now have heavy gospel." On a weightier matter, he assured that "we're doing everything we can do . . . to keep our accreditation in order. However, we belong to you, you do fund us and you tell us what you want the seminary to be. We will keep accreditation at any cost, except your cost."[33]

— Russell Dilday, who spoke of a "dramatic revival" and "spiritual renewal" that is "breaking out in unprecedented ways" at Southwestern Seminary. It's "unlike anything I've ever experienced," Dilday said. "Groups of students and faculty praying together. Classes stopping lectures to pray. Peak attendance in chapel during the annual revival week with Dan Vestal [as the preacher]. . . . Evangelist Freddie Gage attended," Dilday noted and was "deeply moved by what was said and felt. He wrote out a generous check and said take this money and have tapes made of these sermons. . . . We want this Convention to know what God is doing."

— Larry Lewis, who noted that the Home Mission Board "now has the largest number of missionaries [under appointment] ever. More new churches were constituted last year than in any year since 1963." Lewis said the HMB had cut 26 positions — "not what I like to do" — because of financial restraints. "If we're serious about 50,000 churches by [the year] 2,000, we must increase resources."

In a later interview, Lewis said he was encouraged. "There's a renewed emphasis on evangelism, church planting and soul winning [in the SBC]. These are the things that have made us a great denomination. They got put on the back burner, now they're up front again." On another topic, Lewis said, "We carefully screen our mission appointees, to make sure they are doctrinally sound. . . . We ask them, 'Do you believe the Bible is truth without any mixture of error? Do you believe the miracles in the Bible were literal events? Do you believe that the historic narratives of Scripture were literal, not allegorical?'"[34]

— Lloyd Elder, who talked about Bold Mission Thrust and the upcoming "Here's Hope," a cooperative project under direction of the Home Mission Board, revivals. The BSSB, he said, had a goal of a 350,000 net increase in Sunday school across the SBC. A new magazine called Growing Churches was in the works. "A new [innerantist] commentary is being written because there are many who want a fresh scholarly exposition of Holy Scripture." Elder was loudly applauded by several dozen persons seated in the gallery and who left after he spoke. Observers thought they were BSSB employees who had come to show him their personal support.

Jerry Vines, in his President's address, talked about the church and its relationship to the denomination. The New Testament, he said, teaches both the independence of local churches and the interdependence of the churches. He "agree[d] with Dr. [James] Gambrell in his oft-quoted prayer: 'Lord, Southern Baptists aren't much, but they are the best you've got.' At times we may resemble Acts 19:32," Vines admitted. " 'Some therefore cried one thing and some another; for the assembly was confused. . . .' But a fresh wind is blowing in our midst. . . . I'm optimistic about the future of our denomination."

Then he dropped a couple of time bombs:

Vines recalled that he had said "the issue of the Bible is settled in Southern Baptist life. . . . Those who believe there are errors in the Bible are in a pronounced minority." By that he hadn't "mean[t] there are no theological problems in our midst, nor that these problems must not be addressed."

He had recently reread the Peace Committee Report where it "recommended 'that the trustees determine the theological positions of the seminary administrators and faculty members. . .' Accountability," Vines said, "would require that our Convention in session receive an update on this recommendation."

Vines noted that he had asked the EC to "defer" a recommendation on the Religious Liberty Commission. "You graciously granted my request. God honored it and evangelism was the focus in Las Vegas." Vines "believe[d] the time has now come to settle the issue of the Baptist Joint Committee on Public Affairs." He asked that the EC "determine the facts of funding of the Baptist Joint Committee for the Baptist state papers so the people can understand it," and "provide the messengers at the New Orleans convention with the opportunity to settle this issue among us in a clearcut, uncomplicated way."[35]

Vines said the next morning, "It's time that we face the issue. New Orleans is a different ball game [from] Vegas. Let the Executive Committee bring the Baptist Joint Committee before the New Orleans convention [for a vote] and let the majority not gloat and the minority not gripe."[36]

Later that same day the EC rescinded its recommendation to create a Religious Liberty Commission. Then in response to the motion by Rudy Yakym at Las Vegas, former EC chairman Charles Sullivan proposed that the program assignment for religious liberty matters be transferred to the Christian Life Commission. Sullivan's proposal was assigned to the EC's program and budget sub-committee for revision of the program statements of the CLC and the Public Affairs Committee. That sub-committee was also asked to propose a 1990-91 SBC Cooperative Program allocation budget that "takes into consideration" the new program assignments.

A clearly upset James Dunn, executive director of the BJCPA, said the proposal to switch the religious liberty assignment to the CLC would be ignoring the Las Vegas convention vote "not to tinker with the budget" of the BJCPA. Richard Land, executive director of the CLC, said his agency was "prepared to do whatever . . . the SBC wants us to do within the limits of our resources and abilities."[37]

At its September meeting, the EC also declined to vote on the controversial "Memorial" sent by the Virginia convention to the SBC and referred by the Las Vegas convention to the EC. EC members found no historical precedent for a connectionalism that called for the SBC president to appoint to membership on the SBC Committee on Committees persons proposed by the Virginia convention. Nevertheless, the Memorial was assigned to a special committee for further study and conversation with Baptists in Virginia.

Conservative EC members left Nashville in an upbeat mood. EC vice chairman Paul Pressler noted that Las Vegas had increased conservative strength on all boards. A majority at Southern Seminary had at last been reached. "There are 63 members on that board. Thirty-two are now solidly conservative. From 10 to 15 of the 31 remaining are swing votes and 15 or 20 others are pretty solid in the liberal camp."[38]

Pressler's optimism typified the feelings of conservatives who intended to press ahead in establishing their resurgence throughout the denomination. Not everyone, of course, agreed with them. Some at the EC viewed the future with deep concern. One agency executive privately saw "the whole Cooperative Program going down the tube." He held out little hope for the survival of the SBC as it "now functions."[39]

The PAC Report on Americans United

The SBC Public Affairs Committee and the Baptist Joint Committee on Public Affairs met during the first week of October. The PAC which, in effect, had been a paper committee for most of its 50 year existence, was now a known force in SBC life and the subject of much criticism by moderates who had long dominated the SBC religious liberty scene.

The PAC now had a small annual budget of $24,200 which it used for meeting expenses and publication of a respectable quarterly called <u>Southern Baptist Public Affairs</u>. The premiere summer and the fall, 1989 issues of the journal provided articles from a broad spectrum across the religious liberty scene. The fall issue, for example, reported on the Annual Conference of Americans United for Separation of Church and State (AU). The report noted, without using the partisan label, the involvement of leading SBC moderates as officers and trustees in the strict church-state separationist group. These included James Dunn (outgoing secretary of AU's trustees, who was given AU's Religious Liberty Award for 1988-89), Foy Valentine (newly elected AU president), Jimmy Allen, C. R. Daley, Stan Hastey and Weldon Gaddy. The PAC publication further noted that Sarah Weddington, the attorney counsel of the celebrated "Jane Roe" of Roe v. Wade fame, was a member of AU's National Advisory Council.

The PAC periodical reported on two addresses at the AU conference. Paul Simmons, the pro-choice [in abortion] professor of ethics at Southern Seminary termed the Roe v. Wade decision "an exercise in protecting religious liberty." Simmons used the example of Faust (who sold his soul to the Devil) as he decried the involvement of the "Religious Right" in the national political and judicial upheaval over abortion.

Robert Alley, a professor at the [Baptist] University of Richmond, cited the school "prayer initiatives," championed by many SBC conservatives, as "totally irresponsible." Alley, a Baptist liberal on record for saying that the virgin birth is a legend and that Jesus did not see himself as divine, also decried Congressional action in making 1983 "the year of the Bible." "Our elected officials [in Congress]," Alley said, "went on to label the Bible as the 'Word of God' and call for a national study of the 'Holy Scriptures.' How dare they?"[40]

The PAC and BJCPA Meetings

The PAC — consisting of 11 elected members, seven agency heads and the SBC president — met on the evening before the annual October BJCPA meeting in which the PAC held a third of the votes. This year the PAC had a new chairman, Albert Lee Smith, a former U.S. Congressman from Alabama. There were enough conservative members to provide a voting majority on the PAC, but not enough to decide the fate of partisan issues in the BJCPA.

In its meeting, the PAC voted to ask the SBC Executive Committee to rescind its September proposal to expand the program of the Christian Life Commission to include religious liberty matters. PAC member J. I. Ginnings said the CLC "must and should speak on moral issues," but religious liberty and moral issues are "vastly different." The PAC, Ginnings declared, should represent Southern Baptists on First Amendment matters, working through the BJCPA. A number of other PAC members, who favored Ginnings' motion in this instance, did not agree that the PAC should work solely through the BJCPA, but that the PAC should be the primary and direct representative of the SBC in Washington.[41]

In past years the PAC had taken stronger stands on hot button religious liberty and moral issues than the BJCPA. This continued in 1989.

The Right to Discriminate

A PAC resolution concerned the constitutional right of religious institutions to enforce their religious doctrines and practices. The resolution grew out of a controversy over a Senate amendment by Senator William R. Armstrong instructing the District of Columbia government to allow Catholic Georgetown University to deny homosexual students official recognition and support. After his amendment was overturned by a federal court, Armstrong introduced another legislative amendment, called the Nation's Capital Religious Liberty and Academic Freedom Act. It was believed that this amendment could pass court muster while accomplishing the basic purposes of the first one.

The resolution supporting Armstrong's new amendment was adopted by the PAC, but not recommended by the BJCPA resolutions committee for BJCPA consideration. PAC member Ginnings then introduced the resolution from the floor.

BJCPA Executive Director James Dunn said the Joint Committee had not involved itself in the Armstrong matter because it concerned local District of Columbia matters. The BJCPA, he said, had historically focused on national issues.

Ginnings countered that the Georgetown issue might set an important precedent. PAC chairman Albert Lee Smith concurred that requiring a church-related college such as Georgetown to recognize and support a homosexual organization would have "national implications."

Larry Lewis said the real question was whether the government could force a church-related school to recognize homosexuals. Lewis, a former Baptist college president, said he was concerned about the SBC related colleges.[42]

After further debate, the resolution was tabled. Later the BJCPA voted for a watered-down statement supporting "the right of religious institutions to enforce their religious doctrines and practices, including their moral and ethical standards." The

BJCPA resolution noted that by accepting direct government funding (which Georgetown had done), religious institutions would be "compromis[ing]" their "free exercise rights."

Tax Supported Porn "Art"

A third PAC resolution — not adopted by the BJCPA — called for support of the "Helms Amendment" which opposed the use of federal funds "to support and promote pornographic and blasphemous materials." The much-publicized issue had arisen over grants from the tax-supported National Endowment for the Arts to artists for art depicting homosexuality, child pornography and a crucifix submerged in urine.

BJCPA Finances

The BJCPA budget committee's "asking" budget for the coming year included a request that the SBC increase its Cooperative Program contribution from $391,248 in 1988-89 to $403,556 in 1989-90 of the total BJCPA budget of $722,772. PAC member Tom Pratt called the amount contributed by the SBC — one of the nine Baptist denominations making up the BJCPA—a "gross inequity." Pratt said of the requested increase, "We know it is not going to be granted." Nevertheless, the BJCPA adopted the budget as proposed.

More Resignations at Southeastern

One week later Southeastern Seminary trustees gathered for their fall meeting at the troubled school in Wake Forest, North Carolina. Over 18 months had elapsed since the change in administration.

President Lewis Drummond and the conservative trustee majority were still viewed as the enemy by the faculty hired under previous administrations. The faculty — viewed as recalcitrant by many trustees — had unanimously opposed the election of Russ Bush as the new dean and the way he had been elected which they maintained, "violated . . . the criterion of accreditation that calls for the faculty to have a substantial voice in such matters." Although Bush had taught at Southwestern Seminary since 1983 and had a good track record as an author, the faculty faulted him for "bias in his writing, his expectation that this faculty would support inerrancy in some form, his affiliation with the fundamentalist leadership in the Convention and his lack of understanding of the history or traditions of Baptists in this area."[43] Bush was not the kind of dean the faculty had in mind for the seminary.

Shortly after Bush was elected, Donna Forrester, the seminary chaplain; C. Woody Catoe, Jr., the director of student affairs; and

B. Elmo Scoggin, the professor of Old Testament, resigned. Scoggin charged President Drummond with becoming a "puppet" of the trustee majority and the SBC's "new religious right wing," which he said "has wedded itself to the new political right wing." The "power-mad fundamentalists" who now control the SBC, Scoggin declared, "will have to answer to God . . . for what they have done to individual persons; to open, honest theological inquiry among us; and for crippling the greatest missionary outreach program in the history of Protestant Christianity. May God have mercy upon our souls!"

President Drummond simply responded, "I appreciate the fact he has expressed himself fully. I would have hoped that he would not have felt so negatively about our situation."[44]

Victims of Gossip

About the time he was discovered to have cancer, Drummond and his wife Betty became the victims of vicious gossip. Dale Moody, who had been released from teaching in retirement at Southern Seminary after protests that he did not believe in the eternal security of the believer, was among those who naively believed the stories to be true. Moody, once a colleague of Drummond's on the Southern faculty, asked in SBC Today, "Is it Christian for trustees of Southeastern seminary to allocate large sums of money ($110,000 is reported) to remodel president Lewis A. Drummond's home in order to make a place for his prize orchids and expensive furs for his wife, Betty? Does this sound like a Christian woman who is to 'dress modestly, with decency and propriety . . . ?'"[45]

Moody's charge was exaggerated to the point of being ludicrous. The moderate tabloid in which Moody's article appeared was asked to print an apology for the "incorrect . . . attacks upon Drummond."[46]

Genesis History: Unimportant?

Pushing ahead, Southeastern's trustees and administration hired the first full-time teachers since conservatives gained a majority on the board almost two years before. The faculty, with the only opposing vote cast by Dean Bush, voted to disassociate themselves from the hiring because of what they said was their token role in the selection process. Trustee Chairman Robert Crowley was highly pleased with the new teachers. He had "sat in with the instructional committee and. . . . asked if they believed Adam was a real person and if the first 11 chapters of Genesis were real history, to be taken literally. I got an affirmative answer from all three," he said.[47]

Publication of Crowley's remarks brought some stinging rejoinders. Moderate E. Robert Brooks "realize[d] that the criteria used by seminary trustees were prescribed in the report of the Peace Committee. But the [Peace] Committee was neither assigned nor qualified to do this," he said. "Why should Southern Baptists be doomed to have faculties at their seminaries chosen on the basis of unimportant, if not invalid, criteria devised by the [Peace] Committee?"[48]

Another reactor commented sarcastically that he was "thrilled . . . no end to see that the only criteria for becoming a professor at Southeastern Seminary" was belief in Adam as a real person and the historicity of the first 11 chapters of Genesis. "It thrills me because now we can start the hiring of Jehovah's Witnesses, Mormons, a couple of nuns and from what I hear, Jim and Tammy [Bakker] are still looking for full-time employment. T'will not be long and all of our seminaries will look alike, talk alike, smell alike and indeed . . . have the same personality. . . . This old world is looking for an example of sacrifice and we are asking, 'Is the book of Genesis real history?'"[49]

With the October board meeting fast approaching, the standoff between the old order, represented by the faculty and the new order, represented by the substantial conservative trustee majority and the Drummond administration, continued. The two accrediting agencies, ATS and SACS, had issued reports critical of the seminary, to which faculty and trustees had responded without giving ground on their previously established positions on hiring of new teachers.

The ATS asked Southeastern to "show cause why it should not be placed on probation. The American Association of University Professors, which was represented on campus by the faculty, had censured the school. Since conservatives had attained a majority on the trustee board 18 Southeastern professors and administrators had resigned and the enrollment was down from 1,046 students in the fall of 1987 to an anticipated 600 in the fall of 1989.

Faculty Hiring Compromise

The SBC Executive Committee maintained that trustees at Southeastern had "the right to set the 'new faculty' selection policies and procedures without fear of intimidation by a faculty that may want a different procedure (especially one that tends to suggest a self-perpetuating mode of faculty selection) . . . ."[50]

A few days before the fall, 1989 trustee meeting, the administration announced that faculty and trustees would hold a joint workshop, October, 11, "in which we can sit down face to face, discuss our different opinions and hopefully find ways to achieve reconciliation." The faculty endorsed the idea, while calling for a moratorium on selecting new teachers until faculty-selection procedure is "modified to conform" to accreditation standards.[51]

The workshop was held during the fall trustee meeting. With Robert Cooley, president of Gordon-Conwell Seminary, serving as facilitator, the three groups — administration, faculty and trustees — agreed to a three-part "compromise" offered by outgoing trustee chairman Robert Crowley that included,

— Observance of a moratorium on election of permanent faculty members until after the board's March, 1990 meeting.

— A special faculty/trustee task force to propose a new faculty-selection process for trustee consideration in March.

— Maintaining of President Drummond's authority to appoint temporary faculty as needed during the interim.

The trustees took other actions during the meeting which highly displeased the faculty, but did not cancel the agreement:

— They declared that the American Association of University Professors and its chapter at the seminary had "no official standing with the seminary."

— They refused to permit "inclusive language guidelines" drafted by the faculty to be printed in seminary publications.

— They voted to consider in March a proposal that would designate the 1963 Baptist Faith and Message Statement as an official seminary document and would require all new faculty candidates to affirm the statement before election or full-time employment.

Robert Cooley, the outside facilitator who had been suggested by the ATS, was encouraged. "Change," he observed, "is accomplished through crisis, revolution, or process. I have seen in this process some movement toward change." Cooley urged the seminary to adopt a "shared governance" model of operation which would involve faculty, administration and trustees."[52]

Despite the apparent success of the workshop, the SACS accrediting agency put the seminary on "warning" notice, giving the school two years to correct and report accreditation deficiencies.

Dean Bush and new trustee chairman, James DeLoach expressed relief that the seminary had not been put on probation. Faculty member Thomas Halbrooks, president of the seminary's AAUP chapter, saw the situation as "grave" and blamed the problems with accreditation on "changes forced upon the school in violation of established standards in American education."

DeLoach said the seminary would try to resolve the faculty-selection impasse that had developed. As for faculty criticisms of the trustees and administration, DeLoach said, "They have not come up with one circumstance where anyone's academic freedom has been trampled upon. If they will come up with an example, we could respond."[53]

How "Political" Can a President Be?

The Southwestern Seminary board met the week after Southeastern's trustee meeting. This meeting was of high concern throughout the Convention. Many saw it as a showdown between the conservative board majority and President Russell Dilday, Jr. over Dilday's alleged political involvement in the denominational controversy.

At Southwestern Dilday ran a tight denominational ship, refusing to allow non-official organizations — such as Campus Crusade for Christ, Wycliffe Bible Translators and pro-life groups — on campus. After maintaining a strict public neutrality in the denominational controversy, he had come out, in 1984, in opposition to the re-election of Charles Stanley. In December of 1984 he made one of his first speeches to a meeting of moderates when he spoke to "Concerned Southern Baptists" at his old church in Atlanta. The invitation from James C. Strickland, Jr. to those "interested in knowing more about the current problems in the SBC" indicated that this was clearly a partisan meeting. Attached was a list of regional coordinators who were working to get out the vote to defeat Stanley in Dallas.[54]

As the Southwestern board changed to include more activists from the conservative resurgency movement, criticism mounted about President Dilday's alleged political partisanship as a denominational employee. There was no real concern with the seminary's faculty or Dilday's personal theology. It was his strong identification with the moderate-"centrist" coalition and his public declarations that the "independent, fundamentalist" leadership in the SBC was hurting the denomination.

In February, 1989, he was quoted by SBC Today as wishing to have "some input into the process" by which trustees were nominated. "We need people on the [Southwestern] board with management, fundraising and other skills — besides simply their spiritual commitment," he said.[55]

In May, 1989 Dilday spoke to the Baptists Committed Symposium in Nashville on denominational unity. James Dunn, Bill Sherman, John F. Baugh, Dan Vestal and W. David Sapp were also on the program. "We are going in the wrong direction," the Southwestern president said. "There hangs over all our work a melancholy cloud of despondency."[56]

In his president's column in the May issue of the seminary's alumni journal, Dilday said the "decade-long struggle of 'take-over efforts' by some and 'resistance' by others has sapped the spirit of our Baptist family. Young men considering God's call to the ministry are discouraged. . . . Cooperative Program support is diminishing. . . . New leaders must emerge who will challenge us to nobler agendas. . . . Messengers [at Las Vegas] must vote for leaders not because they are on the 'right side,' but because they are more likely to pull us out of the morass."[57]

The Trustees Become Concerned

President Dilday's speech in Nashville and his column in the alumni paper did not set well with many of his trustees who saw the efforts as a not-too-subtle call to get out the vote and defeat Jerry Vines in Las Vegas.

As time for the fall board meeting approached, newspaper stories suggested that Dilday might be formally censured at the October board meeting and perhaps even fired if he did not agree to get out of the political arena. He was quoted in the Houston Post as conceding that board chairman Ken Lilly, a medical doctor in Arkansas, had received at least 20 letters from trustees complaining that the statements in question were inappropriate for a denominational employee. Trustee Pat Campbell, one of the letter writers, said he had first become concerned about Dilday's Nashville speech after reading a critical article in the Southern Baptist Advocate. After getting a copy of the speech, Campbell declared, "Any way you slice it, the comments were an indirect attack on the fundamental-conservative leaders of the past 10 years."[58] Still, Dilday insisted that he "had avoided all political involvement" and that the Nashville speech to the partisan gathering was not intended to be a political statement.[59]

The Dallas Morning News quoted moderate Ken Chafin as saying, "Any effort to get Dilday isn't based on character, doctrine, or administrative ability, [but] on getting Dilday out and someone else in, probably Jimmy Draper."[60]

Trustee officers considered calling a special meeting on August 29 to "deal with Dilday," but then changed their minds, Chairman Lilly said. Lilly didn't "see at this point how [the conflict] with Dilday can be avoided" at the regular October 16-17 trustee meeting.[61]

Two weeks before the board meeting, Lilly mailed to all trustees 86 pages of press clippings which he said were "political" statements by Dilday, dating back to 1983.[62] On October 6, Hugh W. Gilbert, an Atlanta lawyer in the firm that represents moderate John Baugh's food processing company, mailed certified letters to all 36 trustees with copies sent to Baptist papers, threatening litigation against individual trustees if action was taken against Dilday. The attorney said litigation would not be filed against the SBC or any of its entities, but "be taken against individual trustees of the entities whose personal positions will be challenged and whose fortunes will be placed at stake." Gilbert told reporter Ed Briggs of the Richmond (VA) Times Dispatch, "I expressed the views that my [Southern Baptist] clients wanted them to be aware of." Gilbert said neither Dilday nor any other denominational employees had "initiated or are parties to this communication."

Dilday thought it was "tragic the controversy has come to a point where brethren would feel a need to resort to this kind of legal action. It just shows that we are a seriously divided denomination. We need to find some way to get back together or there will be destruction of what we are about." Dilday said he "personally would not use [a suit] because I do not think it is the way to get the job done."[63]

Settling a "Family" Conflict in Secret

Over 200 visitors came for the trustee meeting. Jimmy Draper moved that the board go into closed session to deal with a "family matter" in discussing "some things with the president." After some debate, the trustees voted 22-11 to have the executive session. Dilday then said he would "rather have had the session open, but you [trustees] have voted to do that in a secret and private way. I will work with you in this regard."

Many of the visitors protested the secret session. Chairman Lilly allowed Charles Wade, the spokesman for the group, to address the trustees "if it will allow you to go on out." Wade, a Texas leader in the moderate-centrist coalition, had once been a member of the Christian Life Commission where he had opposed the attempted firing of CLC Executive Director Larry Baker. Wade told the Southwestern trustees, "We cannot leave our president alone to be censured or spoken to in a way that does not respect the great contributions he has made to Southern Baptist life."

Draper objected, saying Wade "has made assumptions that these [trustees] don't love the president. [Wade] has already determined what we will do . . . when we haven't even met yet. This is the kind of circus atmosphere I have spoken of."

Wade's group left the room. They sang the doxology, prayed in small groups and broke into other songs while waiting for the trustees to come out. Trustees who left the executive session briefly told those waiting outside that no mention had been made of firing Dilday.

After an almost five-hour session, the trustees and Dilday emerged. Chairman Lilly read a three paragraph statement:

"Our executive session consisted of healthy dialogue," Lilly said, "in which we all acknowledged our differences and failings.

"We, the trustees and president, hereby affirm one another and pledge our mutual support.

"Because of the sensitivity of the issues involved, we covenant together as trustees and president to cease and desist from making any statements, or writings, or engaging in any activities that could reasonably be interpreted as being intentionally political in nature, all the while seeking to deal with each other and the institution we serve in truth and love."

The spectators responded with mild applause. "That's it," Lilly declared. Then he opened the meeting for regular business.

Dilday also gave a statement to reporters, saying, "It is not likely we will settle those differences in our perspectives about the Convention, the nature of the SBC, or the direction it ought to take. But those differences [between Dilday and the trustees] do not directly relate to the work of this institution . . . [which] continues to remain strong."[64]

Lilly said Dilday and the trustees "will go ahead and go wherever they feel led of the Lord to go. . . . We will do our best to desist and intentionally avoid political issues. . . . Dr. Dilday will certainly say anything in conscience that he needs to say. There is no gagging or changes in his way of doing business."[65]

The Texas Baptist Standard, which covered the Southwestern board meeting, printed a cartoon showing two men reaching long arms across a wide and deep abyss for a handshake. The caption declared: "And they said we could not do it!"

October brought the end of the national board meetings for another year. Moderates and many institutional executives could only breathe sighs of relief. Lloyd Elder and Russell Dilday had survived. No other agency heads appeared to be in danger of losing their jobs. New administrations elected by conservative board majorities were not purging their employee ranks of moderates. Surprise, surprise, Texas pastor Paul Powell, a leader among the Texas "centrists," had been elected president of the Relief & Annuity Board, giving moderate alarmist Bill Self a little crow to eat. Self had once warned that if the "takeover" faction were not stopped the thousands of SBC annuitants might lose their retirement funds. Still another surprise was that some women had advanced in agencies. The Foreign and the Home mission boards each had a woman vice president. That hadn't happened when moderates were in control.

References

1 "Patterson/Parks Disagreement Sparks FMB Trustee Resolution," Word & Way, June 1, 1989, p. 1.

2 Tammi Ledbetter: "FMB Trustees Reject Missionary Candidates," Indiana Baptist, July 25, 1989, p. 1. Art Toalston and Eric Miller: "Ordained Couple Turned Down by FMB Trustees," Baptist and Reflector, July 5, 1989, p. 1.

3 "FMB Trustees Question 'Top Special Assistant' Role," Word & Way, November 9, 1989, p. 3.

4 "FMB Works to Halt Decline in Overseas Appointments," Word & Way, September 21, 1989, p. 3.

5 Stan Hastey: "A View From Washington," SBC Today, October, 1989, p. 27.

6 Dan Martin & Linda Lawson: "SSB Trustees Contribute to Payoff of SBC Building," Baptist Press, February 17, 1989.

7 SBC Executive Committee Minutes, February 20-22, 1989.

8 March 6, 1989. Letter released to press by Larry Holly.

9 President's Update Report [on the] SBC Building and the Cooperative Program to the BSSB Trustee Executive Committee, April 27, 1989.

10 Holly to New BSSB Trustees.

11 Larry Holly: "Retrospective and Prospective," a paper mailed to BSSB trustees, p. 7.

12 Op. cit., pp. 8, 9.

13 Op. cit. pp. 10-12.

14 James L. Sullivan Addresses Question of SBC Turbulence," Facts and Trends, July-August, 1986, pp. 10, 11.

15 Larry Holly: "History of the Presidency," included in Holly's July mailout to trustees.

16 Holly sent me a copy of this material which was distributed at Glorieta.

17 Information and quotes from the August BSSB trustee meeting come from official minutes of the meeting, notes made by a trustee, impressions conveyed to me by other trustees and the Baptist Press report appearing in state papers. I also had available editorials from some Baptist papers and various articles including Lonnie Wilkey: "Tennessee Trustees Discuss BSSB Meeting," Baptist and Reflector, August 23, 1989, p. 1 and Ray Waddle: Nashville Tennessean, "Baptist Board Chief Rebuked," August 11, 1989, p. 3B.

18 Information from a BSSB trustee who was present. Quoted from the Memo.

19 BSSB Minutes, August 7-9, 1989, p. 2.

20 From a tape recording of the trustee meeting.

21 Personal interview with French, Nashville, January, 1991.

22. From a tape recording of the trusstee meeting.

23 Amy Greene: "Campus Crusade for Christ," SBC Today, May, 1989, p. 11.

24 "Elder Calls Withdrawal of Motion to Fire Him 'Depth of Cowardice,' Word & Way, August 24, 1989, p. 12.

25 French to Hultgren, September 21, 1989.

26 August 16, 1989.

27 August 17, 1989.

28 August 22, 1989.

29 August 11, 1989, p. 3B.

30 Julian H. Pentecost: "Strategy of Intimidation Directed Against Lloyd Elder," Religious Herald, August 24, 1989, p. 4.

31 Baptist Standard, September 6, 1989, p. 2.

32 Ibid.

33 Quotes and information on this and other reports at the September EC meeting are from my taped and written notes.

34 Interview, Nashville, September, 1989.

35 From my notes and a manuscript of Vines' address.

36 Interview, Nashville, September, 1989.

37 "Executive Committee Changes Direction of Religious Liberty," Word & Way, September 28, 1989, p. 7.

38 Interview, Nashville, September, 1989.

39 The agency head gave me this gloomy prospect. He asked that he not be identified.

40 In previous volumes of The Truth in Crisis, I dealt extensively with tangled relationships between the SBC, the PAC and the BJCPA. Readers interested in becoming more informed should read especially Chapter 8, "Who Represents Southern Baptists in Public Affairs?" in Volume 3 and Chapter 9, "Tough Times in Public Affairs," in Volume 2.

41 "News Update," Southern Baptist Public Affairs, Fall, 1989, p. 8.

42 Information from "BJCPA Adopts Weakened Resolutions, Rejects Support for Helms Amendment," Fall, 1989, Southern Baptist Public Affairs, pp. 10, 11.

43 Lewis, while president of Hannibal-LaGrange Baptist College in Missouri, had experienced pressure from officials of the Missouri Department of Higher Education to adopt a policy which would have required the college not to discriminate against homosexuals and atheists in hiring practices. The educational officials maintained that this was required because the college was benefiting from state financial grants awarded to students. Only by skilful lobbying of state legislators was Lewis able to keep the governmental "camel's nose" out of the college's "tent" in this instance.)

44 Marv Knox: "Bush Elected, Accepts Despite Opposition," Baptist Standard, March 22, 1989, p. 5.

45 Julian H. Pentecost: "More Resignations at Southeastern Seminary," Religious Herald, April 27, 1989, p. 4.

46 Dale Moody: "Dale Moody Speaks Out on Several SBC Issues," SBC Today, September, 1989, p. 15.

47 Jim Hendricks in "Today's Mail," op. cit., October, 1989, p. 10.

48 "Southeastern Employs New Faculty Despite Faculty Protest Over Process," Religious Herald, July 27, 1989, p. 8.

49 Steve Strickland in "The People's Forum," Biblical Recorder, August 12, 1989, pp. 2, 9.

50 Statement of affirmation by the SBC Executive Committee. Passed, September, 1989.

51 Marv Knox: Southeastern Plans Workshop; Profs Want Hiring Delayed," Baptist Press, September 1, 1989. Marv Knox: "SEBTS President, Faculty Address Accreditation," op. cit.

52 Marv Knox: "Southeastern Takes Step Toward Reconciliation," Biblical Recorder, October 21, 1989, pp. 1,10.

53 Marv Knox and Mark Wingfield: "Accreditors Place Southeastern on 'Warning,' Religious Herald, December 21, 1989, p. 6.

54 James C. Strickland, Jr. to Georgia moderates, December 10, 1984.

55 Amy Greene: "Conflict Affecting All Seminaries," February, 1989, p. 1.

56 Report on the Symposium, Southern Baptist Newsletter, May, 1989, pp. 4, 5.

57 "From the President," Southwestern News, May, 1989, p. 2.

58 "Trustee Officers Ask Dilday to 'Quit Doing Political Things," Word & Way, September 7, 1989, p. 9.

59 Cecile Holmes White: "Southern Baptist Seminary Leader Rankles Trustees," Houston Post, September 2, 1989, p. E-1.

60 Helen Parmley: "Baptist Seminary Leader Under Fire From Fundamentalists, Dallas Morning News September 6, 1989, p. 31A.

61 "Dilday Expects Trustee Confrontation Over His Role in Denominational Conflict," SBC Today, October, 1989, p. 1.

62 "Dilday, Trustees Reach Compromise," SBC Today, November, 1989, p. 1.

63 Dan Martin: "Legal Action Threatened if Dilday is Fired," Baptist Standard, October 18, 1989, p. 3.

64 Dan Martin: "Dilday, Trustees Settle SWBTS 'Family Matters,' " Baptist Standard, October 25, 1989, p. 4.

65 Toby Druin: "Dilday, Lilly Insist Only 'Gag' Will Be 'Sensitivity,' " Baptist Standard, op. cit. p. 9.

Chapter 7

"Struggles in the States Continue"

With the conclusion of the last national board meeting in October, attention swung to the fall, 1989 state conventions where conservatives had been gaining in strength in recent years. Here are brief summaries of what occurred in several key states, followed by more detailed reports of developments in North Carolina, Arkansas, Louisiana and Texas.

Moderate's Maintain Dominance in Virginia

To no one's surprise, moderates won in Virginia, though they were not entirely united. Ray Spence was elected president with only 55 percent of the vote against three other candidates. A resolution was passed that "strongly affirm[ed] the leaders in our convention who have experienced emotional pain in recent months. . . . "[1] Lloyd Elder and Russell Dilday were the ones in mind. Another resolution instructed a committee to investigate setting up an alternative news agency "if censorship or intimidation renders Baptist Press incapable or unwilling" to be as free and responsible as it had been in the past.

Virginia also recommended that its Committee on Boards and Committees nominate two persons "for approval and suggestion" to the SBC President for consideration as Virginia members of the SBC Committee on Committees." Samuel H. Letson, a pastor, opposed the recommendation, saying, "The SBC president must serve within the parameters of his office. We must avoid connectionalism and maintain the autonomy of each Baptist body." The recommendation passed with no one predicting that Jerry Vines would appoint the persons designated.[2]

Close Presidential Vote in South Carolina

In past years, the national controversy had largely been kept out of the South Carolina convention which was considered to be more conservative than North Carolina. Earlier in the year protests had arisen over an invitation for Mahan Siler, a pastor in

Raleigh, to serve on the faculty for the Furman University Baptist Pastors Conference. Siler's stated views on homosexuality had been a factor in the Southeastern Seminary board's decision not to renew his contract as an adjunct professor at the seminary. Siler had declared the Bible to be silent on homosexual orientation and had further chastised Christians for condemning homosexual behavior. Even though state convention executive Ray Rust expressed his "deep concern" about Siler's homosexual views, the invitation was not withdrawn.[3]

More Mercer Problems in Georgia

The Godsey-Mercer issue continued to dominate Baptist affairs in Georgia. President Kirby Godsey and Mercer had weathered the wave of protests over Godsey's alleged universal salvation views. Godsey was now on the griddle for allegedly concealing from trustees over seven million dollars in short-term debt to cover operating expenses. Faculty, students and many others were angry with Godsey and the trustees for closing down Mercer's branch college in Atlanta. A law suit on the issue found the president and trustees guilty of bad faith and breach of contract in voting to close the school.

Mercer claimed to be a Baptist school and received support from the Georgia Baptist Convention (GBC) Cooperative Program. Yet the state convention's power was limited to the election of trustees from among those nominated by Mercer trustees and the Alumni Association. Mercer's sitting trustees refused to consider any charter revision allowing GBC control. Baptists who helped pay Mercer's bills could only offer advice.

The Atlanta and Macon newspapers had supported Godsey and Mercer in the theological dispute with Georgia Baptist conservatives. The papers were now ripping Godsey for the school's debt problems and the closing of the Atlanta campus. The Atlanta Constitution noted, in an editorial, that "two respected trustees have resigned in dismay. Those [trustees] remaining need to recognize that if they fail to get themselves a new president, Dr. Godsey may drag them and their institution down with him."[4]

The fall state convention re-elected incumbent president Dwight "Ike" Reighard by acclamation. Conservatives were also elected as first and second vice presidents. Conservatives now had control of the state convention processes, but they could only make requests of Mercer.[5]

Florida, Mississippi, Tennessee and Missouri

Florida conservatives kept the state convention presidency by electing J. C. Mitchell with 60 percent of the vote to 38% for the moderate candidate.

Conservatives won in Mississippi with Eddie Hamilton. The Mississippi convention passed a strong resolution for freedom of Baptist Press, but tabled a proposal for support of the BJCPA, calling it "a controversial and divisive issue."[6]

Tennessee had been hit in June by the resignation of Clyde Tilley, a Union University religion professor, because he did not hold to the traditional Baptist doctrine of "once saved, always saved." Tilley said one could renounce his salvation and lose it. After resigning, Tilley began writing a column for SBC Today.

In a three-way race for the convention presidency, conservative Murray Mathis received 51 percent of the vote. Mathis said he represented those desiring to "come together as Tennessee Baptists." Conservative Guy Milam was elected first vice president.

Tennessee conservatives failed in their attempt to adopt a constitutional amendment that would have increased the number of years an outgoing Executive Board member would have to wait before being eligible for re-election. Ron Phillips, pastor of the largest SBC church in East Tennessee, said the change needed to be made to keep "the same people" from "filling the same positions over and over and over again."[8] Fletcher Allen, editor of the state paper, declared, "We must pay attention to the sincere calls for broad representation on boards and committees."[9]

Missouri elected Lee Beaver president by a close 440-435 vote in a runoff against conservative pastor Richard Wakefield. Then in a show of unity the messengers elected Wakefield as first vice president. Wakefield called Beaver, "One of the outstanding laymen" in the SBC. Beaver had once served as chairman of trustees at Southeastern Seminary during the Randall Lolley administration.[10]

For the fourth year in a row, the Missouri convention passed a resolution supporting the BJCPA and opposing efforts within the SBC to weaken the denomination's relationship with the agency.

Conservatives Fall Short Again in North Carolina

Conservatives had been gaining momentum in North Carolina, a long-time moderate stronghold. In 1985, conservative Ned Matthews had lost by only 340 votes. Two years later Matthews received enough votes to have won the election in 1985, but lost to a big sympathy vote for Randall Lolley, who nominated the winning candidate. Lolley had just resigned as president of Southeastern Seminary. In 1989, two conservative candidates, Billy Cline and Eugene Ridley, opposed moderate Gene Watterson who had served as first vice president for the past two years.

Cline was strongly supported by a new group called Conservative Carolina Baptists. Formed under the leadership of

M. O. Owens, Jr., the CCB published a thin, issue-oriented monthly periodical. Ridley was promoted by "Baptists United" in which <u>Southern Baptist Advocate</u> editor Bob Tenery was prominent. The difference in the two conservative groups was more in tone than substance; still, the moderate candidate Watterson won by 21 votes against Cline and Ridley on the first ballot. Had there been a runoff, the two conservative groups would have joined forces.

George McCotter, a layman, opposed Randall Lolley for first vice president. McCotter had broken with the moderate Friends of Mission group because they would not support his choice for a convention office. It was even speculated that McCotter might support Billy Cline for president, if the CCB backed him. However, a conservative candidate for first vice president was also nominated and McCotter ran a distant third in the three-man race. Lolley then won by a narrow 51 percent margin in the runoff against the conservative. The multiple candidacies for the two offices indicated that neither conservatives nor moderates in North Carolina operated as a solid bloc.

Moderates generally controlled the voting on other issues. But a moderate-backed resolution was defeated 1,648 to 1,227 that would have requested the Foreign Mission Board to reconsider the appointment of Katrina and Greg Pennington. Steve Hardy, a FMB trustee, spoke against the resolution, stating that the Penningtons had not been rejected because of Katrina's ordination or the protest lodged by the Oklahoma association. Other matters of a "personal" nature were involved, he said, which could not be discussed in public without violating confidentiality.[11]

Intrigue and Defection in Arkansas

Arkansas had been a relatively quiet convention until the summer of 1989. Don Moore, the executive director of the state convention, had been identified with the conservative movement as a pastor. As state executive director, he was striving to keep Baptists working together for common interests in evangelism, missions and Christian education. As for the schools, Southern Baptist College in Walnut Ridge was considered to be clearly in the conservative camp. Ouachita, the other convention school, had strong ties with both conservatives and moderates.

Conservatives were especially strong in northwest Arkansas where they were led by Joe Atchison, chairman of the SBC Christian Life Commission and a Director of Missions in a local association; and Ronnie Floyd, a member of the SBC Executive Committee, president of the Arkansas Baptist Pastors Conference and pastor of FBC, Springdale, the largest church in the state.

A short time after the 1988 state convention, Atchison wrote a two-page letter to about a dozen friends, urging them to begin thinking and preparing for the next year when we will elect "our [conservative] man" as president, "who in turn, will appoint key committees that will begin to make a difference in our state." It was the kind of letter that had been written by partisans from both sides in other states to their friends and leaked to the press. In Arkansas, Atchison's letter was sent by an unknown person to James Scudder of the Arkansas Gazette.

Scudder wrote an article titled, "Baptist Factions Vie for Control of the Convention." Scudder quoted incumbent convention president Cary Heard: "This is basically an offshoot or echo of the same thing that is happening on the national level. . . . I think we're better served by letting people make up their own minds without politicizing and polarizing the nomination." Scudder also quoted from an anonymous "Fact Sheet" that claimed a "small clique of fundamentalist politicians" had been meeting secretly to discuss ways to "achieve the termination" of editor Everett Sneed and the takeover of state convention boards.

The Gazette article quoted Atchison as saying it was "no secret" that some Arkansas Baptists wanted to elect a conservative as convention president and that their choice was Ronnie Floyd "because he sets the role model for Sunday school growth and evangelism and a conservative doctrinal stance." Floyd, according to the Gazette article, said he had been contacted by "many men [from] all over the state" about nomination and "if that's what the brothers feel, I'm willing" to be nominated. Floyd continued to support Don Moore as state executive director, noting that Moore had preached in his church and that the church had "the whole convention staff up to honor them."[12]

Early in September the first issue of a monthly conservative periodical, A Conservative Voice in Arkansas, appeared. Editor Mark Brooks quoted extensively from the Gazette article and the "Fact Sheet." It is evident," Brooks said, that "some . . . in Arkansas are doing their best to counter conservative efforts," . . . . and to make "conservatives look like a reactionary faction bent on personal prestige." Brooks then declared that the new paper was, among other things, "committed to seeing" the SBC "continue its conservative resurgence" and "to supporting Don Moore and the Arkansas Baptist State Convention."[13]

A Secret Tape

About this time news broke that a "conservative" pastor, David Montoya, had secretly taped a conversation between himself, Joe Atchison, Mark Brooks, Ronnie Floyd and Bob Foster, pastor of Gum Springs Baptist Church. Copies of the tape were passed to the Gazette writer, state editor Sneed and a moderate network within the state. Montoya, who said he had been one of eight district leaders in the Arkansas conservative organization, alleged that the conservative group had "attacked Don Moore and other conservatives. I submitted my resignation. It has become a political organization. The issue is not inerrancy, it is power."[14]

Sneed, while declining to comment in print on the growing controversy and the tape, did print a letter in which Montoya again accused the conservative group of "orchestrat[ing]" a movement to elect Floyd as president. Montoya asked, "How is the Bible defended by using appointments for political power, attacking fellow conservatives, or bragging about the power to 'black ball' those who don't bow the knee! Where is the inerrancy in this?"[15]

Mark Brooks got a copy of the tape and offered it to anyone who would send $5 and a self-addressed envelope. The tape reveals, Brooks said, "that a small group of men discussed how many conservative messengers . . . would show up at the fall convention." They "considered how to get fellow conservatives to come . . . and get involved in their convention." They "discussed who they thought would be candidates for the fall convention and who they should recommend for the SBC Committee on Committees."

Montoya, who did much of the talking on the tape, had concealed the recorder in his coat pocket. Montoya apparently had planned on "setting" up the participants in the meeting. At one point he asked, "Let's take the worst possible scenario, something blows up, it looks bad come September, what do we do then?" Montoya, according to Brooks, "did not leave the meeting upset. He repeatedly laughs throughout the tape. He attended two more meetings of conservative men after this tape was made."

Brooks said that after the tape was made, Montoya stopped returning phone calls. "Finally, he called one of the participants and admitted he had a problem with one of the other men in the taped meeting because he felt this man treated him like a child, he never took his advice."[16]

Brooks printed an "open letter" from Ronnie Floyd in which Floyd said the "Fact Sheet" distributed by moderates, before the tape was disseminated, "is filled with lies. . . . The conservatives I know do not desire control, but change. We want [the Arkansas convention] to mirror evangelism, revival and church growth." Floyd was "unsure" about his "life . . . in relation to Arkansas Baptists."[17]

A Call for Revival

The mid-November convention drew 1,602 messengers, the largest number in history. The accusations and rumors that had made headlines in secular papers were not mentioned until the afternoon of the first day when attorney Lane Strother, president of the board of the <u>Arkansas Baptist Newsmagazine</u> spoke of a "backroom network . . . out for control and power," who disapproved of Editor Sneed and Executive Director Don Moore because they would not "lock step to their marching orders." After a few comments from Editor Sneed, many of the messengers broke into sustained applause.

Don Moore preached in the evening session of the first convention day on "Folly in the Family of God." Taking his text from the biblical story of Achan's sin and the Israelite defeat, Moore told messengers there was folly in God's family when anger replaces divine anointing, death and defeat replace deliverance, fright replaces fight in the hearts of God's people, blaming replaces blessing and God's people become more worried about their image with men than with favor before God. Moore said Arkansas Baptists must soon "make a choice between revival and death."

Following the Tuesday evening session, Moore convened a "solemn assembly" to give messengers an opportunity to practice what he had just preached. Several hundred remained to pray, testify and confess sin.

The presidential election came the next morning. Mike Huckabee, a pastor from Texarkana, defeated Ronnie Floyd by a vote of 808 to 443.

Afterwards, Huckabee told messengers that despite the tension of the presidential election, there was no personal tension between himself and Ronnie Floyd. The lordship of Christ, Huckabee said, is the "common ground" on which all Arkansas Baptists should come together. "There is a place for everyone."[18]

Montoya and the Moderates

After the Arkansas convention, David Montoya became a cherished property among moderates. Montoya published an article in the liberal Christian Century titled, "Trading Principles for Power in the SBC." Montoya ripped the "Machiavellian machine" of his former associates for "power politics, focusing not on inerrancy but on personal advancement, prestige, vendettas, power and of course, money."[19] Montoya's Century article was reprinted in the Virginia Baptist Religious Herald and the moderate tabloid SBC Today. He was praised by editors of both publications for his courage.

That was not the end of the Montoya story. Shortly after his article was published, the Southern Baptist Advocate learned that Montoya had "a rather extensive police record" in Texas stretching from 1970 to 1979. Montoya, the Advocate reported, had been charged with auto burglary, possession of marijuana, aggravated assault and delivery of cocaine. According to the Advocate's sources, Montoya had received ten years probation on the cocaine charge in 1979 which in 1982 was reduced to three years, three months and fifteen days probation. Montoya, the Advocate said, had freely admitted to his police record and other things "before he came back to God" and enrolled at Criswell College.

Criswell College officials said they had not known of his police record. A deacon of Montoya's church in Arkansas told the Advocate he had not given them the information when coming as their pastor.[20]Montoya told Baptist Press that he had informed the church.[20A]

In disclosing Montoya's background, Advocate editor Bob Tenery "hope[d] and pray[ed] that there can be healing in Arkansas among the conservative brethren and that there can be a coming together as we face a critical [national] convention."[20B]

A Turnover in Louisiana

The Louisiana Baptist Convention (LBC) in 1989 appeared somewhat like the SBC in 1979. For many years, a coalition of leading pastors and denominational workers had controlled the LBC, with many of the same people coming on committees and boards year after year, while those deemed "uncooperative" were ignored. One prominent pastor had served on the state Executive Board for 20 consecutive years. Two had served on three boards or committees at the same time. Conservatives had been held back for years and were now determined to wrest control from the old establishment and open up the system.

The center of power in Louisiana was in the metro Alexandria area where the convention headquarters and Louisiana College were located. Unlike other state conventions, the LBC hired and paid associational directors of missions, instead of the local associations.

Questions From a Pastor

Ron Herrod, pastor of FBC, Kenner, which led the state in baptisms for 10 years, tried first to break up the old-style establishment's lock on the LBC. In 1983 Herrod was nominated for convention president. He was defeated by a large vote margin, but he did get elected to the board of Louisiana College.

Herrod soon began raising questions about college policy and operations. He objected to a campus concert by a secular rock group. He protested the use of college facilities for a Mormon convention. He opposed the use of a text in Bible classes which he said took a non-historical approach to the first 11 chapters of Genesis. He opposed employment of Catholics as teachers. He objected to the college's giving an honorary doctorate to an Episcopalian without knowing if he drank alcoholic beverages. He protested a speech in chapel by a furloughing SBC missionary who saw no difference between praying in the name of Jesus and making petitions in the name of a Catholic saint.

When it appeared that he was making little headway with the college which his church helped support, Herrod presented his concerns "over the direction" that "our" Baptist college "is taking" in a letter to the editor of the state denominational paper. The editor would not print his letter, even after he agreed to soften his criticisms.[21]

In 1985, Herrod was nominated again for state convention president. As he had in 1983, Herrod refused to permit any organized effort to get out the vote. Herrod lost this second time by a large majority. A major reason was that many conservative pastors had stopped going to the state convention because they felt shut out of the process.

A New Leader for Conservatives

After Herrod moved to FBC, Fort Smith, Arkansas, the conservative pastors turned to Fred Lowery, pastor of the 5,000-member FBC, Bossier City, for leadership. Lowery was a former vice president of the SBC Pastors Conference. His church had been a leader in Cooperative Program giving. Still, he had reportedly not been asked to preach, pray, or say anything at a state convention function for almost five years. He was apparently regarded by many as a radical independent.

In 1987 Lowery consented to be nominated for president. A single pastor mailed a letter to 16 other pastors, urging them to come and bring their maximum number of church messengers to support Lowery. Opponents used the letter to raise the specter of a takeover by radical fundamentalists. Lowery lost and the establishment remained in power. A conservative, Everett Geis, was elected vice president. The elected president did not consult — which he was not legally required to do — with Geis on appointments to the powerful Committee on Committees.

In 1988, conservative Tommy French and a number of other pastors sought to begin a pre-convention pastors conference. The established power structure feared that this might serve as a catalyst for rallying opposition and tried to get a committee appointed to control the program. French sent a questionnaire to every pastor in Louisiana, asking them to indicate the type of leadership they preferred for the pastors conference. Eighty percent voted for elected leaders. French was elected president of the first pastors conference, which was held that year.

The establishment candidate was re-elected president of the convention without opposition. In 1989 the Chairman of the Religion Department at Louisiana College retired. Conservatives urged that a self-avowed inerrantist be hired in the department. One conservative scholar was recommended by over 40 pastors, but he was never contacted by anyone from the college. In fact the trustees did not vote until after the moderate candidate was already at the school and teaching.

In May, 1989, Louisiana College President Robert Lynn was quoted in the Southern Baptist Advocate as endorsing a "covenant relationship" between the school and the convention. This would allow college trustees to be elected from a list of names submitted by the president. The concept was reportedly approved by the college trustees in their September board meeting, but Lynn denied advocating such a plan. Even so, concern spread across the state that the convention might lose control of the college, as had happened in North Carolina with Wake Forest and in Georgia with Mercer.

When the next pastors conference was held, prior to the November, 1989 convention, a group of laymen and pastors who had not been very enthusiastic about the conference showed up to vote. French presided and announced that only pastors would be permitted to vote.

A Close Vote

Two candidates were nominated for conference president, Everett Geis, the former LBC vice president and Perry Sanders, pastor of FBC, Lafayette. Sanders, a theological conservative and a long-time kingmaker, was the establishment favorite. When the votes were counted, it was discovered that Geis had won by a two to one margin.

The 1989 convention was held at Guinn Auditorium at the college, making it more convenient for college personnel and denominational workers from the nearby state office to attend as messengers from their churches. To no one's surprise, a record number of messengers registered. It was apparent that both parties had worked to get their vote out. The coalition of pastors, laity and denominational workers that had been so long in power backed Sid Young, a former president of the State Executive Board. Conservatives supported Fred Lowery again.

The election of officers came on Tuesday. Incumbent President Calvin Phelps permitted the balloting for president to start when some were still registering. A number of persons voted in the hall. There were charges of irregularities. Conservatives later conceded that two of their churches had over-registered by one messenger each, but it was found that 13 "liberal/bureaucrat coalition churches" had registered more than the permitted number.

Gasps were heard when the totals were announced — 723 for Lowery and 719 for Young. Lowery's supporters erupted in spirited applause. The leadership on the platform sat visibly stunned.

That afternoon Perry Sanders nominated Sid Young, the presidential loser, for first vice president. Sanders cited the election of Winfred Moore (after Moore's defeat by Charles Stanley for the SBC presidency) as SBC vice president in Dallas in a plea for unity. Young received over 60% of the vote in defeating the conservative choice.

By Wednesday morning less than one fourth of the 1,660 registered messengers remained. That morning Perry Sanders talked peace and unity at breakfast with Fred Lowery. What the conservatives didn't know was that during the afternoon Sanders had already planned to ask that the LBC bylaws be amended to allow the president and the two vice presidents, instead of just the president, to act as a committee in appointing the Committee on Committees. When Sanders did so protests broke out. Tommy French and Everett Geis opposed the motion. Sanders said this was something he had wanted to do for a long time and that he only wanted to bring more people into the appointment process. The parliamentarian suggested a quorum might not be present. Nevertheless he ruled that a vote on a change of bylaws could be made without a quorum.

The motion passed on a standing vote with about 50 conservatives declaring opposition.

President Lowery appointed a bi-partisan committee to investigate the legality of the bylaw change. The convention lawyer was asked to look at the proposal and make a ruling. The lawyer found the convention constitution authorized the president to make appointments and choose the chairman of the Committee on Committees. The constitution, the lawyer said, took precedence over the bylaws. The change as voted by the small crowd at the convention could not take effect.[22]

Faceoff in Texas

The Baptist General Convention of Texas (BGCT) is the largest state convention in the SBC and consequently has more votes on SBC agency boards than any other state. Texas also boasts the largest Baptist seminary and the largest university in the SBC. It comes as no surprise that the Texas convention is watched closely across the denomination.

Four elements had been active in every Texas convention meeting during recent years: theological moderates (who are generally to the right of moderates in the eastern states), self-styled centrists (who are conservative in theology, but willing to accept moderates as religion professors and work with moderates in convention affairs), conservative activists (who have felt shut out of convention leadership and are committed to reverse a perceived leftward drift in the SBC and in Texas institutions) and Baylor University.

Alleged liberalism at Baylor almost always came up at the BGCT convention. The greatest fear of moderates and centrists was that conservatives would gain control of the Baylor board.

In 1984, Baylor President Herbert Reynolds joined SBC seminary presidents Lolley, Dilday and Honeycutt in public opposition to the conservative resurgency movement. Each year thereafter, in the Baylor alumni magazine, Reynolds spoke against the movement. His printed criticisms and warnings usually came in the May issue with the obvious intent of motivating sympathetic alumni to go to the national convention and vote against the "fundamentalist" candidate for president.

In May, 1989, he charged the conservative alliance with moving to "capture and dominate a convention comprised of 14-15 million people and the billions of dollars of assets that go with such a large organization. . . " The SBC conservative presidents, he said, "have moved closer to Jerry Falwell and the Moral Majority — politically, philosophically and theologically."

Reynolds listed several other organizations "with a peculiar political and theological vision for our nation and for the world," with which he said the SBC conservative leadership was affiliated. These included the American Coalition for Traditional Values, the Religious Round Table, the Jerusalem Temple Foundation and the Christian Reconstructionist Movement, which Reynolds said intended to "replace the U.S. Constitution with the Old Testament through the creation of a theocracy." The co-mingling of SBC "fundamentalists" with these groups, Reynolds said, is "a pretty doggone weird, radical kind of thing, . . . and the thing that we have to fear these days is that these people will be successful to an increasing degree."[23]

Reynolds came back in the October issue of the Baylor student newspaper to complain of an "intractable mindset" in the "fundamentalist camp" that would create "indoctrination centers" out of Baylor and other Baptist institutions. In the same article, the student reporter quoted Paige Patterson's response: "Dr. Reynolds reminds one very much of a little boy with a toothache — sacred to death of the dentist, when in fact the dentist is the only one who can remove his pain."

Later in the article, the writer quoted Patterson as saying of Baylor, "Everybody knows there is a large number of professors in the religion department who believe there are mistakes in the Bible and that concerns us."

The reporter then quoted Reynolds as saying that he believed the Bible to be inspired, but not necessarily inerrant. "I think that there are too many contradictions for that to occur," Reynolds added, "but I believe that the Bible is indeed the inspired Word of God."[24]

Conservatives quickly grabbed hold of Reynolds' statement on inspiration and printed it on a handout for distribution at the convention. Underneath they printed the words " . . . It is impossible for God to lie. . . " from Hebrews 6:18.

Plans for a Pastors Conference

Moderates and centrists were caught off guard in September when conservative pastor Rick Scarborough announced plans for a pre-convention pastors conference. The listed speakers included Jack Graham, Ralph Smith, Jimmy Draper, Stan Coffey, John D. Morgan and Fred Wolfe — all pretty well known names in the conservative movement.

Outgoing BGCT president Joel Gregory, who had enjoyed support from all factions in the state, said the BGCT had no authority "to tell any group of brothers or sisters when or where they could meet and could not meet." Gregory did think it "unfortunate" that the conference had been scheduled at a time when two mission groups, Texas Baptist Men and the state WMU would be meeting.

The "centrist" Concerned Texas Baptist group called the planners "a self-appointed group of young Pressler-coalitionists," a political faction bent on dividing the BGCT. "History tells us that we can expect the Pastors Conference" to "promote their candidate, Dr. John Morgan, for president" of the BGCT "and the two people they choose to run for 1st and 2nd vice presidents, . . . attack Texas Baptist institutions, . . . create distrust and suspicion, . . . promote Ralph Smith and Fred Wolfe as possible SBC presidents, distract us from the spirit of missions," and "encourage churches to follow Dr. Paige Patterson's suggestion to send Cooperative Program funds directly to Nashville, thus bypassing the state convention."[25] It was typical alarmist rhetoric that had been heard before.

Scarbough said he was "aware of criticism that the meeting is of a political nature, but in the environment we are in that is unavoidable."[26]

The pastors conference was held.

Joel Gregory's Concerns

Rumors had circulated that Joel Gregory was concerned about theological problems at Baylor, although Gregory had sought to maintain a strict neutrality in partisan politics during his two years as BGCT president. Gregory, an avowed inerrantist, was one of the few Texas Baptist leaders whom all groups could support. But in a pre-convention interview, Gregory saw a "threat to Texas Baptist togetherness" that "comes from the perception on the part of some that they have no voice in convention life, that they have been shut out of appointments and places on boards, commissions and committees of the denomination." He conceded that "when you look . . . across a 10 to 15-year period or across a longer historical period, there may be more perception than reality. But that is beside the point, because when you have a constituency that perceives that [it has no voice], it quickly becomes reality." Gregory wished that he could "bequeath a kind of inclusiveness" to his successor so "no one will sense that he or she is shut out of the leadership process."

In the interview, Gregory recalled that in his president's message for the 1988 BGCT annual meeting, he had urged critics of Baylor not to criticize every part of the institution, while cautioning the "caring custodians" of the university to listen to the "oft-repeated concerns of responsible Texas Baptists." Gregory said he himself had delivered to Baylor a list of possible teachers, "about 20 conservative, evangelical scholars who had not been actively involved in the Southern Baptist Convention controversy, but who were credentialed, conservative, inerrantist scholars." Gregory said it had never been his "intention" to replace any professor. I am talking about a matter of balance in [the religion] department, which Dr. Reynolds has indicated . . . that it was his desire to do."[27]

New Officers Elected

Ralph Smith, a former president of the BGCT and the SBC Pastors Conference, nominated John Morgan for BGCT president. Morgan was pastor of a large and growing church in Houston and had an outstanding record in missions and evangelism. Winfred Moore, who had been the standard-bearer for the moderate-"centrist" coalition in the SBC, nominated Phil Lineberger as Morgan's opponent. Lineberger's candidacy had been actively promoted by the Concerned Texas Baptists group and the Baylor Alumni Association.

Lineberger won a first ballot victory over Morgan and Bailey Stone, an unaligned pastor. As in past elections, the margin of victory was not disclosed. The moderate-"centrist" coalition then proceeded to elect their candidates for first and second vice president.

At a news conference after his election, Lineberger was asked how he would reach out to those who had not voted for him and who might feel disenfranchised. "I will sit down and talk with them about why they feel they aren't included," he pledged.

Asked about charges regarding Baylor, Lineberger replied, "If our nation could be run as effectively as Baylor, we'd be in good shape."[28]

With the tension of the elections past, controversy erupted only once when Jimmy Draper protested the decision of the nominating committee not to renominate Jim Bolton, a layman in FBC, Dallas, for a third term as a Baylor trustee. Draper said other Baylor trustees had "been far more active in political rallies" than had Bolton whose church was faithful in Cooperative Program giving. "[Renomination] is the right thing to do if we are going to reach out," Draper said.

However, an opponent of the renomination said he had heard Bolton make charges to a group which Bolton had not previously brought before the board. This, the opponent said, was a violation of Bolton's "Christian fiduciary responsibility" as a trustee.

Draper's motion to amend the nominating committee's report was then decisively rejected.[29]

The statement by Reynolds on contradictions in the Bible, as printed in the October 27 issue of the Baylor student paper, was not brought up, but dealt with in a response by Editor Presnall Wood in his "Letters to the Editor" column. Wood responded to a letter from reader Megan Foster of Houston who cited the damaging quote. Wood said he had called Reynolds and asked him about the statement. Reynolds replied, according to Wood: "Some of the translations of the God-breathed scriptures are contradictory but this does not mean that God's original breathing of the scriptures was contradictory; God never contradicts Himself. By saying some of the translations are contradictory I mean such things which have to do with some dates, numbers and chronological order. I say these are contradictions — not error."[30]

So ended another Texas convention. Questions remained about Baylor. Conservatives had not elected a single officer. Because of the tradition of re-electing an incumbent president, conservatives would probably not have a chance for two more years. But they had started an annual pastors conference and in three months they would be buoyed by decisions of two prominent and previously undeclared Texas pastors to join the resurgency movement in electing a conservative president at the 1990 national convention in New Orleans.

References

1 "1989 Resolutions," Religious Herald, November 23, 1989, p. 9.

2 "Crisis Committee Report Draws Little Discussion," op. cit., p. 4.

3 Southern Baptist Issues, June/July, 1989, p. 1.

4 Editorial: "Ending the Godsey Era at Mercer," The Atlanta Constitution, April 28, 1989, p. 22A.

5 William Neal and Albert Mohler: " 'Quiet' Convention Draws Fewer Messengers; Meeting Characterized by Optimism, Unity," The Christian Index, November 23, 1989, pp. 1, 3.

6 "State Conventions Act on Abortion, Cooperative Program and Crisis," SBC Today, December, 1989, p. 2.

7 Lonnie Wilkey: "Union University Religion Professor Announces Resignation," Baptist and Reflector, June 28, 1989, p. 3.

8 "Tennessee Baptists Vote Down change to Constitution," Baptist and Reflector, November 22, 1989, p. 5.

9 "Priority of Prayer and Messenger Concerns," op. cit. p. 2.

10 "St. Louis Layman Beaver Elected MBC President," Word & Way, November 2, 1989, p. 7.

11 R.G. Puckett: "Convention Marked by Close Votes, Major Decisions, Resolutions," Biblical Recorder, November 25, 1989, pp. 1, 10.

12 James Scudder: "Baptist Factions Vie for Control of Convention," Arkansas Gazette, July 1, 1989.

13 September, 1989, Vol. 1.

14 James Scudder: "Southern Baptists Caught in Growing Power Struggle," Arkansas Gazette, October 11, 1989.

15 "Letters to the Editor, Arkansas Baptist Newsmagazine, p. 4.

16 "Responding to the Pirated Tape," A Conservative Voice in Arkansas, September, 1989, Vol. 2.

17 "An Open Letter From Dr. Ronnie Floyd.

18 Mark Kelly: "State Convention: Repentance and Revival," Arkansas Baptist Newsmagazine, November 23, 1989, pp. 4-8.

19 "Christian Century, January 25, 1990, p. 5.

20 Robert M. Tenery: "Sad News From Arkansas," Southern Baptist Advocate, February, 1990, p. 3.

20A Telephone Interview with Baptist Press, April 6, 1990.

20B Advocate, op. cit.

21 More details on Herrod's concerns about Louisiana College are presented in Volume 2 of The Truth in Crisis, pp. 96, 97, 183-186.

22 Information from: Personal Interview, Ron Herrod, Metairie, Louisiana, 1987; Jim Richards: "The Louisiana Hayride," The Southern Baptist Advocate, February, 1990; Sidney Williams: Attorney Disallows Baptist Bylaws' Railroad Job," Alexandria Daily Town Talk, November 17, 1989, p. D 11; "Wrapup Reports of State Baptist Conventions, The Christian Index, November 30, 1989 p. 5.

23 "Reynolds Cites Broader Goals of Fundamentalists," The Baylor Line, May, 1989., pp. 24, 25.

24 Paul Yowell: "Factions Struggle for Control of BGCT," The Baylor Lariat, October 27, 1989, p. 9B.

25 Newsletter, Concerned Texas Baptists, October, 1989, p. 2.

26 Toby Druin: "Conference Causes Concern," Baptist Standard, September 20, 1989, pp. 3, 4.

27 Toby Druin: "Joel Gregory: Texas Baptists Are 'Together,' " Baptist Standard, November 1, 1989, pp. 8, 9.

28 "Ken Camp and Scott Collins: "Lineberger to Stay Course, Vows Inclusiveness," Baptist Standard, November 15, 1989, p. 7.

29 "Toby Druin: 104th Convention: 'Just a Spiritual Meeting," op. cit.

30 "Letters to Editor," Baptist Standard, November 29, 1989, p. 2.

Chapter 8

"Enlarging the Tent"

Dan Vestal, the man who once called denominational politics "immoral," was on the campaign trail, although he sought to be in his church every Sunday. Indeed, he had hardly stopped to catch his breath since the press conference after his defeat in Las Vegas.

Crumpler's Call

On Sunday evening January 14, 1990 Carolyn Weatherford Crumpler came to his church in Georgia and announced that she was willing to be nominated for first vice president. Vestal, who had been urging her since the past October to join his campaign, promptly endorsed her candidacy.

As WMU president for 15 years Carolyn Weatherford had become the best known woman in Southern Baptist life. A compelling speaker, she was a person of no controversy until becoming involved with the Women in Ministry (WIM) group, serving as a member of WIM's National Steering Committee and speaking at WIM meetings. Still she was nominated for first vice president at Las Vegas and received almost one third of the vote. That summer she resigned from the WMU to marry Joe Crumpler, a widowed pastor in Cincinnati, Ohio. Even before her wedding, she said she would not "step out of SBC politics, . . . because I am concerned about the future of our convention and I want [it] to settle down to its main job [of] missions."[1]

In her announcement at Vestal's church, she foresaw the opening of "future doors . . . to continued involvement" in SBC politics. "Yes, I might be a candidate for the presidency someday. But, right now I believe totally in Daniel Vestal and. . . I believe my running for the first vice-presidency will help his candidacy for the presidency."[2]

A Caribbean Cruise

While the moderate-"centrist" coalition was gearing up for New Orleans, conservative leaders were talking candidates. The occasion was a Bible study cruise in the Caribbean. "We didn't go to discuss SBC politics," Adrian Rogers explained later. "But while we (Rogers, Jerry Vines, Charles Stanley, Bailey Smith and a number of other pastors) were there, we did talk about 10 possible candidates. Among these were Morris Chapman, Fred Wolfe and Ed Young."[3]

Wolfe was reportedly the consensus choice as the best candidate. He pastored in Mobile only 150 miles from New Orleans and, according to Bailey Smith had "more exposure nationally" than Chapman." Wolfe agreed to be nominated, "but the closer we got to announcing the decision," Wolfe said later, "the more troubled I got in my spirit."[4]

Bisagno to Nominate Chapman

After returning from the cruise, Adrian Rogers and some others on the cruise were contacted by John Bisagno, who, according to Rogers, said, " 'I believe you're on the right way. I'd be willing to nominate a candidate and use my influence to encourage some of my own kind [to help him get elected]. So we flew to Houston [and met with Bisagno and Ed Young]. John talked to some of the others [in] the broad middle. They said, 'What about Morris?' And that's how Morris Chapman surfaced as a candidate."[5]

Chapman had just observed his 11th anniversary as pastor of the 7,776-member FBC of Wichita Falls, Texas. Both he and his wife, Jodi, had served on important boards, he on the SBC Foreign Mission Board and the Executive Board of the Texas convention, she on the Sunday School Board and as a member of the SBC Peace Committee. Before coming to Wichita Falls, Chapman had pastored FBC of Albuquerque, New Mexico where he served two terms as president of that state's convention.

He "went to Washington for a meeting February 5 and 6 thinking it had been settled. . . . I was confident Fred [Wolfe] would be the nominee." But upon arriving home February 6, Chapman received a call from Wolfe in which Wolfe described himself as "not God's man for the hour."

According to Chapman, Bisagno, pastor of FBC, Houston for 20 years, called the next afternoon, February 7 and "said he believed I was the man who could bring a unifying spirit to the SBC and asked if he could nominate me for the presidential position. I told him events had been moving very rapidly and I was stunned that it was taking this turn but that I was taking [Bisagno's request] as a word from God."[6]

Bisagno's movement, when announced, sent shock waves across the SBC. Moderates had hoped the popular evangelistic pastor of FBC, Houston would at least remain neutral. Conservatives were overjoyed.

Throughout the controversy, Bisagno had sought to steer a neutral course in hopes that he could bring the two sides together. In the fall of 1986, he had urged challenger Winfred Moore and SBC President Adrian Rogers to both "step down in favor of a non-political man, like a Dan Vestal or a Jim Henry." Let Adrian "nominate . . . this type of person and Winfred . . . second and then unify around evangelism and missions."'. Shortly before the 1988 San Antonio convention, Bisagno mailed an eight-page paper to Baptist papers in which he said, ". . . In some ways, both sides are right and both sides are wrong. The Right has [gone] beyond the position of an infallible Bible and . . . imposed certain issues as tests of orthodoxy. . . . The problem . . . of the left is just as real. History has well documented that once you tiptoe down the path of neo-orthodoxy, you will ultimately walk full stride on the liberal highway. The sands of time are strewn with the shipwrecks of once-mighty denominations that drifted from neo-orthodoxy onto the treacherous reef of liberalism. The death of evangelistic fire and missionary zeal are the heritage of the liberalism to which neo-orthodoxy has historically moved. Who should be president of the Southern Baptist Convention? That person who will . . . use all available tools to ensure opposition to the neo-orthodoxy of the Left and the excesses of the Right." Bisagno said then that he "would be willing to nominate such a person, though he did not name anyone."⁸

Bisagno's Bombshell

The day after talking with Chapman, Bisagno issued a five-page press release endorsing both Chapman and the conservative movement.

"It is not unity at any cost that will save this denomination, it is unity around a perfect Lord Jesus and all that we know about Him found in a perfect Book," Bisagno declared, adding, "Too many of us who feel this way have been silent too long."

The Houston pastor quickly focused on the nature of Scripture, as taught in SBC institutions, the issue which moderates and "centrists" had been trying to dodge for 11 years.

He recalled the four "examples" which the Peace Committee determined were "held by Southern Baptists at large"; including, "but not limited to, the reality of Bible characters, stated authorship, the miraculous and historical accuracy [of the Bible]. . . . I believe that . . . at least 95 percent of grass root Southern Baptists affirm those precepts and expect them to be perpetuated at every level of Southern Baptist institutional life." Yet the Peace Committee found that "some" SBC schools were not teaching these and were thus "out of line with historic Baptist beliefs." The PC, he noted, "called upon" SBC "institutions in the future to build their professional staffs and faculties from those who clearly reflect such dominant convictions and beliefs held by Southern Baptists at large. . . ”

Moderates had argued that it didn't matter whether Genesis 1-11 was real history or not. Declared Bisagno: "If Adam is not real, perhaps Jesus is not real. If the first 11 chapters of Genesis are not historical, then Adam and Eve, Cain and Abel, Noah and the flood, the Tower of Babel, Methuselah, Enoch, the origin of sin, the fall of man, the first mention of the Redeemer, the first mention of the blood, the first home, the first family, the first government, the first question, the first answer, the first problem, the first solution, are all swept out into the sea of mythology.

"Add to that a Bible with books claiming to be written by authors not so [designated], miracles demonstrating the power of God not occurring, the historical accuracy of [the books] not existing and you have cut out the heart, the very foundation of our authority for evangelism.”

"Recently a prominent educator wrote, 'It is an absolute and unforgivable tragedy that the Word of God has been used as a weapon this past decade by those who have torn the Southern Baptist Convention asunder.' I totally disagree. In fact, it is an absolute, though correctable, tragedy that any administrator in any Southern Baptist institution has allowed one person under his responsibility to discredit the Word of God by denying its history, its characters, its miracles and its stated authorship.”

Strong stuff. Adrian Rogers would hardly have said it differently. But this was John Bisagno the "neutral," taking his stand in the Convention controversy.

Sure, Bisagno said, both sides had made "mistakes" and given "regrettable statements, within the past 11 years. But sweep away all the secondary issues — politics, control, women in ministry, pastoral authority, the priesthood of the believer, etc. — and the bedrock issue has not changed. Does this Book mean what it says, or not?”

Bisagno recalled that in 1979, "an effort working within the bounds prescribed by our constitution and bylaws began to bring a pendulum swinging much too far to the left back to its conservative roots. The time has [now] come to refocus on the issue and that issue is still the nature of Scripture. . . . Doctrinal integrity is as essential to world evangelism as is an impeccable Savior.”

He came to the headline making part of his statement: "I shall nominate for Convention president a man who will lead us to a broadened togetherness; a man whose major credentials are not only those of character, leadership and superior mission giving, but a commitment to the Word of God — an authoritative, authentic, perfect Bible, brought into being by a perfect God.

"I call upon my fellow Southern Baptists . . . to unite behind the man who can unify us all, without political parameters, around the integrity of Scripture and a perfect Savior there revealed; a man committed to the completion of the correction begun 11 years ago; a man who in 1989 led his church to give 14.5 percent of its budget to the Cooperative Program, totalling $367,111.18, as well as $55,613.58 to the Lottie Moon Foreign Mission Offering; . . . a man whom I intend to nominate for president of the Southern Baptist Convention in New Orleans. . . — Morris Chapman."

The Candidate Presented

Five days later Chapman came to the annual Pastors School and Bible Conference at FBC, Jacksonville, where current SBC president Jerry Vines is co-pastor with Homer Lindsey. There Chapman received a long-distance call from Bisagno, which was heard by the audience of over 3,500.

During the call, Bisagno read an addendum to his statement of the previous week. "I want what I am saying to be dead center, bull's eye, perfectly clear. The goal of the past 11 years and more — that every denominational servant and every institutional staff member not only believe in, but teach and perpetuate belief in, a perfect infallible Bible — must not change."

Homer Lindsey, Jr. called Bisagno's statement and endorsement of Chapman "historic." Many SBC leaders like Bisagno, Lindsey said, who have tried to remain neutral, "are coming to the realization that they can remain neutral no longer." Bisagno, Lindsey said, "is in the process of bringing these men out of neutrality." Lindsey anticipated that others would soon make statements similar to Bisagno's, noting that Jerry Vines had been trying to bring in unaligned pastors, telling them, "to decide 'if, in the Southern Baptist Convention, they want a split or splinter.' If the majority of Southern Baptists believe in this Word," Lindsey added, then they are the ones that should prevail. And if it's the minority that do not believe in this Word, then they are the ones who should keep quiet or leave."

Adrian Rogers also called Bisagno's coming out "the most historic thing that has happened in these 11 years." Rogers urged the Jacksonville group to do "all you can" to elect Chapman president. Rogers called Chapman one who "is doctrinally straight, morally pure, eminently qualified. . . . He has been through the fire. He has paid the price."

After receiving a standing ovation, Chapman declared himself "100 percent, totally committed to the inerrancy and infallibility of the Word of God. I don't know the will of God about the election, but I do believe God will stand with those who stand for the truth," he said.[9]

The Southern Baptist Advocate and the Conservative Carolina Baptist printed Bisagno's statement in full.[10] Baptist Press quoted from the statement in a larger story on Chapman as the conservative candidate, noting that Bisagno "spent most of his statement saying the issue of the 11-year controversy 'is still the nature of Scripture.' "

BP also quoted responses to Bisagno's statement from several SBC conservatives:

Bailey Smith: Bisagno's "strong statement" meant ". . . He wishes he had gotten with this [conservative] movement earlier."

Jimmy Draper: Bisagno's announcement that he would nominate Chapman "represents a broadening of support" for the conservative movement. "Bisagno has been on the sidelines. . . . His coming expresses his willingness to say the cause is right and that there is a broader circle that can be drawn to include more people. We recognize the need to include people who, for whatever reason, have not been identified with us in the past."[11]

Chapman agreed with Draper, saying "my heart's desire is to . . . reach beyond perceived political parameters of our convention to bring us together again. The time has come to enlarge the tent . . . to encompass all cooperating Southern Baptists who are dedicated to perpetuating our allegiance to the Bible as the perfect Word from the perfect God. We must stay the course of this commitment in the spirit of broadened togetherness and shared leadership."[12]

"Who Has Reserved 27,000 Rooms?"

The Executive Committee met in Nashville February 19-21. Al Shackleford, the designated manager for the New Orleans convention, noted that the Super Dome where the convention was to meet in New Orleans would seat 71,000. Shackleford "hope[d] that when we leave New Orleans we will feel as good about the Super Dome as the San Francisco 49ers [who recently won the Super Bowl there].

"There are 27,000 hotel rooms in New Orleans," he noted. "All have been [reserved]." Shackleford couldn't answer the big question: Who had reserved all those rooms?

Bad News for the BJCPA

Of more immediate interest at the February, 1990 EC meeting was a proposed three-way rearranging of allocations and program assignments for representation of the SBC on religious liberty concerns in Washington. A motion by Charles Sullivan had passed at the previous fall EC meeting asking that the Christian Life Commission be given the primary program assignment for religious matters. The proposal, which was referred to sub-committees for study, would clearly call for a reduction in funding for the Baptist Joint Committee on Public Affairs and some adjustment in the assignment and budget allocation for the Public Affairs Committee.

The galleries were full with many standing along the walls when the Program and Budget Sub-committee presented its recommendations during the Tuesday afternoon plenary session. If passed, the recommendations would go before the full convention in New Orleans.

The first recommendation called for enlarging the CLC program statement to include: (1) "Promot[ion] of religious liberty in cooperation with the churches and other Southern Baptist entities." (2) Bring to bear "Baptist statements, convictions and insights in the field of Christian ethics and religious liberty upon important policy-making groups. . . (3) "To relate [the CLC's] emphasis on Christian social ethics and religious liberty to Baptist associations, churches and leaders through printed media."[13]

The second recommendation called for EC adoption of operational guidelines that authorized the Public Affairs Committee to:

— "Address matters of religious liberty and church-state issues concerning the Southern Baptist Convention and the various state Baptist conventions."[14]

— "Represent" the SBC on the BJCPA.

— "Relate to and cooperate with" the CLC "in areas of joint concern" on religious liberty matters.

— Be the "vehicle through which" the BJCPA "makes its budget requests" and "account[s] financially to the SBC and "review" the BJCPA "program and personnel for and in behalf of "the SBC."

The proposed arrangement called for a reduction in the SBC allocation to the BJCPA from $391,796 to $50,000 for the 1991 budget year, with the PAC's funding increased from $23,704 to $96,600 and the CLC's allotment raised from $897,508 to $1,191,236.

Subcommittee Chairman Bill Harrell moved the adoption of the first recommendation. EC member Ann Smith quickly spoke in opposition saying the BJCPA had "earned its money" by, among other things, "stopping a tax on missionaries that saved the Foreign Mission Board $10 million in the last eight years. The recommendations, she said, reflected "tunnel vision" and would "splinter" SBC efforts in Washington. "Some on this Committee," she added, "are so set on political goals that they're willing to sell their Baptist heritage for a mess of pottage."

Wallace Jones of Missouri argued that past convention actions had shown SBC support of the BJCPA. Jones presented a substitute motion to refer the matter back to the subcommittee for discussions with the BJCPA and the PAC. Another supporter of the substitute said three agencies in Washington would mean a "waste of money."

Robert Goode opposed the substitute. The Convention, he said, had not had an up-or-down-opportunity for a clear vote on the BJCPA. Fred Wolfe said it was time to "quit playing games" about religious liberty representation. "We haven't been satisfied with representation given us" by the BJCPA.

Jones' substitute motion lost 53-17 and the original motion then passed. By the time the second vote was announced, many of the BJCPA supporters who had come to view the proceedings were already out the door.

Two efforts were made to amend the proposed budgetary changes. One moved to transfer $72,600 of the PAC's proposed $96,600 funding to the CLC. This lost on a 35-35 tie vote. A second sought to amend the budget by giving each of the three entities a 1.89 percent increase based on the previous year's allocation. This was rejected by a large margin.

During debate on the recommendations an eight-page document was distributed to the EC members. Put together by the EC officers, it was entitled, "Some Reasons for the Southern Baptist Convention 1990-1991 Budget Allocation to Support Religious Liberty and Separation of Church and State." The document was to show "the reasons for" the EC's decision. Steve Brumbelow of West Virginia moved that the paper be printed in the 1990 Convention Book of Reports, the Baptist Program (which is mailed to all SBC pastors) and the Daily Bulletin at the New Orleans convention.

Martin Bradley, recording secretary of the SBC, immediately objected on grounds that the paper lacked balance and ignored decades of service by the BJCPA.

After a motion to table the motion failed 32-31, EC Vice-chairman Paul Pressler spoke for the original motion. "If we fail to publish this . . . rationale for our actions, we can be misled by people putting words in our mouths." Member Stan Coffey also argued for publication, saying that people "are asking, 'What is the rationale for acting as you [the EC] did?' We're not causing these differences [over the BJCPA, etc.]. The differences are already there."

The motion to have the document printed in the designated places passed 39-20.

The EC then voted to permit the "same exposure" for a minority report drawn up and signed by individuals favoring it.

When it appeared that the business relating to future work and funding of the BJCPA, the PAC and the CLC might be done, David E. Hankins moved to reconsider the budget to reduce the PAC's funding to $25,000 with the difference from the original figure going to the CLC. Hankins called this a "third alternative. We're saying we want the SBC to work primarily with the CLC instead of the BJCPA." Despite objections from Paul Pressler, the motion to reconsider was approved 44-25.[15]

With this final action, the ground was cleared for presentation of the EC's recommendations on religious liberty to the convention in New Orleans.

Dilday Talks to Vines

Beside the religious liberty matters, there were two other main topics of conversation at the EC meeting. The first incident related to statements allegedly made by Russell Dilday to Jerry Vines. This happened on Tuesday as Vines and four EC members — Bob Parker, Gordon Graham, Fred Wolfe and Steve Brumbelow — were about to leave the Baptist Building for lunch.

According to the recollection of Vines and his friends, this is what happened:

Dilday walked up to Vines and said, "Jerry, I'm highly upset. You've offended me by a statement made to [reporter Jim Jones] in Fort Worth."

Vines: "How did I offend you, Russell?"

Dilday: "You said you would be very surprised if Russell Dilday takes a personal stance before the [New Orleans] convention."

Vines: "Russell, I made that in light of your agreement with [your] trustees [to stay out of denominational politics]. If I have personally offended you, I apologize."

Dilday: Everywhere I go I'm campaigning for Dan Vestal. I'm going public; I'm doing it right now. I'm going to promote him."

Vines: "What about Daniel [Vestal's] statement that [denominational] politics is immoral? Do you agree that what Daniel's doing is immoral?"

Dilday: "Oh yes."

Vines: "Then what you're doing is immoral."

Dilday: "Oh yes, yes. I publicly endorse Daniel Vestal. I'm with him."

Vines: "You are?"

Dilday: "Yes, I'm working for him every way I can. I'll surprise you how much I'm working for him."

The conversation switched to activities of the conservative group.

Dilday: "Jerry, your group has lied and told untruths."

Vines: "Name someone."

Dilday: "Well, Paul Pressler."

Vines: "I'm amazed that a man in your position would strain at a Pressler and swallow a Baugh."

Dilday: "What do you mean?"

Vines: "Russell, you know what I mean about Johnny Baugh."

Dilday: "This [conservative] movement in the Convention is the most devastating in the history of the SBC. Time will prove that it is far more devastating than [the] Norris movement."

Vines remained quiet while Dilday continued: "The trustees you sent me are objectionable, incompetent and they couldn't even read a financial statement."

Vines: "That's pretty serious. What about Jimmy Draper?"

Dilday: "He'll be the chairman of my trustees."

Vines: "He's not incompetent?"

Dilday: "That's neither here nor there. I don't care one way or the other."[16]

The second matter of corridor interest concerned predictions by several EC members that Joel Gregory, Jim Henry, Ken Hemphill and Peace Committee Chairman Charles Fuller would shortly follow John Bisagno and come out in favor of Morris Chapman for president. This talk continued Thursday, February 22, at a meeting in Atlanta of 255 conservatives from 20 states.

The Meeting in Atlanta

Adrian Rogers moderated the six-hour meeting in a fellowship room of FBC, Atlanta. After explaining the circumstances of Bisagno's statement and his intention to nominate Morris Chapman, Rogers said he expected others "in this broad middle who have been on the sidelines to join our cause. I cannot speak for any man, but I [predict] we will see great numbers of their kind [coming]. This will send shivers in the moderate camp.

"We're saying to these middle men, 'The issue is the Word of God. On that we will not budge one inch. We welcome you with open arms. We are not going to look down on you, [but] you can't distance yourself from those who've fought to get where we are.'

"The coming of these men to join our cause," Rogers declared, "is the most historic [happening in the SBC] during the past 11 years. We're lengthening the cords and driving deeper the stakes. We're seeing [happen] what we've been dreaming and praying for."

Rogers sought to place the SBC conservative resurgence in larger perspective: "As the SBC goes, so goes the evangelical world. As the evangelical world goes, so goes America. As America goes, so goes the west . . . and the world. Even the independents who used to think we [in the SBC] were liberal are now cheering for us."

Conservative Strategy

Most of the discussion at the Atlanta meeting centered on the New Orleans convention. Estimates of attendance ran from "around 40,000" (Paul Pressler) to "bigger than Dallas" (Advocate editor Bob Tenery). "We're moving into the most crucial three-and-one-half months in Southern Baptist history," Pressler said.

Cautioning the group not to "be led down any rabbit tracks," Adrian Rogers urged a three-point strategy in preparation for the June convention.

— Keep the "focus" on the Peace Committee Report, "which is now the Report of the Convention. Some of our seminaries," Rogers noted, "are saying we haven't had conservatives on our faculties and we will put some on. We don't want 'some.' While we've never said we want wholesale firings, we do want purity as a goal."

— "Show the duplicity of moderates." Dan Vestal, Rogers recalled, had once called denominational politicking immoral. "Not since the earth crust hardened has there been more politicking than by those trying to elect Dan Vestal."

Moderates, Rogers said, "will try to move the discussion from the Word of God to personal agendas. Anybody who says we don't have theological problems [in denominational agencies] is either ignorant or dishonest."

— "Get behind our candidate and get your messengers to New Orleans."

Throughout the Atlanta meeting, Rogers and several other speakers kept cautioning the attendees to stick to the issue of the accuracy of the Bible, "avoid ugliness," and not become divided over women's ordination, accreditation problems at Southeastern Seminary, or allegations that Russell Dilday might be breaking his promise with trustees to stay out of politics. "Don't let the issue at the convention be, 'Let's save Dilday's job.'"

The Atlanta group applauded an announcement of the EC's action on religious liberty assignments and funding. Some did express disappointment that the anticipated increase in funding for the PAC had been shelved by the EC. In a telephone call to the group, Jerry Vines did not get into that matter, but said the time had come "for an up-and-down [convention] vote on the Baptist Joint Committee."

Concern was expressed at the meeting over activities by two former agency heads involved in working for a moderate victory in New Orleans. It was noted that former Radio and Television Commission president Jimmy Allen had recently mailed partisan materials to a list of former employees at the Sunday School Board. Allen had recently succeeded Winfred Moore as President of Baptists Committed, which was aligned with SBC moderates.

Concern About the WMU

Fears were expressed that Carolyn Weatherford Crumpler might try to use her WMU contacts in partisan ways. Adrian Rogers warned that "politization" of the WMU could be "a dangerous thing." Oklahoma conservative leader Eldridge Miller noted that he had already talked to a WMU official and been assured that Mrs. Crumpler will "absolutely not" use the WMU to get herself and Dan Vestal elected.

The first issue of a new conservative publication, The Southern Baptist Communicator, was introduced at Atlanta by Editor Fred Powell. "We're thankful for the Advocate," Powell said. "We just felt an additional voice was needed." After noting that a businessman was paying to send the new paper to every pastor and church in the SBC, Powell made a special plea for financial help for the Advocate which he said was entirely dependent on financial aid for publication.[17]

The Atlanta meeting closed with optimism and expectations that announcements would shortly be made by Joel Gregory and other "middle men" who would join John Bisagno in his call for a new "togetherness."

Gregory Comes Forth

The "other shoe" fell on moderates March 1 when Joel Gregory announced that "by the deepest conviction of my life and soul I must endorse [John Bisagno's] attempt for unity with doctrinal integrity." Since his famous "castle and wall" peace sermon in San Antonio, Gregory had been the most popular speaker on the state convention circuit. His inerrantist views were as well known as his declared neutrality in the struggle.

In his lengthy statement, Gregory said he had "attempted to be a peacemaker" in "this controversy" that "could ultimately destroy the denomination. For years I had hoped something would happen to end the controversy. Many of us not visibly involved hoped that a 'third party' would arise which would recognize our doctrinal concerns and maintain convention unity. This is not going to happen."

Gregory noted that the Peace Committee Report had been "adopted by a 96 percent vote" and "it stated that the roots of the controversy were theological.

"I am an inerrantist," Gregory declared. "I believe that the Bible does not err in any area of reality. On the other hand, it has been perceived that some who claimed this view were creating an exclusive group of leadership within the convention."

Gregory termed Bisagno's announcement that he intended to nominate Morris Chapman an "historic breakthrough" that "changed the situation for the first time in 11 years" because "both of these men are committed to reach beyond perceived political parameters of our convention to bring us together again. They have said that the time has come to enlarge the tent . . . to encompass all cooperating Southern Baptists who are dedicated to perpetuating our allegiance to the Bible as the perfect word from the perfect God.

"Dr. Bisagno has called for an 'historic new day' which will bring an end to this controversy and enable us all to fulfill the missionary task. . . . I see what is happening as nothing less than a new coalition to put an end to these painful 11 years."[18]

Even before Bisagno had announced, Gregory set up a conference call with Kenneth Hemphill, Jim Henry, Charles Fuller and Charles Carter, saying that John Bisagno had a statement he wanted to share. Bisagno then read a rough draft of his statement.

Kenneth Hemphill, pastor of FBC, Norfolk, Virginia, gave his statement on the same day that Gregory went public. Hemphill said he had "maintained a strictly neutral posture on all Convention issues which might be deemed political. . . . I have not been aligned with any political faction . . . , nor do I seek such alignment now or in the foreseeable future." Hemphill, who also released his statement on March 1, "pray[ed] that this will be the year Southern Baptists can put political rhetoric, divisive titles and character assassination behind us. I resonate with John Bisagno's call for peace now without compromise on the integrity of Scripture."[19]

Jim Henry, a member of the Peace Committee and pastor of FBC, Orlando, Florida, was more explicit than Hemphill. Henry had hoped that the conflict would "quickly abate. As far as I could tell, all the Southern Baptists I knew believed the Bible was infallible, inerrant and authoritative — the historic Baptist position." Then [the Peace Committee] went to work to find the root causes of our problems. When all of the smoke blew away, there was a unanimous consent that indeed, in certain [SBC] institutions, . . . there were those in the place of instruction and leadership who had drifted far from the heart of our spiritual roots. . ."

Henry "believe[d] that 11 years ago we caught the ship of faith in time to correct her course." During these years of correction, he conceded, "things have been said and done from all points of reference that have caused pain and embarrassment. . . , but we have made decided and constructive progress. I believe we must continue on that path. . . ."

Henry saw "two godly men" as the major nominees for president. "I know and love them both, but I can only vote for one. In deciding for the first time . . . to speak out on a presidential election, I am doing so not on the basis of personalities, but of a far greater concern — a principle: the integrity and nature of Scripture. Our leader must be the one who will affirm the course that will keep us off the reefs of denominational destruction . . . that has polluted and practically destroyed every mainline denomination. . . . I am confident both Dan Vestal and Morris Chapman believe" the Bible to be inerrant. "But, I feel only [Morris Chapman] appears willing . . . to appoint capable men and women who will adhere to the spirit and intent of the Peace Committee Report. . ."[20]

Charles Fuller did not speak until March 17. He supported Bisagno's plan as having "refreshing potential," but like Hemphill, he stopped short of directly endorsing Chapman for the presidency, although Fuller would "not be judgmental" of those who had done so. He too had not "been part of a political coalition or counter coalition," nor did he "seek to be. I simply yearn for a widened tent of leadership and fellowship among us, but held in place by the indispensable cords of a perfect Bible and a Great Commission."

Bisagno's proposal, Fuller said, presents "an alternative to one which has continued to be on an ongoing collision course. No tent of togetherness can be broad enough to house all the extremes among us, but surely the cords are long enough to include all who seriously embrace the convictions, the mission and the spirit of the Peace Committee Report, overwhelmingly adopted by the convention."[21]

Baptist Press Delays the Big Story

The statements by Gregory and Hemphill had appeared in their church papers, March 1. Henry's came March 8. Fuller's was released a few days later. Conservatives were expecting big stories, especially about Gregory, in Baptist Press and the state papers. Several conservatives called BP to ask when BP's report would be on the wire.

BP News Director Dan Martin recalls the sequence of events and BP's handling of the story. "For some time we'd been hearing that some major things were going to happen. We'd even heard that the conservatives had a plan to have a different pastor announce at a press conference every week. We got Gregory's announcement by fax March 6. In considering whether to run a story, we asked, 'Who is Joel Gregory? What has he been elected to?' He had been president of a state convention, but that was in Texas.

"People began calling and saying, 'We hear you're refusing to run a story on Gregory.' We said, 'We're waiting for a person who has held national office.' That in my opinion was Fuller. When he announced, we ran a story on all four pastors.

"We got the information out in a way that we thought was sensitive to the situation in the Convention and that prevented a proliferation of politics, which we saw had great possibilities of happening with a series of endorsements. We would have handled a series of announcements for the other side the same way."[22]

The first published story (to my knowledge) on Gregory's announcement appeared in the March 13 issue of the Indiana Baptist. Managing Editor Tammi Ledbetter quoted 172 words directly from Gregory's statement. The Indiana paper gave no response from Dan Vestal, noting only that he had announced that he would be nominated again in New Orleans.[23] The Indiana Baptist later ran the Baptist Press story, which appeared in other state papers.

On March 15, the Virginia Religious Herald printed in full Hemphill and Fuller's statements in full, under the headline, "Fuller, Hemphill Issue Statements on Controversy." Also, on March 15, the Florida Baptist Witness ran a story by Associate Editor Greg Warner on the announcements by the four pastors, with a response by Vestal. The headline read: "Henry, Gregory Endorse Chapman, Inerrancy Movement," with a subhead declaring: "Vestal Says Endorsements Are 'Political Ploy' to Perpetuate Power of Former Presidents." The Florida paper quoted extensively from Bisagno, Gregory, Henry and Fuller's statements and also included information from interviews by Warner with Henry and Fuller, as well as giving responses from Vestal.

Concern by conservatives for press coverage was most intense in Texas, where Gregory had recently served two terms as president of the state convention. The Baptist Standard carried nothing on Gregory's announcement in its March 7 and March 14 issues, although the latter included several stories relating to the New Orleans convention A two-column article relating to the announcement by Gregory and others then appeared on page 5 of the March 21 issue of the Standard. Bylined by Associate Editor Toby Druin, it was headlined. "Bisagno, Chapman Plan Praised by Some, Criticized by Others." It was not included among headlines of four other articles displayed in a box on the front cover which spotlighted Editor Presnall Wood's editorial for that issue, "SBC Politics Bigger Than Necessary?" In his editorial Wood declared that "a kind of politics that smacks of hateful and hostile negative secularism is a politics that is bigger — or smaller, if you please — than Baptists need."[24]

The Standard article included quotes from the announcements of three of the four pastors and responses from Dan Vestal and Richard Jackson. The Standard quoted directly about 50 words from Gregory's statement, 11 words from Hemphill's and 26 words from Fuller's declaration. Jim Henry was mentioned only as going on record with Gregory to endorse "Bisagno's call to rally around a perfect Bible and Chapman for the presidency."

The article then quoted the responses of Dan Vestal (93 words) and Richard Jackson (62 words) to the statement.

Vestal, according to the Standard, called the new "coalition" a "very clear political strategy. Morris Chapman is going to be nominated because the five former [conservative] presidents want him to be nominated. Southern Baptists don't need a college of cardinals to determine the direction. We particularly don't need a college of cardinals who go on Caribbean cruises and then come back and determine who will have a part in the decision making process. We do not need to be a centrally controlled denomination by a centrally controlling group determining who can and who cannot be part of Southern Baptist life."

Jackson, the Standard reported, decried Bisagno's claim of "inclusiveness." "Nothing has changed," Jackson said. "The same people are still having Caribbean cruises and making decisions for everyone else. I don't believe grassroots Baptists identify much with Caribbean cruises. If they really want to be 'inclusive' and 'broaden the tent of togetherness' why don't they include all the former presidents of the SBC in these decisions, not just those of the last 11 years."

In explaining the Standard's coverage, Toby Druin said in a telephone interview, "We traditionally have not carried political endorsements in our news columns. We really did not think [the announcements by Gregory, Hemphill and Henry] became news until Fuller announced. He's chairman of the Peace Committee.

"[When Gregory's statement became known] we immediately offered him the opportunity to submit a letter for our 'Letters to Editor' page. He felt like as a former president of the state convention that he should have some kind of special entree to our newspaper, but we just consider him a pastor in the same light as all the 5,000 other [SBC] pastors in Texas."[25]

Dan Martin, News Director of Baptist Press, wrote two BP stories, one on the announcement by the four pastors and the other on Vestal's response, which were sent out in the same mailing. The headlines on these articles varied among the state papers. Some examples:

Virginia Religious Herald, two articles, March 22: "Fuller Says Bisagno Plan Has 'Refreshing Potential." "Vestal Says Endorsements Clear Political Strategy." The Herald ran the articles on facing pages.

Missouri Word & Way, two articles on three-fourths of one page, March 22: "Fuller, Others Affirm Inerrancy 'Coalition.' " "Vestal Takes Issue With Coalition, Endorsements."

North Carolina's Biblical Recorder, two articles, March 24: "Fuller Says Bisagno Plan Has 'Refreshing Potential.' " "Vestal Says Endorsements Political Strategy." This paper started both stories on the front page, with continuation inside.

The announcements by the four pastors did not increase the optimism of moderates about Dan Vestal and Carolyn Crumpler's prospects in New Orleans to turn back the conservative movement. Fuller's and Gregory's statements were especially big blows. While Fuller and Hemphill had not directly endorsed Chapman, it was obvious from their statements that they favored the Bisagno plan which called for the election of Chapman.

References

1 Elaine Witt: "After Marriage, Will Weatherford's Life Hold More Missions, Politics?" SBC Today, July, 1989, p. 11.

2 Jack U. Harwell: "Carolyn Crumpler Makes Bid for SBC Leadership," op. cit., March, 1990, pp. 1, 3.

3 Related at meeting of conservatives in Atlanta, February 22, 1989.

4 "Fundamental-conservative SBC Leaders Choose Morris Chapman as 1990 Presidential Nominee," Word & Way, February 15, 1990, p. 4.

5 Conservative meeting, op. cit.

6 "Fundamental-conservative SBC Leaders Choose Morris Chapman . . . ," op. cit.

7 Marv Knox: "Bisagno Promotes Plan for 'Peace' Candidate," Baptist and Reflector, November 19, 1986, p. 7.

8 Marv Knox: "Both Sides at Fault, Bisagno Says of SBC," Baptist Press Report, May 10, 1988.

9 Greg Warner: "Texan Morris Chapman Endorsed as Convention Presidential Nominee," Religious Herald, February 22, 1990, p. 2.

10 It was printed in some other independent conservative Baptist papers. I do not have the full list at this time.

11 "Fundamental-Conservative SBC Leaders Choose Morris Chapman as 1990 Presidential Nominee, op. cit.

12 "Chapman Explains Desire for Election," Indiana Baptist, March 13, 1990, p. 10.

13 Taken from the proposed revision of the CLC Program Statement, February, 1990.

14 Taken from the Program and Budget Sub-committee Report, February, 1990.

15 Most of the quotes and other information presented during the lengthy procedure and debate over the roles and funding of the PAC, the BJCPA and the CLC in handling religious matters were taken from my notes. Some information also came from Toby Druin: "Joint Committee Funds Slashed; Will Go to CLC," Baptist Standard, February 28, 1990, pp. 4., 5. Druin wrote an excellent review of this part of the February EC meeting.

16 I talked with Vines and the others in his group a few hours after the conversation took place. The dialogue is as they gave it to me.

17 Quotes are from my notes taken at the Atlanta meeting. I was quoted indirectly by Baptist Press as saying that conservatives intended to "monitor the WMU to make sure it is not used for political purposes." I did not use the word "monitor." I meant to say and perhaps I was misunderstood, that conservatives intended to watch the WMU to see that it was not used by Mrs. Crumpler for political purposes." At any rate, the statement as printed by BP stirred up a mild furor of which much good will come if more pastors pay more attention to the WMU

and its mission effort. I laud the WMU women for their unselfish commitment to missions.

18 Joel C. Gregory: "The Word for Travis Today," <u>Travis Avenue Baptist Church Newsletter</u>, March 1, 1990, p. 1.

19 Statement by Kenneth S. Hemphill, March 1, 1990.

20 Jim Henry: "With All My Heart: A Time to Be Silent and a Time to Speak," <u>The Beacon</u>, First Baptist Church, Orlando, Florida, March 8, 1990, p. 1.

21 "Fuller, Others Affirm Inerrancy 'Coalition,' " <u>Word & Way</u>, March 22, 1990, p. 6.

22 Telephone Interview with Martin, April 6, 1990.

23 Pp. 1, 10.

24 The editorial appears on page 6 of the March 21 issue of the <u>Standard</u>.

25 Telephone Interview with Toby Druin, April 5, 1990.

Chapter 9

"Compromises and Confrontations in Seminaries"

The six seminaries had been a major concern of conservatives from the beginning. Only Golden Gate and New Orleans had been spared the protests. Conservatives saw Bill Crews at Golden Gate as one of their own. They respected Landrum Leavell at New Orleans — who said he "was preaching the Bible was inerrant before these boys [conservative pastors] ever got ordained," although Leavell had said "neither group [in the controversy] fully represents me."[1]

The Sparkman "Hearing"

Midwestern had also managed to keep a low profile in the controversy. A flare up had occurred in 1986 when trustees held a hearing on Professor Temp Sparkman's theology. Seminary students were kept away from the day-long meeting, although 77 requested "an open dialogue" before "our entire student body." After extensive questioning of Sparkman, trustees voted 21-11 to affirm his writings as being "within the context of the seminary articles of faith."[2]

The Sparkman hearing sent tremors through other seminaries. A week later the six presidents met at the Glorieta Conference Center and affirmed the Bible to be "fully inspired . . . 'God-breathed,' utterly unique. . . . . not errant in any area of reality."[3]

Conservative Takes Board Chairmanship

Conservatives did not move as fast at Midwestern because of President Milton Ferguson's successful diplomacy in shielding his faculty and because a number of trustees did not see any theological problems at the seminary. Finally, on April 10-12, 1990, conservative Richard Adams, a confessed inerrantist, was elected by a two-vote majority to succeed Truett Gannon, a Georgia moderate, as trustee chairman.

The greatest attention continued to be centered on Southeastern, Southern and Southwestern. The continuing Convention-wide struggle was evident in the spring, 1990 trustee meetings at all three schools.

Hanging Tough at Southeastern

At Southeastern, President Lewis Drummond (who was recovering from cancer surgery) and others kept trying to find common ground between faculty and trustees. A compromise was reached on procedures for hiring new faculty by trustee acceptance of a plan that called for a committee of three faculty along with President Drummond, Vice President of Academic Affairs Russ Bush and one trustee to make up a list of qualified candidates for vacant positions. From this list, the President would decide whom to invite to the campus for interviews with professors, students, administrators and trustees. A candidate from this pool could then be recommended for trustee approval by a two-thirds vote of the committee. In case of a tie, the president would make the decision of whom to recommend. Faculty leader Michael Hawn called the new policy "a step in the right direction. . . . We hope to come to a point of collegiality."[4]

Another troublesome matter at Southeastern was a referred Convention motion calling on Southern and Southeastern seminaries to replace their Abstract of Principles articles of faith with the Baptist Faith and Message. Faculties at both schools were unwilling to accept this switch. At their spring, 1990 meeting, Southeastern trustees voted to affirm the 1963 BFM statement and authorize its continued publication in the seminary catalog, as it had been since 1978. Faculty would be guided by the Abstract of Principles which would "not be supplemented, amended or replaced. . . ." However, the Abstract would be "interpreted" by Abstract author Basily Manly's book <u>The Bible Doctrine of Inspiration Explained and Interpreted.</u>

The trustees also approved a statement, offered by attorney member William Delahoyde, that said the "Seminary will endeavor to attract faculty candidates who reflect the viewpoint that where the Bible speaks, the Bible speaks truth in all realms of reality and to all fields of knowledge and that the Bible, when properly interpreted is authoritative to all of life."[5]

A Challenge from President Drummond

The new president was the brightest light on campus. Exuberant and upbeat, he avoided inflammatory remarks and painted a bright future for the seminary. In the spring of 1990 he noted that five new professors had recently been appointed, the enrollment slump looked to be ending, fund-raising was up dramatically and a ten-year self-study on institutional effectiveness had begun. He expected that the study would give Southeastern a clean bill of health with its two accrediting agencies, the Association of Theological Schools and the Southern Association of Colleges and Schools, which had placed the seminary on "warning" status.[6]

Drummond, in a special address to the faculty, enumerated 10 steps "that we can take together to give us a basic direction":

1. "We [will] establish ourselves as a thoroughly evangelical seminary in theology . . . We are people of the Book, God's Holy and truthful Word. That will never change!"

2. "We are determined to become . . . a world missionary-minded evangelistic institution [in which] there is no place for an . . . incipient universalism or syncretism concerning the lostness of humanity. . . "

3. "Academic excellence shall be maintained and even enhanced."

4. "The spiritual life and discipline of the entire seminary family shall be a major and constant concern."

5. "We shall see the church as central to the life of Southeastern."

6. "We will have peace and harmony on this campus. The days of conflict will come to an end."

7. "We will respect our relationship with and dependence upon Southern Baptists [who] created this institution, . . . who own us and fund us . . . "

8. "New innovative ways of delivering seminary training will be undertaken."

9. "In a spirit of mutual respect and Christian love we shall implement these principles. . . "

10. "Jesus Christ will become the center of everything. . . He will be Lord of Southeastern Baptist Theological Seminary."[7]

Dr. Dilday on the "Carpet"

Southwestern trustees met the same week as the Southeastern board and elected Jimmy Draper as chairman. The trustees had no theological concerns about the Southwestern faculty or the programs. During the preceding year, Southwestern had enrolled its 50,000th student since the seminary's founding in 1908.

President Russell Dilday, now recuperating from open heart surgery, was serving as president of the accrediting Association of Theological Schools. Dilday continued to be in trouble with some of his trustees — not for his theology, but for his upsetting remarks.

Prior to the meeting, Steve Brumbelow, a member of the SBC Executive Committee, sent a letter to all trustees about statements of Dilday to the EC that Evangelist Freddie Gage "was so deeply moved" by the campus revival at Southwestern in which Dan Vestal had preached, "that [Gage] wrote out a generous check to me and said [to Dilday], 'Take this money and have tapes made of these sermons and send them out...'"[8] Brumbelow said in checking with Gage, "It was discovered that such had not happened." Brumbelow said that when he confronted Dilday about "his misrepresentation ... he stood by his story until he found out that I knew otherwise. He then admitted to never receiving a check from Freddie Gage."

Brumbelow also noted that he and three other EC members had been present when "Dr. Dilday approached Dr. Jerry Vines in ... the Baptist Building" on February 20. "He immediately began an all out attack on Dr. Vines and all who are in the conservative movement with the Executive Committee. ... We stood there in disbelief at the caustic remarks made by the president of our largest seminary."

Brumbelow asked in his letter to the Southwestern trustees: "Has Dr. Dilday disregarded the agreement reached with the trustees a few months ago in which he promised to remain politically inactive? Does Dr. Dilday believe that it is all right to be untruthful in order to concoct a good illustration for a speech?"[9]

Dilday responded that he had known Gage "since we both fought in the Golden Gloves days." Dilday said Gage had certainly offered to write the check "that very night," but "[I] indicated he could make that gift anytime he wanted. ... [But] the fact is that gift has not come, yet."

As to his alleged remarks to Vines, Dilday told the trustees he was "a little surprised that a personal, informal conversation" had developed into "this kind of public event and concern." Dilday said Brumbelow "did not listen very carefully to the conversation, because his report is not altogether accurate and does not represent the conversation Dr. Vines and I had."[10]

Dilday said he had indicated to Vines his "great" disappointment that trustees were being nominated "these days more because of loyalty to the [conservative] cause than on the basis of qualifications and ability and expertise that could help that agency fulfill its work." Dilday said he also mentioned to Vines an admission by Adrian Rogers that mistakes had been made in trustee nominations and that people had been elected that "he [Rogers] would not have on his church committees".

Dilday said he told Vines he "would keep" the agreement made with trustees at the last board meeting, "that I would not be involved in any kind of [SBC] political activity..., particularly as we look ahead to New Orleans. I let Dr. Vines know that I did have my personal support of a candidate very enthusiastically and that

I would do everything within my ability and within the limits of [the agreement] to see that happen."[11]

Trustee Max Cadenhead said he could accept Dilday's statement that he was not engaging in outside political activity. Cadenhead said Vines had described Brumbelow's recollection as accurate, but that hearing both Dilday's and Vines' accounts of the conversation might be like hearing two blind men describe an elephant.

Kenneth Faught moved that the board receive Dilday's response as "satisfactory." After an effort to refer the matter to the new trustee officers, Faught's motion passed."[12]

The painful meeting of the trustees of the world's largest seminary closed with hopes that questions about "political" remarks and positions by the president had been put to rest.

Professors in "Hot Water" at Southern Seminary

The annual meeting of Southern Seminary's board was scheduled for April. In recent months several incidents had happened that appeared to cloud prospects for a harmonious meeting.

The Chattanooga Times reported Southern professor Glenn Hinson as telling First Baptist Church, Chattanooga that new Southern trustees were hostile to the seminary, didn't know what a seminary is for and came with their own agenda. Should the trustees cut funds, the faculty was "prepared to take a half salary rather than see" the school "turned into something it has never been." The paper quoted Hinson as saying that the "fundamentalist trustees . . . want indoctrination rather than education. We [at Southern will] go through pain to overcome the problems." Hinson, according to the paper, called Adrian Rogers, Jimmy Draper and Jerry Vines "satellites of [Jerry] Falwell. They are all linked together. That is why Falwell disbanded the Moral Majority. It is no longer needed. He has the SBC. . . "[13]

Asked about the Chattanooga story, President Honeycutt said he would "determine whether or not the reporter quoted [Hinson] correctly. . . . If [so], then there are serious implications concerning the inaccuracy of some statements and the impropriety of others."[14]

Paul Simmons, another Southern professor, stirred up pro-life Southern Baptists in a speech to the annual meeting of Planned Parenthood in Charlotte, NC. Simmons, as quoted by the Charlotte Observer, termed opponents of abortion rights "dogmatic" and "chauvinistic... These are not people who embrace the tenets of religious liberty. They . . . come out of medieval Roman Catholicism, . . . or out of New England Puritanism, as with Jerry Falwell, or others in the Jesse Helms' camp. . . . Each of them [has] a theology that women are simply inferior."

Both of Hinson's and Simmons' reported speeches would gain a place on the board's April agenda.

Darkening Mood on Southern Campus

The upcoming April 23-25 trustee meeting was the talk of the campus. Conservative control of the Southern Board had been slow in coming because trustees could serve at Southern up to ten years instead of a maximum of eight in other agencies. Board moderates had thus far been able to keep conservatives off the executive committee, which involved 21 of the 63-member board, Conservatives now had the numbers for the April, 1990 meeting and a foreboding was in the air.

Bill Leonard, professor of church history, spelled out the issues in the controversy as he saw them during Southern's Denominational Heritage Week. Leonard said SBC confessions of faith "originally used by denominationalists to preserve unity and avoid schism [had] become a source of division as groups debate the definition of specific dogmas." Leonard saw the problem as "representatives of one particular theological viewpoint [seeking] to impose their interpretation on the entire body." [15]

Jerry Johnson's "Cover-Up" Paper

Not since the 1987 demonstrations at Southeastern, had there been such apprehension on an SBC seminary campus. Then a few days before the trustee meeting, the youngest board member mailed to trustees, President Honeycutt and the Southern Baptist Advocate a 16-page paper titled, "The Cover-Up at Southern Seminary." The author was Jerry Johnson, a 25-year-old Colorado pastor who had graduated from Criswell College and Conservative Baptist Theological Seminary. A picture on the front of his paper showed the youthful, dark-haired trustee posing with the silver-haired President Honeycutt as they examined the seminary's Abstract of Principles.

Johnson framed his paper around criticisms of Southern made by Missouri editor Bob Terry in a 1986 editorial. [16] Terry had written his editorial after the Peace Committee completed investigations of the six seminaries. Investigators "cleared" New Orleans, Golden Gate and Southwestern, with "questions" remaining at Midwestern, Southeastern and Southern. Following the committee's report, several Southern faculty came under heavy criticism from Indiana editor David Simpson and many other conservatives. [17]

Terry said, "Those who had complaints about Southern Seminary generally interpreted the public response as a blanket rejection of their concerns. They felt they had not been heard. We believe an opportunity to improve communications between

Southern Seminary and her [Peace Committee] questioners was missed." Johnson said the term "blanket rejection" represented "a coverup" — thus the title of his paper.

Johnson quoted Terry as further noting, "Opportunity to address issues such as sensitivity of professors to different views and articulate teaching about his or her position on doctrinal matters was not available.'"

Terry, Johnson, said had not gone far enough. "One must pull back the blanket and go beyond the cover-up to find the root cause of division concerning the seminary and our Convention." Starting at the top, Johnson turned to some of Honeycutt's writings.

"One Would Have to Be as Blind as a Mole ..."

Honeycutt, Johnson charged, "does not personally believe the account of Moses and the burning bush. . . . Jesus certainly did." Honeycutt also "scoffs at the historical reality" of "the rod in Moses' hand which became a serpent" and several other historical incidents in Exodus and I and II Kings, including Elijah's calling down of fire from heaven and Elisha's restoration of life to the son of the Shunamite woman. "Honeycutt," Johnson said, "displays a. . . bias against the supernatural in the Bible. One would have to be as blind as a mole not to see that Dr. Honeycutt just does not believe the Bible." Honeycutt's signing of the Baptist Faith and Message — which his faculty had not signed — to ward off criticism was "an illusion."

Johnson alleged "more serious doctrinal aberration" among other faculty. Molly Marshall-Green, he said, had asserted that "one can be saved by Christ without knowledge of Christ." Glenn Hinson "recoil[ed] at the idea of a unique and exclusive gospel," found non-historical "embellishments" in the Gospels and "doubt[ed] the historical reality of the resurrection."

Charges of "Insensitivity"

Citing Terry as reporting that some Southern personnel had shown "insensitivity" by "highly emotional and provocative" statements, Johnson cited 20 instances, over a period of four months, in which a professor had used profanity in his class. Johnson noted that the professor and Dr. Honeycutt had apologized to the offended student who took down the remarks. Johnson did not mention that the professor was then going through a dark hour when his wife was critically ill. Johnson noted Paul Simmons' "work . . . for the pro-abortion movement," characterization of pro-lifers as part of the "fanatic fringe" and his support of the Supreme Court's Roe v. Wade decision which made abortion legal.

Another example of insensitivity, Johnson said, was Glenn Hinson's statement in <u>SBC Today</u> [18] where he called "fundamentalism . . . the back side of atheism." Johnson termed this "a slap . . . in the face" to Southern Baptists, "most" of whom "believe in the fundamentals of the faith and biblical inerrancy."

Johnson cited Terry as saying that the "attempt . . . to stop unkind political comments from being batted about in Southern's classrooms has not been altogether successful." Johnson then noted several quotes from President Honeycutt which had appeared in newspapers. In 1984, Honeycutt had declared a "holy war" upon conservatives, Johnson noted. "Honeycutt said he used the term 'holy war' because of 'my conviction that unholy forces are at work in our midst. . . . The inerrantist political party' is seeking to 'hijack the [SBC].' " In 1985 and 1986, Johnson recalled, Honeycutt had referred to conservatives as " 'hostile forces' of harassment."

Terry, Johnson said, had cited "shock confrontation" by seminary personnel on social issues. Terry "fails to reveal the magnitude of the problem," Johnson said. Johnson quoted from Molly Marshall-Green's lecture "on Feminist Theology, . . . in the presence of a trustee and his wife: 'For God so loved the world, that she gave her only begotten daughter, that whosoever believeth in her should not perish, but have everlasting life.' " Johnson called this "divisive" and "deceptive."

Johnson asked, "What are these blankets which have been so effectively used to cover-up the problems at Southern?" One, he said was "neo-gnosticism" or "intellectual elitism . . . . If grassroots Southern Baptists do not call professors into accountability for what they write," Johnson warned, "we will watch every seminary go down the drain."

The second, Johnson said, "is the aberrant view of The Abstract of Principles which Honeycutt and others hold.. It clearly is their chief line of defense. . . . It should be the measure; but they have warped the ruler." They have "read into" the Abstract "the broadest contemporary meaning possible. This is wrong. Southern Baptists should demand and the administration should seek what every court seeks in every legal text: the original meaning of the words."

Johnson called for the Abstract to be interpreted in the light of author Basily Manly's book, <u>The Bible Doctrine of Inspiration</u>, as Southeastern Seminary's trustees had already done. "Manly," Johnson said, "was an inerrantist who said the idea that the Bible is not 'free from error' is a 'fallacy.' " This "is the issue on which ultimately everything will be determined." The problems at Southern, Johnson declared, had resulted from the seminary departing from the doctrine and "designs" of Manly and the school's founder, James Boyce, also an inerrantist.

The 8700-word paper received no detailed rebuttal. Indeed, most of the allegations and quotations had been presented before. Angry reactions came quickly from President Honeycutt, the faculty, the pastor of the adjoining Crescent Hill Baptist Church, denominational editors and other supporters over Johnson's statement, "One would have to be as blind as a mole not to see that Dr. Honeycutt just does not believe the Bible."

The "Heat" is Put on Jerry Johnson

The seminary's Faculty Club expressed "moral outrage" at the paper and termed it a "malicious attack" on President Honeycutt and the professors cited. Hundreds of students repeatedly applauded Faculty Club president Bill Leonard as he read a call from the Faculty Club, approved by 60 of 78 full-time faculty members, for Johnson's resignation. The professors charged that Johnson's article used "innuendo, misstatement of fact, personal attack and distortion of views." Most of the charges, the faculty claimed, had been made years before and resolved.[19]

Johnson's youth, graduation from a non-SBC seminary and less-than-one-year tenure as a trustee did not add to his credibility.

Johnson told reporters that he published his paper only after presenting his concerns to Honeycutt. When Honeycutt failed to "take the lead" in dealing with the professors, "I felt like I needed to take his response back to my constituency, the Southern Baptist Convention." Johnson said he was "not obligated to respond to the faculty request for me to resign. They have no authority. However, if they feel I need to [resign], I invite them to bring it to the Convention."

Honeycutt confirmed that Johnson had talked with him the previous September when Johnson came to the seminary for new trustee orientation. But Honeycutt "had no recollections of his discussing persons. He only discussed problems. We discussed his problem with Article I of the Abstract of Principles on Scripture and specifically his interpretation of 'inspiration' to mean inerrancy. He did discuss the necessity of adding only inerrantists to the faculty.

"I don't think he discussed anything other than his general unhappiness. He may have mentioned a litany of names as a general expression of his unhappiness, but I would not consider those surface discussions adequate to say he discussed the 16-page document with me. . . . . "[20]

Johnson said he had not tried to remove Honeycutt. "While they're calling for my resignation, I'm not calling for anybody's resignation." Asked if he would urge his fellow trustees to oust Honeycutt, Johnson replied, "No comment."[21]

Conservative Majority Takes Charge

The trustee meeting which followed was "very volatile," according to conservative trustee Gary Taylor. The moderate-conservative division was obvious from the first session on. As at Southeastern three years before, students crowded into the meeting room, leaving an overflow milling around outside. Many wore T-shirts proclaiming, "Maintain the Vision" as a symbol of loyalty to the faculty and administration.

The hold-over moderate executive committee presented three persons to fill vacancies on the board with the understanding that the three would serve for only the one trustee meeting. Conservatives countered by nominating three from the slate due to be presented by the SBC Committee on Nominations at the upcoming New Orleans convention. The three conservative choices received a majority of votes at the April meeting, but because a two-thirds majority was necessary for seating, the positions would remain vacant until voted on in New Orleans. Even so, the conservatives felt their majority would hold for the April meeting.

Spotlight on the "Cover-up" Paper

The controversy over the Johnson paper overshadowed the three-day meeting. It had been rushed into publication by the Advocate and copies were available all around the campus. Conservative trustee John Michael said he had heard that the moderate executive committee was going to try to meet with Johnson to discuss his article. Michael moved that the full trustee body become a committee of the whole to discuss the paper. This motion was adopted.

Against protests from moderates, the trustees moved into executive session to debate possible responses to the Johnson document. The session hardly proved to be closed; much of what took place was later leaked by a number of moderate trustees to the media.

Conservative Wayne Allen said he was "concerned" about trustee discipline and needed time to study the Johnson paper. Allen moved that any action on the paper be postponed until the 1991 trustee meeting. Moderate trustee Julian Pentecost, editor of the Virginia denominational paper, objected, calling Johnson's paper vile and vitriolic in places. Pentecost wanted immediate action. In a secret-ballot vote, trustees voted 30-27 to delay action on the paper.

President Honeycutt Speaks

Immediately after this vote, a resolution of appreciation for President Honeycutt was introduced with "our enthusiastic hope that he will continue to serve" as president "for many years to come." An amendment by trustee Jerry Mahan, lauding Honeycutt for his "fidelity to Scripture," was ruled out of order. But an amendment affirming Honeycutt's handling of seminary affairs, was accepted along with the resolution.

Honeycutt then told trustees that he could not live for a year with questions unanswered about his commitment to the Bible. He said he would make a statement the next day in open session rather than in the closed session. Honeycutt later said that by postponing action on the paper for a year, the trustee majority "did exactly what they accuse us of doing — covering up."

The next day, Honeycutt declared that he had spent 44 years in serious study of the Bible and had "never known a time when I did not . . . seek to live out its revelation. . . . It was the Bible which brought me the good news of Jesus in salvation, voiced my call to ministry and still sustains daily through circumstances such as these accusations"

Claiming that one Johnson criticism hung on the interpretation of six Hebrew words, Honeycutt said, "You can tell me you disagree with my interpretation of Scripture, but please don't tell me you disagree with my belief in the Bible."

Students in the room responded with a standing ovation. Trustee Johnson told reporters he was "not satisfied" with Honeycutt's explanation. Johnson said he stood "completely and totally behind" the truthfulness of the charges made in his document. "The future," Johnson predicted, "will vindicate my article."[22]

Simmons and Hinson on the "Griddle"

As expected, the extra-curricular activities of professors Paul Simmons and Glenn Hinson, were brought up in the closed sessions.

Simmons had already written a letter saying he would henceforth refuse interviews with the media on abortion and avoid inflammatory rhetoric in responding to persons who take different positions. Still the academic personnel committee expressed "disappointment, disapproval and deep concern over the harm done this seminary" by Simmons' speech that had lambasted pro-life activists. However the committee found "no grounds for dismissal" from the faculty.

Trustee Ron Herrod introduced a substitute motion calling on Simmons to "repent of his teachings on abortion as being unscriptural," adding that if Simmons did not repent, then the board could "prayerfully ask him to consider resigning. . . " Trustees reportedly rejected the substitute motion by about 10 votes, then amended the original committee report by adding "that his continued activities" in the abortion area "may be considered sufficient grounds for dismissal. . ."

Hinson had also written a letter to Honeycutt saying the Chattanooga Times' article was "a garbled account of what I told" the Chattanooga church. . . . I am deeply embarrassed by it and offer sincere apologies." Trustees, in response, expressed to Hinson their "deep concern" about his "intemperate comments about controversial issues which negatively affect the public perception of Southern Seminary . . ."

Faculty Promotions

Trustees considered a number of personnel recommendations in the executive session. They elected Doris Ann Borchert, an ordained deacon, as an associate professor of Christian education with tenure, after she said the Chicago Statement on Inerrancy accurately described her position of Scripture, although she preferred not to use the term inerrancy. However, some trustees were concerned because Mrs. Borchert reportedly did not answer directly about the historicity of Genesis, while expressing belief "in everything Genesis teaches."

Six of seven faculty were quickly awarded promotions. The seventh, Molly Marshall-Green, had been the target of previous questions relative to statements in her doctoral dissertation. Trustee Michael Harris asked if she believed Jesus was the only way to heaven. Marshall-Green reportedly told him that she had previously stated to trustees her belief that Jesus was the only way of salvation. She was voted the promotion against some opposition.

Abortion and Classroom Taping

The "volatile" meeting was far from over. In open session trustees adopted a strong anti-abortion resolution despite opposition. Two trustees, George Steincross and Jess Moody, questioned the appropriateness of a seminary board making a statement on the issue. Others thought abortion was not the major moral problem of the country. They asked if the resolution was intended to lead to the discipline of faculty or staff who might differ with trustees on abortion. Proponents of the resolution said the resolution expressed only the feelings of the trustees and would not be coercive.

A motion passed allowing student taping of classroom lectures, despite "caution" by Honeycutt about "telling how a professor must conduct a class." Trustee Harry Dent, a former Nixon White House counsel, recalled the Watergate tapes and said recording lectures would help professors "consider what they present in sober judgment and not from the seat of their pants."

Johnson's Motion on the Abstract Postponed

Trustee Johnson moved that the book The Bible Doctrine of Inspiration Explained and Interpreted become the official interpreter of the seminary's Abstract of Principles, since Basil Manly had authored both. Johnson said the statement in the Abstract about inspiration does not mean "what I understand many of our faculty to mean when they talk about inspiration."

President Honeycutt opposed the motion, saying that Baptists had never permitted the writings of one man to interpret a confessional statement. If trustees had questions with individual faculty, Honeycutt said, they should use processes already in place. Trustees debated the motion for more than an hour and adjourned the session without agreement. Johnson later moved that his motion be postponed indefinitely.

Trustee Carroll Karkalits moved that the seminary pay for Jerry Johnson's defense if a lawsuit should be filed. Karkalits said he had heard that Johnson would be sued by Professor Simmons because of charges made against Simmons in Johnson's paper. Chairman Alton Butler ruled that the motion was speculative and thus out of order.

Election of New Officers

Even though conservatives were clearly in a majority, they chose not to challenge the nomination of first vice chairman Sam H. McMahon, Jr. as the new chairman. McMahon was elected. Conservative Wayne Allen was then elected first vice chairman, with Larry L. Adams and John G. Hicks elected second vice chairman and secretary respectively. Conservatives also took control of the executive committee for the first time.[23]

Media Reaction

Headlines in the secular and denominational media indicated the significance of the April board meeting at the SBC's oldest and most prestigious seminary. The liberal Christian Century declared: "Another Seminary Falls to Fundamentalists." The Louisville Courier-Journal declared, "Conservative Trustees Move to Remold Baptist Seminary."

Responses to the shift from moderate to conservative control ran along party lines in the larger SBC conflict. Glenn Hinson called the trustees "an absolutist group" with "a very authoritarian style." The conservatives "have shown their hand that they do not represent the heart and vision of Southern Seminary" declared Stephen Shoemaker, pastor of the church in which many seminary people held membership. Moderate trustee Henry B. Huff "saw" the recent board meeting, as "a right-wing takeover, . . . the beginning of a complete change at Southern — and it will come quicker than many people believe, too." Southeastern Seminary faculty said they were "compelled by conscience to express . . . solidarity with" Southern faculty . . . in response to actions by Southern trustees. Southern alumni officers, headed by president-elect Bob Terry, were "convinced that the hope and heritage embodied in Southern Seminary . . . ultimately will be victorious. . ."[24]

However, conservative trustee John Michael said the votes at the meeting did not constitute a takeover, but showed that "the conservative influence was felt more clearly." Trustee David Miller "was pleased with the meeting from start to finish."[25]

Virginia editor Julian H. Pentecost, himself a trustee, said "aggressive insistence on certain biblical-theological code words" will "greatly complicate the processes which have served Southern well for many years. . . Continuation of the new majority's recent inclinations will doubtless have disturbing consequences for the seminary because accrediting agencies pay particular attention to questionable entanglements of trustees in institutional administration."[26]

President Honeycutt Answers the "Cover-up" Paper

Although the trustees had postponed for a year action on Jerry Johnson's "cover-up" paper, President Honeycutt published his more detailed response in a 28-page booklet titled "Response to 'The Cover-up at Southern Seminary.'" Thousands of copies were mailed free to those requesting the booklet.[27]

Honeycutt said "most of the accusations relate to events which occurred years ago." The trustees in 1986 had "dealt" with the issues. A trustee committee had found "no evidence justifying the dismissal of any professor." The Peace Committee had found "absolutely no evidence to substantiate charges of dismissal." There had been no cover-up.

Honeycutt devoted most of his rebuttal to defending himself against charges that he denied the "historical reality" of certain passages in the Old Testament. "My love and reverence for the Bible," he said, "flow so deeply through my life I am offended by the suggestion I take such an attitude toward the Word of God."

He affirmed the "burning associated with the bush" in the experience of Moses, although "persons may disagree with me about the source of the flame."

He noted "significant similarities" in his writing on Exodus in The Broadman Commentary with notes in The [W.A.] Criswell Study Bible, which was edited by Paige Patterson. Example:

Criswell Study Bible: "Egyptian magicians had long ago mastered the art of inflicting a temporary paralysis on a cobra, making him appear stiff and rod like. However, their 'rods' were swallowed by the 'rod' of Aaron, which should have been a message to Pharaoh of the direction of events for the coming days"[28]

Honeycutt Commentary: "... It is important to note that [the rod turning into a serpent] could be duplicated by the Egyptian magicians. Driver suggests that modern Egyptian serpent charmers possess unusual power over serpents and that the practice is alluded to in Psalm 58:5; Jeremiah 8:17; Ecclesiastes 10:11[29] Probably some such practice constituted the nucleus of the sign described in Exodus 4:2 ff. However, there are elements of the present narrative which go beyond such explanation. For example, Moses assumedly began with the rod in his hand, probably the shepherd's staff which became the symbol of his authority[30]; then the rod became a serpent"[31]

After comparing other comments on Exodus events from the Criswell Study Bible with views in his commentary, Honeycutt asserted, "I reject categorically trustee Johnson's statement that 'Honeycutt also scoffs at the historical reality of the plagues.' " Honeycutt said the writer of Exodus held a "view of nature miracles" that saw "the whole of the created order, man and nature ... subject to the providence of God."

Honeycutt denied "express[ing] disbelief in the account of Elijah calling down fire," as Johnson had charged. Honeycutt quoted himself: " 'Few persons would defend the morality of calling down fire from heaven upon a group of fifty as in the [Elijah] narrative.' "

As to Johnson's allegation that he did "not believe the miracle of the restoration to life of the son of the Shunamite woman," Honeycutt noted that he had written: " 'Through the personal ministration of Elisha the life of the child is restored' . . . The narrative suggests that Elisha did in fact restore the life of the child." But Honeycutt conceded that he had written: "That this is most likely a wonder story in the category of saga and legend is most probable. The use of technical language such as saga and legend may be misleading. Yet, it is common in literary studies, including the Bible, to classify literature by different types or forms. . . . Contrary to popular current attitudes, they transmit the record of historic events which stand at their core."

Honeycutt did not attempt to answer Johnson's statements about members of the faculty cited in the paper. He used only three pages in disputing other charges about himself. He did take seriously his signing of the Baptist Faith and Message and the Southern Seminary Abstract. And he had not rejected the Glorieta Statement in which he and five other seminary presidents had affirmed that the Bible is "not errant in any area of reality."

He thought it did little good in the 1990's to "recall the extreme rhetoric from both sides of the controversy in the early eighties." He "never declared a 'holy war,' but rather said we had been involved in that conflict since its inception by Mr. Pressler. . . ." The Seminary had adopted the "recommendations submitted by the Peace Committee" in its report in St. Louis.

In summation he noted that (1) Johnson had written the article without talking to seminary leadership about "how the seminary dealt with concerns raised by the Peace Committee," and (2) "had not talked to any of the principals to discuss specific charges" before noting them in his paper.

Honeycutt feared that the "cover-up" paper would "extensively sabotage the seminary for this century" and "cause enduring personal damage to members of the faculty. . . . Most of all I grieve for the crucifixion of the truth, the abdication of trusteeship and the abuse of free speech which characterize trustee Johnson's attack on the President, the Board of Trustees and the Faculty" of the seminary.

Honeycutt was bombarded by invitations to speak from Southern alumni. One meeting, publicized by word of mouth, drew over 500 in Decatur, Georgia. Honeycutt defended himself against Johnson's charges, calling the take-over paper a "document of misstatement of fact, innuendo and distorted view" that shows what years of controversy can do." David Sapp, a moderate leader in Georgia, called the paper "the reincarnation of the spirit of the Spanish Inquisition and the Salem witch trials. It must be stopped."[32]

Conservatives were not silent. Eldridge Miller, an Southern alumnus and member of the SBC Executive Committee, circulated a paper that recalled a story from an Old Testament class. "The professor — one of the most conservative I had — was explaining that Jonah was probably was not a real historical person. . . . He referred to the book of Jonah as 'an anti-separatist tract' written by some unknown scribe to discourage Israel's exclusivism. At this point I heard the sound of pages being torn and the exclamation, 'There goes another one!' The professor stopped his lecture and asked an explanation from the student. 'There goes another book out of my Bible,' the student said in defense of his action." Miller recalled another student friend who "came into my dormitory room and plopped down on my bed. 'I'm going home,' he said dejectedly. . . . 'After this semester I don't have anything left to believe or preach,' were his last words as he left my room."[33]

Shortly after the board session, off-campus directors of Southern's Boyce Bible School came to Louisville for a meeting. Boyce provided ministerial training for persons without college degrees.

Mark Coppenger, executive director of the State Baptist Convention of Baptists in Indiana and director of the Boyce extension centers in his state, had previously been critical of Southern. Coppenger heard Seminary Provost Willis Bennett say that he expected each Boyce director and teacher not to make any public statements, inside or outside the classroom, which would diminish trust in Southern.

Coppenger, in a lengthy column in the Indiana Baptist, said he "observed" to Bennett that Boyce teachers were short-term contract workers and didn't "belong to the seminary as full time professors did. One could be loyal to the seminary itself without supporting its current direction."

Coppenger cited Southern alumnus W.A. Criswell as an example of one who was "less than enthusiastic over Southern's look in recent decades," yet "nonetheless loyal to the seminary itself. He simply had a different notion of what was best for the seminary." Bennett, according to Coppenger "didn't blink in ruling Dr. Criswell out of bounds."

The Indiana denominational executive, who had previously been a trustee at Southern before moving to Indiana, cited numerous examples from faculty writings which he said were doctrinal aberrations, including Glenn Hinson's assertion that "some embellishment undoubtedly occurred" in the Gospels. "There are dozens and dozens of such [faculty quotations]," Coppenger said, "which could set typical Southern Baptists' teeth on edge.... And that is why the struggle properly continues though we are all weary. Woe to us if we ever reach the day when we are too 'sick and tired' to attend to these matters.' . . . . The cause of biblical inerrancy is worth it."

Coppenger recalled the Peace Committee's findings of "significant diversity" in SBC seminaries. Coppenger noted President Honeycutt's remark that Southern trustees had, in 1986, interviewed 14 Southern professors "whose work was questioned by the Peace Committee" and in Honeycutt's words given the seminary 'a clean bill of health.' But, how then did the report pass muster?" Coppenger asked. "Easy. 'Loyalists' controlled the Board. ... In fact, they filled the [Board's] executive committee completely. When I went to my first Board meeting . . . in 1988, there were no 'disloyal' people on the Executive Committee," even though "there had been, by this time, nine straight SBC [conservative] presidential victories."

President Honeycutt had also addressed the Boyce directors and, according to Coppenger, "made some comment about newer Board members who were ignorant of the Seminary's heritage. Let me suggest," said Coppenger, "that anyone who understands the value of commitment to an inerrant Bible has an admirable and sufficient notion of the Seminary's heritage. There is more to learn, indeed, but all right thinking about Southern must begin there. And only on those terms is there true ground for royalty."[34]

Provost Bennett did not take kindly to Coppenger's remarks. Declared Bennett: "Dr. Coppenger will never be satisfied with Southern Seminary until decisions are made his way and interpretations of Scripture are in agreement with his own views .... Loyalty does not rule out criticism, but it does not sow distrust," he said in a response to Coppenger. "It is apparent that we shall not be able to operate an effective Boyce Bible School Center [in Indiana] with Dr. Coppenger as director."[35]

Calling the break "painful," Coppenger accepted Bennett's decision. "But I do believe that it will prove to be providential in that it frees us to establish a school of our own, one designed to meet the particular needs of Indiana Baptists." [36] The school Coppenger had in mind, was subsequently opened as an extension center of Oklahoma Baptist University.

The seminary extension center in Indiana closed May 31, barely two weeks before the meeting of the national convention in New Orleans. The Boyce incident marked another chapter in the convention-wide controversy and the growing differences between Southern Seminary and its conservative trustee majority.

More struggles between seminary personnel and trustees lay ahead.

References

1 Interview, Southern Baptist Convention, Dallas, June, 1985. Landrum Leavell: Column, The Vision, Spring, 1985, p. 9.

2 I was at the hearing. My detailed report appears in Volume 2 of this series, pp. 113-118.

3 Dan Martin: "Six Seminary Presidents Make Reconciliation Try," Baptist Press, October 24, 1986.

4 R.G. Puckett: "Southeastern Seminary Faculty,Trustees Reach Compromise," Biblical Recorder, March 24, 1990, pp. 1, 5.

5 Marv Knox: "Seminary Trustees Focus on Doctrinal Statements," Biblical Recorder, March 31, 1990,pp. 1, 4.

6 "Southeastern Has Second Milestone, Advance Background Story," Southern Baptist Convention Newsroom, June, 1990.

7 "Dr. Lewis A. Drummond Speaks Candidly to the Southeastern Faculty," Southern Baptist Advocate, April, 1990, p. 9.

8 A tape of the September EC meeting confirms that Dilday made this exact statement.

9 From a copy of Brumbelow's letter sent to Southwestern trustees.

10 Vines and others in the group told me in interviews that Brumbelow's allegation was accurate.

11 Quoted from a transcription of a tape by Norman Miller of Dilday's remarks to the trustees, March 12. 1990.

12 Toby Druin: "Southwestern Trustees OK Pro-Life Statement," Biblical Recorder, March 31, 1990, pp. 1, 4.

13 Ruth Robinson: "Professors Brace Themselves for Hardships," November 25, 1989.

14 Honeycutt to Floyd L. Battles, Sr., December 22, 1989.

15 Church History Professor Notes Loss of Tolerance Within Denomination, Religious Herald, April 26, 1990, p. 16.

16 "A Word About Southern Seminary, Word & Way, July 17, 1986, p. 2.

17 See Vol. 2, The Truth in Crisis, pp. 108-111.

18 SBC Today, July, 1986.

19 Statement by Faculty Club. Also Bill Wolfe: "Irate Professors Want Seminary Trustee to Resign," Louisville Courier-Journal, April, 1991.

20 Marv Knox: "Seminary Faculty Responds to Attacks," The Christian Index, May 17, 1990, pp. 1, 3.

21 Bill Wolfe, op. cit.

22 Baptist Press, April 26, 1990.

23 The April, 1990 Southern Seminary trustee meeting was well-covered by media. Besides the Baptist Press report, I found articles by Bill Wolfe in the Louisville Courier-Journal and Bob Terry in the Word & Way to be helpful. The Louisville paper published a number of articles by Wolfe during the week of the trustee meeting. Editor Terry's report in the May 3 issue of the Word & Way is the most comprehensive.

24 Quoted from Julian Pentecost: "From a 'Correction of the Convention' to a Denial of Historic Baptist Belief and Practice," Religious Herald, May 10, 1990, pp. 4, 5.

25 Bill Wolfe: "Two Professors Denounced at Baptist Seminary," The Courier-Journal, April 26, 1990, pp. 1, 7.

26 "Editorial: A Critical Time at Southern Seminary," Religious Herald, May 3, 1990, p. 4.

27 It is still available by writing to the seminary, 2825 Lexington Road, Louisville, KY 40280.

28 p. 81

29 cf. Mark 16:18.

30 4:17; 7:20

31 p. 333.

32 Ruth Robinson: "Honeycutt of the Baptist Seminary Refuses to Yield," Chattanooga Times, pp. F-1, 3.

33 Quoted from Miller's paper issued after the 1990 trustee meeting.

34 Indiana Baptist, May 8, 1990, pp. 3, 12, 13.

35 G. Willis Bennett: Letters to the Editor, Indiana Baptist, May 22, 1990, p.2.

36 Mark Coppenger: "A Timothy School?" <u>Indiana Baptist</u>, May 22, 1990, p. 3.

Chapter 10

"Countdown to New Orleans"

Nineteen ninety was the 12th year since Adrian Rogers' fateful win in Houston. Moderates were running Dan Vestal again. Conservatives rallied behind Morris Chapman, pastor of FBC, Wichita Falls, TX. Most moderates considered New Orleans their last chance, for at least a generation to come, to turn the convention back. Not since Dallas in 1985 was there such intense pre-convention political activity for the presidential vote.

A Look at the Candidates

John Bisagno, who planned to nominate the conservative candidate, Morris Chapman, said in April, ". . . We are looking at a splinter or a split. . . If Dan Vestal wins, I think that the conservatives will become even more vocal and the struggle will continue endlessly. But, if the true conservatives that have been standing in . . . the middle ground where I've stood and the true conservatives on the right get together in a shared leadership committed to the same common goal without flinching, then you have a coalition that forms what is a true picture of this convention theologically and that is more like a 90/10 instead of a 50/50. If that happens, then those that are on the far left tip may choose to splinter off."[1]

Paige Patterson looked further ahead. "When you change trustees, you change the potential to change. When you change agency heads, you change the agency. During the next five years five more aging presidents will retire. That will bring 10 conservative agency heads." The big difference in New Orleans, Patterson said, would be the "new day" inaugurated by Joel Gregory and other "centrist" pastors who had pledged to support Chapman. Gregory, Patterson said, "had walked into a telephone booth and come out with an S on his chest."[2]

Chapman, a former president of the SBC Pastors Conference, had been a conservative stalwart from the beginning of the resurgence. He had nominated two previous convention presidents, Jimmy Draper and Charles Stanley; his wife, Jodi, had served on the Peace Committee and as a trustee of the Sunday School Board.

The year before, in Las Vegas, Chapman had probably nailed down the 1990 nomination with his convention sermon on the Bible. Noting the [moderate] cry "for us to return to our Southern Baptist heritage," he cited educational reports to the 1913, 1922 and 1925 conventions that acknowledged the Bible as inerrant. Thunderous applause resounded when he shouted, "We are people of the faith who believe in the inspired, infallible, inerrant Word of God and we need professors in our Baptist schools, seminaries and colleges who believe in the inspired, infallible, inerrant Word of God."[3]

Dan Vestal had been in the media limelight for over a year, since he was running for the second time. Having called "denominational politics" immoral when serving on the Peace Committee, Vestal was clearly the more politically active before the New Orleans Convention.

Both Chapman and Vestal were inerrantists. The churches pastored by both men gave liberally to the Cooperative Program, although Vestal's previous congregation in Texas gave more. Vestal had been identified with conservatives during the early years of the resurgency movement. In 1982 he served as Chairman of the SBC Committee on Boards; in 1985 he was elected to the Peace Committee. Yet, oddly, he told a moderate rally, " . . . Deliberately, intentionally, for eleven years they've excluded me."[4]

Vestal called the endorsements of Chapman by Bisagno, Gregory and other "centrist" pastors a "very clear political strategy. . . . The college of cardinals is reaching out to a select group of influential pastors in order to perpetuate control of the past eleven years by enlisting fresh leadership into it."[5]

Vestal declined to say if he would appoint persons who believed the Bible had errors. Time and again, Chapman said he would not. Said conservative editor Gary Ledbetter: "Morris Chapman . . . has clearly stated the point at which he will stand firm. Dan Vestal has been more evasive on the matter. Clearly, as a man of conviction, there must be a point at which his toleration ends. However, with a coalition that runs the gamut from the extreme elements in the Southern Baptist Alliance and Women in Ministry to the more mainstream, [to the] flawed vision of Southern Baptists Committed, we must wonder where Vestal draws his line."[6]

Conservative patriarch Criswell was more blunt: "These liberals — alias moderates — have chosen a pawn — a man they can handle or control — [whom] they will support for the presidency."

Vestal's running mates for first and second vice president respectively were Carolyn Weatherford Crumpler, the retired executive director of the WMU and Steve Tondera, a former lay president of the Alabama Baptist Convention. Raymond Boswell of Louisiana, an announced candidate for second vice president, was also acceptable to moderates.

Among a field of four first vice presidential candidates at Las Vegas, Crumpler came in second to the conservative choice, Junior Hill, receiving 32.62 percent of the vote. After her linkage with Vestal for New Orleans, some conservatives expressed fears that the WMU might become involved. One isolated instance was reported in Georgia by Thomas M. Atwood, a pastor, stating that his church's WMU Director had received a political mailing puffing Crumpler from the WMU Director in Vestal's church.[7]

Crumpler's stature increased when a month before the convention she was elected general secretary of the North American Baptist Fellowship. She was also active on the speaking circuit, claiming that the future of missions was at stake if conservatives won again.

Crumpler was "not moderate about anything. . . . If you're going to label me, label me a missions-concerned member of a local Southern Baptist Church." She used an illustration from putting clothes in a dryer to illustrate why she was running. "If you know where a problem is, you ought to do something about it. I think the Convention's lint trap needs to be emptied."[8]

The conservative choices for first and second vice president respectively were Douglas Knapp, a retired career missionary and Fred Lowery, pastor of fast-growing FBC, Bossier City, LA. Lowery had been elected president of the Louisiana Baptist Convention in 1989 by a close vote. Knapp had witnessed the founding of 403 churches and 58,000 professions of faith in Kenya. Knapp had declined nomination in Las Vegas — in deference, he said to Carolyn Weatherford. Knapp believed "the drift to liberalism [has] to be corrected. . . . If everyone had experienced what I did, they would rise up and demand change." Knapp said he had been "stunned by what I was being taught" at Midwestern Seminary in 1963. "It took me years to get over this. I was taught to doubt the validity of the Scriptures."[9]

An endorsement of Vestal by 304 retired Southern Baptist missionaries hit the headlines in state papers. Finlay M. Graham, retired from service in the Middle East and North Africa, personally telephoned missionaries over a ten-day period and said "98 percent of those I called were enthusiastic in their support of Vestal."[10]

Knapp didn't "believe" the retired missionaries had "heard both sides of the issue, but a number apparently allowed themselves to be included in a poll of support for Vestal. I wonder who paid for all those phone calls . . . "[11]

Baptists Committed's newsletter also printed a statement by 18 former state presidents, saying they were opposed to "the . . . takeover movement" of which "Morris Chapman has been a vital part . . . since its inception in 1979." The 18 "saw no evidence" that the endorsement by Gregory, Bisagno and the other "centrist" pastors for Chapman marked "a historic new day."

"Sons and Daughters"

Meanwhile, another special interest group was rounding up Baptist college students. Organizer David Burroughs, a student at Southern Seminary, said he was motivated to form the Sons and Daughters of the Southern Baptist Convention by a speech given by Home Mission Board staffer Nathan Porter, calling for Baptist students to "wake up . . . Our denomination is stagnated with Bibliolatry . . . Legalism, power and control are the current reality." [12] Burroughs and fellow students chose six regional directors, one from each SBC seminary, including the daughter of the new WMU executive director, Dellanna O'Brien and FMB staff member Bill O'Brien.

A mailout to 1100 Baptist Student Union directors identified the group as Baptist students "concerned about the future of our [SBC] home. Both of our mission boards have experienced major budget cuts this past year. Our seminaries are experiencing unnecessary scrutinization and mistrust has replaced cooperation as a Southern Baptist byword. Our controversy has caused a polarization leading to the illusion of vast theological differences. Students must begin leading our denomination away from the struggle of the past eleven years and toward a refocusing of purpose for Southern Baptists." The mailout included a petition for student signatures, instructions for organizing prayer partners and a covenant card for students to fill out

Daniel Vestal could not have written a better statement for moderate campaign literature. Conservatives, while not doubting the sincerity of the students, were further upset by a March 31 speech by Burroughs at the Louisiana BSU Spring Assembly. Louisiana editor Lynn Clayton reported. that Burroughs had cited "several examples of how he believes freedom has been restricted within the SBC during the past eleven years. Included were restrictions against appointing divorced people as missionaries, a proposal to cut most of the SBC's funding of the Baptist Joint Committee on Public Affairs, biblical inspiration and women in ministry."

According to Clayton, several students asked Burroughs if his views did not favor SBC moderates. Burroughs said they represented the Sons and Daughters group.

After the meeting, Louisiana BSU Director Gene Hendrix said he regretted that Burroughs' presentation involved partisan statements." Contacted later by Baptist Press, Burroughs "apologize[d] for causing trouble. . . . The objectives of our organization . . . . are not incredibly political. I overstepped my boundaries. . . ."[13]Advocate writer Dr. Larry Holly called Burroughs "a fine young man who holds personal convictions different from this writer." Holly said Burroughs had expressed regret for taking advantage of the Louisiana BSU meeting to present his personal political agenda. Holly called for the organizers of the Sons and Daughters to "be very candid with the SBC about their true motives." They have the right to "oppose the conservative consensus," Holly said, "but they must not couch this desire in a call to prayer," and "they must understand that they WILL NOT be allowed to use the BSU as a forum to advance their political motivations, if any exist." Holly further warned that the Sunday School Board's "National Student Ministry Department and BSSB employees must hear loudly and clearly that [using national student meetings to advance the moderate agency] must be stopped."[14]

The moderate's SBC Today called the Advocate's "latest blast . . . another example of intimidation being placed on the BSSB's Department of Student Ministries. . . ."[15]

The Wall Street Journal Article

Press coverage of controversy-related events before New Orleans was extensive. Most of the articles in the metro papers were well balanced. However, a gloomy front-page story on SBC troubles in the Wall Street Journal, titled "House Divided," became a major point of contention among conservatives. Author R. Gustav Niebuhr had recently come to the Journal from Atlanta where he had close contacts with SBC moderates. The sub-head for his story declared, "Southern Baptists Lose Members and Impetus in an Internal Struggle." Niebuhr quoted only two conservatives, Pressler and Patterson, against nine moderates who gave the standard gloom-and-doom shibboleths on the effects of conservative dominance. Moderates mailed out thousands of copies of Neibuhr's piece in an attempt to show that the conservative "resurgence" was leading the SBC to ruin. SBC Today called Neibuhr "a scintillating writer" and an "outstanding Christian reporter and religion analyst" who has given "an accurate but depressing portrayal of how the rest of the world views Southern Baptists. . . ."[16]Advocate editor Bob Tenery called the Journal piece "a study in bias, prejudice and distortion from the headline to the last paragraph." Tenery said Niebuhr was short on facts: "nine out of ten areas in Southern Baptist life reported gains in 1989. That doesn't sound like 'impetus' is lost."

Neibuhr said the controversy was forcing SBC agencies to cut their staffs and postpone salary increases. Tenery cited annual salaries and fringes for the top executives of three boards and seven agencies. Five earned well over $100,000. The five, according to Tenery, were Lloyd Elder, President, Sunday School Board, $157,086; Harold Bennett, President-Treasurer, Executive Committee, $151,079; Larry Lewis, President, Home Mission Board, $113, 582; Keith Parks, President, Foreign Mission Board, $113,000. The Annuity Board declined to report renumeration for its newly-elected president, Paul W. Powell. Tenery further noted that the top six men at the Sunday School Board, where Tenery is a trustee, were paid $715,475 in salary and benefits. "Does this appear as if Southern Baptist employees have been denied a raise?" Tenery asked. "It is apparent that we take care of our workers quite well."[17]

"Independent" Papers on Review

A number of small independent publications circulated in state conventions. The small papers, with the exception of the Carolina Conservative Baptist, came out infrequently. The problem was money. In funding they could not compete with denominational papers which received a state convention subsidy.

SBC Today, the Southern Baptist Advocate and the new Southern Baptist Communicator published monthly on a national level. All three were distinctly partisan in editorials, but there was a distinct difference in tone, style and length of articles. Southern Baptists Committed made occasional — and expensive — slick, multi-colored campaign-type mailings.

The Advocate, which had the largest readership, was supported by gifts and mailed free to every Southern Baptist church, plus several thousand other persons. Sixty-nine percent of researcher Nancy Ammerman's clergy respondents said they got news about the Convention from the Advocate. A businessman paid for sending the first issues of the Communicator to the church list. Fred Powell then began moving the paper toward a subscription basis. SBC Today operated on both subscriptions and gifts. The Communicator and SBC Today printed the names of board members; the Advocate did not.

The Communicator was the mildest of the three in tone and featured statements from leading conservative figures. The Advocate — particularly Bob Tenery's editorials — did not mince words. Examples:

Russell Dilday's "false charges about trustees and his calling of five honorable men 'liars' is reprehensible."[18]

"Many Southern Baptists are still reeling under the shock they experienced when they learned that Dr. Vestal, who had described politics as immoral, actually purchased time on a Las Vegas television station and carried his political campaign into the convention city itself. There he was, for the whole world to see, participating in the 'immorality' that he condemned. . . . Maybe it is time for Southern Baptists to ask the question of Gary Moore from past decades: 'Will the real Dan Vestal please stand up?' "[19]

SBC Today, as well as the Advocate and the Communicator, picked up some stories from Baptist Press. Editor Jack Harwell and Walker Knight, the founder of SBC Today, shared the editorials which could be as partisan as Tenery's.

SBC Today featured some political cartoons as vitriolic as some appearing in secular newspapers. One showed three witches stirring a brew in a black kettle labeled "SBC." The caption read: "A good dose of right-wing politics, a peck of distrust, a heap of destruction, a pinch of lust-for-power, a sizable portion of secrecy: a handful of deception. . . "[20] SBC Today printed excerpts from an advance copy of Nancy Ammerman's Baptist Battles which indicated the "liberal" lifestyle of some moderates.

"The use of an occasional four-letter word seemed a kind of defiant badge of liberation. I have never heard a moderate use God's name in a profane way, nor have I heard any sexually explicit language, but other 'four-letter' words can be heard on occasion. . . . Likewise, a glass of wine with dinner was not uncommon . . . But they would surely take care that they were unnoticed. Room service was heavily used in Southern Baptist Convention hotels. While moderates wanted to proclaim their liberation from puritanical standards, their freedom to express themselves fully or to drink in moderation was hampered by their knowledge that most of their Southern Baptist brothers and sisters did not approve."[21]

The difference in the papers was never more obvious than when they were reporting the same event. Take the March 14th National Affairs Briefing by President George Bush. SBC Today said the briefing was supposed to be hosted by the Baptist Joint Committee on Public Affairs as a "regular service" for Baptist editors. The denominational editors were "angered" that Bush sat between Paul Pressler and Albert Lee Smith, chairman of the SBC Public Affairs Committee. "One editor said to SBC Today, 'Neither Pressler nor Smith is an editor. What were they doing there?" SBC Today quoted "one SBC analyst" as calling this "one of many recent episodes which document the frightening influence of Christian Reconstructionism on Presidential politics."[22]

The Advocate showed the seating arrangement and reported the story as if no controversy was involved in setting up the briefing. Editor Tenery, who was also at the briefing and sat next to Smith, wrote, "When the President first entered the room he thanked Judge Paul Pressler, Vice-chairman of the Southern Baptist Executive Committee, for arranging the meeting." Tenery also said, "It is refreshing to note that the Public Affairs Committee has such access to the White House in light of the fact that the

Baptist Joint Committee on Public Affairs has been so hostile to the White House in recent years."[23]

The independent papers existed for partisan purposes. The state convention papers were supposed to be fair, yet the Peace Committee found "some" had shown "prejudice against the conservative political activists." The PC cited no instance of unfairness to moderates in the denominational papers.

Gregory, Montoya and Baptist Press

In Chapter 9 of Volume One and Chapter 11 of Volume Two in this series I examined the editorial and news handling practices of state papers in detail. Those chapters also explained how the Baptist Press system networks with agency public relations persons and state editors. Baptist Press and several state papers came under heavy conservative fire in the spring before New Orleans for news handling of two stories. The critics charged that BP and some of the papers had dragged their feet on getting out a story on the announcement by Joel Gregory and other "centrist" pastors that they would support Morris Chapman, while moving with great haste to spotlight conservative "defector" David Montoya's proclaimed intent, as a member of the Committee on Nominations, to present in New Orleans alternate nominees for some on the Committee's list. Conservative Mark Coppenger called Montoya Baptist Press' "latest darling."[24]

Joel Gregory said that on March 5 he faxed a copy of his announcement from his church paper to BP offices in Nashville. BP did not acknowledge receiving the document. On March 9, "I finally called to ask if they had received the statement. . . . They said they did not know where it was." Gregory faxed another copy which was "acknowledged, with no promise of carrying the story. . . . After an incredible number of inquiries," BP "finally relented," Gregory said and carried a brief story about two weeks later on the announcements made by Gregory, Ken Hemphill, Charles Fuller and Jim Henry.

BP, however, quickly released a long story about Montoya's protest of the Committee on Nominations report. Baptist Press, Gregory charged, "would not carry a single word of my individual statement but has given extensive coverage to everything Mr. Montoya has said."[25]

The Committee on Nominations met March 22-23 in the SBC Building in Nashville. After the meeting, Montoya told reporters that he had "asked . . . to present a minority report. They voted that down. I was the only person in the room that asked for a minority report." Montoya said he would present alternates to about half of the nominees in New Orleans. Complaining of "hardliners" in the report, Montoya said conservative leaders "are using the issue of inerrancy as an opportunistic base . . . to gain political power." Montoya said he would start contacting state executives, denominational leaders and "anybody I can find" to assemble a list of alternate nominees — "middle-of-the-road, non-political Baptists out there who need to be appointed."[26] He would make them public when the Committee released its report in late April.

The BP story on Montoya — to cite only three papers — covered over a page in the Texas Baptist Standard;[27] two thirds of a page in the Missouri Word & Way[28] and was front-paged by the North Carolina Biblical Recorder[28]

Montoya called a press conference to announce 32 alternate nominations, after the Committee on Nominations made public its nominations the following month. BP and several state papers gave Montoya's second announcement big play, along with a BP release on the Committee's nominations. SBC Today, in an editorial, noted three "examples of the types of nominees Montoya wants removed from nominations to SBC leadership": Lee Roberts nominated for the Executive Committee, "who led a major assault on Mercer University in 1987" and who was reported by the Atlanta newspapers as having "23 court judgments against him for various financial losses. . ."; Bob Tenery, nominated for another term on the Sunday School Board, "editor of the Southern Baptist Advocate, flagship magazine of the fundamentalist party in the SBC and Curtis Caine, nominated for another term on the Christian Life Commission, a "trustee who made outrageous racist remarks in 1988. . . and so unacceptable to most Baptists that a 1989 messenger moved that Caine be removed from the CLC."[30]

In a sort of tit for tat, the Advocate noted that Montoya's proposed alternates from North Carolina "come from the most left wing elements of this state." Betty Gilreath, he said, was from the church "which was instrumental in the founding of the Southern Baptist Alliance." John Hewett "is one of the most strident critics of conservatives in the Convention. . ."; William E. Poe, "a member of the Peace Committee from the Moderate/Liberal wing, . . . was one of the men who fought so hard to have the Report watered down and weakened before it was brought to the Convention"; and Leon Smith, elected President of the North Carolina Convention as the candidate of the Liberals right after Randall Lolley resigned at Southeastern Seminary. . ."

"If this is Montoya's ideas of 'Centrist' candidates," Tenery said, "we surely would dread to hear his idea of what a Liberal candidate really is!"[31]

Montoya had published an article in the liberal Christian Century, January 17, titled, "Trading Principles for Power in the SBC." He accused SBC conservative leaders of "unethical practices" and "political demagoguery." The article was reprinted in SBC Today and in at least one state paper, the North Carolina

<u>Biblical Recorder</u>, in its April 14 issue, one week after Montoya announced that he would challenge the official Committee report.

In April, the <u>Advocate</u> ran two long follow-up articles to its February story on Montoya which alleged "a rather extensive police record" by Montoya in Texas from 1970 to 1978 before "c[oming] back to God" and enrolling at Criswell College. [32] One of the April articles, by Montoya's former compatriot Mark Brooks said Montoya, in making charges against former associates, had "take[n] facts and twist[ed] them to suit his purpose." [33] The other by Larry Holly said Montoya had made himself a martyr and was being used as mouthpiece by some state editors. Holly repeated the allegations that Montoya "has eight felonies," saying that his "last arrest for cocaine trafficking" had come when "he was already preaching the Gospel."[34]

Montoya later said the investigation of his alleged crimes had been faulty and that he had only one felony on his record. Montoya attributed the additional felonies to other "David Montoya's living in Dallas during that time."[35] However, another observer says that a study of the police records throws doubt on Montoya's explanation.[35A]

Mission Board Presidents Speak on Controversy

During the weeks before New Orleans there was much concern that agency personnel might try to influence votes. Larry Lewis, for example, told Home Mission Board staff that they "must not" become involved in partisan politics on any issue.

While not involving himself in partisan activities, Lewis did make a statement to his board in their March meeting about the SBC situation in the context of citing increases in baptisms, home missionaries, volunteers and chaplains. Then after noting that HMB staff had "reaffirmed our belief in an inspired, infallible Bible 'without any mixture of error,' Lewis said:

"Though painful and even hurtful at times, I believe the conflict of the '80's has reaped good as well as ill for our denomination and for the Kingdom. A reaffirmation of our historic commitment to the authority and authenticity of the Scripture was needed and that reaffirmation was made. Belief in an inspired, infallible Bible cannot be considered a peripheral doctrine of little concern to Southern Baptists. Baptists feel deeply and strongly about the Bible and will not allow that historic doctrine of the faith to be eroded. For this, I believe Southern Baptists should be thankful."[36]

Though reporters were present, the denominational media all but ignored the statement.

Foreign Mission Board trustees met in San Diego about two weeks later and elected Bill Hancock, pastor of the largest SBC church in Louisville, as their chairman to succeed Mark Corts. Their meeting was held in conjunction with an appointment service for 29 new missionaries. At the close of the service, 75 persons responded to an invitation from board chairman Keith Parks to consider mission service. The meeting was reportedly upbeat and harmonious, although the board voted acceptance of a committee report stating that "the time is not right" to establish another central seminary in Europe. By a vote of 23 to 18, the board rejected a proposed amendment by trustee Paige Patterson that the report be delayed for further consideration at the trustees' July meeting.[37]

About a month before the New Orleans convention, trustees received by registered mail an open letter of concern by Keith Parks, which Parks said he was sending to all denominational editors. Remembering that Parks had opposed the election of Charles Stanley in 1985, some trustees took the letter as an attempt by the FMB president to re-enter presidential politics. "He did the same in opposing Charles Stanley," trustee Ron Wilson noted. "He just didn't name anyone this time."[38]

"For the sake of three and a half billion lost people," Parks wrote, "I plead with Southern Baptists to rise above our controversy and recommit to sharing Christ with the whole world. . . . But many signs indicate we may forfeit our greatest challenge. We are seeing the most results ever in our work overseas. But at home, our conflict is depriving us of the additional resources that are urgently needed . . .

"The effort to control has excluded many major supporters of cooperative missions. We are losing the wholesome balance that has been our convention's strength. Historically, we have always been a mixture of two major groups. We need full participation of both if we are serious about reaching the world for Christ. . . . More and more churches and individuals are noting the controversy as a reason for withholding support."

Parks noted "a decline of appointments" with "many missionary candidates . . . increasingly concerned about the direction of our convention and turmoil on seminary campuses. We were once known as a people of evangelism and missions. Now, even internationally, we are headlined as a people of controversy. Our witness of love and hope is less effective."

The solution, Parks said, is to "humble ourselves, pray, seek God's face and turn from our wicked ways. Hopefully, it is not too late for healing."[39]

The conservative trustees harmonized with the call for revival and more mission concern. Some — perhaps a majority — were upset by Park's negativism and the call for greater inclusiveness in appointments, particularly because Parks did not say where the theological line should be drawn in seeking a "balance" in appointments and nominations for boards.

Parks mailed the letter before trustees could have input. State editors gave the letter big play. A reply by former FMB trustee chairman Mark Corts did not get nearly as much attention in most papers.

Corts join[ed] with Parks in calling for an urgent commitment to share Christ with the whole world." While Corts "deeply respect[ed Parks] and his sacrificial commitment to world missions," he "question[ed] both the timing and conclusions of his comments."

Corts conceded that the controversy had "taken some focus off missions," but thought it "unfair for the controversy to be the scapegoat for our failure. . . . In addition , we must ask, 'What role does our soft national economy and troubled economic times in the oil belt, which traditionally provides strong Baptist support, play in this decline in mission giving?' "

Furthermore, Corts said, "if major supporters of cooperative missions are no longer supporting missions because they feel excluded, their very withdrawal proves they may not actually be supporters of cooperative missions." Corts recalled conservatives had felt "systematically excluded" in the past, nevertheless, "they were exhorted by many to continue their support for missions in spite of their concerns. If it was appropriate then, cooperative support for missions is appropriate now."

Corts said the SBC had "always been a mixture of more than two major groups. There is a wide variety of Baptists with many concerns. . . . There is a large number of loyal Baptists concerned about a loss of biblical authority who believe that the decline in missionary activity in many mainline denominations [results from] the decline in biblical orthodoxy. Their history serves a clear warning . . . that we cannot separate our mission mandate from confidence in the integrity of the Word of God which provides that mandate."

The BJCPA Fights to Preserve Funding

Next to the presidential contest, the hottest item on the agenda for New Orleans was the Executive Committee's recommendations that the BJCPA's SBC allocation be reduced from $391,796 to $50,000 and the CLC's allotment raised from $897,508 to $1,191,236, with the CLC becoming for the first time "a" religious liberty voice for the SBC in Washington and the SBC Public Affairs Committee given permission to "address matters of religious liberty and church-state issues."

The PAC would also continue to represent the SBC on the BJCPA. The EC was recommending only a small increase in PAC funding so as not to complicate the situation further.

There had been attempts to drastically cut the funding of the BJCPA before, but not until 1990 did the EC include the funding changes in the budget which would go before the upcoming convention.

Majority and minority reports from the Executive Committee on the BJCPA issue were printed in full in the May issue of the Baptist Program, which went to every SBC pastor. President Jerry Vines then ruled about a third of the minority report "out of order" because it included violations of the Convention parliamentary authority, Robert's Rules of Order and said only the remainder could be printed in the Convention Bulletin.[40]

BJCPA executive director James Dunn was now speaking and writing to every person he could reach, in an effort to persuade New Orleans-bound messengers to reject the transfer of funds. In a two-page spread in the Virginia Religious Herald, Dunn said "outrageous accusations" had been made against the BJCPA by "civil religionists" who seek "to advance their own agenda" by "engag[ing] in a campaign of dubious tactics, distortions and misrepresentations to justify takeover of the religious freedom assignment."[41]

Dunn and the BJC staff were working harder than some supposed. On April 26, Mississippi pastor John Voss reported receiving a call from Don Chenevert in the BJCPA office, asking Voss to call several pastors "to explain the actions of the Executive Committee" and to urge them to bring messengers to New Orleans to support the BJCPA. When Voss asked his relationship to the BJCPA, Chenevert said he was "on loan" from the HMB. Complaints also came from other pastors that a HMB worker was soliciting support for the BJCPA.

HMB president Larry Lewis says he was sick at home with pneumonia when he received a call about the reports. "Do you have anyone with the Joint Committee?" the caller asked.

"No, I'm sure we don't have," Lewis said. "Wait, we might have one of our semester missionaries up there." Lewis recalled that a few student interns worked jointly for the HMB and agencies or state conventions for a college semester, receiving academic credit for completion of the assignment. "I'll check into it," Lewis promised. He immediately called Paul Adkins, vice president of the HMB's ministry section and learned that the HMB and BJCPA had worked together in such a program for years. Lewis then instructed Atkins, "Call that young man up and tell him immediately to cease that calling. Call Jim Dunn and tell him that we are very upset that he has assigned this HMB semester missionary to make these calls and gotten [the HMB] into a controversy. And find out when the young man's term ends and terminate him at that point."[42]

Oliver Thomas, general counsel for the BJCPA, defended the activity of the intern: "We feel there is no greater threat to religious liberty and to the convention as a whole than the effort to defund the Baptist Joint Committee. Everyone on our staff from the Executive Director to the semester intern has tried to communicate that to Southern Baptists." However, Thomas said "far less than five percent" of the intern's time was spent "alerting" Southern Baptists about concerns of the BJCPA.

Dunn then told Bill Berry, the HMB supervisor of the semester interns, that the BJCPA would no longer need a semester intern from the HMB. When Lewis learned of this decision, he said he would not refer the matter to HMB trustees because "it is not necessary."

Dunn and the BJCPA continued to receive strong support from the Vestal ticket, moderate pastors and most state editors. They touted the BJCPA's record in "protecting" churches from the encroachment of big government. They warned of dire consequences if the budget cut should be approved. They promised that any cut would be made up by sympathetic state conventions and individuals and that the SBC Public Affairs Committee representation on the BJCPA would be reduced from 18 to 11 members.

The PAC, operating with only a $23,704 budget, remained very much in the picture with a journal, committee meetings, recognitions and press contacts. The PAC grabbed headlines in April when it voted to give Senator Jesse Helms its Religious Liberty Award. Helms had been battling with the National Endowment for the Arts over public funding of obscenity. At the PAC award luncheon, Senator Tent Lott called Helms, "a man of great integrity, ethics and religious commitment. He fights for family values and moral concerns." Larry Lewis also had "tremendous respect for Senator Helms. He has led the nation in many social and moral issues." But Lewis told fellow PAC members that the award "embroils us in volatile political issues that do not do us any good. . . . We might win a battle and lose a war" in New Orleans.[43]

Conservatives kept making Dunn's past associations an issue, particularly his involvement with the left-leaning People For the American Way and the ACLU. They cited allegations that Dunn and the BJCPA had been much less than neutral in supporting legislation, such as the Civil Rights Restoration Act, which many believed would force churches, schools and private industry to hire homosexuals. And they continued to remind audiences that the BJCPA was not an SBC agency, but a committee answerable to nine Baptist groups, even though the SBC had been by far the largest contributor for many years. The CLC, under Richard Land, conservatives kept saying, would provide the most efficient and responsible religious liberty representation for Southern Baptists in Washington. And the SBC would not be opting out of the BJCPA, but simply reducing the BJCPA's funding to a reasonable level.

Beneath the funding and turf battles, the differences in principles regarding religious liberty matters remained the same. The BJCPA and its SBC supporters took a strict separationist stance, often taking the same positions on legislation as People For the American Way, the ACLU and Americans United. SBC conservatives wanted more recognition by government of the nation's Judeo-Christian heritage and stronger defenses against the encroachment of secular, non-biblical values into American society.

Politics Pick Up

Denominational papers during the weeks before the 1990 convention were filled with reports of political activity. Supporters of Roy Honeycutt and James Dunn urged sympathetic pastor friends to bring their maximum number of messengers to the convention. Students from the Sons and Daughters group spoke on campuses. The candidates crisscrossed the country, speaking to rallies of supporters. Heated rhetoric — more from moderates than conservatives — darkened the air. Moderates kept warning that New Orleans would probably be their last chance for a generation to save the SBC from division. Conservatives, while hoping to win, said if the EC recommendations and the Chapman ticket lost, they would be back in 1991 in force. A few conservatives became jittery at hearing stories of moderate successes in advance recruiting: Russell Dilday, someone said, was predicting 3,000 churches would send ten messengers each to vote for Vestal; Baptists Committed was promising to deliver 23,000 messengers; 27,000 rooms had reportedly been reserved in New Orleans by millionaire John Baugh. Baugh later said he had reserved only one room for himself and his wife[44]; a conservative Southern Seminary student told his pastor that a group of students at Southern were writing churches to send messengers to fire Jerry Johnson as a Southern trustee; several moderate networks were offering to pay $200 per messenger who would commit to vote for Vestal.

Whatever the truth in these stories, moderate confidence ran strong. Conservatives were edgy. A conservative activist in Florida predicted a 52-48 percent moderate margin in the presidential vote, based on 130 phone calls he had made.

There was common agreement on one thing: The 1990 New Orleans convention was crucial to the future of the denomination.

References

1 Fred Powell: "Interview with John Bisagno," Southern Baptist Communicator, April, 1990, p. 4.

2 Meeting of Kansas-Missouri conservatives, April 12, 1990.

3 "Search the Scriptures," Las Vegas, June, 1989. Printed in the Southern Baptist Advocate, April, 1990, pp. 1, 6.

4 Florida Baptist Witness, January 25, 1990, p. 5. Cited by Southern Baptist Advocate, June, 1990, p. 5.

5 Jack U. Harwell: "Political Rhetoric Swirls Across the SBC," SBC Today, May, 1990, p. 1, 24.

6 "A City Without Walls," Indiana Baptist, June 5, 1990, p. 2.

7 April 12, 1990. Cited by Southern Baptist Communicator, June, 1990, p. 4.

8 Sarah Zimmerman: "Baptists Encouraged to Clean Out Lint Trap," The Baptist Messenger, April 5, 1990, pp. 3, 4.

9 James L. Holly: "Conservatives to Nominate Real Missionary, Douglas Knapp, as First Vice President of SBC," Southern Baptist Advocate, June, 1990, p. 2.

10 "Vestal Endorsed by 300-plus Retired Foreign Missionaries," Baptists Committed . . . Newsletter, May, 1990, p. 1.

11 Southern Baptist Advocate, op. cit.

12 Cited by James L. Holly: "A Prayer Seminar That Turned into a Political Speech," Southern Baptist Advocate, April, 1990, pp. 8, 10. In a rebuttal to the Advocate article in the May issue of SBC Today, p. 24, Burroughs did not rebut this statement by Porter, although SBC Today says Holly "attack[ed]" Porter.

13 "Seminarians Organize; Call for End to SBC Strife," Indiana Baptist, April 26, 1990.

14 Southern Baptist Advocate, op. cit.

15 Jack U. Harwell: "An Editorial Viewpoint," May, 1990, p. 24.

16 "Secular Media Look at Baptists Deserves Review," June, 1990, p. 8.

17 "The Wall Street Hoax, Southern Baptist Advocate, June, 1990, p. 8.

18 "Where is the Last Straw?" April, 1990, p. 2.

19 "Vestal's Duplicity," February, 1990, p. 5.

20 SBC Today, June, 1990, p. 8.

21 Rutgers University Press, New Brunswick and London, p. 108.

22 "Editors Angry at Bush," May, 1990, p. 9.

23 "President Bush Briefs Baptist Editors and PAC Members," April, 1990, p. 11.

24 "Loyalty to Southern Seminary," Indiana Baptist, May 8, 1990, pp. 3, 12.

25 Fred Powell: "Interview With Joel Gregory," Southern Baptist Communicator, June, 1990,p. 20.

26 Word & Way, op. cit.

27 Baptist Standard, April 4, 1990, p. 4.

28 Missouri Word & Way, April 5, 1990, p. 4.

29 Biblical Recorder, April 5, 1990, pp. 1, 8.

30 "SBC Challenges to Nominations Merit Support," June, 1990, p. 8.

31 Editorial: "Conservative Bashing in the Biblical Recorder," June, 1990, pp. 4, 5.

32 Advocate, February, 1990, p. 3.

33 Advocate, April, 1990, p. 7, 12.

34 Advocate, op. cit. p. 12, 23.

35 Montoya related this to me in November, 1990, at the Baptist General Convention of Texas meeting in Houston.

35A This observer is a highly reliable source whom I have chosen not to name.

36 Quoted from Lewis' report to his board, March, 14, 1990.

37 Robert O'Brien: "Foreign Mission Board Trustees Elect Hancock," Religious Herald, April 26, 1990, p. 10.

38 Telephone Interview, May, 1990.

39 "Dear Southern Baptists: Foreign Mission Board Leader Pleads for Peace," Biblical Recorder, May 26, 1990, p. 3.

40 Vines: Part of Report Out of Order, Biblical Recorder, May 12, 1990, pp. 1, 9.

41 "Reject Cut in BJC Funds, Says James Dunn," March 29, 1990, p. 6.

42 Telephone Interview with Lewis, March, 1991.

43 Marv Knox: "Senator Jesse Helms Receives PAC's First Annual Religious Liberty Award," The Christian Index, May 3, 1990, p. 3.

44 Baugh told me this in a letter several months after New Orleans. He was upset that I had taken note of the 27,000-room rumor in Volume 5 of The Truth in Crisis. I apologized to Baugh for not contacting him at the time.

45 First Baptist Reminder, May 25, 1990. Cited in Julian H. Pentecost: "Another Regrettable Criswellian Excess," Religious Herald, June 7, 1990, p. 4.

Chapter 11

"The Twelfth Win"

The advance staff came first: Al Shackleford, vice president for public relations and the designated convention manager, to check out the facilities in the Louisiana Superdome; Dan Martin, news director of Baptist Press to prepare the press room for over 600 pre-registered media representatives; Radio and TV Commission technicians to string wires and set up the sound system and the floor mikes; Sunday School Board people to unpack books for sale; Foreign Mission, Home Mission Board people and employees of other agencies to prepare promotional displays; Registration Secretary Lee Porter to train his local committee and set up the counters for issuing voting credentials to an expected 35-37,000 messengers, down sharply from earlier estimates that ranged as high as 60,000, but way up from the 1982 New Orleans convention which registered only 20,437.

The first significant scheduled pre-convention event — the National Prayer Conference — began Thursday at New Orleans Seminary. For three days about 150 people prayed and listened to messages of concern. Organizer Avery Willis and other leaders saw prayer and corporate repentance as the only way to salvage America and the Southern Baptist Convention."1

Foreign Mission Board trustees met on Saturday before the convention. Chairman Bill Hancock called trustees and staff to prayer after Keith Parks spoke about the ill will he felt had arisen among some trustees following his open letter of May 15. Parks sought to clear the air. "I would plead," he said, "that somehow we could resolve this 'something-against-me' kind of feeling. I believe it is biblical [and] necessary for the Spirit of God to move among us and to bring us together."

Parks "had not said or meant that the board was to blame for the problems. . . . I was trying to say to Southern Baptists that missions, in my estimation, is hurting. And every time we get together and irresponsibly tear at each other, . . . this hurts our witness again."

Hancock urged all who held animosity toward another to reconcile it "before this day is done." Hancock later said that rumored trustee action on Parks' letter was now "history." "I've been praying the Lord would give us the wisdom to bring a positive response rather than reaction."

At dinner, Parks and Mark Corts linked arms in a gesture of friendship. Corts, the former trustee chairman who had written an open letter in response to Parks', "reaffirm[ed]" his "love and appreciation for Keith Parks."[2]

Saturday also marked the second annual evangelistic witness to the convention's host city. Morris Chapman, Dan Vestal, Larry Lewis and about 1,000 others braved New Orleans heat for five hours of "soul winning." Officially sponsored by the Louisiana Baptist Convention with support from the Home Mission Board, the blitz resulted in 521 professions of faith.[3]

At a Saturday evening rally of Hispanic Southern Baptists at New Orleans Seminary, Vestal recalled an experience during the blitz. "At the fifth house, a young black mother came to the door. I asked her, 'Are you a Christian?' She said, 'No.' I asked if I could tell her how to be a Christian. She said, 'Yes.' I showed her from the Scriptures how to be saved, then we joined hands and prayed as she accepted the Lord. That black woman," Vestal said, "didn't care about the controversy in the Southern Baptist Convention. She knew only that she needed Jesus Christ."

Vestal asked the audience to stand while he read about Paul's indebtedness to the world to share the Gospel. "We [also] owe the Gospel to all humanity," he declared. "But while we . . . are embroiled in an internal struggle, we are continuing to lose touch with [the lost] in America."

Morris Chapman also spoke at the Hispanic rally — the only occasion when he and Vestal appeared together in New Orleans before the convention.

"My desire," Chapman said, "is to perpetuate our long held belief in the perfect Word of God, which is infallible and inerrant in the original manuscripts. . . . While speaking the truth in love, we must perpetuate God's perfect Word through the institutional life of Southern Baptists. We must complete the course correction and return to the faith of our forefathers."[4]

Vestal also spoke to the Monday night Sons and Daughters of the SBC "Homecoming Rally " which Chapman could not attend. "The more you grow as a Southern Baptist," Vestal said, "the more you realize [what] you owe to those who have given their lives to forging Baptist distinctives." If "in the providence of God" [I should be elected president, I will] "enlist all Southern Baptists . . . to pay a debt to a lost world."

Keith Parks, WMU executive director Dellana O'Brien and Larry Lewis also spoke to the group. O'Brien worried about the effects the controversy might have on young people, but she encouraged them to play a part in the "noble cause" of "world evangelism."

In reference to reports that some moderate pastors might lead their churches to boycott the Cooperative Program, Parks "plead[ed that this cooperative] plan [not be destroyed] until you come up with a better plan."

Larry Lewis also expressed concern about a moderate boycott of the Cooperative Program. He encouraged students who were unhappy with the way things are going within the SBC to work for change. There are a number of ways to effect that change, he said, "but holding our missionaries hostage is not one of them."[5]

Vestal, Parks and O'Brien received enthusiastic applause. Vestal was given a standing ovation by a few students. Lewis' remarks were received less enthusiastically. The mixed applause and the Catch the Vision buttons which many wore, suggested that Vestal would win if the election were decided by this group.

Everybody had to already know where Chapman and Vestal stood. Their views had been in all the state papers. Chapman was committed to "enlarging the tent so that all Southern Baptists who believe in perpetuating a commitment to the infallible, inerrant Word of God will know they are a part of the [SBC]." Southern Baptists can walk together within the parameters of the Peace Committee report where 85 to 90 percent of Southern Baptists stand, Chapman asserted. If there are people in key denominational positions who stand outside these parameters, "it would be the desire of most Southern Baptists that [they] be removed or replaced" through attrition, retirement or resignation."[6]

Vestal was committed to ending the "exclusiveness" practiced by conservatives. "I am a biblical inerrantist," he said, "but biblical inerrancy is not a central issue. It is whether one will pledge continued control of the SBC by the [conservative group]."[7]

As at Las Vegas, Vestal made himself more available to the secular press at New Orleans than did the conservative candidate. Vestal made these points to the Religious Newswriters Association in New Orleans:

He conceded that conservatives "have captured the issue of the Bible. They have painted everybody who does not support them, a liberal. . . . We have not somehow been able to counter that to say, 'I believe the Bible is the Word of God as much as you do.' . . . That has hurt us."

He was "deeply offended" that the secular press had cast him as "moderate. . . . That word 'moderate' hurts and offends a lot of Baptist people. What you call a moderate movement is . . . not monolithic."

He promised, if elected, to appoint a blue-ribbon commission to study and recommend to the Convention how to limit the powers of the presidency.

If elected, he saw the "possibility of healing." If he lost, conservatives should not expect "to continue to shut people out of this convention and expect them to continue to cooperate. . . . You will begin to see some kind of mechanism put in place for different funding . . . of missions and theological education . . . with significant funds going into it."[8]

The conservative-dominated Pastors Conference, which elected Richard Lee as their president, drew some 20,000 preachers; the alternative moderate Forum attracted only 2,000. Moderates hoped the differences in the crowds would not be a barometer of registration for the convention.

Speakers at the Pastors Conference declared some firm convictions:

Adrian Rogers: "It is better to be divided by truth than to be united in error. . . . We have some today who would jettison truth on the altar of cooperation. . . .There is no way to preach the truth and be loved by everybody. In the Bible, anybody worth anything had enemies."

John Bisagno: "There is no way to overstate the disdain God has for the person who tampers with the integrity of the Word of God."

Morris Chapman: "We live in a world in bondage to a personal devil. And the time is running out. The whole world needs to hear the message of John 3:16."[9]

Speakers at the moderate Forum spent much of their time attacking conservatives:

David Montoya: "[My involvement in the conservative movement became] not a search for piety," but an exercise in "vendettas, blackballing, threats, kingmakers and a ministry of money."

Randall Lolley, former president of Southeastern Seminary: "[Leaders of the conservative faction] rule from their saddles. Never expect a cowboy to do a shepherd's job. . . . Every sect has established itself in this same way, whether the Moonies, the Mormons, Jim Jones in Guyana or Father Divine in New York. They select a few texts, disregard their context, bend their interpretation and make them normative for faith and practice."

Herbert Reynolds, president of Baylor University, called conservatives "ambitious malcontents" with a goal "to control and manipulate a large mass of people to satisfy their own unhealthy personality needs. . . . The fundamentalist tactic is simple; hatred, bitterness and condemnation of all whom they despise."[10]

The Pastors Conference and Forum concluded on Monday evening. That same evening a meeting of moderates was held uptown at St. Charles Avenue Baptist Church. The street car that ran past the church was crowded with seminarians and moderate messengers. A conservative trustee happened to be on one car and overheard a young woman say, "Did you go to any of the Pastors Conference?" "No," the other student replied, "but I heard that they had this huge Bible on the convention floor and all those fundamentalists marched around it." Everyone in the party laughed loudly. Then the one who had spoken first declared, "They're Fascists. It's just like worshiping Hitler."[11]

Tuesday morning, June 12, messengers streamed into the Louisiana Superdome. As they formed long lines to register, many picked up free papers and brochures with a partisan twist. A conservative pastor observed one well known moderate pastor stuffing copies of the Advocate into a trash barrel. "Brother, what you're doing is of the flesh," he reminded him.

SBC Today headlined in their June issue, "304 FOREIGN MISSIONARIES ENDORSE VESTAL." The "convention issue" of the Advocate front-paged answers to moderate claims made in a mailout to every SBC church. A sampling of the Advocate's rejoinders: "Baptisms are lagging says the slick puff sheet, but why should liberals worry about baptisms? All those who have led in baptisms for 50 years are conservative inerrantists. . . . In states like North Carolina and Virginia, many of the liberal [SBC] churches are receiving members who have never been baptized."

A brochure by the new Religious Liberty Council, established to prevent funding cuts from the BJCPA, cited endorsements of the BJCPA from 12 state editors. "Such defunding defies the wishes of the convention," said South Carolina's John Roberts. ". . . Baptist freedom may indeed be what is at stake," worried Mississippi's Don McGregor. "The 'rationale' adopted by the Executive Committee [for the funding cut] to justify its actions is trivial and misleading," declared Florida's Jack Brymer. Among editors in the old south states, only Georgia and Alabama's were missing from the endorsers.

Ten thousand copies of the conservative Baptist Sentinel from Texas were stacked by entry ways. Editor Norman Miller printed the entire text of "The Cover-Up at Southern Seminary." Fred Powell's Southern Baptist Communicator front-paged Adrian Rogers' "Why I Support Morris Chapman." Among the inside pieces was a challenge by John Bisagno: "Let every Southern Baptist seminary and university professor promise that he will teach only in accord with dominant convictions and beliefs held by Southern Baptists at large in the four areas of theological concern cited by the Peace Committee and the battle is over."

The satirical SBC Inquirer included among the "new Broadman books available," How to Become an Instant Celebrity by David Montoya and The Relative Vision Capabilities of the Common Mole by Jerry Johnson.

At 9:20 a.m. the choir from Jerry Vines' church began warming up the crowd with "Love Like a River." From the high press box, where David Montoya, wearing a Baptist Joint Committee button, sat chatting with reporters, the platform personalities looked far away; still a trim red handkerchief could be seen peeping above

President Vines' lapel pocket. To reach the platform from any side, one had to walk across the bare floor for over 50 yards.

Except for a cancellation by President George Bush, the program for the 133rd session in the 144th year of the Southern Baptist Convention was set. The invitation to the president to speak had reportedly been issued after a member of the White House staff said Mr. Bush wanted to address the convention. Bush apparently declined after some Southern Baptists criticized a White House invitation for leaders of homosexual and lesbian organizations to attend a bill-signing ceremony. White House religion liaison Doug Weed said the president had not known the gays were even there. Nevertheless, Bush sent his "warmest greetings" to the convention, calling the SBC "a vital source of spiritual strength, guidance and fellowship for millions of Americans."[12]

At 9:40 President Vines called the convention to order. Behind him stood the chief parliamentarian, Barry McCarty and four assistants, John Sullivan, Jimmy Draper, Joe Reynolds and Jimmy Jackson. Registration Secretary Lee Porter reported that "as of three minutes ago, this convention had registered 31,856 messengers; at some time this morning we will become the third largest convention in history." Porter, in his deep sonorous voice, moved that the "duly elected" messengers "be recognized as members of this convention."[13]

Jack Burton of Texas immediately moved an amendment that "the convention deny seating to messengers from the Emmanuel Baptist Church of McAllen, TX, because the church has not given anything to the Cooperative Program this fiscal year." A burst of applause was countered by groans. It was already known to many that the pastor of this Hispanic church was Roland Lopez, chairman of the Committee on Nominations. An article had been published in the Texas Baptist Standard about the church.

President Vines was prepared. He nodded to Lawton Searcy, Chairman of the Credentials Committee.

"Mr. President, the members of [the church] have agreed to withdraw their request as messengers in compliance with Southern Baptist Convention bylaws."

More applause rippled across the stadium.

Vines presented Ike Reighard, chairman of the Order of Business Committee. Reighard moved that the printed order of business be adopted.

Microphone Four was flashing red. "State your name, your church and your motion." Vines would repeat this request dozens of times in the long contentious hours ahead.

Pat Pearce from North Carolina asked that the president's address be moved from before to after the election of the new president.

Moderates had tried this stratagem before. Vines ruled that a fixed order of business could not be changed.

From the applause received by both Pearce and Vines, it appeared that the crowd was about evenly divided. The first big test came at 9:40 when Bill Harrell of Georgia presented Recommendation One from the Executive Committee, calling for extension of the Christian Life Commission's program statement to include promotion of religious liberty. This, as everyone knew, was to prepare the way for the 87.24 percent cut in the previous year's appropriation to the BJCPA and a 40.70 percent increase to the CLC. The funding transfers would be included in the larger budget contained in Recommendation Three.

Harrell explained the EC's reasons for the enlargement of the CLC's program statement: This will "strengthen the work of Southern Baptists in the area of religious liberty." The CLC can "provide [the leadership we need] in religious liberty and work with such groups as the Baptist Joint Committee and the Public Affairs Committee. The CLC can [thus] speak [with increased influence] to important moral and social issues, such as abortion, the National Endowment to the Arts and pornography. We feel," Harrell said, "that a body of almost 15 million people should have its own [voice in Washington speaking on these critical issues]. This revised program statement will solve some of the problems of recent years regarding funding and accountability. . . . This will be a positive step, a forward step in the area of religious liberty concerns."

Microphone Three was flashing. "Mr. President I have a motion which takes precedence over the motion here." Vines conferred briefly with Parliamentarian McCarty and said, "Your point of order is not well taken. The messenger must push the 'motion' button."

Vines now recognized lawyer Frank Ingraham of Tennessee, a former member of the Executive Committee, at Microphone Five for a substitute motion.

"Mr. President and fellow messengers, it is [appropriate] that we congratulate the Christian Life Commission and its trustees for their work in morality and social ethics in Washington, D.C. However, this recommendation expresses frustration rather than common sense. The issue is separation of church and state. . . . It reminds me of crossing a railroad with a jack rabbit. You don't know what you're getting."

Former EC Chairman Charles Sullivan opposed the substitute motion. "We had the Baptist Joint Committee speaking for a bill. The CLC was against it. The reason: One was told they could speak for religious liberty; the other was told they could speak only for Christian ethics. We need a common voice representing our convention."

John Lee Taylor of Georgia favored the substitute. "The Christian Life Commission already has more than an adequate program of [moral and social concerns]. We'll be adding religious liberty to an already crowded agenda."

Charles Stanley took an opposite view. "Too much emphasis on religious liberty is not possible. It is unthinkable that Southern Baptists do not have their own voice for religious liberty and separation of church and state.... Let's take a giant step forward."

Ron Sisk from California said "taking money from the BJCPA will in many ways damage the work of the Baptist Joint Committee. The Christian Life Commission already has more than it can do. I know, I used to work there. If it ain't broke don't try to fix it."

Loud partisan applause had been given each speaker. Vines evoked groans when he ruled that the time had expired for discussion of the substitute motion. A vote by raised ballots was inconclusive. Vines ordered a ballot vote.

Counting the ballots would take at least an hour. EC Chairman Sam Pace noted that because EC recommendations 1-4 were closely related, they would move to Recommendation Five, while the votes for Ingraham's substitute motion were being tallied.

This recommendation called for a bylaw change that would preclude the possibility of cronyism by the Committee on Nominations: "The Committee [on Nominations] shall not nominate a fellow committee member or the member's spouse or a member of the previous year's Committee on Committees or the member's spouse for a first term on [a board or committee]." In the past, particularly before 1979, there had been instances of committee members nominating one another and spouses. "This will further remove any possibility of cronyism," EC member Eldridge Miller said.

Before a vote could be taken, Messenger Greg Clements from South Carolina called for a point of order. He wanted "verification" of Vines' "explanation of the previous balloting on the substitute motion." Vines repeated his directions and clicked off the mike. Clements punched the button again. "Sir, I need an explanation. . . " The mike went dead again. Boos and moans rolled across the stadium. Other requests for points of order were made, taking valuable time from the business schedule.

Recommendation Five and four other routine EC proposals passed easily; among other things, it was agreed by "common consent" to invite the Forum and Women in Ministry to participate in the 1995 Sesquicentennial Celebration.

The ballot count for Recommendation One was still going on. President Vines moved to "miscellaneous business." A flurry of motions were introduced.

— One asked the Executive Committee to study the feasibility of establishing a SBC accrediting agency for seminaries and colleges.

— Another requested the EC to study and determine how the terms "cooperating Baptist church" and "in friendly cooperation with" the SBC relates to the SBC.

— Another — obviously aimed at Jerry Johnson — asked that trustees be at least 30 years old.

— Another requested that an announced presidential nominee be forbidden to publicize himself. This was later declared out of order.

— Another would allow state conventions to elect members of the Committee on Nominations. Most of these and other motions were referred to the EC or the appropriate agency.

Forty-two resolutions were read into the record. With the ballots on the substitute motion to Recommendation One still not counted, Adrian Rogers introduced Jerry Vines for his presidential address, "The Glory of the Church."

Vines warned against "doctrinal error" in the church. "Those denominations that affirm the inspiration, inerrancy and infallibility of Scripture have a bright future. But those that do not are destined for the garbage dump of denominations," he declared. "It is better for Southern Baptists to debate and settle the issue of Scriptural inerrancy today than to someday debate whether homosexuals are suitable in our pulpits."

Churches, he said, must not allow themselves to be intimidated by "bureaucratic bullies" in the choice of programs and literature. Yet independence should be tempered by interdependence with like-minded churches cooperating in missions and benevolence. "We can do together what we cannot do alone."

Messengers punctuated Vines' sermon throughout with heavy applause. For many, he saved the best till last when he quoted revered B.H. Carroll's dying charge to L.R. Scaraborough, Carroll's successor as president of Southwestern Seminary: " 'I want you, if there ever comes heresy in your faculty, to take it to your faculty. If they won't hear you, take it to the trustees. If they won't hear you take it to the conventions that appointed them. If they won't hear you, take it to the common Baptists. They will hear you. And I charge you in the name of Jesus Christ to keep it lashed to the old Gospel of Jesus Christ.' "[14]

Before Vines finished the last sentence, hundreds were on their feet applauding, cheering and shouting. Around them sat other glum messengers who had stayed to hear the report on Frank Ingraham's substitute motion to derail the Executive Committee's recommendation for broadening the program of the Christian Life Commission. This would be a strong indicator of future votes on partisan issues.

The choir from FBC, Jacksonville, FL was singing "Tis a Glorious Church Without Spot or Wrinkle," when Lee Porter signalled that he had the vote count. Porter, as on previous occasions, kept the messengers in suspense until the last second: "On the substitute voting this morning, we had voting 27,417 messengers out of 32,120 messengers registered; 85 percent of the messengers voted. Voting yes on the substitute motion, 12,829 for 46.06 percent..." Foot-stomping applause, cheering and shouting broke out again as Porter tried to continue. Voting no, 14,788, 53.94 percent."

It seemed evident now, at about 12:30 p.m., that the BJCPA would lose other votes and that a conservative would be elected president for the 12th year in a row. Nevertheless, some moderates held out hope, saying, "All our people haven't registered yet."

Conservatives were ecstatic. Jimmy Draper was "very pleased." Eldridge Miller said he had told Bill Harrell, " 'We'll win [this one] by 2,000 votes.' and that's about what happened. We may win the presidency by 3,000."[15]

The Tuesday afternoon business session saw more motions. The potentially most explosive, made by Lamar Wadsworth of Maryland, asked "that Jerry Johnson of Colorado be removed from office as a trustee of" Southern Seminary, "and that his trustee position be declared vacant." Thousands of Southern Seminary supporters gave a standing ovation. Discussion was postponed until later in the convention.[16]

Nomination of presidential candidates came at 2:30. Phil Lineberger, president of the Texas Convention, nominated Daniel Vestal. "For Daniel Vestal the Bible is not a law of works, but a way of life," Lineberger said. "In our world we have seen walls coming down everywhere. God has provided for us the greatest open door for evangelism in the history of the world. We must walk through that door together. Let's elect a man who promises to take us through together — Daniel Vestal, just like you, one of us."

John Bisagno, another Texan, began in a softer tone than Lineberger. "My dear brothers and sisters in Jesus, it is with God's given promise stirring within . . . my soul that I rise to nominate Morris Chapman for president of the Southern Baptist Convention. . . . We hold in our hands the opportunity this day to put this [Bible] issue to rest once and for all. . . . The man is Morris Chapman, . . . God's man."

The applause for Chapman died. The ballot was taken.

It was time now for the Committee of Nominations report of 263 persons nominated to serve on boards. Roland Lopez who, along with other messengers from his Hispanic church, had withdrawn as messengers, came to present the list of nominees. He thanked the convention "for the opportunity to serve." The committee, he said, had "worked, prayed and asked the Lord's wisdom and guidance in reaching nominations." He recommended that four on the list be replaced, including two from his church because that church is no longer considered to be a "cooperating" SBC church, he said sadly.

Microphone four was now blinking. "Mr. President, my name is Greg Clements and I have a point of order. . . . The body is in violation of Bylaw 16, paragraph one, last sentence. . . . I say that members of the nominating committee must be members of cooperating Southern Baptist churches."

Jerry Vines stepped back to confer with the parliamentarians, then returned to the podium. "After consultation the chair rules that the chairman of this committee was elected last year by this convention [when] he was a member of a cooperating Southern Baptist church. The chair rules that the point of order is not well taken."

Vines recognized committee member David Montoya at Microphone Four, who moved for the substitution of his minority report of 30 persons.

Vines conferred with his parliamentarians, then asked assistant parliamentarian John Sullivan to explain why Montoya's motion was out of order. "Roberts' Rules of Order [the official SBC parliamentary manual], clearly says that under the procedure of nominating from the floor, no one may nominate more than one person for an office. It is clear in Roberts' that [persons presented] in any minority report with recommendations have to be treated one at a time and must be nominated one at a time."

Vines: "Does the messenger at Microphone Four [Montoya] wish to make a nomination?"

Montoya: "I wish to strike the name Ronnie Floyd from Arkansas and substitute John McClanahan from Arkansas [for the Executive Committee]." Floyd, pastor of the largest church in Arkansas, had been one of Montoya's associates before Montoya switched to the moderate camp.

"Mr. President, if there are no further nominations, I have some other names."

Vines came back. ". . . . Does the messenger wish to speak for his nominee?"

"No Sir, I do not."

"Does the committee wish to speak in favor of their nominee?"

Don Perkins from Arkansas noted that Floyd had served one term "faithfully and loyally. Tradition has it that people are elected for a second term, if there are no specific reasons against. There is no reason for Ronnie Floyd not to be renominated. Since coming to Arkansas, the church he pastors has led our state in baptisms. His church supports the Cooperative Program at approximately 10 percent of their budget." Perkins closed amidst loud applause.

On a raised ballot vote Vines ruled that Montoya's nominee had lost.

Vines recognized Microphone 11. Floyd Parker moved to send the name of nominee Walter Carpenter [to the HMB] "back to committee in view of the fact that Second Baptist Church, Houston already has a representative on the Executive Committee. . . . I believe that in 37,000 churches we can find people to serve without having two from one church."

Parker's motion lost on a raised ballot vote.

During both the morning and afternoon business sessions, frustrated moderates had kept the microphone lights flashing, raising questions and asking to speak on a "point of order." When the speaker merely wanted information, Vines usually said "your point of order is well taken" and tried to respond. At other times he conferred with his parliamentarians, before stating that the point of order was "not well taken."

Some of the points of order were raised in regard to a previous vote. At Vines' request, McCarty declared that "the point of order must be called at the time the business is before the body. Each time the convention moves to another item of business, the box [must be] cleared [of previous business], or we could spend all day going back and back and back to previous points of order."

The suspenseful afternoon wore on. With the tellers still tabulating votes for president, the business moved back to recommendations from the Executive Committee. The substitute motion having been defeated, the messengers now voted on Recommendation One to enlarge the program statement of the CLC. The motion passed on a raised ballot vote. The CLC could now speak for religious liberty.

Recommendation Two, calling for a deletion of the PAC program statement because only agencies have program statements, also passed. The action called for the PAC to function under guidelines drawn up by the Executive Committee for research, study and public relations on religious liberty matters and to serve as SBC representatives on the BJCPA.

EC member David Hankins presented Recommendation Three, the proposed 1990-91 Cooperative Program Budget which called for a 40.70 percent increase for the CLC and an 87.24 percent decrease for the BJCPA.

"This convention has approved giving a religious liberty assignment to the Christian Life Commission," Hankins said. "It is now appropriate to grant them the funds to do the job we have assigned to them."

Microphone Three called for a point of order. Once again, McCarty explained that "the point of order must be made at the time the breach of order occurred. . . . The parliamentary authority also states that when points of order are being used to obstruct the business of the convention, they are dilatory." McCarty's explanation was answered both by shouts of "No!" and applause.

Moderate David Sapp spoke against Recommendation Three. "Several state conventions are on record [as planning] to designate money directly to the BJCPA, in the event of such a motion as this. There may be some damage to the Cooperative Program. Second, this convention, four of the last five years, has voted down a similar action directed at the BJCPA. Why should we have [to vote] again on a matter we've spoken about so many times before?"

Malcolm Yarnell spoke for the motion. Frank Ingraham moved to amend, proposing that the BJCPA, the CLC and the PAC each receive only 1.89 percent increases in line with budget increases for other SBC entities. After debate, Henry Green of Florida called for a ballot vote. It would be another hour or more before the results would be announced.

The presidential vote was still not in. Charles Sullivan moved a resolution of appreciation for Darold H. Morgan, on the occasion of his retirement as president of the Annuity Board. Finally, Lee Porter signalled that the vote tally was completed. For over a decade, this had been the highest moment of expectancy during a convention. Porter gave the number of messengers voting, 37,334. A tense quiet prevailed as he paused. "Of that number, 15,753 or 42.32 percent voted for Daniel Vestal . . . "

"Praise God! Hallelujah! Glory!" Shouts and applause interrupted Porter who waited patiently. ". . . And a total of 21,471 or 57.68 percent of those voting cast ballots for Morris Chapman."

The shouting and applause began again. Conservatives joyfully hugged one another while moderates sat in dismay. Some threw down their programs in disgust. Some cried as they walked out. Never before had so much time, energy and money been spent for a candidate. Now they had lost by a much larger margin than almost anyone had expected.

"The Chair," Jerry Vines announced to a roar of approval, "declares Morris Chapman elected as president."

Many people were already out in the corridors, still expressing amazement at Chapman's margin of victory. Inside, business moved on. Thirty new resolutions and 17 additional motions were presented. Some of the motions were obviously meant to annoy the conservative majority. One asked that "our president and convention officers identify by name [the inerrant] Bible so that we all may have access to it." This motion was later ruled out of order.

The presidential vote made the elections of the vice presidents predictable. Doug Knapp defeated Carolyn Weatherford 16,348 — 60.47 percent to 10,688 — 39.53 percent. Fred Lowery won with 63.90 percent.

At the Tuesday evening Home Mission Board session, HMB president Larry Lewis presented a plaque to Richard Jackson as pastor of North Phoenix Baptist Church which had led SBC churches in baptisms for seven of the past ten years. The year before Lewis had welcomed Jackson, twice the moderate candidate for the SBC presidency, to the HMB Board of Directors. The messengers gave Jackson warm applause.

The partisan business resumed the next morning. Frank Ingraham's motion to amend the propsed budget had failed. Recommendation Three now passed. The big budget cut for the BJCPA was now official.

Martin Bradley, Recording Secretary and Lee Porter, Registration Secretary, both were opposed for re-election for the first time in many years. Bradley received only 46.63 percent of the vote in losing to David Atchison, son of CLC board chairman, Joe Atchinson. Porter handily survived a challenge by Bob Mowery, a conservative Nashville pastor.

Seminary presidents Russell Dilday and Roy Honeycutt, along with six other agency heads, gave reports Wednesday morning. It happened that messenger Michael Haley had overheard Dilday use the word "satanic" while giving a press interview the day before. Haley asked Dilday to clarify what he had meant. "The comment I made," said Dilday, "was that the methodology used in the takeover of the convention in these past 12 years — the crass, secular, political methodology — does have satanic, evil qualities [to] which I am desperately opposed."

Honeycutt was asked by Michael White, a 1990 graduate of Southern Seminary, if recent charges against him [by trustee Jerry Johnson] had not previously been "laid to rest" by the SBC Peace Committee. Honeycutt said Southern trustees had voted 41-11 in 1986 that there were "no charges worthy of dismissal" represented in the committee's concerns.[17]

The motion for removal of trustee Jerry Johnson was brought back. SBC legal counsel James Guenther noted that the convention's parliamentary material "require that the procedural steps of a notice and a hearing must be met before a trustee can be removed from office. Mr. Johnson has not had legal notice of the charges made against him, nor has he had an opportunity to respond to those charges." Therefore, it would be "out of order to consider" Johnson's removal.

Accepting Guenther's judgment, President Vines said, "If the messenger who made the motion would like to move that the matter be referred to the board of Southern Seminary, the messenger may feel perfectly free to do so."

Messenger Wadsworth made this motion and deferred to President Honeycutt who favored referring the motion to the trustees. The referral was authorized by raised ballots, averting a possible bitter battle for the moment.

The convention recessed for Wednesday afternoon with conservatives having won every vote in the 1990 "Battle of New Orleans." Reporters played catch up on typewriters in the news room. Some messengers went home. Others attended traditional alumni luncheons.

A Southern Seminary class "taking" the convention for credit gathered in the public registration area to hear a lecture by Registration Secretary Lee Porter.

The grandfatherly Porter, a design editor at the Sunday School Board and a former pastor, had previously served as first- and second-vice president of the SBC and as convention parliamentarian. He had never before been reported as speaking publicly on the controversy, though he had rankled conservatives by past suggestions of ballot violations. He had devoted much time to the task of training clerks and overseeing the registration process for many years. When he went to speak to the class, he was clearly upset with the challenge to his re-election and the way the convention had gone.

The class was in an open area where people were coming and going. While Porter was talking, Tammi Ledbetter, Managing Editor of the Indiana Baptist, came to obtain the local address of an Indiana messenger. Ledbetter was waiting at the counter when she heard Porter say, "The man [Mark Coppenger] in charge of Indiana wouldn't mind if Southern [Seminary] closed tomorrow." Porter's reference to Coppenger — Ledbetter's boss — grabbed her attention. She immediately began taking notes. Messenger Alma Ruth Morgan was already there. Morgan, a trustee of the Christian Life Commission and a former administrative secretary to Winfred Moore, heard Porter's stern voice and began taking notes. "Fundamentalists could have controlled everything if they had quit five years ago," they wrote. "They're like Hitler and Khomeni. They just overkill. . . . They have all the answers, but when your daughter has to have an abortion, they don't know how to react — there's no grace, no forgiveness. Make one mistake and you're gone. . . ."

"They want you to agree with every book in the Bible. . . They want indoctrination, not education. Your degree won't be worth a nickel if we do that. We may lose our institutions. They don't care.

"They will kill Southeastern [Seminary]. If they take over Southern . . . you'll finish up where you are and hope you don't get your degree destroyed."

Porter, according to Ledbetter and Morgan's notes, alleged that cheating had taken place in past elections, suggesting that pastors had been among the chief culprits. He intended to personally review every registration card after New Orleans, checking for irregularities. . . . "Pastors are the biggest liars in the world," he reportedly said.[18]

The two women later compared notes. Mrs. Ledbetter talked to her husband, Gary, editor of the Indiana Baptist. They decided to use Porter's remarks in a later series on "how the next generation of Southern Baptist leaders are being educated regarding the denomination."

The Wednesday evening session, with its emphasis on foreign missions and recognition of past SBC presidents, had once been a highlight of conventions. In New Orleans, only a few thousand heard Keith Parks talk about mission opportunities in once atheist countries "beyond anything ever [known] before.... You and I have taken our luxuries and wasted our wealth, not only on ourselves, but on our religious activities," Parks said. "This is God's right time," he declared. "We must not do wrong."[19]

Thursday's crowd dwindled to around five thousand — not enough for a quorum, the parliamentarians said. No business, including several important resolutions reported out by the Resolutions Committee, could be voted on. Only reports and messages could be given.

Throughout the convention a dark cloud had hung over Committee on Nominations chairman Roland Lopez and Emmanuel Baptist Church in McAllen, TX, whose messengers had been disqualified. Thursday morning, Bill Sutton, who pastored in the same association as Lopez, was recognized on a point of personal privilege to lift the cloud.

Sutton noted that before going to McAllen, Lopez had pastored a church in Lubbock, TX that was in "friendly cooperation" with the SBC. It was at this time that he was elected to the Committee on Nominations. "He went to Immanuel," Sutton said, "on November 15, 1989, one month after church letters were to be submitted to our association.... Just prior to the departure of the former pastor, [Immanuel] church started a new mission as a part of Bold Mission Thrust. This less than wealthy congregation determined not to allow this mission to fail while they were leaderless. With this in mind, Emmanuel gave $300 for the next year to the Cooperative Program. ... But it was not recorded in the correct year. During that next year the church operated pastorless and supported their new mission with $15,000. I believe this is a part of Bold Mission Thrust and friendly cooperation."

Sutton asked the messengers to remember that "our uniform church letter is an Anglo English document. While without a pastor, our Hispanic brethren were trying to deal with a document that was not of their culture. Please, let's not make them live up to all of our expectations. The Rio Grande Association unanimously commended [Roland] Lopez for his work and the loyal commitment that he had made." Sutton then asked that "this assembly ... send a message of appreciation and encouragement ... to this Hispanic congregation."

The messengers responded in prolonged applause with many standing. Vines said the letter would be sent.

The crowd was even thinner for the final message, a stirring evangelistic sermon in which Evangelist Jay Strack talked about caring for lost souls. "What has to happen before we wake up to eternity? What will make us care about those who die without Jesus? Must they cry out in despair, 'No man cared for my soul' "?[20]

President Vines announced a final unaudited registration of 38,478 messengers. Messenger Steve Hensley led in prayer. The few remaining trickled out.

So ended the 12th straight convention victory in the conservative resurgence. But the struggle was far from over.

References

1 Terri Lackey: "National Prayer Conference," Baptist Press, June, 1990.

2 "Parks Clears Air Among Trustees," The Christian Index, June 28, 1990, p. 5.

3 The HMB coordinated the pre-convention evangelistic effort in 1989 in Las Vegas and was preparing to do so again when LBC staff asked to take the lead. A story circulated that the LBC promoted the project lightly to lower the incentive for conservatives to come to New Orleans for the convention. The story was false and I regret repeating it in a letter.

4 From my notes at the Hispanic rally.

5 Kathy Palen: "Sons and Daughters Rally," Baptist Press, June 1991.

6 Bob Terry: "Chapman: 'Perpetuate Conservative Resurgence,' " Word & Way, Convention Preview, June, 1991.

7 "Vestal: SBC Needs Inclusive President," op. cit.

8 From a tape of the RNA meeting with Vestal.

9 Jim Lowry and Tim Nicholas: "Pastors' Conference Wrapup," Southern Baptist Convention News, June 11, 1990.

10 Art Toalston: "SBC Forum Wrapup," Southern Baptist Convention News, June 11, 1990.

11 Alma Ruth Morgan, a trustee of the Christian Life Commission, shared this conversation with me.

12 Quoted from the letter from President Bush.

13 Unless otherwise indicated, information and quotations from speakers during the business sessions are from my written notes and tape recordings and official minutes of the convention.

14 From my tape and Ken Camp: "President's Address," Southern Baptist Convention News, June, 1991.

15 Interviews with Draper and Miller after the announcement.

16 Kathy Palen: "Motions Tuesday Afternoon," Southern Baptist Convention News, June 12-14, 1990.

17 Robert O'Brien: "Dilday, Honeycutt Respond to Questions of Politics," The Christian Index, June 28, 1990, p. 7.

18 From Ledbetter and Morgan's notes.

19 Mark Wingfield: "Foreign Mission Board Report," Southern Baptist Convention News, June 12-14, 1990.

20 From a printed copy of Strack's sermon.

Chapter 12

"The Firings at Baptist Press"

The media left no doubt about the outcome of New Orleans. "Holy War Ends," declared Time. "The Southern Baptists Choose a Fundamentalist Future." Time quoted moderate Jack Harwell, "We're fixing to enter the darkest period in our history," and Morris Chapman, "[The Bible battle has been settled once and for all and the SBC] will become an explosive force for Christ around the world."[1]

State denominational editors agreed that conservatives were firmly in the saddle:

Bill Webb of Illinois: "Ballot tallies — and an applause meter would substantiate — that conservative leaders remain in control of the convention."[2]

Bob Terry of Missouri: "The overwhelming victory of Morris Chapman . . . effectively ended the confrontive politics of the past 12 years."[3]

Julian Pentecost of Virginia: "The 1990 annual convention . . . will have the dubious distinction of being known as the occasion fundamental-conservatives drove the final nails in the coffin of the SBC as it historically has been known, loved and supported."[4]

The two biggies in the New Orleans voting victories were the shift of funds from the BJCPA to the CLC and the election of Morris Chapman.

Dunn and Land Speak About The Future

Before New Orleans, James Dunn had vigorously campaigned to prevent the transfer of funds from his agency to the BJC, saying, it would be "impossible [for the CLC] to be a watchdog [on church-state matters] and an advocate [of social issues] at the same time." The CLC's Richard Land had responded, "Dr. Dunn's views represent one perspective on the issue of the Christian Life Commission's program assignment. Others would see . . . [the CLC's] proposed expanded program assignment as a preferable alternative."[5]

After his jarring defeat, Dunn said the BJCPA would "continue in the tradition of [John] Leland and [George] Truett who would not compromise on religious liberty. Everything has changed; those who now mouth things about accommodation want to take a little tax money. We haven't changed and we're sticking by that [no compromise] agenda."

Dunn wasn't worried about financial support. "Messages . . . are coming from Texas, Kentucky, Tennessee, North Carolina, South Carolina and Georgia [that] they intend to support us most significantly. . . . Those who genuinely believe in Baptist heritage will support us."[6] Land spoke in a conciliatory tone. "Before [New Orleans] we could not address the religious liberty and church/state separation issues. Now we can and this frees us to work more closely with the Baptist Joint Committee on joint statements."

The CLC, Land said in a press conference, would add three new staff members in Washington and more office space. The CLC would support SBC-adopted resolutions on abortion and prayer in public schools. However, he expected that the Supreme Court's upholding of the free access clause for student religious organization in schools would result in lessened concern for public school prayer.[7]

Views of Chapman and Vestal

Morris Chapman and Daniel Vestal gave their perspectives on the future. Chapman spoke as an "optimist" to a crowded press conference after the announcement that he had been elected president.

"It is a great honor . . . and awesome responsibility, particularly in these days . . . to be president . . . I do pray for God's wisdom and courage that I might be the man of God who will lead us to more peaceful and harmonious days. We have a great convention and I believe that we are on the threshold of our greatest days ever in missions and evangelism. For these last several months I have stated over and over that once the issue is settled on the nature and authority of God's word, that Southern Baptists will become the most explosive force for Christ in all the world. . . . We have some very wonderful days before us.

"My heart's desire is to enhance the cooperative spirit among Southern Baptists by standing steadfastly for Biblical truth. . . . Our compassion must reach out and touch all the peoples of the world, including our own Southern Baptist brethren.

"For 12 consecutive years, Southern Baptists have been sending a signal to the leadership of our agencies and institutions that . . . we must come home to the faith of our fathers. Southern Baptists are a people of the Book and our belief in the inspired, infallible, inerrant Word of God must be perpetuated through the institutional life of our beloved Convention. For peace and harmony, . . . elected officials and paid personnel of the denomination must gain a better understanding of each other. . . . I look forward to meeting individually with all presidents of our agencies and institutions. . . . to listen to their heartbeat and for them to hear mine."

After his statement came the usual flurry of questions.

Q. "How do you interpret the largest winning percentage [for election of president] in many years?"

A. "I believe it is the establishment of a trend which could be interpreted as the heartbeat of rank and file Southern Baptists. . . . All of us are weary [of] struggling against one another. Our heartbeat is to be a witness to the world for the Lord Jesus Christ and it is my heart's desire . . . to depoliticize this convention."

Q. "Do you think there needs to be a more specific statement, like the Peace Committee report, on the Bible?"

A. ". . . The Peace Committee report was adopted overwhelmingly by the SBC. . . It is a Convention statement more than a committee statement. The Peace Committee has done a great favor to all Southern Baptists in helping to describe [the] infallibility and inerrancy of God's Word. Second, they asked us to move beyond perceived political parameters."

Q. "There's been a lot of talk about widening the umbrella. Will you . . . appoint such people as [moderates] Ray Allen or Jim Slatton from Virginia?"

A. "My commitment [is to] appoint those persons who believe in the perpetuation of an allegiance to the perfect Word of God and those who believe within the parameters of the Peace Committee report."

Q. "How will you reach out to the 40 percent who didn't vote for you?"

A. "I do not feel that we're really facing a matter of encompassing 40 or 60 percent; our potential is to encompass at least 90 percent of all Southern Baptists. I do believe that as we move forward in this process, we will find that there are many denominational employees who do believe in the infallibility and inerrancy of God's Word."[8]

The next morning, Vestal received three standing ovations when he spoke to about 700 persons attending a Baptists Committed breakfast. He could not explain the unexpected wide margin. The election, he said, was not about believing the Bible as the infallible Word of God, but "about the future — whether we will be a united convention that recaptures a vision for cooperative missions, evangelism, . . . the priesthood of all believers, congregational polity, religious liberty and separation of church and state. That vision failed," but we did "what is right."

Vestal asked for:

— Baptists Committed to set up a forum where invited participants could hold formal dialogue on the future of the SBC.

— Those who voted for him to practice Christian charity and focus attention on a sovereign God and the leadership of the Holy Spirit.

— Those who voted for Chapman "to accept the rest of us as brothers and sisters and stop accusing us and implying we do not believe the Bible just because we don't agree on interpretation of Scripture or support your political movement."

— All Southern Baptists "to let the love of Jesus Christ fill our hearts so that it overflows to other people."

— Chapman and the other presidents of the SBC for the past 12 years to "broaden the tent of involvement in the SBC" as they have suggested publicly.

— John Bisagno, Joel Gregory, Jim Henry, Charles Fuller and others to live up to their pre-convention promise "of a historic new day" in the SBC.

— Trustees of SBC agencies to affirm, trust and support denominational executives and stop embarrassing publicly "these good and godly men."

The key question now, Vestal said, is "where do we go from here?" He offered five scenarios for the future: (1) The present leadership could . . . bring Southern Baptists back together by balancing appointments to committees and boards. (2) The leadership could maintain "its present rigid posture" and some churches would leave the SBC and affiliate with American Baptist Churches and/or the Southern Baptist Alliance. (3) The SBC could return to a "societal" approach. (4) New organizations might develop to provide continuing educational and political involvement. (5) State conventions might secede or change the way they support national agencies through their Cooperative Program. Vestal did not advocate any of these scenarios, but said he was just echoing ideas he had recently heard.[9]

Views of Hastey and Pressler

Stan Hastey, Executive Director of the Southern Baptist Alliance, told reporters, "Southern Baptists will never be the same." He predicted that "a lot of the energy [will] dissipate in moderate efforts to get out the votes. That doesn't mean there aren't a lot of moderates out there who will not pursue a political solution. That will go on, but clearly there's no room for defection from the moderate movement. Any dropouts [in SBC life will] insure the inevitable that this is a different, a new kind of denomination and that for the foreseeable future there won't be a political solution for moderates, which means that the boards . . . will be totally dominated by" conservatives. "They can then afford to wait [for agency and institutional administrators] to retire on schedule, if they choose to go that way."

Hastey sensed "some sentiment for a new denomination. . . . What I'm hearing from a lot of moderate people is an enormous reticence to give up on the Southern Baptist Convention. . . . But some moderates are beginning to say, 'We need to start talking about new structures.' " The SBA, he said, now "projected opening (the alternative) Richmond [Theological Center] in the fall of '91. . . . We have about $600,000 committed. We need more than that to get off the ground. . . . The majority of trustees will be Alliance people. We'll be joining a consortium with two Presbyterian schools and an American Baptist school."[10]

Some reporters were testy with Paul Pressler. "Why won't you meet and talk with Reynolds, Dilday and others?" one asked.

"I have letters in my file from Russell Dilday, Herb Reynolds and others saying they don't want to meet," Pressler replied. "I'm always willing, within my time schedule, to meet with them — so we can work together in missions and evangelism based upon the fact that the Bible is God's inerrant Word. I will welcome any discussion; the more dialogue, the better off our denomination is."

Another asked, "What is your program?"

"I'm a judge and have lots of other things to do. I just want the Convention to move in the right direction. I serve on the Executive Committee. My second term expires next June. Somebody asked me what I hoped to get out of [the denominational conflict] and I said, I hope to get out of it as quickly as possible. . . . I want missions and evangelism. I have listened to 12 years of Southern Baptists clearly speaking and I recognize that they want our institutions to be taught on the basic conviction that the Bible is truth. That's not talking about interpretations, but on the basic conviction that the Bible is true."[11]

Many moderates continued to see Pressler and Paige Patterson as the arch villains in the conservative movement. Conservatives, of course, held quite the opposite view. One who particularly appreciated them was "Cactus" Cagle, an attorney in South Texas.

The Cafe du Monde

Cagle had read a recent story about the SBC controversy in the Wall Street Journal where writer Gus Niebuhr had asked Patterson: "What do you want out of this?" Patterson replied, "I don't want anything [for myself], Gus. I just want the work to be done." When Niebuhr kept pressing, Patterson, according to his remembrance, laughed and said tongue in cheek, "If they want to do something for me and for Paul, they could put a plaque down at the Cafe du Monde to remember when we met down there [in 1967] and talked about this situation." Niebuhr quoted Patterson as simply saying, "We think they should put a plaque there."[12]

Cactus Cagle read the story and, without telling Pressler and Patterson, had two plaques of appreciation prepared. He printed up invitations for a party at the Cafe du Monde on Wednesday night during the New Orleans convention when the plaques would be presented.

Patterson says he didn't learn about it until he arrived in New Orleans and was handed a copy of the invitation. "At that point," Patterson says, "I knew it was not a good thing to do from the point of view of people understanding it because there would be some down there at the Cafe du Monde who would not be great fans of ours. But what do you do? There were several hundred invitations out, and we couldn't very well refuse to go to a place where somebody was going to say thank you to us."

After the evening convention session, the cafe was filled with around 300 people, including some moderates and other diners. A smiling Paul Pressler walked in and began going about the tables shaking hands. Patterson arrived, then Jerry Vines and chief parliamentarian Barry McCarty whose assignment was to stay with Vines throughout the convention. Someone said, "We need somebody with a loud voice who will call this to order." "I've got a loud voice," McCarty said and stood upon a chair and laughingly called, "Order, order, I call this party to order." Then the plaques were presented and the group sang, "Victory in Jesus."

Several moderates sitting nearby began shouting, "Shame! Shame!" The group kept singing. Afterwards, Kentucky messenger Jay Robison told Pressler that the presentation was inappropriate. Pressler tried to explain that he and Patterson had not even known until arriving in New Orleans that it was going to take place. The next day at the convention Robison asked for a point of personal privilege in which he raised the question of McCarty's involvement at the Cafe du Monde party. Vines ruled that a point of personal privilege had to relate to the body of the convention itself, and the point of order was therefore not relevant.

The Baptist Press story, headlined, "SBC Parliamentarian Participates in Victory Celebration," appeared in a number of Baptist papers and was also cited in The Christian Century by moderate Bill Leonard as a "celebrat[ion] of victory." Leonard also said that the next day when a messenger questioned whether the parliamentarian's activities at Cafe du Monde had compromised his objectivity, the messenger's microphone was abruptly turned off and his point ruled 'not well taken.'[13]

Responding to criticism of McCarty, Indiana editor Gary Ledbetter said, "If McCarty had been serving moderate presidents for the last few years, I don't believe that the coverage of such a meeting and his part in it would have been as extensive or bitter. It is as though, unable to win Southern Baptists over to their viewpoint, moderates will try to nibble to death anyone who even cooperates with the majority. . . . It is nasty because the quarrel is not with [McCarty] but with SBC leaders. . . . The issue is not what but who. McCarty would do his job the same way for Dan Vestal as he will for Morris Chapman. The main difference is that a moderate victory celebration would have probably taken place in a building owned by Southern Baptists."[14]

FBC, Fort Worth Comes "Home"

On Sunday evening after the convention closed in New Orleans, the First Baptist Church of Fort Worth, formerly pastored by J. Frank Norris and called by some the "mother church" of the independent Baptist movement, voted to join the local Tarrant County Association and also resume participation in the Southern Baptist Convention. The pastor, Bill Ramsey, had just returned from attending his first meeting of the Southern Baptist Convention. This came 66 years after the Baptist General Convention of Texas excluded Norris from its fellowship. On Monday, Jimmy Draper accompanied Ramsey to the associational pastors' conference where he was enthusiastically welcomed.

Ramsey emphasized that the church was "burning no bridges with our past, just building some bridges for the future." Ramsey said he began praying about the matter about two years before when he became "excited about the movement" within the SBC "toward its historic moorings." He researched Norris' papers at Southwestern Seminary and found "the issues were essentially the same issues today as they were even then, in as far as inerrancy goes." Ramsey said he also found no record that the church had ever voted to disassociate itself from Southern Baptists. . . . Someone has said Norris left by eviction rather than conviction and I think that is pretty accurate."

Ramsey said he saw "too many good missionaries [in the Baptist Bible Fellowship] not able to reach their respective field for lack of support." In Southern Baptists he saw "evangelistic fervor along with structure. . . . We just didn't fit where we were."[15]

The decision shocked the BBF to which the church had been "loosely connected," the term used by James O. Combs, editor of the Fellowship's Baptist Bible Tribune. Combs said he had implored Ramsey not to make the move, but Ramsey had been wooed by conservative leaders in the SBC.[16]

Lee Roberson, who had led the Highland Park Baptist Church of Chattanooga out of the SBC some 50 years before, noted that other fundamental Baptist churches . . . are becoming weak and fearful," and "are leaving the independent ranks and joining the SBC. . . . In the SBC, they've lifted some good men to top offices. [But] the SBC hasn['t changed one single bit. . . . They have the same school system they've always had."[17]

The success of the conservative resurgency movement continued to draw strong reactions from moderates who went home and gave their churches a different view on the controversy from that of other Southern Baptists. Messengers to New Orleans from FBC, Amarillo, TX, presented a history of the controversy as they saw it. Conservative leaders, they said, were guilty of "character assassination" in accusing some denominational teachers of liberalism. "After thorough investigation, the answer as to whether there is widespread theological liberalism in SBC colleges or seminaries is a resounding 'no.' " The goals of the "takeover movement are more political than theological." The leadership "now shows open support for the goals of the Reconstruction Movement with its plan of taking dominion over America and establishing a theocracy. . . . " [18]

The executive committee of Baptists Committed and leaders of the Southern Baptist Alliance met in Dallas the following weekend, in response to Dan Vestal's call at New Orleans. They voted to call a national meeting of moderates in Atlanta for August 23-25 to (1) draft an alternate funding plan for dividing the Cooperative Program Budget, with "respected" SBC leaders as trustees, (2) formulate a structure for a new fellowship to give continuing leadership to the movement, (3) plan for a national convocation in the spring, to recommend ongoing budgets and programs and structures beyond 1991. The meeting place was to be the Sheraton Atlanta Airport Hotel, not a large facility because only a few hundred were expected to attend. The attendance, however, would turn out to be much larger, sparked in part by the Executive Committee's firings of the director and news director of Baptist Press. [19]

The Widening Gulf with Baptist Press

Conservatives had felt for years, with considerable justification, that Baptist Press was biased toward moderates in the convention controversy. Part of the concern lay with BP's connectional relationship with the agencies, which allowed agency public relations people to write "news" for BP. The director of Baptist Press functioned also as director of public relations for the Executive Committee.

W.C. Fields showed his intense partisanship after retiring from BP early in 1987. Fields called the conservative resurgency movement "an evil force" that had arisen "right out of the abyss." [20] Conservatives hoped to elect one of their own to succeed Fields — many preferred David Simpson, editor of the Indiana Baptist, but did not have quite enough votes in the Executive Committee to head off the candidacy of the well-liked Alvin Shackleford, editor of the Tennessee <u>Baptist and Reflector</u> whose nomination was made by EC president Harold Bennett. Bennett was viewed by some conservatives as at best a neutral in the controversy.

Paul Pressler came to the EC meeting when Shackleford would be voted on with a sheaf of photo copies of clippings from the Tennessee paper "to show" an eight-year "pattern of unfairness toward conservatives." A substitute motion to postpone action on Shackleford lost on a 29-29 tie vote. Pressler thought "that [after the tie vote], Bennett would back away so as not to polarize the Executive Committee."[21] Bennett, however, quickly moved for Shackleford's election. Pressler then decided "not to present my evidence, in order to avoid an angry confrontation . . ."[22] Shackleford was then elected by a 32-26 margin and pledged to be "fair, objective and balanced." He asked for "a year of grace to see if I can fulfill your expectations."[23] Pressler pledged to "prayerfully support him and carefully observe him."[24] Adrian Rogers was quoted as saying, "The proof of the pudding is in the eating."[25]

Two years passed during which it was generally agreed that Shackleford was fairer than Fields, though some conservatives remained dissatisfied. Then the TV "documentary" on the SBC controversy by former Southern Baptist Bill Moyers set conservative blood pressure rising. Pressler argued with Moyers over the partisanship of the program. Moyers harshly attacked Pressler in a fax message to Baptist Press and asked to speak to the EC during the 1989 convention in Las Vegas. The EC chairman refused to permit Moyers to appear. Pressler asked Shackleford not to publish Moyers' "attack." Shackleford refused and BP sent Moyers' statement to news media. This incensed many EC members, causing the EC's six officers — chairman, vice chairman, secretary and chairs of the three sub-committees — to request of Shackleford that BP be more fair in the future. In the mind of some, they had put Shackleford on notice.

The following year, Shackleford and BP news editor Dan Martin, who had served seven years under Fields, delayed reporting the announcement by Joel Gregory and other conservative "centrist" pastors that they would vote for the conservative candidate in New Orleans, while giving quick and prominent play to David Montoya's dissent from the Committee on Nominations Report.

Another incident centered on Southern Seminary's severance of its extension relationship with the State Convention of Baptists in Indiana a few weeks before New Orleans. An article from the editor of the Indiana Baptist, with quotations from the Indiana extension director and the Indiana Convention's executive committee, was declined by BP news director Dan Martin in favor of a report on the happening by Southern Seminary writer Pat Cole. Martin, according to the Indiana Baptist, said, in using the seminary p.r. man, that BP was deferring to the "way we've always done it."[26]

Plans for Dismissals

Martin was already feeling pressure. According to Sam Pace, the new chairman of the EC, Martin, two weeks before the New Orleans convention, "specifically by telephone and in person" asked for an appraisal of his work and his prospects for continued employment. Pace says he said to Martin, "Dan, if you tell me in New Orleans that you want to resign, I'm going to accommodate you."[27] Pace also recalls that in 1987, Shackleford had asked for "a year to prove he would be fair, equitable and balanced with Baptist Press." Pace was quoted as saying that during the three years since, the "vast majority" of the EC had come to perceive that "the very opposite has proved to be true."[28]

In the press room at New Orleans, Martin appeared anxious about his future. A story circulated that the EC's officers had instructed EC executive Harold Bennett on Wednesday, June 13 to dismiss Shackleford and Martin. Pace later said the officers sought to avoid "a very unpleasant confrontation" in the EC that afternoon and decided to allow Bennett to handle the matter "quietly and graciously." Bennett was said to have been "instructed" at three p.m. to tell Shackleford and Martin to either resign or they would be "dealt with harshly." Shackleford said later that Paul Pressler had informed him, " 'We told you what you had to do.' "[29]

Pace said later that neither the EC officers nor Bennett had used the phrase "dealt with harshly. Nor did we or Dr. Bennett use the word 'instructed,' " Pace said.[30]

On Tuesday, June 19, Bennett gave the request, which Shackleford later termed an "ultimatum," from the EC officers for Shackleford and Martin to resign. Instead of responding to the request, Shackleford told Bennett on June 26 that a secular paper had become aware of what was happening and that BP would release a story the next day on the requested resignations. Bennett did not try to stop the story. Shackleford and Martin said in the BP release that the EC officers through Bennett had promised that if they resigned quietly, they would be continued on the payroll through the end of the fiscal year, September 30, but neither were to attend the September 17-19 EC meeting at which their resignations would be announced. Then if they did not find other employment, they would receive "up to six months salary and benefits after September, but only on condition that they did not make an issue of their leaving."

In the BP release Shackleford said the call for their resignation was "an attempt to control the right and responsibility of Baptist church members to know what is happening in their denomination." Baptists, he said, "have the right to know that the officers of the Executive Committee do not trust them with the truth and are seeking to deprive them of their access to a fair, objective and balanced news service."

Martin told the Baptist Standard's Toby Druin that he was not surprised by the officers' action. "I have thought for some time that the new conservative majority would want its own minister of information, . . . and that has come. . . . Now news will be to tell their side of the story and no dissent will be allowed."

Martin said he had promised Paige Patterson and Paul Pressler "the first week I was here" that "I will be as fair as I possibly can. . . . I am not ashamed [of my performance since]."[31]

Chairman Pace broke the silence of the EC's officers. Pace said in a statement sent through BP that the officers had thought "the denomination would be better served by handling this quietly and graciously."[32] As to the role of Paul Pressler, Pace said, "Paul is a very influential person, but he does not believe in this anymore than the other five of us [officers]. We mutually agreed on a course of action." Pace predicted, "You're going to read that all this came out because of the strong vote for Morris Chapman in New Orleans. This is not true. This was in the mill before we ever got to New Orleans. We had meetings with Al. We corresponded with him. Our biggest concern with Al and Dan was balance. It is our view that what we were doing was valid and fair and Christian. We just came to the place where this termination was inevitable." Asked about the delay in reporting on the statements by Joel Gregory and others, Pace said, "That's just one illustration of the unfairness — the downplay of Joel Gregory and the upplay of David Montoya."[33]

State Editors Respond

Most state editors took the side of Shackleford and Martin. Presnall Wood of Texas said the call for the resignations was "a clear case of an attempt to suppress a free press. . . It is a case of shooting the messenger for bringing the news."[34] Virginia's Julian Pentecost called the officers' requests "galling" and "brazen" and said Pressler had consistently sought to "intimidate" BP.[35]

Reacting swiftly, the Southern Baptist Press Association met July 6-7 in Irving, Texas and with only one dissenting vote passed a resolution praising BP for 44 years of "professional service," commending Shackleford and Martin for "excellence," expressing "grave concern with publicly announced plans to remove" them from office and calling upon the EC to provide the two "an open forum for a discussion of any and all charges against them."

Tammi Ledbetter of Indiana, the lone dissenter, could "endorse much in this statement," but could not "in good conscience affirm" everything. The resolution, she said in the Indiana Baptist, "fail[ed] to acknowledge any . . . failures" in BP reporting on the denomination.[36]

Coppenger's Analysis

The same issue of the Indiana Baptist carried a lengthy analysis of the Baptist Press system by Mark Coppenger, Executive Director of the State Convention of Baptists in Indiana. Coppenger offered "$100 to the first person who can convincingly demonstrate that even 10 percent of the 80 [editors, associate editors, etc. in the BP state paper system] favored the election of Morris Chapman in New Orleans. On the other hand, I would not dare offer $100 to one who could demonstrate that dozens of these editors and writers favored Dan Vestal's candidacy. I don't have money to burn."

Coppenger saw "an overwhelming weight of perspective that rules our denominational press. Some of the editors are aggressive and outspoken in their disdain for the conservative resurgence. Most of the others would not lift a hand to challenge their interpretation of affairs. So what you have is a pretty cozy network" with "a shared conviction that affects the choice of stories, assignment of interviews, length and frequency of quotation, spin of headlines, publicity of gaffes and foibles and typification of personalities as, say, victim or villain, sage or fool."

Coppenger cited as an example the refusal of a new Southeastern Seminary professor, James Cogdill, to sign a statement by Southeastern faculty of support for the "embattled faculty" at Southern Seminary and critical of Southern trustees. Cogdill, Coppenger noted, was then finishing his Ph.D. at Southern. After Cogdill declined to sign the statement, 18 Southern professors abstained from approving his degree. "The abstention of those 18 stood as unpleasant but revelatory behavior for Baptist Press to report," Coppenger said. "There was, though, no report. Would there have been coverage had conservatives moved to deny an earned Ph. D. to one who would not sign their petition? We would have seen apoplexy in print."

Coppenger noted that near the same time, BP ran a story from Southern on Grady Cothen's commencement sermon, castigating SBC conservative actions as "fear and intimidation masquerading as orthodoxy, . . . intellectual violence rooted in religious arrogance and intemperance" and conservatives as a "handful of self-appointed guardians of the faith."

"How does such venomous talk get into print while the Cogdill fiasco doesn't?" Coppenger asked. "It's simple. The public relations office at Southern prefers Cothen's perspective to Cogdill's. So their writer, Pat Cole, serves up a generous helping of Cothen while avoiding the embarrassing Cogdill story. A compliant Baptist Press hurries Cothen's remarks on down the line to a number of equally compliant state editors. And before you know it, 400,000 Southern Baptist households, who'll probably never hear of Jim Cogdill, will be coached to despise conservatives."

Coppenger "urge[d] those state editors who cry for a 'free' Baptist Press to begin at home by publishing . . . stories on the personal failings of your own [state] Board members. . . . Why are you demanding of the SBC Executive Committee what you do not demand of your own state executive boards?"[37]

The Vote to Fire

The EC officers called a special meeting of the Executive Committee for July 17 to consider the BP Situation. Chairman Pace and former EC chairman Charles Sullivan then contacted Shackleford and Martin a second time and offered the same severance package as proposed earlier, adding that if they resigned, the called meeting would not take place. Both declined the request. Shackleford said by resigning he would be turning his "back" on the conviction . . . that God had clearly revealed to him [in 1987] that he should accept the position with Baptist Press. Shackleford said he had wanted to sit down and discuss the "whole issue" with "honorable men of good will and common sense," but "rather than discussion and dialogue, I have a demand to leave."[38]

Stories spread that as many as 1,000 persons might be coming to Nashville to protest the expected firings. According to Sam Pace, the EC officers feared that the crowd would exceed the legal building occupancy limits established by the fire marshall's office. They hired off-duty policemen, instructing them "to request politely that only Executive Committee members enter" the meeting room and "to help evacuate the building should any emergency situation occur. They were told that under no circumstances were they authorized to use force. The men were not carrying weapons because of any request of the Executive Committee, but were armed in accordance with police department policy." Pace cited EC policy, adopted in 1985, for meeting in closed session to handle "personnel matters which could not be handled wisely in open session."[39]

On the morning of July 17th, committee members threaded their way through a crowd of about 200, which included a large number of secular journalists and denominational media. The visitors remained for the next three hours at the request of Attorney Frank Ingraham, a former member of the EC, who said he was there as a friend of Shackleford and Martin. Shackleford and Martin had been invited to speak for five minutes to the administrative subcommittee which met before the full EC. Both gave a two-sentence response in declining: "As journalists who are committed to openness, we cannot in good conscience participate in your closed executive session. As employees, we submit to you our written statements to do with as you please."[40]

Shackleford told reporters the issue was "the control of the right and responsibility of Baptist church members to know what is going on in the denomination." Martin said his goal had been to provide for Southern Baptists "the most free, the most accurate and most balanced news possible. . . . I wanted a BP that was fair to all."[41]

When the three-hour session ended, the EC members solemnly filed out. None talked to the press. Ernest Mosley, Executive Vice President of the EC, distributed a brief statement: The committee had voted 45 to 15, with one abstention, to terminate the employment of Shackleford and Martin. The meeting had been held in private "to preserve" the EC's "privilege of conducting a full and free debate on personnel matters without fear of causing our employees a legal injury."[42]

Chairman Pace later described the proceedings as "respectful" with no strident rhetoric. . . . It was a time when all Executive Committee members could freely and carefully weigh information in an effort to know the truth and to lay falsehood to rest. This could not have been done in a public forum. No specific charges were leveled against either man, but the opinion of many was that irreconcilable differences did exist. Accepting the fact that the journalists had been operating in ways consistent with their own consciences, to [have required them to] do otherwise would have been unconscionable. By the same token, the majority of the Executive Committee members could not continue in good conscience to operate Baptist Press as it was. To do so was unconscionable to them. . ."

Pace said the existing secretarial staff would continue to operate the national office of BP. Ernest Mosely would work with the remaining BP staff and the five bureau offices in Atlanta, Nashville, Dallas, Richmond and Washington."[43]

Pace and other EC members mentioned no names to fill the positions from which Shackleford and Martin had been removed. Pace said the EC was thinking of taking a bold step which many professional journalists had urged for years. "We think we ought to separate public relations from Baptist Press: have a vice president for public relations and a vice president for Baptist Press. The p.r. man would help the whole denomination. The Baptist Press man would see that the news is reported fairly."[44]

Attorney Ingraham, Shackleford and Martin held a news conference following the end of the closed meeting. Ingraham called the concern of the EC to protect Shackleford and Martin's reputation as "a false guise, . . . a farce." Both of the fired employees reiterated previous defenses. Asked how the controversy might be related to the firings, Shackleford said, "One can assume that this is another step in which permission to be diverse has been denied."

Many state editors spoke their dismay. New Mexico's J.B. Fowler called the firings "a great injustice," and said the EC should apologize to Roger Williams and other pioneers in religious and press freedoms. Mississippi editor Don McGregor called the action "the final destruction of freedom of the press amongst Baptists."[45]

The secular press took up the cry. Some ran editorials. The newspaper in Rome, GA, where Jerry Vines once pastored, said, "It is regrettable that Southern Baptists now must travel through the long night that always accompanies a loss of journalism. It is an event that serves only the power of darkness and not the power of light."[46]

Less than a month after the firings, several state editors and other interested persons met in Nashville to set up a new "Associated Baptist Press." State editors had talked about such a move in the past, in the event of a "takeover" of Baptist Press.[47]

A New Press Service

Bob Terry, editor of Missouri's Word & Way, presided at the ABP organizational meeting until officers were chosen. Terry said the new ABP should not be identified as a "moderate Baptist" news agency, but as an uncensored source of information for Southern Baptists. Charles L. Overby, president of the Gannett Foundation and a former Pulitzer Prize winning newspaper editor, was elected "chairperson." Two state editors — Puckett of North Carolina and McGregor of Mississippi — were elected to the board. Pentecost of Virginia was named treasurer. Al Shackleford was also elected to the 15-member board which included a number of prominent SBC moderates.[48] Though it was not official, a story spread that Dan Martin would become news editor for the new press service.

Fallout From The Firings

Moderates made the Shackleford-Martin firings a cause celebre. The Executive Committee was painted as the enemy of a free press. Paul Pressler became again the chief villain, even though he was in Europe with his family when the called meeting was held.[49] The EC, among other things, was lambasted for using "armed guards" to keep concerned Southern Baptists out of the July meeting and for wasting $50,000 for the called meeting. The actual cost of the meeting, according to Ernest Mosley, was $23,992.97 for travel, lodging, meals, telephone calls and security, plus $600 for the off-duty policemen hired to keep order.[50]

Martin and Shackleford now became martyrs in the moderate camp. Martin told the North Carolina chapter of the Southern Baptist Alliance that he would "never work again for a Southern

Baptist Convention agency. . . . As far as you and I are concerned, the Southern Baptist Convention as we have known it is dead. . . . We're not talking the same language. . . . We don't mean the same things by . . . First Amendment, women in ministry."[51]

Terry Davis, the Maryland/Delaware member of the EC, resigned in protest over the firings. "The situation is such that I don't want to be part of the Executive Committee any longer," he said. "I believe Al and Dan are only the first two. There are going to be many more [terminations in Southern Baptist agencies]", he predicted.[52]

By and large, SBC conservative leaders tended to support the firings as painful but necessary. EC member Eldridge Miller of Oklahoma said, "It had to happen." Miller said he and Shackleford were "personal friends" with family members in the same church. "I called Al up and talked to him a half hour before the meeting. The situation was basically a matter of how Al and Dan perceived what was going on [in the SBC]."

Home Mission Board president Larry Lewis saw the firings as "a mistake, coming at a time when the convention desperately needed reconciliation. Many people came away from New Orleans totally frustrated and defeated. Some magnanimous gesture at this point would have been a very healing ministry. Instead we learned that right on the heels of New Orleans, these two journalists had been terminated. The timing was very bad." Lewis, however, was "not sure that [Shackleford and Martin] really had [taken] an objective stance in reporting the conservative resurgency throughout the decade. I'm very sure they made a bad mistake in not reporting [right away] the support of Joel Gregory for Morris Chapman."

Lewis said he could not support the new Associated Baptist Press. "I would have to have board action before I would authorize [use of ABP] by the Home Mission Board. I would be inclined to think my board would not allow it. I think that would be true of most of the agencies. Our agencies pay newspeople who lend their services to Baptist Press. This is a good investment. We get our news releases published. But I'm not at all sure that the agency boards would want to pay people [to write for ABP]."[53]

With the Shackleford-Martin firings coming in mid-July, all agreed on one result: The incident fired up moderates for the planned August 11, 12 meeting in Atlanta. Before the firings, only a few hundred, at most, were expected. The event would draw over 2,000 and would be marked by some as the beginning of a schism within the denomination.

References

1 *Time*, June 25, 1990, p. 52.

2 Illinois Baptist, June 20, 1990, p. 2.

3 Word & Way, June 21, 1990, p. 2.

4 Religious Herald, June 21, 1990, p. 6.

5 Scott Collins: "Dunn Evaluates Expanded CLC Job," Indiana Baptist, May 8, 1990, p. 9.

6 From a tape of Dunn's press conference at New Orleans after the vote.

7 Jim Newton: "Land Outlines Plans for CLC Expansion," Christian Index, June 28, 1990, pp. 1, 4.

8 From my tape of the press conference.

9 Jim Newton, Southern Baptist Convention News, June, 1990.

10 From my tape of Hastey's remarks.

11 From my tape of Pressler's remarks.

12 R. Gustav Niebuhr: "House Divided," April 25, 1990, pp. 1, 10.

13 "SBC Fundamentalists Enforce Their Rule, June 27-July 4, 1990, pp. 620, 621.

14 "Murder in the Baggage Train," Indiana Baptist, July 17, 1990, p. 2.

15 Earl Fredericks: "Interview With Dr. Bill Ramsey," Southern Baptist Communicator, November-December, 1990, p. 6.

16 Toby Druin: "FBC, Fort Worth, Votes to Return to SBC Fold," Baptist Standard, June 27, 1990, pp. 3, 4.

17 Lee Elder: "Independent Baptist Fundamentalists Lament Loss of Norris Church," SBC Today, November 16, 1990, p. 3.

18 The First Baptist Reporter, July 6, 1990.

19 "Moderate-Conservatives Announce Plans for Convocation in Atlanta," Religious Herald, July 26, 1990, p. 2.

20 Biblical Recorder, May 2, 1987.

21 Telephone interview with Pressler, March, 1987.

22 Telephone interview with Pressler, May, 1987.

23 "Fight Erupts Over [BP] Head," SBC Today, March, 1987, pp. 1, 2.

24 Personal Interview with Pressler, Houston, February, 1987.

25 "Fight Erupts over [BP] Head," op. cit.

26 Tammi Ledbetter: "Objectivity of Baptist News Service Tied to Network of Reporters," Indiana Baptist, March 26, 1991, p. 8.

27 Telephone interview, July, 1990.

28 Toby Druin: "Baptist Press Director, News Editor Ordered ...," Baptist Standard, July 4, 1990, p. 4.

29 Druin, op. cit. I was also in the press room and heard that Bennett had been instructed to proceed with the dismissals.

30 Telephone interview, July, 1990.

31 The most complete report on the request for the resignations and Shackleford and Martin's response was written by Toby Druin for the

July 4th Baptist Standard. Other state papers gave the BP story wide play.

32 Associated Press: "Fundamentalists Now Restricting Baptist Press," Hannibal Courier-Post, July 7, 1990, p. 14.

33 Telephone Interview, July, 1990.

34 "Baptists Deserve a Free Baptist Press Service, July 4, 1990, p. 6.

35 " 'Freedom of the Press' But Not Baptist Press," Religious Herald, July 5, 1990, p. 4.

36 "Indiana Editor Witholds Support of SBPA Resolution," p. 17, July 17, 1990.

37 "Tinkers to Evers to Chance," Indiana Baptist, July 17, 1990, pp. 16, 17.

38 Lonnie Wilkey: "BP Staffers Decline Reconsideration," Biblical Recorder, July 21, 1990, pp. 1, 10.

39 Sam Pace: "News Release," July 24, 1990.

40 Tammi Ledbetter: "Shackleford, Martin Fired by Executive Committee," Indiana Baptist, July 31, 1990, pp. 1, 9.

41 "Baptist Press Leaders Issue Final Statements," op. cit. p. 10.

42 "Shackleford, Martin Fired by Executive Committee, op. cit.

43 Tammi Ledbetter: "Pace Responds to Executive Committee Criticism of Termination Proceedings," Indiana Baptist, July 31, 1990, p. 11.

44 Telephone Interview, July, 1990.

45 "Shackleford, Martin Fired by Executive Committee," op. cit.

46 Editorial: "No Faith in the News," Rome News-Tribune, Rome, GA, August 14, 1990, p. 4.

47 Jack Harwell told me this when he was editor of the Georgia Christian Index.

48 "News Agency Divides Baptists," St. Louis Post-Dispatch, September 15, 1990, p. 6D. The report of the organization of the ABP ran in all state papers. Most mentioned all of the principals. However, the Missouri Word & Way did not note that its editor had presided over the proceedings.

49 Pressler says he bought his tickets in February and left July 9, remaining in Europe for seven and one half weeks.

50 Reported in Baptist Standard, November 14, 1990, p. 2.

51 Post Dispatch, September 15, 1990.

52 Bob Allen: "Maryland/Delaware Member Resigns from SBC Executive Committee," Indiana Baptist, July 31, 1990, p. 11.

53 Personal Interview, Nashville, September, 1990.

Chapter 13

"The Cooperative Program in Peril"

Many moderates gave up on the SBC political process after losing in New Orleans. The Baptist Press firings turned frustration to anger. The announcement in mid-August that the Sunday School Board was stopping the publication of Professor Leon McBeth's history of the Board further inflamed passions and roused louder cries of censorship.

Tough Times for Moderates

Denominational moderates had simply been voted out of board leadership. Forty-two percent of the presidential vote didn't mean, according to SBC bylaws, forty percent of the appointments. It was that way before 1979 when moderates controlled the Convention. They loved it then and kept conservative activists off boards. They hated the bylaws now that the conservatives had the vote. The elected president appointed every last member on the Committee on Committees, which from 1979 on meant people who would propose a Committee on Nominations that would look for change-minded trustees. In 1990, there were still many moderates with important denominational jobs, but resignations and retirements had brought many conservatives into key offices.

Churches were autonomous, but many moderate pastors were no longer immediate choices for writing and speaking assignments once taken for granted. Cecil Sherman, for example, lamented, "Once I wrote for the Sunday School Board. Not anymore. I've opposed these people. Once I traveled here and there speaking [to denominational assemblies]. Not anymore. . . . I have opposed the wrong people."

Sherman, pastor of the Broadway Baptist Church near Southwestern Seminary, said he had talked with seminarian church members who had been turned down for jobs "simply because of their association with a 'liberal church like Broadway.'" Sherman blamed all this on the loss of freedom, even though conservatives had suffered restrictions in the "golden days" — to use W.C. Fields' term — when moderates were the "beautiful" people in the halls of influence and power.[1]

It was not that moderates hadn't been thinking about their future. The SBA was moving full steam ahead on plans to open the new Richmond seminary. Wake Forest University's planned divinity school had received pledges by June 30, 1990 of more than $1.1 million. Baylor University was also laying plans for an "alternate" seminary, if needed. "Baptist Houses of Study" were being considered by Duke and Emory universities. If conservative boards changed the seminaries too much, there would be more accommodating places for moderate ministers to train.

Mercer University Press was publishing theological books. The cover of the fall/winter catalog carried, of all things, a quotation from the Muslim Koran in large type. Score one for greater theological diversity![2] Another alternative publisher, named in honor of two Baptist pioneers for religious liberty, John Smyth and Thomas Helwys, was planning to release its first book, Studies in Acts, by T.C. Smith. The board advisors included Frank Stagg, C.R. Daley, Samuel Balentine, Bill Leonard, Randall Lolley, Mollie Marshall-Green and Cecil Sherman — all luminaries in the moderate camp. SBC Today was already publishing books. The next release, authored by Clayton Sullivan, would, according to Frank Stagg, "demonstrat[e] that the claim of biblical inerrancy does not make sense."[3]

With opportunities to write for denominational publications drying up, moderates — especially those to the left of the Baptist Committed group — were using their literary energies to write for SBC Today, which was publishing "alternate" Sunday School lessons; the liberal Christian Century; the journal of the Baptist Professors of Religion and other publications.

Differences of Opinion

In one notable article, Princeton Seminary professor Alan Neely, a founder of the SBA and its first director, suggested that "since 1879, the year Crawford H. Toy was forced to resign" from the Southern Seminary faculty "because he sought to interpret the Old Testament historically, there has been a conscious conspiracy, acquiesced to by those who know better, to shield Southern Baptists from critical biblical study and to obliterate their historical-critical awareness. The present state of affairs in the [SBC] is, therefore, the inevitable legacy of a century of self-imposed obscurantism."

As an example of "obscurantism," Neely cited a "Lottie Moon" foreign missions editorial by editor Presnall Wood in the Baptist Standard. Wood — by no means a fan of Pressler and Patterson — asked, among other things: "Are those who have never heard the gospel of Jesus Christ lost and doomed to hell? Yes! They are lost."[4]

Neely sent Wood's editorial to 30 Southern Baptist professors of religion and theology, asking two questions. To the first, "Does Presnall Wood's view generally represent your own perspective?" Six answered "yes," 13 "no" and three were ambivalent. To the second, "Do you sense that [Wood's] is the predominant view of Baptists you know?" 14 replied "yes," two "no" and six were unsure.

Neely said, "This may be Presnall Wood's theology. It may be the theology of most Southern Baptists. But it is not my theology and the reason is that it reflects arrogance, ignorance and superficiality; arrogance about his own theological understanding, ignorance of the principles of sound exegesis of the New Testament and superficiality in regard to the nature of God and the nature of salvation."[5]

Planning for Atlanta

Baptists Committed almost certainly included more "moderates" who agreed with Presnall Wood than with Alan Neely and others in the SBA. Yet Baptists Committed was committed to inclusiveness. So Dan Vestal, Jimmy Allen and others with Baptists Committed met with SBA members and the staff of SBC Today to plan the "Consultation of Concerned Baptists," scheduled for August 23-25 at a hotel in Atlanta, although Baptists Committed were listed as conveners of the meeting. Vestal said he called the meeting because "many of us have lost confidence in the decision-making process of the SBC, but we still believe in the causes and institutions of the denomination." The consultation, he said, would be an open forum of discussion at which proposals would be made for alternative funding mechanisms for denominational giving, an "interim budget for division of these gifts," a new leadership structure and an executive committee for future plans and structures."[6] Plain and simple, they were planning their own version of the Cooperative Program.

With registrations climbing, following the Baptist Press firings, the planners moved the meeting from the hotel to the Inforum in Atlanta's Technology Exposition Center. The venerable Duke McCall, one of several retired agency heads identified with Baptists Committed, "dream[ed] of a way for 'moderate' Southern Baptists to keep on working together in a way which will send our CP gifts from state conventions "through Atlanta instead of Nashville," with "SBC agencies like the Foreign Mission Board and other causes such as the Baptist Joint Committee . . . supported by cooperating 'moderates.' . . . Let us 'moderates' stay together in our Christian witness," in the SBC "if conscience permits — and the majority allows."[7] This was nothing less than an alternative Executive Committee, not elected by the SBC.

Talk of alternate funding mechanisms set alarm bells ringing. Denominational papers in July and August were filled with statements of concern about the future of the Cooperative Program and even the denomination.

Concern for the COoperative Program

Denominational "statesman" Herschel Hobbs, who called himself "an old-time Southern Baptist" who "has never been on either side," defended the CP as "revealed" by divine guidance. "It has spent over 65 years in reaching its present potential. We could destroy it in a day! . . . We need no new agency through which to channel our missionary giving. We need to use the one we have and which has served kingdom causes so well."[8]

"Now is the time," pleaded Morris Chapman, "to enhance our cooperative spirit through substantial participation in the Cooperative Program. We must be certain that we do not damage our world mission effort. . . . I caution churches against choosing to bypass certain national agencies and seminaries and likewise caution state conventions against choosing to selectively designate funds on a national level. Such action could lead local churches to decide to support the national organizations to the exclusion of state organizations."[9]

Many state editors joined in the plea. Presnall Wood, speaking to both moderates and conservatives, called for careful consideration before changing the CP. Wood quoted Paige Patterson as saying that if losses are felt in the national convention budget, then some churches "would be forced to give around the state conventions."[10]

Georgia's Albert Mohler was equally concerned. "The Cooperative Program has shaped the SBC to such an extent that a substantial change in the CP will also be a change in the shape of the denomination."[11]

Jess Moody, a well-known unaligned conservative pastor, cited "research which indicated that the SBC was following a 20-step process toward denominational division." Moody called for the Atlanta meeting to become "a repentance, confession and prayer time on the part of moderates. The Fundamentalists must — right now," he said, "reciprocate in kind."[12]

The Atlanta "Consultation"

Publicists claim 3,000 attended the rally. Ron Wilson, a conservative onlooker, says he "counted only 2,300 seats, and they were never all filled at any time.[13] At least one-third, according to Georgia editor Al Mohler were Georgians. Around 300 came from Texas. Far fewer came from other states.

Jimmy Allen, president of Baptists Committed, chaired the meeting. Allen claimed that more than half of the 10 congregations contributing most to SBC programs were represented. Former agency heads present, besides Allen, included Duke McCall, Southern Seminary; Grady Cothen, Sunday School Board; Larry Baker and Foy Valentine, Christian Life Commission; Carolyn Weatherford Crumpler, WMU; and Darold Morgan, Relief & Annunity Board. With many pastors and laity active in the moderate movement, the gathering brought together the leading voices from the coalition of Baptists Committed, the SBA and Women in Ministry.

Besides a large press corps, a number of "observers" came. One was Keith Parks, the only sitting agency head in attendance. However, Parks was not on the program.

The "Consultation of Concerned Baptists" began at one p.m., Thursday, August 23 and ran into Saturday morning. Dan Vestal said in his opening address that "many of us" left New Orleans "crushed in spirit. . . . I saw grown men weep and others act numb and stunned." They "have told us . . . that if you don't believe in [the conservative resurgence] and won't work for it, you have no place among them. . . . I do not believe I have left the [SBC], but rather the [SBC] has left me." Yet "I still believe in much of our . . . . institutions and ministries. . . . I am looking for ways to support [these enterprises] without violating . . . basic foundational truths.

"We're not here to form a new denomination, to plan political strategy, . . . to wish anyone ill or harm. But we are here to explore how we can cooperate for the cause of Christ in ways that do not violate our conscience. . ."[14]

When Randall Lolley, another keynote speaker, talked about "Hardliners," everybody knew who he had in mind in the SBC. "Hardliners were always coming after" Jesus. "Their weapons were always the same: legalism, literalism, chauvinism and intimidation." Hardliners, Lolley said, were strict literalists — "hypocrites, blind guides, snakes, . . . fools," who insisted that the Old Testament Law be observed, even if it meant that people went hungry and remained sick. In seeking to trap Jesus on a legal question, they were "going for the jugular!"

Baylor University President Herbert Reynolds called for a plan that would "preserve the integrity of state conventions while continuing to support worthy SBC causes. We must work closely with our state conventions so long as they are not under the control of the Presslerites," he said.

Interspersed between sermons, workgroups sought to reach a consensus on subjects of concern. These included a new alternative funding mechanism, support for seminaries and theological education, literature for the local church, missions and evangelism, denominational and local church relations, alternatives in ethics and public policy and an alternative information [press] system.

The workgroup on alternative funding gave an "overwhelming positive" reaction to a proposal presented by Grady Cothen. The former Sunday School Board head said a plan should be mission directed, flexible and simple and provide free choices for churches. Churches would remain affiliated with the SBC, with relationships with the Annuity Board maintained. The pastors and churches need to retain a voice in the associations and state conventions and can do so if they remain in the SBC relationship to "protect their own interests" and "insure that their influence be felt and voice be heard in crucial issues. . . "

Fear was expressed that trustees of Southern Seminary "may try to terminate Dr. Honeycutt" and "create new rules/creeds for faculty to sign, so as to make dismissal more likely." Another speaker said, "If we think there is not going to be a wholesale bloodbath at Southern [Seminary], we've got our heads in the sand. It's time for this group to take action."[15]

The seminary study group was not optimistic about Southeastern's future. A student from Midwestern reported "an environment of suspicion in the classroom." A trustee from New Orleans said the faculty there was safe, with harmony existing among trustees. The group saw "great value in our free-standing seminaries, but the development of [alternative] divinity schools and Baptist houses [of study on university campuses] is most hopeful. Given the direction of the [SBC], the latter could well become the mainstay of quality theological education for moderate Southern Baptists."

Participants in another group registered numerous criticisms of Sunday School Board literature. "The quality of the literature has diminished," they agreed. It is "often . . . out of touch with reality." It "emphasizes evangelism too much." The "application is too narrowly defined." Proposals were made to use curriculum by American Baptists, Kerygma Press and David C. Cook, or "produce your own curriculum [with] desktop publishing."

The workgroup on ethics and public policy agreed with Foy Valentine who said "acceptance of some sort of designated giving to enable concerned Baptists to pick up the ball of Christian ethics and run with it is now required."

The workgroup on "information" saw the new Associated Baptist Press as a "viable alternative" to Baptist Press and urged support of ABP and SBC Today.

The workgroup on denominational and local church relationships encouraged "networking," formation of local groups, "town meetings," writing letters to state papers and heads of boards of agencies, sending news releases to secular press, producing videos on the "takeover and new alternatives" and using the Bill Moyers' video, "Battle for the Bible."

The workgroup on accelerating missions and evangelism talked about "a climate of fear" among missionaries and expressed "widespread concern about the future of the Foreign Mission Board and the Home Mission Board and the integrity and openness of the missionary appointment process." It was felt that "global missions" could not "be accomplished adequately through existing structures due, at least in part," to increasing control by "fundamentalist trustees and . . . the growing distrust engendered by the takeover movement."

A New Funding Mechanism

The larger assembly, by an "overwhelming margin," agreed upon two major actions. Three weeks earlier, Duke McCall and 11 other directors had filed articles of incorporation for a "Baptist Cooperative Missions Program" with the Georgia secretary of state. The Consultation voted to accept the new BCMP "funding mechanism" and elected Dan Vestal to develop a permanent "fellowship" organization that many saw as the core of what could become a new denomination. Then they elected a 60-member Steering Committee — compromised of 39 men and 21 women — to oversee the plan. The committee included former agency heads McCall, Cothen, Weatherford Crumpler, Allen and Morgan, along with Winfred Moore, Stan Hastey, Cecil Sherman and other notables.

The BCMP plan would begin receiving mission gifts from churches October 1, 1990. Nineteen trustees would distribute the monies to SBC causes as each church directed, or hold gifts in escrow if a congregation wished. The steering committee would later develop a long-term formula for distributing these and other funds, either to SBC causes or new ventures or both. This formula would then be approved at the next meeting of the Consultation in the spring of 1991.

During the final session, Page Fulgham of Georgia proposed the name, "Cooperative Baptist Fellowship." However Jimmy Allen urged participants to simply refer to themselves as "The Fellowship." This was accepted.

Participants in the new "Fellowship" left in high spirits. "We weren't there to fight," said Gary Parker, pastor of FBC, Jefferson City, MO. "You didn't have to put on a flak-jacket to be there. It was positive and inclusive."[16]

The most common media question during and after the Atlanta meeting was: "Is this the beginning of a new denomination?" Jon Stubblefield of Louisiana, a member of the Steering Committee, thought "the prospects for a new denomination are remote. We [in the SBC] are one people and we can work our way through this and become united again."[17] LaVon Brown of Oklahoma said the possibility of a separate Baptist body would "be determined in the next three to five years. . . . If our group continues to be ignored and told to get out if we don't like the way things go, then you might see something take shape."[18]

"It is not time to leave the SBC," Cecil Sherman cautioned in his church newsletter. "We have too much invested. We have too many friends who are deeply entangled in the mission and education parts of the denomination. But does that mean we have to put our money in the hands of an Executive Committee we do not trust?" Sherman said no.[19]

Fears for the Future

Seedbed for a new denomination or not, there was general agreement across the SBC that the Atlanta meeting marked a critical juncture in the SBC controversy. New Mexico editor J.B. Fowler said, "Although speakers played down the concept that a new convention was being formed, that was exactly what it was." Fowler predicted that "unless a miracle of reconciliation takes place, . . . perhaps in no more than three to five years" the budget of this group "will be so sizable that Cooperative Program work as we have known it for 65 years will sharply decline. . . . In the light of all this," Fowler's "word was the same as it has always been: stay with the Cooperative Program."[20]

Two weeks after the Atlanta Consultation, Jimmy Draper and eight other SBC leaders — Morris Chapman, Adrian Rogers, Charles Fuller, John Bisagno, Joel Gregory, Russell Dilday, Keith Parks and Harold Bennett — met for six hours at the Dallas-Fort Worth airport to discuss a cure for what Draper diagnosed as a "sick" denomination. The nine had known each other for 30 years. Draper, who called the meeting, hailed it as "one of the most fruitful times . . . I have ever seen." No press were invited. Draper said there would "be a time, . . . when and if we are successful" that the group would make public their recommendations."[21]

John Bisagno did not wait for others to speak. Ten days later, on September 17, he proposed his own plan: (1) Let President Chapman appoint an ad hoc committee to recommend mutually satisfying names for the two parties. (2) Let every president and board head of every SBC agency and state Baptist college and university "acknowledge that the truth of the Bible is not negotiable," and "that any discrepancies in Scripture are discrepancies in appearance only." (3) Let "every conservative church" raise its CP giving by at least one percent. (4) Let messengers to state conventions make every effort to depoliticize and defuse controversy in upcoming state conventions. (5) Let Chapman and Vestal join with the Home Mission Board in planning and leading a nationwide solemn assembly "to seek God's power, healing and blessing."[22]

Meanwhile, Back in Nashville

The Executive Committee was then meeting in Nashville and was unaware of Bisagno's challenges which he had mailed to the Baptist Standard. Corridor talk hummed with reports of responses by the churches of some of the leaders in the Atlanta meeting. A straw vote in Dan Vestal's Atlanta church to endorse the program of the new Fellowship, reportedly failed by a 60-40 percent margin. Walnut Street Church in Louisville, pastored by Kenneth Chafin, reportedly said "no" also and even voted to raise their CP giving one-half of a percent.

A Nashville newspaper article described SBC leaders as "reeling" from the threat of the alternate funding plan, although Cooperative Program giving was up over two percent across the Convention. James Jones, an EC member from Kentucky, said, "We're not reeling. We're thanking God for how He's going to bless us." Jones then introduced a resolution which called on "all Southern Baptists to stand together in support of the Cooperative Program," and urged "every local Baptist congregation" to consider prayerfully following the excellent example of "those churches which have recently increased their giving to the Cooperative Program."[23] FMB president Keith Parks cautioned that it would "take more than a resolution" to preserve a strong Cooperative Program. "Leaders in the convention somehow are going to have to restore some trust." The resolution passed unanimously.[24]

The EC changed a bylaw that would permit EC officers to fill the vacancies at Baptist Press and the office of vice president of business and finance. EC president Bennett confirmed what chairman Sam Pace had mentioned earlier. Public relations and Baptist Press would be separated, with a vice president for each area. The EC also requested the BJCPA not to reduce the SBC representation on the 54-member committee from 18 to 11

The EC authorized further study on the qualifications for churches to participate in the annual convention. This was related to the confusion over the qualifications of the messengers from Roland Lopez's Hispanic church whose credentials were questioned at New Orleans. And the committee requested that Southern Seminary's trustees "consider amending the provisions related to the power of that board to remove trustees." This was related to the motion at New Orleans to fire trustee Jerry Johnson. Southern Seminary trustees had previously adopted amendments to its bylaws to provide for the direct election by the SBC of the seminary's board of trustees. In the past, the seminary board had re-elected those elected at the convention.

The EC, which acts between conventions for the SBC, held a three-hour solemn assembly for prayer and confession of sin. "I have had deep resentment against moderates who think we're stupid and can't discern God's will," one member said with voice breaking. "I want to be free of any resentment."[25]

Morris Chapman gave the customary presidential address. "Perhaps we are finding ourselves in a broken state," he said, "so we can realize that God is sovereign and our resources are in Heaven. Our great need is not financial resources, but spiritual resources. It is time to put away bitterness and speak kindly of one another."[26]

Chapman's Plea

At this point Chapman began reading from his prepared manuscript. He called "all present and all Southern Baptists" to a "passion for truth and a compassion both for fellow believers and unbelievers." He asked "all Southern Baptists," including denominational employees "to restudy the Peace Committee Report. The 'enlarged tent,' " he said will encompass persons who are (1) "cooperating Southern Baptists," (2) "committed to the perpetuation of allegiance to God's perfect Word through the institutional life of Southern Baptists," and (3) "in agreement with the Peace Committee's 'Statement on Scripture.' "

Chapman restated the issue from the PC report: "The Bible is God's perfect Word which means that it is not errant in any area of reality. When the Bible speaks it speaks truth and nothing but the truth historically, scientifically, philosophically and spiritually. This conviction is foundational in Southern Baptist life and it can only remain so if we teach it in the classrooms of our educational institutions, preach it in the pulpits of our churches and print it in the published pages of our literature."

Amidst a continuing chorus of loud "Amens," Chapman said, "If in your heart you agree, the time has come to say so." If the SBC family "will stand side by side . . . on this single issue," we "will make a quantum leap beyond excessive politics."

Chapman urged churches "inclined to abandon or drastically reduce" CP gifts "to make no decision in haste. A funding program designed to go around the Cooperative Program is unacceptable to mainstream Southern Baptists and may well lead to a permanent break from the convention. The two great traditions of Southern Baptists are conservative theology and cooperative methodology. We must remain true to both traditions."

He moved on to talk about spiritual control in conflict, missions, evangelism, prayer and revival. He had appointed Jim Henry, pastor of FBC, Orlando, FL to head a task force to "further encourage Southern Baptists to engage in solemn assembly." He cited Home Mission Board consideration for a volunteer "Crossover America" project in a city like New York in 1993 and Foreign Mission Board agreement to sponsor "Cross Overseas" volunteers for the summer of 1991.

"Now is the time for reduced rhetoric, for Christ-like attitudes and for gracious communication," he said. "Now is the time to focus on spreading the Gospel, . . . to boost our world-wide mission outreach, . . . to encourage cooperative participation."[27]

This upset a number of EC members. EC members praised Chapman's address as one of the best they had ever heard on bringing unity to the SBC. However, a front-page story in the Nashville Tennessean highlighted his statement that the alternative funding program "may well lead to a permanent break from the convention."[27A] Paul Pressler called the Tennessean story the only "sour note" during the EC meeting. "I don't see how the reporter could have heard Morris speak last night and write the article he did." [28] The EC voted to ask state editors to print Chapman's "entire speech in full." "It was more than a fireside chat," said EC member Eldridge Miller. Most papers, however, printed only summaries and a few salient quotes.

Agency heads gave their customary reports. Willis Bennett, reporting for Roy Honeycutt who was recuperating from bypass surgery, said, "These are the best of times and the worst of times" at the seminary. He spoke of stable enrollment and funds raised for a new student center. Problems, he said, included student and faculty "anxiety over the future of the seminary. Pray that we will work with our trustees and resolve the loss of trust among Southern Baptists. . . . Conservative teaching," he said, "has always been" at Southern. The Executive Committee gave Bennett no applause.[29]

Larry Lewis Speaks Out

Most other agency executives, in their reports and interviews with reporters, tended to steer clear of comments about the Atlanta meeting, although they did affirm the Cooperative Program. However, HMB president Larry Lewis was not reluctant to declare his feelings about the alternate financial plan in a tape-recorded interview.

Lewis was "upset beyond words" at the number of former agency heads, who once supported the Cooperative Program and lived off it for years and who are now leaders in the renegade effort to promote an "uncooperative program."

He conceded that the alternate plan "does give a steam valve for these fellows who are just so upset they would [otherwise] leave the Convention. This gives them an opportunity to support the things they want to support. But they're really setting up another Executive Committee. They've always had the right on the local church level to directly fund what they want."

However, Lewis saw a "distinction between what a church has a right to do and what is right [for it] to do. We need to affirm that every church has a right to support missions in whatever way they feel most appropriate. [At the same time], I think that the Convention should expect of every church that names and uses the name Southern Baptist, that it will support our world missions program. We also have to affirm that the state conventions have the right to set up an alternative plan, like the Virginia Plan, but even though it's their right to do it, I think it's wrong to do it. The Cooperative Program has proven itself through 65 years, through good times and bad, to be an excellent program for mission funding.

"When a church escrows, withholds or reduces funds, they're not really speaking to political issues. What's bothering them is not what they're addressing; it's the missionaries who are hurting, not Paul Pressler or the SBC Executive Committee.

"This is why I'm speaking so vocally in saying that it is not proper for any agency to give any kind of endorsement at this point to any kind of renegade alternative plan."

Still, Lewis didn't think the alternative funding plan would ever become a "serious threat to the Cooperative Program and I'll tell you why," he said. "When these guys go back home, their churches, which have heard the gospel of the Cooperative Program preached for 65 years, will be very reluctant to change that support system just to accommodate some good old boys who have not been elected at the convention. What that's going to do is to divide and split some churches. They're going to have to decide, 'Is our church going to go with the Cooperative Program or the Uncooperative Program?'"

Lewis had heard of one church, whose pastor had been prominent in the Atlanta meeting, where the plan "didn't go over. After an hour of rather heated and volatile discussion one group said let's go with this new plan; another group said let's go with the other plan; the vast majority said let's not change anything. I think that any church that wants to go with the new plan will no doubt have members who will be upset and some will leave. There is also the possibility that some moderates might leave conservative churches, but conservative churches will not have to vote to do anything; they can go right on as they've been doing, supporting the Cooperative Program."

Lewis noted that he and Keith Parks had been invited to speak to a specially called meeting of the WMU board, composed of WMU presidents from every state convention, in Richmond. "The WMU is under strong pressure to not only promote the Cooperative Program, but to also promote this Uncooperative Program. They've asked us to come and say what we think about it. I'm going to be as outspoken there as I am right here with you and your tape recorder. I'm going to say I think it will be absolutely disastrous for the WMU to position themselves as an advocate of any kind of an alternate [funding] program."[30]

Lewis and Parks Address the WMU Board

Speaking to the WMU board the following week, Lewis reported that Home Mission Board trustees had recently passed a motion affirming the right of church and state convention autonomy in giving and the CP as "the preferred method of world missions funding," while opposing alternate plans. He then presented six reasons for opposing the alternate plans.

1. "It will increase the division and polarization even more. We certainly don't need another issue to drive us further apart."

2. "The reasons for the alternate plan are somewhat questionable. The rationale suggested in recent days is that anyone who was not a right wing political activist on the Patterson-Pressler political agenda has not been placed on any board or agency." Calling this a "false assumption," Lewis named several HMB trustees, including Richard Jackson, who could not fit into the above category.

3. "These alternate plans will divert funds from needy agencies. . . For every moderate church that determines by some kind of new funding mechanism to exclude a certain agency, there will be that many more conservative churches to jump on the same bandwagon and say, Hot diggety dog, this is what we've been looking for all these years, a way to keep from funding agencies we really don't like and never have. We are opening a Pandora's box and there will be no end to confusion and frustration that I think will result."

4. "It will destroy our historic, systematic, cooperative approach to missions" and "encourage a reversion to the societal plan. Each of us will have to make our pitch and go with hat in hand, trying to generate the support we need to do our work. I fear that day."

5. "Alternate plans will tend to devastate bookkeeping and budget planning."

6. "This will destroy our . . . Convention as we've come to know it. We will have two conventions with two political parties, two agendas, two systems of funding, two fellowships, two pastors' conferences, maybe even two women's organizations. . . . I don't like what I feel will be the results."

Lewis asked that "the WMU, the Home Mission Board and every SBC agency refrain from giving support, approval, promotion of and encouragement to alternate funding plans."

Keith Parks was less resolute. "The potential in world missions has never been greater," he said. Yet, there has been since 1985 a "very disturbing drop in missionary appointments."

Happenings in the Convention, he said "have affected this," though he "did not know how much and some don't like to acknowledge that and don't like for me to express that. I only do it because I know it's true."

Parks said he had received many letters and phone calls from people. "There are growing numbers . . . say[ing] to us, 'Until we see a little more clearly where we're going as a denomination, we're just not ready yet to follow through with our missions commitment.'"

Parks reported some missionaries were "demoralized" with happenings in the SBC. He cited one missionary as saying he had received eight letters in one month from significant churches saying we're going to escrow our funds until we see what's going on. You talk about demoralizing. [This missionary] told of one experience when his whole family was sick. . . when he got a letter asking him what he believed. He said it's no longer enough to give your life for the Lord, you've got to do it believing the right thing."

There was "no question" in Parks' mind, "if we have our options, that any of us want to change the combination we have in the Cooperative Program and the special mission offerings. Every mission group in the world envies that; none have suggested a better plan."

The question is "can we do what we want to do and is that feasible [within the current Convention climate]?" I've been asked by board members and others, 'What about just rejecting any funding that comes through alternate funding plans?' I've said, 'You've got to be kidding. . . . I don't believe we've ever checked the orthodoxy of any individual or church that wanted to send money to the Foreign Mission Board.

". . . Certainly I concur that our Cooperative Program is the preferable plan, but the question . . . is, 'Will it remain intact?'"
Parks didn't "believe there's ever been a time when there's been so many churches writing to us about alternate ways of giving. My response is a very simple letter, saying that for generations there have been at least six ways you can give to foreign missions," including the Cooperative Program — "our preferred way," Lottie Moon, designation by a church for a particular project or missionary, designation by an individual for a missionary, or designation for special capital needs.

Parks said he was now hearing such things as, " 'Some of the folks that are emphasizing our Cooperative Program are from churches that already have a designated alternate plan of giving for the majority of their funds and send such a small percentage through the Cooperative Program, that they already have an alternate missions plan they support.'

"Some are saying 'We've been giving virtually all our funds through the Cooperative Program. We're going to give less through that channel and do some things with more of our money as many other churches are doing. . .'

"Some are saying, 'If all Southern Baptists are to be equally supportive of our cooperative plan, as we've been in the past, then there ought to be the give and take and representation, rather than the controlled representation from one segment of our denomination. And unless there is recreated trust and inclusiveness, we're going to find another way to do it.'

"You can interpret that politically if you want to," Parks said, ". . . I'm simply telling you what I'm hearing."

Parks reiterated that "one simple cooperative way is the best way." But "suppose [that] to insist that you do it that way means that a significant portion of churches that traditionally have provided the main part of our Cooperative Program decide they will pull out entirely, that they will direct money totally away from [SBC agencies]. I don't like that scenario either and I guess, no I know, I prefer an alternate plan of giving that would still support our agencies to a restriction that would cause many churches to decide to do for home, foreign and state missions unilaterally.

" . . . I guess the question I'm asking is, can we maintain the status quo simply by saying to people we ought to maintain the status quo. Or, are there underlying things that need to be addressed in order that we can recreate the sense of trust and involvement? I'm convinced that if that trust and involvement . . . and the perception of inclusiveness cannot be restored, that we're all facing some of the sad situations that Larry [Lewis] has already described.

". . . There's never been a time," Parks emphasized, "when prayer has been so desperately needed as right now. . . . We are at a point where nothing but the intervention of the Lord is going to hold us together and move us forward."[31]

The WMU Board Takes a Position

After a question and answer time with the two mission leaders, the WMU board approved unanimously a lengthy statement relating to "one of the most crucial and pivotal points" in the history of the WMU and the SBC. This marked the first time the national WMU leadership had addressed the SBC controversy.

The board members affirmed their love and support for home and foreign missionaries. "We will be your staying force when you fear all others might abandon you." They called for WMU members to pray "like you've never prayed before." They issued an "urgent, strong call" for prayer for unity within the denomination. They "regret[ted] any suspicions that the WMU might be politically involved in the denominational strife," but they could not remain silent any longer.[32] They then affirmed the traditional channels of missions giving, while affirming as well the "right of individuals, churches and state conventions to choose other plans for cooperative missions giving."[33]

Three former national WMU presidents — Helen Fling, Christine Gregory and Dorothy Sample — and two former WMU executives — Alma Hunt and Carolyn Weatherford Crumpler — endorsed the action taken by the WMU board.

The WMU action did not set well with many other Southern Baptists. Judy Felkins, WMU director for Maytown Baptist Church in Alabama, was "shocked and disappointed. . . . By taking this step, the WMU has not remained independent and out of the fray' but only added fuel to the flame of dissension."[34] Executive Committee member Eldridge Miller asked if the time had not "come to consider allowing the present WMU to become the auxiliary of the Atlanta Fellowship while our convention moves boldly forward to forge a Women's Missionary Commission which will have the same relationship to our convention as our Baptist men?"[35]

On the first day of the called WMU meeting, the biggest bombshell ever to hit the SBC's largest state convention fell in Texas. Baylor University trustees met on September 21 and voted 30-7 with one abstention to, in effect, secede from control by the Baptist General Convention of Texas. Barely two weeks before, Stetson University had asked the Florida convention to reduce its funding in exchange for giving up the right to approve the nomination of Stetson trustees. Then, on October 15, Furman University trustees, by an 18-6 vote, declared themselves a self-perpetuating board with sole governing power over the school that had been founded by South Carolina Baptists in 1826.

Three days after Baylor voted to sever "control" ties with Texas Baptists, Southern Seminary trustees voted to wipe the slate clean of previous accusations that some faculty members had been teaching outside accepted Baptist doctrine and the seminary's governing theological statement. They then voted 36 to 14 to add the Peace Committee report — "both findings and recommendations" — as a guideline for hiring new faculty and for promoting or granting tenure to existing faculty. The faculty responded by unanimously asking the trustees to rescind the more restrictive employment and promotion policy.

Meanwhile, the pot was bubbling over at the Sunday School Board where the controversy over the withdrawn McBeth history and the disclosure of Lee Porter's lecture to students in New Orleans, was driving the wedge deeper between many trustees and Board president Lloyd Elder.

With the official passing of summer, the SBC climate grew even hotter. Division deepened over the alternate funding plan when moderate leaders presented a proposed budget that eliminated the Executive Committee, the Christian Life Commission, the Public Affairs Committee and Southeastern Seminary from receiving allocations. North Carolina and Virginia would vote in November on alternate state giving plans. And across the denomination a number of heavy Cooperative Program giving churches were preparing to vote on changes in their funding patterns.

References

1 Cecil Sherman: "Fear and Career in the SBC," The Window, Broadway Baptist Church, May 24, 1990, p. 2.

2 The quotation: "Seest thou not how God hath coined a parable? A good word is like a good tree whose root is firmly fixed and whose top is in the sky. And it produces its edible fruit every season, by the permission of its Lord." The Koran 14:24-25.

3 Ad, SBC Today, November 16, 1990, p. 11.

4 Baptist Standard, December 6, 1989, p. 8.

5 Alan Neely: "Baptists and Peoples of Other Faiths," Perspectives of Religious Studies, Fall, 1990. A paper presented to the Southeastern Regional Meeting of the NABPR, Charlotte, NC, March 16, 1990.

6 R. Albert Mohler Jr.: "Moderates Explore Their Options in Atlanta Meeting," Christian Index, August 23, 1990, pp. 1, 3.

7 "Dream it Again!" Religious Herald, August 23, 1990, p. 4.

8 "Save the Cooperative Program," Religious Herald, August 23, 1990, p. 4.

9 "Chapman Urges Support for Cooperative Program," The Christian Index, August 10, 1990, p. 3.

10 "Carefully Consider Before Changing CP," Baptist Standard, August 15, 1990, p. 6.

11 "Decisions on Cooperative Program Affect Future of the Convention," The Christian Index, July 26, 1990, p. 2.

12 "R. Albert Mohler, "Moderates Explore Their Options in Atlanta Meeting," op. cit. August 23, 1990, pp. 1, 3, 4.

13 Telephone Interview, December, 1990.

14 Quotations and other information from sermons and reports are, unless otherwise indicated, taken directly from the minutes of the Atlanta Consultation.

15 This second statement is quoted from Jim Newton: "Southern Baptist Moderates Organize New Fellowship," Biblical Recorder, September 8, 1990, pp. 1, 10.

16 "Missouri Baptists Share Reactions," Word & Way, August 30, 1990.

17 C. Lacy Thompson, "Louisianians Respond to Action of Atlanta Meeting," Baptist Message, September 6, 1990, pp. 2, 6.

18 Bob E. Matthews: "Oklahoma Participants Reflect on Atlanta Meeting," The Oklahoma Baptist Messenger, pp. 4, 5.

19 "Protecting Your Conscience," The Window, September 13, 1990, pp. 1, 2.

20 A Call for Cooperative Program Support," Baptist New Mexican, September 8, 1990, p. 2.

21 Toby Druin: "Draper, Others Huddle, Seek Cure for 'Sick' SBC," Baptist Standard, September 26, 1990, p. 5.

22 Toby Druin: "Bisagno Offers Plan for SBC Reform, Renewal," Baptist Standard, September 26, 1990, p. 4.

23 "Cooperative Program Affirmed," Word & Way, September 27, 1990, p. 3.

24 Ibid.

25 "SBC Executive Committee Addresses Bylaw Changes," Word & Way, September 27, 1990, p. 3. Also Robert H. Dilday: "Executive Committee Officers May Elect Staff," Religious Herald, September 27, 1990, p. 3.

26 From my notes of Chapman's remarks before he began reading from his manuscript.

27 President's Address, September 17, 1990.)

27A Ray Waddle: "Baptist Leader Warns Split May Be on Way, September 18, 1991, p. 1.

28 Personal Interview, Nashville, September, 1991.

29 From my notes of Bennett's report.

30 Personal Interview, Nashville, September, 1990.

31 Quotations from Lewis and Parks are from a tape of the called WMU board meeting.

32 Karen Benson: "For First Time, National WMU Leaders Address Controversy Within Convention," The Alabama Baptist, October 11, 1990, p. 5.

33 Former WMU Leaders Endorse Board's Action," Biblical Recorder, October 13, 1990, pp. 1, 7.

34 Letters to the Editor, The Alabama Baptist, October 11, 1990, p. 5.

35 Letters, Word & Way, November 8, 1990, p. 2.

Chapter 14

"The Resurgence Sweeps On"

Before turning to the developments at the Sunday School Board which led to the resignation of Lloyd Elder as president, we will look at significant happenings in other agencies during the last months of 1990.

The CLC in Washington

Thanks to the increased funding voted in New Orleans, the Christian Life Commission took a quantum leap in raising the agency's profile and influence in Washington. The Washington office was expanded and two new staff members added, attorney Michael Whitehead and journalist Tom Strode. By press releases and personal contacts, the CLC was fast becoming known as the agency which was allied with the SBC Public Affairs Committee in directly representing the largest non-Catholic denomination in the nation on matters of moral and social concerns and religious liberty. The PAC, which had taken some strong stands, was still limited by a minuscule budget and no paid staff. The CLC had agency status and the money to operate on Capitol Hill.

When CLC executive Richard Land spoke, federal officials listened. In marked contrast to the style of the BJCPA's James Dunn, Land participated in the giant 1990 Rally for Life. Land personally urged President Bush to exert more visible leadership on the abortion issue. Land warned that if the government did not clean up obscenity in tax-funded art, then the CLC would call for the abolition of the National Endowment for the Arts. The BJCPA had declined to take a stand on NEA grants. Land protested White House invitations for leaders of homosexual organizations to attend White House bill signing ceremonies. The BJCPA had been virtually silent on the explosive issue of homosexual rights. Land joined other evangelicals, including Morris Chapman, in asking Bush to issue an executive order affirming the traditional family and opposing homosexual rights. "We certainly will be pursuing this matter with the administration until we receive a satisfactory response," Land declared.[1] SBC conservatives cheered. It was a new day for them in Washington.

The BJCPA Seeks More Funds

SBC funds to the BJCPA had been slashed from $391,796 to $50,000, in New Orleans despite opposition from virtually all of the old guard agency leadership in the SBC and editorial pleas from almost every state editor. James Dunn said in October that the beleaguered BJCPA "is alive and well..." The BJCPA adopted a 1990-91 budget of $666,794, down from the $729,772 budget for 1989-90. Dunn was counting on $508,959 from Southern Baptist individuals and entities, including state conventions. This meant that Southern Baptists would still be contributing far more than all the eight other Baptist bodies in the BJCPA combined. At its October meeting, the BJCPA rejected a request from the SBC Executive Committee and cut the number of SBC members from 18 to 11, giving the seven seats to the Religious Liberty Council, which was formed to represent contributing state conventions, local churches and the Southern Baptist Alliance.

The October, 1991 BJCPA meeting was held in conjunction with the committee's Religious Liberty Conference, where about 150 attenders heard Dan Martin, Gustave Niebuhr, Stan Hastey and ABC TV's Sam Donaldson expound on religious and press freedoms.

Martin and Hastey flailed the SBC Executive Committee for the Baptist Press firings. Martin said that the EC had made a "cripple" of a good news service, whose "credibility" has been "destroyed" by "guerrillas at the gate."[2] Hastey called the actions a violation of the fundamental right of the press. BP, Hastey added, "[has been] emasculate[d] by a band of leaders" who show "ignorance of Baptist history and contempt for Baptist values." Hastey suggested that all Baptist editors should stand in fear of losing their jobs.[3]

Few good words were spoken for SBC conservatives at the BJCPA's 1990 meeting. Dunn minced no words himself in writing the caption for a page-sized cartoon which first appeared in Newsday and was reprinted in the October issue of the BJCPA's Report From the Capital. The drawing showed the entrance to a "Fundamentalist Baptist Church" with footprints stamped on a carpet labeled "Bill of Rights." Dunn wrote: "There's a 'fundamentalism' that is simply honest and faithful to the Bible and another 'Fundamentalism' that is the stuff of theological terrorism and spiritual and political tyranny. What irony, then, that the religious radicals called Baptists, who contributed so significantly to the Bill of Rights should now be represented among its detractors on the eve of the bicentennial of that document. Pulitzer Prize-winning cartoonist Doug Marlette of Newsday has captured the essence of the way the world sees Baptists."[4]

On the seminary front attention focused on Southeastern, Southwestern, Midwestern and Southern. Academic life and governance at Golden Gate and New Orleans encountered no problems of consequence.[5]

Better Days at Southeastern

"Southeastern Born Again as Conservative Institution," headlined the Raleigh, NC News & Observer. Paige Patterson, the speaker for a two-day "preach-a-thon" that kicked off Southeastern's new year, predicted the genesis of a "national revival" could come on "this campus." Moderate forecasts of the seminary's demise, Patterson said, were "wishful thinking."[6]

The turmoil that accompanied the changeover in power had dissipated. Trustees invited faculty to officially observe and give input to the workings of the board — something which had never happened before. Newly elected trustee chairman, Roger Ellsworth, thought "the new spirit of cooperation between faculty and trustees will continue and increase. I think the trust level is coming back."

Shared governance was on everybody's lips. Trustees, for example, asked faculty and administration to join in developing guidelines for student taping of faculty lectures. The selection process for four new faculty appeared to be working. The Search Committee, which included three faculty, the dean, the president and a trustee, prepared a "short list" of applicants from which the president would select those he wanted to bring to the campus for interviews with members of the committee. Then the president would make recommendations to the trustees for employment.[7]

In an earlier interview, President Drummond reported that progress was being made with the seminary's two accrediting agencies. The school had not been put on probation, he said, although the Southern Association of Colleges and Schools had issued a statement of warning. "We're getting into our self-study," he noted, "which comes automatically every ten years."

Drummond said some lessons had been learned from the difficulties at Concordia Lutheran Seminary after that denomination voted to enforce the affirmation of inerrancy. "They gave the faculty a choice to sign a statement of inerrancy or resign. Thirty five of 40 faculty resigned and 350 of 400 students pulled out to form Seminex [their seminary in exile]. The new seminary has since been absorbed into another seminary. Concordia's president told me two years ago that their enrollment was up to 700."[8]

On December 12, SACS noted "significant improvement" at Southeastern, but said the agency's "warning" status would continue for another year. Drummond said, "This leaves our accreditation fully and completely intact. We believe we will be able to resolve all of their concerns in the next year."[9]

Conservative Trustees Move at Midwestern

"At Midwestern, we seek the truth," said President Milton Ferguson at New Orleans, adding, "I do not presume to claim that I am always right."[10] Three months later, at Midwestern's fall convocation, Ferguson received a standing ovation when he declared, "We are a family in trouble [and] distress. We must, therefore, acknowledge the conflict" and not "run from it. . . . However, that does not mean we are hopeless. . . . Let's ask God to deliver us from becoming petty tyrants, seeking to impose our truth on each other."[11]

Conservatives now held a solid majority on Midwestern's board. They expressed "confidence" in the faculty and administration that "they are acting within the spirit of the Baptist Faith and Message and the Peace Committee Report." They voiced "appreciation" to President Ferguson for his commitment to the trustees that he will seek teachers to "fill vacancies who will bring balance to the faculty and . . . be acceptable to all areas of concern of the trustees."

They then voted to have the board's executive committee "study the method by which faculty are elected and, if feasible, recommend a plan by which the trustees can be involved earlier in the process of faculty selection." Trustee Sid Peterson, who made the motion, said that by the time the faculty selection process went "through the dean, the president, the faculty, everyone has already determined who's going to be here except the trustees, whose duty it is to elect the faculty."

Trustee Jerry Davenport followed with a motion to permit students "to tape record class lectures and chapel sessions." Davenport withdrew his motion after Ferguson told the board the seminary did "not have any regulation that prevented such taping. . . . If the professor is agreeable," anyone can tape. Ferguson then urged trustees "to get to the point," saying, "if a professor feels that [someone] is taping him in order to get evidence to charge him with heresy, then that professor is obviously going to be skittish. The issue is not whether or not he can be taped. The issue is the professor's teaching in accordance with the Articles of Faith?"

Davenport responded by saying 15 or 16 students with "conservative views of Scripture" had told him they had been "intimidated in classes" and "threatened with being thrown out." Davenport's evaluation was that "this school is not where Southern Baptists are. It is to the left. . . . When I came on as a trustee [in 1982], there was not one [faculty member] to my knowledge . . . that had a high view of Scripture. We do not have very many today, as I am aware."

Ferguson "challenge[d] your charge that these professors don't have a high view of Scripture." Ferguson said he "would lay their view of Scripture alongside yours, mine and others. . . . I'm beginning to think that when people say they want 'balance,' what they really are saying is that they want everyone to be just like them."

Ferguson said that "some students [who can't do the work] take refuge behind the complaint that, 'If I tell how I really feel, I won't get to graduate. . . . That is an attack on the integrity and quality of these faculty members and that is irresponsibility. There is no evidence that any student has ever been punished or penalized . . . because of his theological views. I stand ready to be confronted with any evidence to the contrary."

Trustee Graydon K. Kitchens, Jr. reacted to the spirited discussion by calling the resolution passed earlier to affirm the faculty "grossly hypocritical . . . I don't think we ought to be sending them any more [resolutions like this] until we resolve how we really feel about it."[12]

The board moved on to more harmonious matters, but clearly the die had been cast for a tighter policy on future faculty hirings.

Dilday Survives at Southwestern

As for Southwestern, feelings ran so strong about President Dilday's "satanic" remark at New Orleans that some expected a called board meeting before the regular October time at which Dilday might be fired.

Instead, board chair Jimmy Draper and Dilday met for three hours, with both reporting they had settled the issue. Dilday stood by his explanation in New Orleans that by "satanic" he meant to characterize the activism of both sides in the struggle. Dilday called their discussion "frank and productive. . . . We can be a model for the rest of the convention in these troubled days." Draper said he was "a lover and not a fighter. The president and I have talked and I'm ready to move on with the business of the seminary."[13]

Still, the October meeting, held in a hotel away from the campus, was not all honey and spice. Some trustees came ready to turn down nominee Bruce Corley — who described himself as "a born again conservative" — as dean of the School of Theology because of a misquoted statement that had him calling dispensationalism a doctrinal heresy. Corley recognized "a kind of central conservative coalition no longer representing the fragmented edges, but the great middle of Baptist life. Southwestern," he said, "may be the place where a new consensus will be seen."

After discussion the trustees voted unanimously that Corley be hired. However, repeated efforts were made to set up a process that would allow trustees greater and earlier input in the hiring of faculty, permitting trustees to talk with nominees before the meeting in which they were due to vote on them. One trustee said this would work both ways: it would give the faculty an opportunity to meet trustees earlier and perhaps establish a better working relationship in the future.

In the closing session, Dilday apologized for any offense his remarks might have caused. "[I] feel badly about the language used and the way it offended some of you." Satan, he said, is capable of "having his way in my life" also. Draper responded by going to the podium to thank Dilday for his apology, then urged trustees and administration to find a way to work together, saying, "It's going to have to be more than words."

Although trustees never ordered Dilday to remain silent, some did hope that this year's peace treaty would last longer than the previous year's. Trustee Vice-President T. Bob Davis urged that Dilday recognize that he is under the authority of the convention through the trustees and avoid "placating, pleasing platitudes that attempt to appease us without producing results."

The meeting produced a great deal of frank discussion about public and private criticisms of one another. One trustee was in the midst of saying that he had found some of Dilday's remarks inappropriate, when another broke in and urged him to confront Dilday privately, in a biblical approach, before presenting such concerns before the full body. This happened a number of times and it wasn't always the same people involved.

Another trustee urged that if Dilday "has something critical to say about us," let him "say it to us personally" — not behind our backs. Trustee Bill Grubbs declared, "It won't hurt any of us if you" — trustees or administrators — "can't think of anything kind to say to keep your mouth shut. . . . There's been a lot of rhetoric on both sides, enough to go around. All of us have to resist the temptation to talk when we haven't formulated the right statement. Our solution is very simple: Keep our mouths shut and get on with our business."[14]

The Gap Widens at Southern

As in the spring, the real seminary hot spot in the fall was Southern where trustees had called a special meeting for September 24. Talk had spread about a mass exodus of professors and students to a new seminary which would be located on the old Tift College campus in Georgia. "We would all like to stay at Southern," Bill Leonard said, . . . but after this spring and the Johnson document, we don't know that we can stay."

Glenn Hinson. who first proposed the Tift possibility, thought more than half of the faculty and 1,000 of the 3,200 students might relocate. He estimated the move would cost about $30 million. "Divide that into 3,000 churches giving $10,000 each," he said. "That doesn't sound unreasonable."

"If all the seminaries in the SBC offer primarily one kind of instruction, where will the Baptist students go who do not conform to that kind of instruction?" Hinson said. "Fundamentalists asked that question and that's why Mid-America and Luther Rice seminaries were started. I guess moderates can ask that question, too."[15]

President Honeycutt called the idea of relocation "premature," noting, "We are not at that point of desperation." Provost G. Willis Bennett said the seminary had "no intention of leaving Southern Seminary or Louisville" and wouldn't engage in discussion of such a proposal.[16]

Amidst such actions and reactions, Stephen Shoemaker, pastor of Crescent Hill Church, to which many Southern people belonged, announced the formation of Alumni and Friends of Theological Education Inc., a non-profit foundation which Shoemaker said would provide a way for alumni and friends to support the seminary, even though they do not agree with the trustee majority. Shoemaker saw it as a "possible model for all SBC agencies and institutions, so they can receive money from people who would feel skittish otherwise."[17]

Hinson and Leonard's talk about an exodus from Southern did not set well with convention conservatives. Houston attorney J. Walter Carpenter urged the trustees to "terminate" the two professors "for cause." Carpenter had heard through the grapevine that "they have indeed encouraged potential donors to Southern Seminary to withhold their largesse until the new seminary is formed." Such reported actions, "are enough to conclude that they no longer have the best interest of [the seminary] at heart." Hinson and Leonard neither retreated nor resigned. "The timing of a move depends on Southern's trustees," Hinson said. "If our trustees in their September meeting do not create any big waves as they did last April, we will look to April [1991] and see what will happen."[18]

Jerry Johnson Apologizes

The trustees met in executive session, September 24, when President Honeycutt was still recuperating from open heart surgery. Jerry Johnson presented an apology. Before New Orleans he had "felt it was my responsibility to attempt to express some deep concerns. Now, there is no doubt in my mind but that I demonstrated lack of judgment in several respects." Some of the language, he said, was "ill-chosen and too harsh." [I] should have expressed these "concerns," through board committees, instead of a "public forum." Johnson still believed his "citations were accurate," but "I should and must sorrow over inappropriate expressions. . . . I ask for your forgiveness." Johnson then closed by "personaliz[ing] this apology to Dr. Honeycutt. . . . I did not mean to suggest that Dr. Honeycutt categorically did not believe the Bible but only to suggest that the two of us believed it in a different way. This area of difference is our problem."

The trustees accepted Johnson's apology and forgave him, "with the hope that this will be the first step in the healing process, not only within this Board but in the [convention] as a whole." [19] Provost Bennett called Johnson's paper a "dead document." [20]

Tough New Guidelines for Faculty

But the breach became wider when the trustees voted, by a 36-14 margin, for the Peace Committee report, including "both findings and recommendations" to "serve as a guideline for the employment of temporary and permanent faculty, the promotion of existing faculty and the granting of tenure." [21]

Trustee Julian Pentecost called the new guidelines a violation of freedom and the beginning of "a sad, new chapter . . . for Southern Baptists' 'Mother Seminary.' " [22] Trustee John Michael disagreed. "When we say we are going to hire people who believe and teach according to our confessional statements there has to be some interpretation of what that means. I see the findings and recommendations [of the PC] as giving us that guidance. . . " Michael did not spell out the four examples in the PC report — belief "in direct creation of mankind and [that] therefore . . . Adam and Eve were real persons," etc. But all knew they were included and would be part of the criteria for promotion and granting of tenure to present faculty and the hiring of future teachers.

Reaction across the SBC came swiftly. Jerry Vines was "very pleased" and called use of the report "just a logical step in the whole process of turning the SBC in a more conservative direction." Dan Vestal said, "This makes the Peace Committee report exactly what we said it would not become — a creed and litmus test of orthodoxy. When you add these things, you narrow in such a way to become creedal rather than confessional." Charles Fuller, PC chair, said the PC report had not been intended to be a "creedal supplement," but "to be taken as a whole." [23]

Officers of Southern's alumni association opposed the new policy. They expressed confidence that the faculty was dedicated to biblical authority by "signing the seminary's Abstract of Principles and, more recently the Baptist Faith and Message." This "is the first time that specific interpretations of God's Holy Word have been required of any Southern Baptist educational institution." The statement was signed by Bob Terry, present association president; Floyd F. Roebuck, immediate past president; and president-elect Emmanuel L. McCall. [24]

Faculty association president Bill Leonard said, "The trustee action in effect establishes a new creedalism at Southern Seminary that is the result of the Peace Committee action. This is for the moment . . . But given the change, we don't know what it will be next year." [25] Southern faculty backed up Leonard and on November 1 unanimously asked the trustees to rescind the new policy on guidelines. The faculty statement said the trustees' action creates "significant problems" in the faculty's relationship with the trustees, "misuses" the SBC Peace Committee report and "introduces ambiguity and confusion" into the seminary's instructional process.

The faculty said the new guidelines present "serious implications" for the seminary's accreditation, "negatively impacts" recruitment of faculty and students and jeopardizes major seminary programs because of its "exclusionary impact" on employment of part-time professors."[26]

Mark Coppenger of Indiana disagreed. "Some are now crying 'creedalism. They were content with the original 20 clauses [in the Abstract of Principles]. That wasn't creedalism. But now we have creedalism with the addition of new clauses. . . . Why add clauses? Because some scholars can be so ingenious in undermining doctrine, who can anticipate their maneuvers? . . . . Nobody is suggesting that you be excommunicated if you say that everyone on earth will go to heaven or that Paul's epistles are errant. They are simply saying that Cooperative Program money should not be used to fund your efforts to indoctrinate generations of students in this direction. Some church will take you. They may even make you pastor. But not at our expense, thank you. It's just that simple."[27]

Just as had happened at Southeastern, the faculty outcry at Southern caught the ears of the seminary's two accrediting agencies. It was announced that staff members from both ATS and SACS would be coming to investigate reports related to actions by trustees at its April and September meetings.[28]

References:

1 "Evangelicals Meet With President," The Christian Index, November 15, 1990, pp. 4, 6.

2 "News & Notes: Religious Liberty Update," Southern Baptist Public Affairs Journal, Fall/Winter, 1991, p. 12.

3 "Baptist Joint Committee is 'Alive and Well,' Dunn Declares," Word & Way, October 11, 1990, p. 11.

4 Report From the Capital, October, 1990, p. 7.

5 For a current overview of problems and challenges in American seminaries from a more liberal perspective, see Paul Wilkes: "The Hands That Would Shape Our Souls," The Atlantic Monthly, December, 1990, pp. 59-88.

6 Erin Kelly, September 8, 1990, pp. 1B, 2B.

7 "Shared Governance Emphasized in Southeastern Trustee Meeting," Indiana Baptist, November 20, 1990, p. 5.

8 Personal Interview, Nashville, September, 1990.

9 "Accrediting Agency Retains Warning Status for Southeastern Seminary," Religious Herald, January 3, 1990, p. 10.

10 Brenda J. Sanders, "Midwestern Seminary Luncheon," Southern Baptist Convention News," June, 1991.

11 "Ferguson: Deal With Conflict Constructively," Word & Way, September 20, 1990, p. 5.

12 "Midwestern Trustees to Study Faculty Selection Process," Word & Way, October 25, 1990, p. 5.

13 "Draper: Issue Concerning Dilday Comments Settled," Word & Way, August 9, 1990.

14 I was not at this trustee meeting. However, an experienced journalist shared notes of the discussion. Other sources were Tammi Ledbetter: "Southwestern Trustees Herald New Era of Openness" and "Corley Approved as Seminary Dean With Full Support," Indiana Baptist, October 23, 1990, pp. 1, 12.

15 Marv Knox: "Southern Seminary Profs Consider Move to Georgia," Western Recorder, August 7, 1990, p. 1.

16 R. Albert Mohler Jr.: "Prof's Proposal Suggests New Seminary at Tift," August 9, 1990, p. 6.

17 Marv Knox: "Foundation Established to Receive SBTS Funds," Western Recorder, August 28, 1990, p. 2.

18 Letter to Trustees, August 22, 1990.)

19 Statement of Acceptance, September 24, 1990.

20 Bill Wolfe: "Provost Calls Trustee's Attack on Baptist Seminary a 'Dead Document,' Louisville Courier-Journal," September 26, 1990, pp. B1, B4.

21 Quoted from Julian Pentecost: "A Sad, New Chapter Begins for Southern Baptists' 'Mother Seminary,' Religious Herald, October 4, 1990, p. 4.

22 Ibid.

23 Dan Martin and Marv Knox: "Fuller: Committee Report Not to be 'Creedal,' " Baptist Standard, October 17, 1990, p. 4.

24 "Southern Trustees Differ Over Employment Guidelines," October 11, 1990, p. 11.

25 Marv Knox: "Policy is 'Creedal,' Says Professor," Religious Herald, October 4, 1990, p. 2.

26 "SBTS Employment Policy," Word & Way, November 15, 1990, p. 11.

27 Coppenger column, Indiana Baptist, November 20, 1990, p. 3.

28 "Accrediting Agencies to Visit Southern," November 15, 1990, p. 11.

Chapter 15

"Showdown at the Sunday School Board"

A gala parade inside the Super Dome at New Orleans launched the centennial celebration of the SBC's most influential agency. A Dixieland band led a promenade of Sunday School Board employees and trustees, with mule-drawn carriages carrying actors representing the early presidents of the Board. James L. Sullivan and Grady C. Cothen, the only two living ex-presidents, rode in cars contemporary to the times of their Board service. After the parade, President Lloyd Elder talked about the many ways in which the Board "touches the lives of Southern Baptists."[1]

Starting with only the elected president, J.M. Frost, in 1891, the Board now had 1882 employees who had shipped 72,225,088 pieces of church literature and grossed $171,986,000 during the past fiscal year. The Board's new Centennial Tower office building was altering the skyline of Nashville. A centennial "Heritage and Hope" history was scheduled for publication in the fall. The personable Elder anticipated that the greatest years were ahead for the world's largest religious publishing house.[2]

From 1891 to 1991 the Board had only seven presidents. The fifth, James L. Sullivan, 1953-1975, was a pillar in the pre-1979 SBC power structure. However, his reputation lost luster among conservatives over publication of the Elliott and Davies commentaries. Even so, after his retirement, Sullivan was elected president of the SBC.

A Celebrated Court Suit

Grady Cothen, a former president of New Orleans Seminary, served as BSSB president from 1975-1984. Cothen inherited some serious personnel problems which came to light during litigation of a $1.5 million suit filed against the BSSB by former personnel department employee Donald Burnett for alleged assault and battery, wrongful discharge, outrageous conduct, false arrest, imprisonment and defamation. Trial testimony brought out that Burnett had conveyed to Cothen complaints from employees of sexual harassment and other misdeeds of superiors. According to Cothen, Burnett reported having "dreams and visions," and said that he was "God's person to clean out the board."

At Cothen's request, Burnett was examined by a psychiatrist who pronounced Burnett paranoid schizophrenic. The psychiatrist happened to be the next door neighbor of a high Board executive who was later asked to resign by Cothen. When Burnett refused to keep silent, Cothen, in consultation with "competent [legal and medical] advice," he said, but without notifying Burnett's family, arranged to have the employee committed involuntarily to a mental institution. The scheme went awry. Burnett escaped and filed suit. The case finally went to a jury trial five years later with no trustees present to observe. After the judge dismissed all charges except the one on defamation, the jury quickly brought in a guilty verdict, recommending that Burnett be awarded $300,000 in compensatory damages and $100,000 punitive damages. The damages were subsequently reduced by the judge to $80,000.

A bare bones story was written by a Board employee and sent through the Baptist Press system as news. The BSSB writer and BP news editor Dan Martin failed to note that several high board officials, about whom Burnett relayed complaints to Cothen, had previously resigned.[3] By this time Cothen was already suffering serious health problems. He took medical retirement in 1983 with a $58,812 a year Board pension, plus other perks. That same year, he lost as the moderate candidate for SBC president to conservative Charles Stanley. From this time on, Cothen was solidly identified with the moderate party.

Lloyd Elder Becomes Board President

Cothen earned $115,000 during his last year at the helm of the BSSB. His successor, Lloyd Elder, was hired in 1984 to start at $90,000. Selected from about 70 nominees, Elder, age 50 and the youngest of 13 children, was a doctoral graduate of Southwestern Seminary, a pastor for 23 years, Assistant to the Executive Director of the Texas convention's Executive Board for five years and Executive Vice President at Southwestern under Russell Dilday since 1978. He was elected when the Board still had a moderate majority. Noting "problems" in the SBC, the search committee said that "the Sunday School Board and its president must act as a major reconciling force . . . to constantly emphasize the all important things that unite us."[4] Though his theology was acceptable to conservatives, Elder's career would be marked by publishing problems and struggles with his trustees that culminated in his resignation, January 17, 1991. Reflecting back seven years later, trustee Tommy French, thinks Elder "was chosen" by the moderate establishment, "because . . . they needed a tough-minded fighter to hold the Board where it was until they could turn back the conservative resurgence."[5]

The road was indeed rocky, as indicated by the string of incidents related in previous chapters, including Joe Knott's unplanned motion to "fire Dr. Elder and declare the presidency vacant," following Elder's attack on trustee Larry Holly. [6] The worst came after the 1990 New Orleans convention when (1) Elder faced a groundswell of protests over printed allegations that Lee Porter, a BSSB editor, had likened conservatives to Hitler and Ayatollah Khoemini, while also hinting that conservatives had been guilty of vote fraud and (2) a trustee investigation and evaluation of Elder's business managements and his handling of the controversial BSSB history.

Consequences of a "Lecture"

Porter's explosive "lecture" to the seminary class in New Orleans, as reported in a previous chapter was made known in the September 11 issue of the Indiana Baptist. Before printing the article, Managing Editor Tammi Ledbetter sent a draft to a few "friends," saying, "This is probably the most sensitive article we've ever run . . . and I need your input." Every advance reader agreed that the paper should run the article, according to Ledbetter.[7]

Ledbetter quoted line after line of Porter's remarks, taken from her's and Alma Ruth Morgan's notes. However, she did not name Morgan as a source.

Shortly after the article appeared, Ledbetter, as was her custom, took a stack of the latest issue of the paper to the SBC Executive Committee meeting in Nashville. Unknown to Ledbetter, someone copied the Porter story and placed a copy on the desk of every committee member.

Many Sunday School Board trustees had already read the story and were incensed. BSSB trustee Larry Holly wrote Elder, with copies going to other trustees and Porter, that Porter had dropped a "hot potato" in his lap. "You and I both know that there are [BSSB] employees and perhaps executive staff who agree with the things which Dr. Porter said, but they have the wisdom not to say them publicly. Dr. Porter's statements are insubordination and I believe warrant his summary dismissal."[8] On this same day, Holly wrote BSSB trustee chairman Bill Anderson, asking him to call an emergency meeting of the board. "[Porter] has thrown the gauntlet down and has asked to become a martyr," Holly said. "I believe that we ought to give him his wish."[9]

Elder immediately wrote trustees that he "deeply regret[ted] and strongly disagree[d] with some of the reported private opinions and remarks of Dr. Porter." He was also "deeply troubled" by Holly's "accusation about our employees" and certainly did "not know," as Holly had alleged, that "there are employees and perhaps executive staff" who agreed with what Porter had said."[10]

A number of other trustees wrote Elder demanding action. Arkansas trustee Mark Brooks called Porter's remarks "abominable" and deplorable." His remarks about voting fraud are "wholly unsubstantiated. If he knows of fraud, then he should quickly produce the facts. As it is, he has cast an unwarranted shadow upon the voting integrity of thousands of Southern Baptists." Brooks urged Elder to ask Porter to resign immediately.[11]

That same day Ledbetter joined other state editors for a routine briefing by the Sunday School Board. Here she was requested by Porter's supervisor to provide more information on the incident in New Orleans. She declined to share her reporter's notes, saying that she stood on her printed story. Then after returning home, she and her husband Gary received a letter from Lloyd Elder checking on the accuracy of remarks alleged to have been made by Porter.

Handling an Apology

On October 5, Porter "extend[ed] to Elder, trustees, Board employees and others my sincere apology for any hurt, pain, or problems my remarks to the students of Southern Seminary . . . and the subsequent publishing of a story concerning those remarks in the Indiana Baptist have caused." Porter maintained that "though I did not say everything reported in the Indiana Baptist, I know that those remarks [may] have caused problems for [the Board] and others." Porter "now realized[d]" that he "was not just speaking [to the class] as a Convention officer, but also as a Baptist Sunday School Board employee." He had violated BSSB policy and "made an error in judgment in making such remarks," He "pledge[d]" to avoid making such statements in the future.[12]

The BSSB trustee Executive Committee was scheduled to meet October 25. They would consider Porter's remarks and his apology then. The day before that meeting Tammi Ledbetter wrote the chairman of the committee, Gene Mims her concern with "misinformation conveyed to trustees through Lee Porter's apology." Her husband, Gary, she said, had been "contacted by several trustees" indicating that "Porter claimed he did not say all of the things for which he was quoted in the Indiana Baptist." Ledbetter said she had "very careful notes from two sources [herself and Alma Ruth Morgan] which validate the statements" in the Indiana paper. "Every statement was presented in context. . . . Hard as it may be for some to believe, we protected Mr. Porter by not printing them as they included references to the character of prominent individuals. I am offended that some in the Sunday

School Board administration have blamed us for causing this problem. We simply reported what was publicly proclaimed."

Ledbetter urged that Porter's apology be released to the press. "For 90 trustees to receive a letter of apology which in effect calls us liars is an accusation that demands an open retraction. If there are falsehoods, . . . we would like to have them specified or such accusations withdrawn."[13]

The Ledbetters left for vacation believing the committee would deal adequately with the situation. Upon checking into their motel, they received a message from an Oklahoma trustee offering to fly them to the committee meeting for the next day. In explaining why they did not go, Gary Ledbetter said they had tried to "let the news reported be the issue, not the reporting of it by the Indiana Baptist and besides, the next day was our daughter's birthday."[14]

When Porter's apology was considered by the trustee committee, questions were raised about the accuracy of Ledbetter's report. Shortly after the committee met, Porter released a statement through Baptist Press. The BSSB administration, he said, had advised that "it would be unwise for me, as a Board employee, to continue to hold an elected office" in the SBC. "I regret that my comments to students as a Convention officer involved me in denominational politics. I am sorry for the pain and disruption caused by my remarks. I accept the position of the administration."

Porter said he had "served" for 14 years as Registration Secretary "with honesty and integrity" and had followed Convention bylaws and "the principle of treating every individual fairly. . . . If the Lord should lead me to another position, . . . then I would be most happy working [again] as Registration Secretary."[15]

What the Denominational Press Did Not Say

A week later President Elder announced through Baptist Press that Porter had been moved from his position as a design editor of adult Sunday School materials and "assigned to a non-editorial" job. The release also noted that Porter had apologized to the administration and trustees. The BP story, written by a BSSB employee, did not quote directly any of Porter's remarks printed in the Indiana Baptist which had set off the furor among BSSB trustees, noting only that Porter had made "critical interpretations and personal comments on a wide range of issues in the 12-year SBC controversy." Board officials, BP said, had "reviewed the matter and concluded . . . that Porter violated the established parameters" of the BSSB "for acceptable employee conduct. His use of inflammatory language has impacted his performance as an employee and the board's relationship with its Southern Baptist constituency." BP presented a paragraph from Porter's apology and noted that he had "affirmed his total allegiance to the

trustworthiness of the Bible." The release quoted Elder as saying
that the Porter affair "has been dealt with fairly and firmly as a
personnel matter."[16]

No other Baptist state paper reprinted the Indiana Baptist
article that set off the fireworks. Missouri's Word & Way ran a
half-page piece covering trustee reactions, administration
decisions and Porter's response. The article did not include any
remarks which Ledbetter alleged Porter had made to the seminary
class.[17] The Virginia Religious Herald, in a shorter piece, said only
that Porter had "made critical interpretations and personal
comments on a wide range of issues in the SBC controversy."[18]
This pattern was followed by most other state papers.

Only readers of the Indiana Baptist, along with BSSB trustees
and administrators, saw the report based on notes taken by
Ledbetter and Morgan at the scene. Several state editors,
according to SBC Today, "voiced outrage that the Indiana paper
would wait three months to print the story, then release it just
before the SBC Executive Committee session" in September. SBC
Today slammed BSSB administrators for "muzzling Porter and
finding a menial 'research' job for him until he retires; he is now
60. He was also told to announce . . . that he will 'not be available'
for re-election as SBC registration secretary next June. . . . And
the beat goes on. . . ."[19]

We will now move to the controversy over the BSSB's
centennial history, Celebration of Heritage and Hope.

A Historian for the Sunday School Board

The selected author, Harry Leon McBeth, had taught church
history at Southwestern Seminary since 1962 and was highly
regarded by his peers. Besides various articles for the BSSB and
scholarly societies, he had previously published eight books,
including the centennial history of the First Baptist Church of
Dallas with which he had "no" problems. Nor "did Dr. Criswell
seek to influence, directly or indirectly, what I wrote, what I
omitted, how I researched, or how I interpreted the historial
data."[19a]

In recent years he had touched on the denominational
controversy in his writings. In 1981, for example, in an address to
the BJCPA, he feared that Baptists were "softening their historic
stand on religious liberty." He saw the "politicizing of conservative
religion — a far-reaching trend" of "the past decade . . . ."[20]

In 1982, he linked Landmarkism — a revolt against SBC
structures beyond the local church — with "some of the views of
the theological controversies confronting Southern Baptists in the
20th century. Elevating doctrinal differences to crisis levels,
refusal to accept as brethren those who differ, elevating minor
issues to major importance and the driving need to create a chasm

between 'them' and 'us,' all too familiar in Southern Baptist history, have their counterparts in recent old Landmarkism," he said. The "old Landmark emphasis" on the local church, to the exclusion of the denomination and its missionary agencies, "lives today in the 'de facto' independence of some SBC superchurches. . . ."[21] McBeth obviously had in mind certain large churches, pastored by Biblical inerrantists, that had not been as active as others in denominational life. He did not note that the pastors of some of these churches had been "shut out of SBC affairs" by the pre-1979 controlling establishment.

In 1983, he seemed to link the 19th century loss of numerous Baptist churches to the "Disciples" movement, led by Alexander Campbell, with SBC conservative activists: "Baptists believe the Bible and always have," he said. "but we have always been vulnerable to people who misuse the Bible, while loudly affirming its infallible authority."[22]

The History Controversy Begins

Let us now jump ahead to the summer of 1990. Shortly after the New Orleans convention the newly elected BSSB trustees came to the Board for orientation. While there they met with President Elder and other top officers. In informal conversations some of the executives reportedly commented that they were having problems getting the new history ready for the printer. This raised eyebrows among the trustees.[23]

In late July, with the full board meeting due for August 13-15, Larry Holly asked for and obtained from Elder a copy of the history manuscript. Several other trustees got copies in like manner. The trustees had previously passed a motion which required Board officials to provide any information requested by a trustee to accomplish his fiduciary duties. The only exceptions were sensitive personnel records and other matters which might cause a legal problem.

Holly, a medical doctor who also holds a degree in history from Baylor University, prepared an "incomplete" ten-page critique which he mailed to trustees urging them to request the book from Elder.

In a letter to Elder, Holly expressed his "general disappointment with the quality of this book. . . . It is not a history, but more an apologetic for the Board." Holly "hope[d] that Don Moore's sub-committee [on publishing] will recommend that publication . . . be suspended and that a true history of the Board by an objective historian be commissioned by the trustees."[24]

Holly expressed to the other trustees his hope "that no facsimile of this book is published by another source as a history of the Board." Holly further "hope[d] that the trustees will commission an objective history, written by a Southern Baptist historian who does not have an axe to grind either for or against the president of the Board or for or against the trustees of the Board."[25] Writing to the new trustees, Holly said he "believe[d] that you and I as trustees should withdraw this book from publication, not as an act of censorship, but as an act of correction of the errors and distortions contained in it." Holly noted that Don Moore, chairmen of the sub-committee on publishing, would "review" the history and "bring a proposal to the trustees." He urged the new trustees to become informed and voice their concern at the sub-committee meeting.[26]

Dr. Holly's Critique

In his 10-page critique, Holly charged, "It is not history, but advocacy." The chapters "which deal with the administrations of Grady Cothen and Lloyd Elder are wholly inadequate." McBeth "totally ignores the very significant ways in which Lloyd Elder has failed" in his assignment by the search committee which recommended him to "act as a major reconciling force in the SBC to constantly emphasize the all important things that unite us. He has further polarized the convention by pressing the moderate-liberal agenda in a number of ways."

Holly's "incomplete" critique covered 35 items in two chapters of a 58-page section titled by McBeth, "The Lloyd Elder Era."[26a] Examples:

P. 335: McBeth reported the Search Committee which recommended Elder as calling on each trustee to "act, think, work as an individual rather than as a representative of a special interest group."

Holly: "The fact that Trustees had always functioned as a 'special interest group,' and that for the administration, is ignored."

P. 340: "Elder really does believe in and practice the 'servant leader' model . . . ."

Holly: "Again there is the effusive, non-critical praise of Lloyd Elder. One begins to wonder how the Board survived for 100 years without him."

Pp. 342, 343, in the context of protests against material in the February and August, 1985 issues of The Student which led to the resignation of the editor: "[The resignation] raised concern among a segment of Southern Baptist constituency that the Board was caving in to a small pressure group."

Holly: "Throughout this 'history' there is this implication, never documented or examined, only assumed. This is not history, it is editorialization called history. Who is the 'small pressure group' and how is doing what is right 'caving in'?"

P. 343: "[The resignation of the editor of The Student] also sent a chill through other editors of the Board's many publications who wondered if something similar could happen to them."

Holly: "... This is not history unless and until it is documented by concrete evidence, either in interviews or documents which are available to the public."

P. 346: "Those who say the Sunday School Board [administration] ignores criticism are mistaken."

Holly: "Judgment and conclusion, not history. The author has abandoned his role as objective historian and has become an advocate..."

P. 361: "By no means should [resolutions passed at conventions] be regarded as an expression of 'Southern Baptist opinion,' and they do not constitute 'directives' to the SBC agencies. ... Some feel that when a few thousand SBC messengers adopt a resolution that 'Southern Baptists have spoken.' "

Holly: "This derogatory view of the SBC in annual session, which is the only time the Convention exists, has been orchestrated by the liberals in an attempt to ignore the clear grass-roots beliefs of Southern Baptists. After 12 consecutive years of the same resolutions, their protest that this is 'not what Southern Baptists REALLY think' becomes laughable."

P. 381: The context is the parliamentary interactions after the motion was made to fire Elder at Glorietta in 1989. "When the tide in the trustee meeting seemed to turn toward Elder, a motion was offered to withdraw the motion to dismiss him. A parliamentary wrangle ensued in which some said the motion belonged to the house and must be acted upon...."

Holly: "When the motion to withdraw was made, Dr. Elder himself shouted, 'You can't do that, that motion belongs to the house.' While he was correct procedurally, his intervention in the trustee process and his usurpation of the role of the Chairman of the Board was characteristic of his style of managing the trustees."

Holly mailed his critique to trustees about two weeks before their August meeting.

At the meeting, the sub-committee on publishing, chaired by Don Moore, reported that they had reviewed the manuscript and counseled the administration not to publish it. Moore said they did not "want to fan the flames of controversy" within the SBC. Moore called the book "unbalanced." Johnnie Godwin, Vice President of General Publishing, said the trustees and administration were partners in ministry, not adversaries. Godwin said he would accept the counsel of the committee not to publish the book; indeed, he had stopped the publishing procedures at the first trustee request for a copy. The Board, he said, had paid the author and owned the manuscript.

Godwin expressed concern about any manuscript copies being sent out, because the Board did not yet have a publishable book he said. Trustee Tommy French moved that everyone who had a copy or a portion of the manuscript be asked to return it. Trustee Gene Mims mentioned that some might have written notes on their copies and would like for them to be shredded. Godwin said that could be done, however he would like all copies returned for both legal and historical records. The motion carried unanimously."[27]

Baptist Press printed a response from McBeth, who was not at the meeting: "I stand by the book. . . . It is a balanced interpretive history of the first 100 years of the Baptist Sunday School Board, ... I had the understanding the fundamentalist trustees wanted a harsh treatment of Lloyd Elder. . . . The attempt . . . to manage history will backfire."

Trustees Under the Gun

Trustees took most of the heat in the press for the Board's decision not to publish the book. The lead sentence in an August 1, Nashville Tennessean story declared: "A new history of the Baptist Sunday School Board is so liberal and controversial that it should be shredded or placed under lock and key, not published, trustees concluded Wednesday."[28] The Fort Worth Star-Telegram quoted McBeth: "I feel as though I have suffered a literary abortion and for no good cause." The same article quoted James Pleitz, a prominent Dallas pastor: "I think it represents another effort to control the press."[29]

An Associated Press report, apparently picking up from the Tennessean article, said the manuscript would "be destroyed." The AP writer said McBeth had lost "a contract" and quoted moderate Cecil Sherman: "What [the trustees] want is their own point of view whether it's right or not. They want to rewrite history just as the Russians did."

Larry Holly responded to the AP story in his hometown Beaumont Enterprise. McBeth had not lost "a contract," Holly said. "He was paid the full amount of his [$18,000] commission. . . . The truth is," Holly continued, "senior administrative officials at the BSSB alerted trustees to the inadequacy of McBeth's book. Trustees then read the manuscript and, after a rigorous review of McBeth's book, counseled the administration not to publish the manuscript. The administration then made the decision not to publish. This decision was not because of controversy; it was because McBeth did not fulfill his commission. He did not write a centennial history; he wrote a book that reflects his personal bias of events in Southern Baptist life. . . . The publisher . . . determined that McBeth's book did not achieve its commission and it was not consistent with the policies and purposes of Broadman. Therefore, appropriately, it is not being published."[30]

Faculties at Southern on August 22, and at Southwestern on August 24, leaped to McBeth's defense by unanimously passing resolutions affirming McBeth and, in effect, condemning the trustees for the book's cancellation. Southern faculty said the trustees had "(1) undermined the academic credibility of Broadman Press, (2) questioned the editorial integrity of the Broadman . . . staff, (3) heightened the atmosphere of tension and mistrust" in the SBC (4) and "repudiated the work of one of Southern Baptists' premier historians." Southwestern faculty blamed the trustees for "this arbitrary act of censorship, which we utterly deplore."

Responding to the faculty actions and the continuing negative news stories, Holly sent letters to BSSB trustees, BSSB administrators, every faculty member and trustee at Southern and Southwestern, several news publications and others. He quoted his response to the AP story, adding that the issue was not McBeth's abilities as a good historian or writer. " . . . His book fails because he apparently used the conclusions of others from which to draw his conclusion." He "failed to interview principal participants in the events about which he made judgments and . . . reported conclusions without adequate and often without any documentation . . . . His methodology was flawed." His "book was not rejected by Broadman because of objectionable material," but "because of unacceptable and objectionable method." The faculty resolutions, Holly charged, "had gone beyond affirming "one of your own," to "impugning the motives and actions of the trustees of another SBC agency . . . ."[31]

Trustee Tommy French, who graduated as a history major at Baylor, sent a letter to state Baptist editors: "When I was informed by the administration of the Sunday School Board about problems with the manuscripts, I requested a copy. After reading the manuscript very carefully, I came to the conclusion that Dr. McBeth did not fulfill his assigned commission." French was concerned that Southwestern's faculty, "not having read the manuscript, would charge" BSSB trustees "with making an 'arbitrary act of censorship.' "[32]

Holly then wrote Elder, on September 5, suggesting that he issue a statement to "help dispel the illusion that the Trustees of the Board have started a 'book burning' project." Holly said his "extensive communication" had "been required to document for future historians what has been done with the McBeth manuscript."[33]

On September 15, Elder spoke to a forum of state Baptist editors at the Board. Tammi Ledbetter's article on Lee Porter's "lecture" to the Southern Seminary class in New Orleans had appeared in the Indiana Baptist only five days earlier. Ledbetter now wrote an article on Elder's remarks to the editors regarding the McBeth book. Elder, according to Ledbetter, said McBeth had not "fail[ed] in his commission." Elder commended the leadership of general publishing committee chairman Don Moore and trustee chairman Bill Anderson for their leadership in handling the book. Ledbetter reported Elder as "disput[ing] exaggerated descriptions of the book being shredded," saying, "The intention of the trustees is to have a copy in the archives." Elder said he and Johnnie Godwin, vice president for general publishing, had determined they would not be "in an open, adversarial position with trustees as they make their decision. . . . Even though we try to stick to our knitting," Elder said, "there are times when we are called to accountability by our own trustees or by Southern Baptists in general."

Still, Elder said, "it is troubling for this Board not to publish their centennial history." Elder then indicated, according to Ledbetter, that Southern Baptists might, through the trustees, still appeal the decision.[34]

Trustees Get Tough

Elder's remarks to the editors, Holly wrote his fellow trustees on October 3, "places the Trustees . . . in a position of needing to have first hand knowledge" of the McBeth manuscript. In August, the trustees had affirmed the action of its general publishing committee. "Now, however, it seems that an appeal to the Trustees has been solicited by the President in order to force this book's publication." Get the facts, Holly urged, and "vote your conscience at the next trustee meeting in February." Holly then asked trustee chairman Anderson to request that Elder send a copy of the manuscript to every trustee.[35]

The manuscripts were sent. Holly now requested of Elder full documentation on written interchanges between Board editors, administrators and attorneys concerning the development of McBeth's manuscript for publication. Elder notified Holly that he was referring the request to Chairman Anderson.[36] Elder wrote Anderson that Holly had a legal right to have the documents and that he was filing the copies with two Board attorneys. Anderson thought it best to let the previous Board decision stand, but said Holly was entitled to the information.[37] Holly got the material and then wrote an analysis of the internal documents which he sent to fellow trustees who also had access to the information.

Copies of these documents and parts of the manuscript leaked to the press and other outsiders. I received a bundle of material in an envelope without a return address. Ray Waddle, religion editor of the <u>Nashville Tennessean,</u> and probably other writers as well, had some access to the memos. References were also made to some items during a later open trustee meeting.[38] An attorney, who serves as a BSSB trustee, assured me that, in his opinion, these were not privileged materials since they deal with the official business of an agency under the ownership and control of the Southern Baptist Convention through duly elected trustees. In making reference to various communications, I have chosen — except for a few key persons — to use titles instead of personal names of the employees.

A Trail of Concern

Written notes reveal that the proposed BSSB centennial history was discussed as early as September 17, 1986 in a conference between Lloyd Elder and six other key executives. Elder mentioned the need for a documented "serious" history with "some sequence reporting, interpreting and analysis" and "some attention" given to "p[ublic] r[elations] — not a history majoring on rabbits and conversations." The SBC controversy is not mentioned in these notes. The first names of four possible authors are jotted on the last page. The name, "Leon," is circled.

A Broadman administrator called Leon McBeth on August 27, 1987 and again shortly thereafter to confirm the Board's interest in him as the author. McBeth said, in a letter dated November 23, 1987, that if he were to write the story, he would want to do both a "factual" and "interpretative" history. McBeth initially declined, then after some negotiations accepted the project in May, 1988. At the same time he requested a "candid" conference about the book. He would later say that he was told "over and over," in a taped interview with Dr. Elder and in later letters from both Elder and another Board official, that he was to write an interpretative history.

The contract between Broadman Press and McBeth was executed on September 16, 1988. The non-royalty agreement called for Broadman to publish the manuscript when it "is completed in a form satisfactory to both parties . . . ." The writer would be paid $18,000 in three increments, $6,000 at signing; $6,000 when an acceptable manuscript is submitted; and $6,000 at publication in 1990. For this the writer granted to the publisher "all rights." An in-house information sheet attached to the contract described the content as "an interpretative history of the Sunday School Board."[39]

Internal communications reveal the uncertainties of the editors and other key parties about the extent of Elder's involvement with the author and the manuscript. Elder wrote McBeth on January 31, 1989 that he was "so very, very pleased you have been chosen to write the history . . . ." McBeth wrote the project editor on September 22 that he had had a number of meetings with Elder, the most recent coming on September 21, 1989. These were "research sessions" during which Elder "discussed recent events at the BSSB from his own memory and perspective." Elder had affirmed that the author would be free to interpret data in the context of SBC history. Elder, on October 3, 1989, had written Johnnie Godwin, vice president of general publishing: "My input on the [B]SSB history was at the very front end and not much since then."

The manuscript was due to the editor October 1, 1989. At least some material was delivered before then. On September 15, the project editor wrote McBeth expressing her concern that "quite often you go beyond the facts to make interpretations, about causes, underlying motives, possible consequences and so on. I have softened some of your statements. However, it is my understanding that you and Dr. Elder have discussed your freedom in writing this history and that he is comfortable with allowing you to make evaluations and interpretations that can be supported by the evidence in your research." Still she had praise for McBeth's work: "It's really a marvelous piece!"

On November 7, an administrator wrote the editor's boss of his feeling that "some trustees will be concerned that Leon might have been given access to information they have requested but have been denied — for example, the Burnett case." The administrator said "some of the language is questionable — even though in the minds of some, accurate. Leon refers to ultraconservative, faction and similar terms when describing trustees and SBC climate. . . . Broadman might not be aware of understandings Leon had with the administration. We know Leon met with the president; we do not know all they talked about or agreed upon."

The Broadman Press people continued to be puzzled about this relationship. On November 21, a supervisor wrote an executive: "The author feels a freedom in his writing beyond what a typical Broadman author would feel. He may be working from an understanding given to him outside of Broadman."

The concern that the book was unbalanced was felt outside of the Broadman area. A highly regarded board executive wrote the vice president of general publishing on December 17, 1989 that he was "sure" the author had "tried to be objective, but I'm afraid he failed to do so on many occasions. . . . He is writing out of a moderate mindset and I believe that will be seen by . . . trustees if not corrected by administration."

The editor continued to wrestle with the manuscript. In a February 5, 1990 memo to her supervisor, she said, "Generally, we agree that Leon has not provided us with a publishable manuscript." She had "difficulty with Leon's use of in-house memos like [Clifton] Allen's recommendations to ignore trustee instructions and to reinstate Vol. 1 of B[roadman] B[ible] C[ommentary]." She noted the author's extensive reliance on interviews with James Sullivan "for the later chapters in the book. In many ways, I fear that this has become Sullivan's history of the

Board. . . . We are missing the Celebrating and the Hope. We have improved the manuscript we have. It could be published with little risk. My question is what about the manuscript we don't have — the positive side." She suggested that the project be delayed so the author can "expand on the positive." Source references to the two chapters covering the Cothen era indicate that the author relied heavily on this living president also. Twenty-six of 33 sources are taped interviews with Cothen. The SBC Annual is cited as a source in four instances, Facts and Trends, the BSSB newsletter for two and an office memo for one.

Inter-office communications during the early months of 1990 indicate continued struggle among editors, administrators and the author to get a "publishable" manuscript. Everyone agreed that there were many positives in the book, but fears continued to be expressed that it was biased toward the moderate side in the controversy.

Two Board public relations reviewers commented that "the style differences" between Chapters 1-8 and 9-16 — dealing with the Sullivan, Cothen and Elder years — are greatly different. This "might give the impression that the history written about living people was highly selective history. . . . Criticism could be raised that some of the living historical figures — Sullivan, Cothen and Elder — were allowed to interpret their own historical involvement while other significant persons were not even mentioned."

Board attorneys Norm Finney and Robert Thomas also reviewed the manuscript. Elder's executive assistant relayed to Elder a November 3, 1989 phone message from one of the lawyers: "Thomas wants to make sure Elder is aware that he sees it as heavily slanted in the anti-conservative way. Lengthy detail on Job, Burnett, Bramlette, Butler. I told him Elder has now read those pages and has similar concerns [and] — will be dealt with."

Four days later Thomas wrote Finney his concerns. Thomas, not a Southern Baptist, said his firm had been general counsel to the BSSB for over 30 years and for the last 16 years "I have been the partner in charge for this particular client." Thomas' greatest concern was "a noticeable bias on the part of the author against the conservatives" in the SBC. Thomas did "not want to give the impression that I might be catering to one faction within the [SBC] as opposed to another, but I could not remain silent on a matter of this significance."

By April 19, in the words of one executive, the book "seems to be coming along well." He noted to Elder that Broadman people would be "deleting" from Elder's forward, "any references that specifically indicate or imply that you've read the manuscript itself." It was obvious now that the projected release date, May 25, could not be met. The editor advised her supervisor on May 21 that an October release "should still be possible . . . , if all goes well."

We know of course that this did not happen. Acting on counsel from the trustees' publishing sub-committee, administrators stopped publication. Strong criticism of the trustees ensued. Larry Holly and other trustees obtained copies of the manuscript and relevant in-house communications. A number of trustees requested that Chairman Anderson call a special meeting of the Board for January 17, 1991 to consider President Elder's future relationship with the Board.

President Elder's Performance Under Review

Prior to that meeting, a five-member workgroup of the General Administration Committee met on December 13 to review Elder's performance as president. The entire 17-member GAC then met January 4 to consider the report of the workgroup. Elder was already under heavy burdens. He had just demoted Lee Porter. His wife Sue was scheduled for open-heart surgery on Christmas Eve. And now with internal documents on the handling of the history circulating among trustees and others, talk was in the air for his dismissal. One trustee called the inter-office communications "the smoking gun" and said, "Lloyd's goose is cooked this time." [40]

The GAC was reportedly incensed that Elder and his administration had failed to disclose to the trustees these internal communications which in GAC chairman Don Collins' words were "fully supportive of the trustees' counsel not to publish the manuscript."[41]

The closed GAC meeting on January 4 reportedly lasted until well past midnight. Friday, January 11, the Nashville Tennessean reported that Elder's future was "clouded," although, Elder, the paper said, had dismissed as mere rumors reports that he was being removed.[42] Saturday, January 12, a Nashville reporter obtained a copy of Elder's confidential letter to the GAC committee, in which he reportedly declined to resign. That same day, the Tennessean quoted trustee W. Gene Henderson: "It's common knowledge among the trustees that a special meeting would be for the singular purpose of dismissing Dr. Elder." [43]

Baptist Press also released a story on January 12, quoting trustee chair Bill Anderson about the content of the GAC's workgroup meeting: "We discussed at length some issues that have arisen, particularly the McBeth book." Anderson declined comment on whether the GAC had asked Elder to resign or retire. "The committee is still discussing options, all kinds of options." The GAC, he said, would meet at 10 a.m. Thursday, [January 17] with the full board convening at 7 p.m.[44]

Tuesday, January 15, the Tennessean headlined: "Festive Baptist History Book Now Timebomb for President." The writer cited the internal memos: "Some memos say that editorial efforts were made to 'tone down' some anti-conservative language in McBeth's manuscript, while others deemed it 'not publishable' in the SBC's current climate of controversy." Trustee Eugene Mims was quoted as saying, "We came away looking like censors in August. But it's clear now we didn't dream it up."

Wednesday, January 16, the Nashville Banner reported that a group of moderate Southern Baptist ministers, led by Bill Sherman, had gone to the Board to show their support for Elder.[45]

Trustee chair Bill Anderson spoke to the BSSB employees chapel on the day of the called meeting. "I am pledging to you as best I can and as best we can," Anderson said, "to act in good will and good faith with good judgment and with good sense."

The Showdown Vote

At seven p.m. trustees were already at their desks in the J.M. Crowe Room when Lloyd and Sue Elder entered to the rhythmic applause of a group of employees. Press perched on chairs behind a long narrow desk. Other visitors stood around the walls and spilled over into the outside halls.[46]

President Elder sat at the front with Bill Anderson and the other Board officers. Anderson read from James 1:5: "If any of you lack wisdom, let him ask of God . . . ." After prayer, the secretary called the roll. Anderson then explained that the meeting was to evaluate the "performance of our president. Eighteen months ago at the [August, 1989 meeting at Glorieta] the General Administration Committee selected a smaller committee to evaluate President Elder. That committee came to some conclusions with perceived impasse. The GAC studied the recommendations of that committee and decided we had some problems." The GAC, Anderson continued, had spent many hours since with Elder. "The results of those discussions led to this discussion."

Elder had been expected to contest his dismissal. Many were caught by surprise when Anderson announced that Elder's attorney had presented a proposal for early retirement because of an inability to move beyond a stalemate with trustees on management issues. The GAC, Anderson said, would later spell out a recommendation in detail.

Invited to speak first, Elder drew chuckles with a Jerry Clower story about a hunter needing "relief" from an angry coon. "The last six to eight weeks have been difficult for all of us," he said. "We have looked at what is best for the . . . Sunday School Board, . . . for our Southern Baptist family, . . . and for Lloyd Elder's effective leadership."

Conceding "substantive disagreement" between himself and trustees, Elder then proceeded to give "an account of my stewardship," presenting slides and overhead projections that illustrated his seven years of accomplishments. He spoke of employee relations, the Centennial Tower, the New American [Inerrantist] Commentary, the new Baptist hymnal, Growing Churches magazine, the new Breakthrough Sunday School literature and other achievements. BSSB literature he said, is used by 96.3 percent of those enrolled in SBC Sunday Schools.

The BSSB, Elder said, had a hundred times more opportunity to make mistakes than a large church with a $1.9 million budget. He conceded that mistakes had been made with the centennial history. He should have involved a "small group" of trustees in author selection and at other points. The manuscript should have been held up "until every effort was made by the author to produce an acceptable balanced manuscript for publication. Not having achieved that, the administration should have stood with the trustees to lay down the matter quickly and quietly as was intended by the trustees in action last summer." Still, "no breach of integrity or willful coverup" had occurred.

"Let us enter the second century with our hope in God," he said. "Let us obediently accept the authority of the Scriptures in our life, for this is a Bible Board." Whatever his future, Elder "pledge[d] . . . to be . . . faithful in my role."

When Elder sat down, Dan Collins, chairman of the GAC, said the committee had met for over 30 hours, studying numerous documents and talking with Elder. "We have reviewed and unanimously accepted the attorney's proposal for Dr. Elder's early retirement," he said.

Lloyd Elder's "Golden Parachute"

The agreement stated that the "parties acknowledge and agree" that the retirement "is a result of honest differences of opinion between [Elder] and the Board with regard to management style, philosophy and performance." Elder would continue in office as president until January 30, 1992, or 30 days after the election of his successor, whichever came first, after which he would serve as consultant on call until April 1, 1993 when he would take early retirement. Elder would receive $10,000 to pay the legal expense for executing the agreement and his full annual salary of $135,800 for the two years. When he reached retirement at age 60 in April 1993, he would be given his company car and specified office furniture and receive lifetime health insurance and annual retirement pay of approximately $67,900 each year. Should he die before Mrs. Elder, she would receive $67,900 for the rest of her life. As for Elder, he agreed that "during the period he is receiving compensation or benefits, . . . he shall not make any statement or take any action not in the best interest of the Board." Violation of this agreement would result in Elder "forfeit[ing] all amounts payable to him."[47]

There were also "genuine concerns" about financial and business mismanagement. Collins said. The Board had suffered "real" sales declines, excluding the effect of price increases during five consecutive years. Three Board enterprises had suffered cumulative losses of almost $25 million.

There were also allegations, backed by affadavits, Collins said, that Elder had taped some phone conversations with trustees and even with Board attorney Thomas, without permission of the callers. However, Collins assured, the GAC had already determined to accept Elder's proposal, with the financial package, to retire before trustee chairman Bill Anderson and Collins disclosed the taping allegations.

Trustee Moves for Elder's Immediate Resignation

The motion to accept the agreement was made and seconded. Trustee Roland Maddox then moved an amendment to ask for Elder's "immediate resignation," arguing that it would not be in the best interest of either party "to drag out" Elder's tenure over a year.

An opponent to the amendment feared that the Board's sales might be affected by perception of the amendment receiving "quick passage late at night." Another urged that Elder be allowed to continue so that he might dedicate the new Centennial Tower, "which is largely due to him." Still another said, "If [the GAC] says they can work with him another year, then let's take their recommendation."

Trustee Larry Winn said to "drag out the process" of Elder's tenure "will limit the Board in doing its job." Danny Strickland said, "If we wait a year, concern in the Convention will mount." Joe Knott said the amendment was "not being unkind to Dr. Elder. We're being very generous. He will still be paid." Larry Holly, citing internal documents relating to the ill-fated history, said there "are other issues of accurate reporting, integrity and forthrightness with trustees which would preclude Dr. Elder from continuing with full powers. . . ." Holly favored "the financial package; it shows there's no acrimony among us." Elder "can still serve as a consultant." Holly also named some of the Broadman Press people whom he thought ought to receive praise for their work on the centennial history.

Among other things, Elder denied having "taped a personal conversation with anyone of you," except for "conference calls" and "when we are on a speaker phone" and all parties knew it. Chairman Anderson replied that he hadn't known his conversation was being taped, and noted, "I asked another trustee if he knew he was being taped and he said, 'No.' "

Morris Chapman, a BSSB trustee by virtue of his convention office, "believe[d] it is in the best interests of our Board and the convention that we defeat the amendment." Chapman was "willing to trust" Elder to abide by the agreement "as long as he should live."

Elder was given the opportunity during a 10-minute recess to consider if he could accept the changed conditions if the amendment passed. He declined to speak. Several trustees later cited Chapman's statement and the recess as having a negative impact on the vote to require Elder to step down immediately. At 9:38 p.m. the amendment lost 41-31. The original motion then passed with two negative votes and a number of abstentions.

Following the vote, President Chapman "express[ed] thanksgiving to God that He has led us through this time. We all had our vote. We will support the trustees." Chapman turned to Elder. "I trust that in your remaining time [in office] you will do all in your power to lead this body, . . . and discourage anything that will bring dissension to our convention."

Conflicting Reactions to the "Settlement"

After the meeting ended, a long line of Board employees and friends expressed sympathy and love to Lloyd and Sue Elder. Moderate pastor Bill Sherman sharply dissented with the trustee action. Sherman told Dan Collins, "The only reason that you dismissed Dr. Elder is that he has a position that you want on your agenda. I can assure you that Baptists will not favorably look on it." Collins retorted that "the issue of a successor, other than on an interim basis of someone within the board," had "not been mentioned in the deliberations."

"They'll try to put a pretty face on this thing," Sherman told reporters, "but this vendetta has been the goal of [Larry] Holly and [Bob] Tenery since they came on this board. . . . It's an abominable disgrace — a hypocrisy."

Attorney Thomas also talked to reporters, saying one of his phone conversations with Elder had been taped without his knowledge. Asked about the memo in which he had warned that the centennial history was biased against conservatives, he said, "It was and I am not even a Southern Baptist."[48]

A later joint statement by Elder and the four trustee officers acknowledged that Elder's office had taped three conversations without the knowledge of the other parties. Elder said the taping had been done by his executive assistant for business purposes and accurate follow-up action. There was no evidence that any other calls had been recorded without the consent of the parties. The trustees and Elder wanted "everyone" to "know that in the future telephone conversations will not be recorded without the consent of all persons spoken to. . . ."[49]

Denominational editors reacted in print. Southern Baptists, said Presnall Wood of Texas, "who have not recovered from last summer's firing of the two Baptist Press editors, have been given another fellowship crisis by the Sunday School Board trustees."[50] However, Indiana's Gary Ledbetter could "not imagine how a non-comatose board of any political persuasion could have been more generous or taken a more minimalist approach to the problems this board faced."[51]

State editors received a number of letters from laity voicing shock at Elder's salary and the finanicial settlement. Twenty-two members of the Rock Creek Baptist Church in Double Springs, AL signed a letter to the Alabama Baptist[52] stating that Elder's salary was "greater than the state's governor, budget director, or education superintendent. They asked, "Should a religious leader receive a retirement salary that is eight to ten times greater than that earned by the average retired family. . . We want to support God's work instead of affluence for men."

Early in February, BSSB trustees elected a 10-member presidential search committee. Rumors immediately began circulating about whom the committee would nominate. At the same meeting President Elder reported that income for the first quarter of 1990-91 was running above that of the same period during previous year. "Agreement [between the president and trustees] to disagree," said Elder, "does not need to mean the end of our kingdom work. . . . "[53]

Early in April, the first chapter of an eight-part "original" series on the history of the Sunday School Board for the Southern Baptist Press Association appeared in several state papers. McBeth said in an April, 1991 phone interview that he had "turned down" the assignment "twice" before agreeing to do the series of articles. "I would have done the series, even if my book had been published. This is a different sort of thing. It will speak to multitudes of people who do not read books."

Reflecting on the ill-fated book project, McBeth said, "Some people think I did a puff job on [Lloyd] Elder. I did not. I didn't interview Elder as much as I did [presidents] Cothen and Sullivan. I interviewed Sullivan more, partly because he was available and served so long and so much happened [during his tenure]. I interviewed Cothen one time, a lengthy interview. I interviewed Elder twice for shorter periods. I also had access to tape recorded interviews, from Board archives, which others had made with Cothen.

"It was untrue," McBeth said, that he had not talked to any trustees. "I talked with some of the persons, including [then trustee chairman] Warren Hultgren, involved [in the 1989 trustee meeting in which a motion was made to fire Elder]."

McBeth said "editors" at the Board, "left both the positive and the less than positive comments about Cothen," in the book, while they "edited out any statement about Elder except the most positive. Then when other people read that, [they] had no way of knowing" what the editors had done." That "made it look as if I had written a sort of puff job on Elder, . . . which I did not."

McBeth was "not bitter" over the book. "I cannot see the problems in it that some people seem to find. I stand by the work. . . . I think it's one of the better things I have done. . . , a fair and honest, interpretive history, . . . although I'm the first to admit that there are many places it could be improved. I believe that some day the manuscript will come to life and if it does, I think I will be vindicated."

As for the Sunday School Board, McBeth said, "It has been the great shaping influence on all Southern Baptists and my life," as well. "I would never do anything to hurt that Board." [54]

The McBeth series appeared just before press time for this book. BSSB trustee Mark Brooks, a member of the Search Committee for a new president, said, "It's news to me, but I have no qualms whatsoever about any article or series on the Board, as long as it is fair and objective to all parties. Our people need to know the rich heritage of this Board which has done more than any other agency to shape Southern Baptist life." [55]

References

1 "Pageant Brings Back Memories," June 27, 1990, Baptist Standard, p. 10.

2 The Sunday School Board Report to the 1990 Southern Baptist Convention, p. 2. Also "General Information" for Press.

3 For a detailed report on this sad experience in BSSB history, read James C. Hefley: "Former Southern Baptist Sunday School Board Officer Wins Settlement," Christianity Today, October 2, 1981, pp. 46-50.

4 Report of BSSB Presidential Search Committee, 1983.

5 Personal Interview, Nashville, January, 1991.

6 Information from a BSSB trustee.

7 Telephone interview with Ledbetter, August, 1991. I was among those to whom Ledbetter sent the draft.

8 Holly to Elder, September 13, 1991.

9 Holly to Anderson, September 13, 1991.

10 Elder to trustees, September 17, 1991. Elder's letter quickly became less than "confidential" as it was circulated to a number of outsiders, of which I was one.

11 Brooks to Elder, September 17.

12 Porter's apology was faxed to state papers on the same date he released it.

13 Ledbetter to Mims, October 25, 1991.

14 Telephone interview, October, 1991.

15 Press Release by Porter, November 30, 1990.

16 December 7, 1990.

17 "Lee Porter Demoted for Comments About Controversy," November 15, 1990, p. 3.

18 "Sunday School Board Reassigns Lee Porter," November 8, 1990, p. 5.

19 "Porter in Eye of Storm Over New Orleans Remarks," November 2, 1990, p. 8.

19a McBeth to Hefley, April 11, 1991.

20 Address given October 6, 1981. Adapted for an article by the Baptist Standard, December 2, 1981, pp. 12, 13.

21 James Lee Young: "SBC Controversy Said Linked to Expansion," Baptist Standard, May 5, 1982, p. 3.

22 "Baptist Pulpit in a Church of Christ," Baptist Standard, April 27, 1983, p. 24. Reprinted from the Louisiana Baptist Message.

23 A trustee related this to me in Nashville on January 18, 1991.

24 Holly to Elder, August 1, 1990.

25 Holly to other Trustees, July 30, 1990.

26 Holly to New Trustees, August 1, 1990.

26a Pp. 333-390.

27 From Minutes of Trustee Meeting.

28 Ray Waddle: "Baptists To Scuttle 'Unfair' History," The Jackson Sun, August 16, 1990, p. B-1. Reprinted from the Nashville Tennessean.

29 Jim Jones: "Baptist Author Calls Book Cancellation a 'Literary Abortion,'" Fort Worth Star-Telegram, August 21, 1990, p. 10..

30 "Baptist Story Was Wrong," August 29, 1990.

31 Holly to Russell Dilday, President of Southwestern Seminary, September 6, 1990.

32 Letters to the Editor, Indiana Baptist, October 9, 1990, p. 2.

33 Holly to Elder, September 5, 1990.

34 "Elder Commends Moore for Trustee Leadership," September 25, 1990.

35 Holly to Anderson, October 3, 1990.

36 Elder to Holly, November 7, 1990.

37 Anderson to Holly, November 10, 1990.

38 January 17, 1991.

39 From the Memorandum of Agreement.

40 Telephone Interview, December, 1990.

41 Earl Fredericks: "Dr. Elder's Resignation Handled with Truth and Fairness, an Interview with Dan Collins," The Southern Baptist Communicator, March, 1991, p. 11.

42 Ray Waddle: "Sunday School Board Chief's Future Clouded," January 11, 1991, p. 8B.

43 "Baptist Board's Leader Faces Jury of Trustees," January 12, 1991, p. 1.

44 Linda Lawson, "BSSB Trustee Meeting Called Regarding Elder's Presidency."

45 Francis Meeker: "New Baptist Trustee Promises to Be Open-minded on Elder," p. B-3.

46 The account of the meeting is taken from mine and Joni Hannigan's notes and tapes and from Tammi Ledbetter's detailed story in the January 29, 1991 issue of the Indiana Baptist.

47 "Employment and Consultation Agreement" between Elder and trustees.

48 From my tape of these conversations.

49 R. Albert Mohler Jr.: "Joint Statement Clarifies Confusion Over 'Taping' Charges," The Christian Index, February 7, 1991, pp. 1, 3.

50 "Sunday School Board Action," Baptist Standard, January 23, 1991, p. 6.

51 "The Art of the Deal," Indiana Baptist, January 29., 1991, p. 2.

52 Alabama Baptist, March 28, 1991, p. 3

53 "BSSB trustees Elect Presidential Search Committee," Word & Way, February 14, 1991, p. 3.

54 Telephone Interview, April, 1991.

55 Telephone Interview, April, 1991.

Chapter 16

"Baylor University: Saved or Stolen?"

W e return now to Baylor University where the SBC controversy over the truth of Scripture began almost 70 years ago. On September 21, 1990, a majority of Baylor trustees secretly amended their charter to declare independence from governance by the Baptist General Convention of Texas. Some saw the action as a grand theft; others said Baylor had been saved from a "fundamentalist takeover." Baptist Standard editor, Presnall Wood, said the unilateral charter change had "create[d] a crisis not known in the history of both Baylor and the Baptist General Convention of Texas."[1] The Baylor action is not unique among state convention schools. Some have already taken the same step. Others are weighing the pros and cons of separation from their funding Baptist body. Hence, the Baylor crisis is much larger than Texas.

First, a look at the significance and history of Baylor. With 12,019 students from all 50 states and 54 foreign countries, Baylor is by far the largest in enrollment of the 48 senior Southern Baptist colleges and universities. With a cluster of prestigious graduate schools and a 1.3 million-book library, which includes the world's largest collection of the works of poet Robert Browning, Baylor is the "crown jewel" of Texas Baptist life. Chartered the year the SBC was born, Baylor has graduated more evangelical ministers and missionaries than any other school in America. Baylor alumni are scattered around the world. Almost 50,000 live in Texas alone. Some are household names in the Lone Star State.

Baylor's Checkered History

Baylor was founded in the historic town of Independence, where patriot Sam Houston lived and was baptized into the membership of the Independence Baptist Church The idea of a Baptist university came from William Tryon, one of the two missionaries sent to Texas by the American Home Mission Society to placate Southern complaints of neglect. Judge Robert Emmett Bledsoe Baylor dictated the first charter while Tryon wrote it and penned the name Baylor University. The charter was certified on February 1, 1845 by the

Ninth Congress of the Republic of Texas. Later that year Texas became the 28th state of the USA. Among the first contributors were Baylor, who gave $1,000, and Houston who donated $330 and the use of his law library.

Classes began May, 18, 1846 with 24 students, male and female. Henry Gillette, an Episcopalian and the first teacher, directed the school until the Baptist president, Henry Lea Graves arrived from Georgia. In 1851 Baylor divided into male and female departments with one president and a principal for each. Disagreement over spheres of authority resulted in the second president, Rufus C. Burleson, moving the entire faculty and the senior class of the male department to Waco Classical School which Burleson rechartered as Waco University.

In 1863, the women's department at Independence separated to become Baylor Female College, the first women's college west of the Mississippi and later renamed Mary Hardin-Baylor College. In 1882 a tornado almost destroyed Baylor University at Independence. Some Texas Baptists urged the merging of Baylor and Waco universities in Waco. Baylor's president, William Carey Crane bitterly opposed the union. A sudden attack of pneumonia killed Crane in 1885. Later that year the Baptist State Convention and the Baptist General Association of Texas consolidated as the Baptist General Convention of Texas. The BGCT Executive Board and the trustees of Baylor and Waco universities voted to move the Independence school to the Waco campus in 1886 where it became Baylor University at Waco. Fifty years later "at Waco" was dropped from the name.

After 1886 Baylor trustees were elected by the Baptist General Convention of Texas, which managed to survive both theological attacks and ecclesiastical feuds. J. Frank Norris' attacks on Baylor and the BGCT are well known. Less known is the bitter rivalry between rival editors J.B. Cranfill and S.A. Hayden who drew guns old west style and fired without hitting each other.

Baylor Administration Sides With SBC Moderates

From the 1920s on there were occasional criticisms of what was being taught in the religion department. It was complaints from students that led to a visit by Paul Pressler to the Baylor campus and the conclusion by Pressler that some professors were teaching a less-than-orthodox view of scripture. The Baylor administration first publicly opposed the SBC conservative movement in 1981 when Abner McCall, then president of Baylor, was nominated as the moderate candidate for SBC president. McCall got less than 40 percent of the vote. That was the year when Dan Vestal told his church that he had almost lost his faith while a ministerial student at Baylor.

Named Chancellor, McCall was succeeded by Herbert Reynolds, who had been his executive vice president. Reynolds, who held a doctorate in psychology and was a former military instructor, came out swinging against conservatives in 1984, saying there are those "who say, 'If you do not see this Book as we see it, then you're not a first-rate Christian."[2]

A month later, in November, 1984, Reynolds was asked by motivational speaker Zig Ziglar, a Sunday School teacher at FBC, Dallas, why Baylor had a Mormon on the faculty. Reynolds responded that the Mormon taught only foreign languages and had pledged not to proselyte his students. A few days later a small group of conservative students at Baylor presented Reynolds a "manifesto" against permitting the teaching of "theistic evolution," R-rated movies, songs with "immoral themes," a lecture by a professor on the advantages of being a homosexual and other "unchristian" activities on campus. The "manifesto" hit the media and put Reynolds on the hot seat. Charging the students with using "KGB" tactics, he said he was doing all he could to investigate their accusations. Behind the students, he said, lurked "a priestly and self-anointed group [Ziglar, Pressler, Patterson, et. al.] out to make "clones" by controlling the SBC educational system.[3]

The heat remained on Baylor. The next year, Zig Ziglar, included Baylor among six state Baptist colleges — the others were Wake Forest, the University of Richmond, Stetson, Furman and William Jewell — which Ziglar said had departed from the purpose for which they were founded.[4]

X-Rated Films

The worst was yet to come. In May, 1986, Lee Roberts, chairman of the SBC Committee on Nominations, got into a public wrangle with Baylor trustee Paul Powell in which Roberts charged that Powell and Winfred Moore, also a Baylor trustee, had "recently voted to allow the continued showing of pornography depicting homosexuality, sadism, nudity, explicit sex and the use of our Lord's name in vain" at the university.[5] Roberts cited Baylor trustee Paul Martin as his source for the vote on the so-called pornographic films being shown at Baylor.

Martin said he had come to the trustee meeting with "no idea that Baylor University was showing pornographic films. . . . But [trustee] Jim Bolton said that he went out and picked up the very films that were being shown by the Baylor Film Society, under the auspices of Baylor University, and these films . . . had explicit sex scenes in them. . . "

According to Martin, when this was brought up, "President Reynolds said that the "'three [professors] in charge'" of the films were " 'fantastic Christians,' and he was sure the films were fine and there was no reason to stop what the Film Society was doing."

Martin at that point moved that the trustees direct the administration to quit allowing films that had explicit sex scenes. Trustee Dewey Presley, according to Martin, "instantly jump[ed] up) and made a motion to table my motion, which is exactly the same as voting it down." Trustees Powell and Moore were among those voting to table.

Trustee minutes show that the Film Society continued to show some of the films for three months. Only after a conservative honor student complained to trustees were the showings stopped. For his objections, the student was derided in local newspapers as a "member of the Fundamentalist KGB."

Reynolds explained to the trustees that the student officers of the Film Society had not followed orders from the faculty sponsors to stop the film showings. Reynolds said he had suspended the Society until the Baylor Communications Media Committee could "recommend to me clear guidelines to govern the Society's future and existence." Reynolds assured the trustees that he was "opposed to pornography [and] to anything that would mitigate against the Christian development of our students here."[6]

Homosexual Professors Resign

A year later, just before the 1987 fall state convention, Baylor was in trouble on another front. Les Csorba, a member of the SBC Public Affairs Committee, alleged in a column that five or six Baylor professors had "resigned" following allegations that they had engaged in homosexual activity. Baptist Standard editor Presnall Wood reported Reynolds as saying that during 1985-86 some students had been dismissed for soliciting homosexual acts and in 1986 a staff member and three of the faculty had been offered a hearing after university security discovered them to be homosexuals. The four chose to resign. "Incidence of homosexual activity on our campus is rather small when compared to communities of the same size," Reynolds said.[7] To Reynolds great relief the resignations did not come up at the Convention.

In the March, 1988 Baylor alumni magazine, Reynolds said that "fundamentalists" are out to gain control of Baylor. "Those who take the view that the Bible is absolutely accurate from historical and scientific standpoints ultimately address such things as the exact ages of [mankind] and our earth," he said. "Their mentality would permeate the entire institution. . . . If we can get the number of messengers to San Antonio from Texas that we need, . . . we have the possibility of returning the Convention to the hands of mainstream Baptists . . ."[8]

Reynolds' use of the alumni magazine for political means greatly upset some conservative trustees and alumni. Alumnus Ron Wilson, a pastor in California, called Reynolds' campaign against conservatives "nonsense and outrageous."[9]

President Reynolds Says ". . .Contradictions in the Bible."

After his side lost in San Antonio in 1988, Reynolds continued insisting that SBC conservatives were moving to "capture and dominate" the entire SBC. The next year Reynolds was quoted in the Baylor student paper as saying "there are too many contradictions in the Bible for the Bible to be inerrant."[10]

At the 1989 Texas Convention, BGCT president Joel Gregory was rumored to be concerned about theological problems at Baylor. Gregory said he had delivered to Baylor a list of possible teachers, "about 20 conservative evangelical scholars" who had not been actively involved in the SBC controversy. Gregory denied that he was out to replace any professor. His concern was only with balance in the religion department.[11] Baylor hired no teachers from Gregory's list.

The Secret Charter Search

Unknown to Gregory and others, Reynolds already had six lawyers investigating the possibility that Baylor trustees could amend the university's charter and become a self-perpetuating board. The lawyers researched law books, historical documents and minutes of trustee and convention meetings. They found that the university had been "chartered" twice, in 1845 and in 1886 and that the charter had been amended a number of times since the move to Waco.

The BGCT's 1886 charter plainly said that Baylor did not have freedom to remove itself from the BGCT's control without convention approval. However, the lawyers said, Baylor had been founded before the convention and the trustees had later given the convention the authority to elect trustees.

Chancellor McCall, a former dean of the Baylor Law School, said later: "No statements in any other organization's charter or bylaws can control what the trustees can do. And once trustees are elected, their obligation is to the trust — not to those who elected them."

McCall said he had "looked into the possibility of such action 25 years ago. I found out then that there was no question about the right of the trustees to change the charter. . . . The [Baptist] conventions," he said, "don't own the . . . institutions. . ." They "are set up as independent, nonprofit, eleemosynary corporations. They are all public trusts, dedicated to public purposes. . . . Once they are dedicated to such purposes, it is an irrevocable dedication. Baylor's relationship with the denomination," he maintained "has been a voluntary, cooperative relationship."[12]

Reynold's Rationale

Many, if not most of the 48 trustees, had been kept in the dark on the legal search. Reynolds says he began thinking it was time to act when SBC conservatives won the denominational presidency for the 12th year in a row. A "reliable source" tipped him that the national leadership planned to make Texas their next target, he claimed. [13] "After they fired the Baptist Press guys, we were even more dismayed. So we looked at the lawyers' findings and decided we had to . . . . continue to be a part [of the BGCT]" and "at the same time . . . to have a board that could not come under the domination of this extremist or fundamentalist group." [14]

The 48-member BGCT-elected Baylor board, Reynolds said, had from 8-14 members who "might vote in sympathy with the fundamentalist faction or do their bidding" on certain issues. With 16 trustees to be elected at the November, 1990 convention in Houston, Reynolds says he saw the possibility that an alternate slate could be substituted, giving the more conservative group a majority.[15]

Reynolds worked closely with Randall Fields, the son of the former director of Baptist Press and a Baylor trustee by virtue of being president of the alumni association, to prepare the alumni for the anticipated secret action. The September issue of the alumni magazine ran a four-page feature under the headline: "Fundamentalists Threaten Baylor Takeover." In that event, readers were told that Baylor's student body would be cut in half and academic freedom stifled by "thought control." An editorial from the <u>Waco Tribune-Herald</u> was reprinted that commended Reynolds for comparing "certain fundamentalist leaders to Nazis in their myopia and intolerance" and warning that they wanted to "convert the world-renowned university into a second-rate Bible college."[16]

The Covert Action

At least five trustees — John Baugh, Glen Diggs, Randy Fields, Winfred Moore and Dewey Presley — came to the September 21 meeting well informed. Knowing nothing of the plans to amend the charter, a number of other trustees walked into the meeting to face the "insiders" with their battery of lawyers. Ten trustees did not attend the meeting.

A motion was made to set aside the announced order of business. Dewey Presley then moved the adoption of the proposed charter amendment. Trustees Diggs, Baugh and Fields all seconded the motion.

The lawyers handed out 17 typewritten pages of projected questions and answers. They told the trustees that Baylor was a "public trust," dedicated to education. It was not owned by the

BGCT but was only under the "patronage and general direction" of the convention. Trustees, they argued, could legally change the charter to provide for a self-governing and self-perpetuating board of regents. The plan called for a three-year transfer of governance from the present 48-member board of trustees to 24 regents, with one-fourth of the regents chosen by BGCT-elected trustees and three-fourths by the sitting board. The three-fourths' self-perpetuating majority would effectively end BGCT governance. BGCT-elected trustees would mainly serve in public relations and fund-raising roles.

In the discussion that followed it was emphasized that the amended charter stated that in the event of Baylor's dissolution, all assets would revert to the BGCT. Furthermore, 75 percent of the regents would have to be Texas Baptists and all be Southern Baptists. However, the lawyers admitted that the charter could be further amended by the regents to allow non-Baptists to serve.

After two hours of discussion the motion to amend the charter passed 30-7 with one abstention. The seven who voted against the charter change were Hal Boone, Bill Grubbs, William D. Agee, Reida R. Stewart, Jack Fields, Donald H. Wills and Fred Roach. Trustee Grubbs told a reporter afterward, "It was a beautiful job — a classical story on how to steal a school. The whole trustee meeting was railroaded."[17]

When the vote was announced, Baylor counsel Basil Thomson called a law firm in Austin where Baylor Vice President James Netherton and Treasurer Howard Dudgeon were waiting with a copy of the amendment. Netherton and Dudgeon signed the document and had it notarized. Netherton and Dudgeon then took the document to the Texas Secretary of State's office and received a certificate of amendment. By mid-afternoon the deed was done. The trustees-turned-regents were now wholly responsible for the university with its $459,005,617 in assets and $203,751,433 in endowment funds.[18]

Before the meeting, President Reynolds reportedly had the fax machines in all administrative offices disconnected to prevent outside knowledge and the possible filing of an injunction to head off or at least delay the charter change. Once assured that the charter had been certified in Austin, Reynolds' office faxed a press release to the Baptist Standard. "This is an historic and courageous initiative by the board of trustees," he said. "This action will maintain Baylor's academic excellence and continue its world-wide Christian emphasis," while "freeing Baylor from an attempted takeover by its special interest group." The Standard telephoned the news to William M. Pinson Jr., Executive Director of the BGCT Executive Board. This was Pinson's first "awareness" of what had happened.

BGCT Officials React

Pinson, shocked, told the Standard it "would be premature for me to elaborate on the situation before consulting with [BGCT officers]. I do hope that Baylor will maintain its historic relationship with the [BGCT]."[19]

Pinson immediately informed the BGCT officers and the directors of the BGCT's Coordinating Boards of Education and Welfare, which related directly to funding for Baylor. He asked the officers to meet with him as soon as possible. Pinson says Reynolds called him the next day to tell him that "a highly confidential legal study initiated two years ago had [showed] that trustees had legal authority under the laws of the state of Texas to amend the charter of the institution without convention approval." Reynolds, according to Pinson, said "the reason for this action was to remove the university from the denominational controversy in the SBC . . . and to prevent a hostile take-over by a group in the SBC. He indicated that Baylor wanted to remain close to Texas Baptists. . ."[20]

On the same day that Reynolds called Pinson, the 80,000 member Baylor Alumni Association's Board of Directors met and approved a resolution affirming the "courageous and historic step to assure Baylor alumni that Baylor University will remain true to her historic mission. . . " The resolution was printed in the October magazine which headlined: "Baylor Charter Change Thwarts Threatened Takeover by Presslerite-Fundamentalists." The issue also featured editorials from three newspapers acclaiming the action and saying the trustees had acted to save Baylor.

Reynolds now sent a folksy videotape message to thousands of Texas Baptist pastors, saying, "I want to be straightforward with you folks." The trustees had amended the charter, he said, to save Baylor from people who "would destroy our convention" and to ensure that Baylor would not become "an indoctrination center" where students and faculty "would walk lockstep with extremists." Baylor, he said, wanted only to "serve" Texas Baptists as "we have for 145 years."[21]

Contrary to what Reynolds and the Baylor public relations people were saying, the threat of a conservative takeover of the BGCT did not seem real. The 1989 convention had refused to re-elect Baylor trustee Jim Bolton because Bolton had spoken negatively about Baylor to outsiders and violated his "Christian fiduciary responsibility" as a trustee. Yet the convention re-elected a number of moderate trustees who, in Jimmy Draper's words, had "been far more active in political rallies" than had Bolton.[22]

Phil Lineburger had been elected BGCT president in 1989 and was expected to be re-elected at the November 13, 14 1990 convention in Houston. Lineburger had nominated Dan Vestal for

SBC president in New Orleans. Moderates — also prominent in the SBC struggle — were clearly in command of the BGCT structure, even as Reynolds was warning of a takeover from those not in charge.

The secrecy of the trustee action was galling to both conservatives and many moderates. Lineberger was "caught . . . totally by surprise" by the charter change which he called "very unsettling."[23]

Presnall Wood, editor of the Baptist Standard and no supporter of the SBC conservative movement, said, "Not conferring with Texas Baptist leadership or even letting them know such was about to take place smacks of a betrayal of a long relationship of Baylor with Texas Baptists. . . . What the Baylor administration and trustees have done and the way they have done it makes their claim of wanting to maintain close 'relationships with Texas Baptists' sound very hollow." The BGCT, Wood said, had "for now lost 'sole control' of the governance of the university."[25]

Trustees called "Robber Barons"

Aroused Texas "conservatives" registered their disapproval in stronger language.

Joel Gregory, who earned the B.A. and Ph.D. degrees from Baylor and named his two sons after Baylor professors: "They have walked off with the crown jewel of Texas Baptist life . . ."[24]

Jim Parker: "It's a cunning Machiavellian move, . . . a diabolical act of treachery" in which "the bank guards became the thieves. Do they really think that they can get away with a $750,000,000 'jewel heist?'"[26]

Paige Patterson: ". . . Here is a group of robber barons who were not happy with the way that the Baptists, who were paying the bills all these years, were managing the university."[27]

Jimmy Draper: "They are saying, 'We don't trust the people, but only ourselves.'"[28]

A retired Baylor employee for 31 years: "I have a friend who transferred because she could not stomach the teachings in the religion dept. I am sick over the action of trustees. We got assurance Baylor would not leave the Baptist fold but now the gate is open until it will be completely severed from Baptists, like Brown, Colgate and Wake Forest."[29]

Many Baylor students and their parents, according to local press reports, appeared to be confused. "I think they totally ignored the students, the parents of students and most of the pastors of the students," said Marisol Madrazo, a junior English major. "Everyone was talking about it. A lot of us were suspicious — not exactly disgusted, but suspicious. We wanted to know why."

"They said they did it so fundamentalists couldn't take over Baylor," said Norman Eng, a junior religion major. "To me, that's the weakest excuse I've ever heard."

Madrazo, Eng and some other students who were interviewed, voiced their disappointment with the religion department. "They teach the Bible like it was Grimm's fairy tales or something," said Madrazo.

However, journalism major Christine Mason, who supported the move, said, "Christian organizations are always going to be [at Baylor]. Also, the principles of the administration I don't think will ever change."[30]

Funds Escrowed, a Committee Appointed

Meanwhile, top BGCT officials conferred and "put in motion a process to utilize appropriate channels and persons within the framework of the Baptist democracy to address this matter."[31] The Administrative Committee of the Executive Board acted to escrow payments to Baylor until the legal standing of the convention with Baylor could be determined by counsel. The BGCT had budgeted $5.8 million for Baylor's $120-million budget for the fiscal year.

The BGCT Executive Board met October 17 in a called session, with the SBC Executive Board's attorney James Guenther from Nashville as special counsel, to respond to the Baylor matter. President Reynolds spoke, insisting that Baylor was still a Texas Baptist institution and repeating that the action had been taken to avert a takeover by "fundamentalists." Many board members expressed doubts of Reynolds' rationale and said the secret procedure indicated a lack of trust in Texas Baptists.

There was general agreement that the Baylor trustees had acted in direct violation of the BGCT constitution. A resolution calling on the Baylor trustees to meet before the Houston convention and rescind their action narrowly failed. The Board appointed a 26-member committee, with Dr.Robert Naylor as chairman, to study and recommend "with all deliberate speed" a response to the unauthorized charter change. Naylor, a revered elder statesman, was a past president of Southwestern Seminary. Special counsel Guenther said any attempt at the convention to ratify the Baylor action would be ruled out of order, since the BGCT constitution required prior approval of charter changes by the Executive Board.[32]

The special committee met October 30 for five hours in Dallas. They affirmed the escrow of Cooperative Program funds for Baylor. They appointed a sub-committee to attempt bilateral discussions with Baylor regarding the BGCT/Baylor relationship. They approved a motion that said nothing the convention should do in Houston would in any way signify approval or acquiescence in Baylor's action and that Baylor trustees should not assume office as defined under the amended Baylor charter unless directed to do so by the BGCT or its Executive Board.[33]

The Houston convention was now just two weeks away. Since September 21, Baylor had been promoting attendance of alumni, faculty, students and other supporters. The October alumni magazine said, "Texas Baptists have been able to keep these takeover architects . . . at bay — largely because Baylor alumni attend the BGCT en masse." The alumni journal urged the re-election of Phil Lineberger as president and said, "We cannot afford to let up in our commitment to keep Baylor true to her Baptist heritage and to keep Texas Baptist institutions and agencies out of the hands of the Presslerite-Fundamentalists. You are needed in Houston!"

Lawyers Challenge Reelection Of Trustees

Meanwhile, seven concerned Baptist attorneys, who opposed the Baylor action, were worried about the special committee's statement that appeared to encourage the re-election of 16 trustees who had voted for the charter change. J. Walter Carpenter, who had "the highest respect for Dr. Naylor," wrote committee counsel Guenther November 7 that the election of trustees "increases the risk that a court would deem the convention action to be acquiescence to the Baylor action. . . ." "By analogy, if you instruct a disloyal agent or fiduciary not to do something that he has already done and shows every indication of desiring to continue to do, you can hardly be heard to complain when he disobeys you, as you had ample warning of his intentions. . . . It is abundantly clear," Carpenter said, "that the nominated individuals who voted for the action, particularly those slated to be regents, will disobey the instructions of the convention if they are to be consistent with their previous action."[34] Carpenter believed "the only safe approach" would be "for the BGCT to decline to re-elect any individual . . . who voted for this action or abstained from voting. . . ."[35] Other attorneys wrote Guenther much the same.

Carpenter was given space in the November 13, Houston Post, on the morning of the convention, to address the Baylor issue. "This gang of 30 [trustees] who voted in the new charter," Carpenter said, "breached their fiduciary obligations to those who elected them by unilaterally taking action to strip them of an asset worth over one billion dollars." The "real reason" of Reynolds and his "cabal of elitists" want to "divorce themselves from the [BGCT] has nothing whatever to do with their alleged fear of 'fundamentalists." It has to do with the simple fact that much more money will become available to them through governmental and foundation grants than would be possible with a sectarian institution. . . . So to determine what's really happening, take the advice of 'Deep Throat' in the Watergate scandal: Follow the Money!"

Carpenter then quoted from the late George W. Truett's 1909 Baylor homecoming address in which Truett noted "an ominous trend today to separate" schools "from the control of religious denominations. . . . But what has Baylor to say to such a trend. She does not hesitate for a moment to give her answer. And that answer is that no amount of money can for one moment tempt her to submit to a divorcement between culture and faith. The religious convictions of the human heart are the profoundest convictions of the human heart and at the same time the broadest. Baylor will not barter these for any mess of pottage, however large."

Carpenter added, "Amen, Dr. Truett, I hope you're right."

Conservatives held a pastors conference before the convention which began on Tuesday. A committee was due to recommend that the convention opening be moved back to Monday in 1991 and 1992, with no pre-convention meetings recommended. Conservatives saw this as an effort to prevent a pastors conference from bringing more conservative pastors to the convention.

The special committee met Monday afternoon with counsel in the Hyatt Regency Hotel. With several Baylor attorneys monitoring the meeting, the committee voted to give the convention the go-ahead to re-elect the Baylor trustees, with the qualification that they should not perform the office of "trustee" as redefined under the amended Baylor charter, unless directed to do so by the BGCT or its Executive Board.

This was precisely what Carpenter and the six other attorneys had warned against. "They're taking a severe legal risk in giving Baylor a defense which Baylor did not have before that action," Carpenter said after observing the meeting. "I wrote Guenther to this effect. He called to thank me for writing. I never dreamed that he would not forward my letter of warning on to the Naylor committee that they would be giving Baylor great legal defenses in saying that the convention could go ahead and re-elect the Baylor trustees who have participated in the charter action. This was either the height of arrogance or he was playing some game of his own. In my opinion," Carpenter said, "Mr. Guenther and his associates are providing incompetent legal counsel. I believe the only honorable thing is for Mr. Guenther to disqualify himself. . . "[36]

In an interview, Naylor identified himself as "a fundamental person of faith. I'm to the right of these guys who think they're right. No suit against Baylor has been filed or authorized," he said. "That's the reason we [will] have two committees [from the BGCT and Baylor] talking. No options are closed." The committee did not "accept the actions of the Baylor trustees" who would be voted on for re-election by the convention. "We do not presume that we are approving them as regents of Baylor." When asked what would happen if the re-elected trustees proceeded to act as regents of

Baylor, Naylor declared, "That's their own business. They will answer to their own consciences. We don't have to accept what they do. We're marching to different drummers."

The Great Baylor Public Relations Machine

Tuesday morning, the Baylor booth was the center of attraction in the downstairs convention exhibit hall. President Reynolds' videotape to pastors played on an elevated TV. Workers in the booth passed out big, bold Baylor buttons and the November alumni magazine, with a featured cover story on "Understanding the Charter Change." Baylor alumni jammed the aisle, talking about old times and new times. One held up a copy of The Dallas Morning News, pointing to the lead editorial that declared the "actions of the trustees," to save Baylor from the "fundamentalist .... threat" to Baylor's "independence and academic excellence were proper."[37]

Not all of the booth visitors favored the charter change. An attorney, with a son in Baylor, frowned at Reynolds on the TV and remarked with wry amusement, "I dreamed last night that I was in a room with Saddam Hussein, Muammar Quadafi and Herb Reynolds. I had a gun with only two bullets." Then pausing for effect, he grimaced, "I shot Reynolds twice."

The theme of the convention, which would register a record 7,500 in registrations was "Texas Baptists Celebrating the Family." Upstairs in the big convention hall, officials were introducing their spouses, children and even grandparents.

Pinson and Naylor Report

The first major report was given by Bill Pinson, Executive Director for the Executive Board. Pinson told the messengers, "We are gathered here to celebrate, deliberate and to dedicate" — to "celebrate" the success of "consolidation" of rival state conventions and colleges into "one Baptist family," to "deliberate" on the "action of the Baylor Board of Trustees to unilaterally amend the Baylor charter to provide for a self-perpetuating board of directors to govern the university rather than trustees elected by convention," and to "dedicate ourselves to the mission of our Lord."

Pinson recounted the events following the Baylor separation. Funds budgeted for Baylor had been escrowed, he said because Baylor trustees "had not abided by the constitution of our convention which states that 'boards shall submit any and all changes or amendments to an institution's charter to this convention for approval in its annual meeting. . . . '

"We need to make wise decisions. . . . We can, . . . if we follow God's Word and speak the truth in love. Remember, Satan is our enemy, not one another. Don't allow controversy to dominate. Let's stick to the main task the Lord has set before us. Texas Baptists, don't give up!"[38]

The venerable Robert Naylor spoke for the special committee. Naylor — "more than 70 years a Southern Baptist, with two children and two grandchildren graduates of Baylor and two great-grandchildren who look like they're headed there" — called the Baylor action, "a shock to all of us. . . . No prior discussion of any kind with the convention . . . Private. Secretive. Filed within hours with the secretary of state. Finished? Not quite. There can be no dispute about the constitution of this convention. . . . No agency can change its charter without the prior approval of this body."

Baylor's relationship with the BGCT that "stood for 100 years" is "now unilaterally settled," Naylor said sadly. "A hundred years when we've walked through the storms and sunshine, [and] suddenly we discover in the morning paper that the relationships changed."

Members of the Baylor board, Naylor said, "are Texas Baptists. In many cases personal friends [of mine]. We belong to each other. Their acquiescence in the amendment of the charter saying Baylor is not responsible to the governance of this convention . . . speaks to the level of trust . . . among Texas Baptists. . . We've always had trust. The constitution of the convention is our covenant by which we live. . . . We stand on common ground. . . . We belong to each other. There are no unimportant Baptists and there are no important Baptists. We belong to each other."

When the applause died, Naylor said the committee had been charged to "study the decisions of the trustees at Baylor to amend the charter, recommend responses and examine the financial, legal and relationship responses to that action. . . . . A financial response [of escrow] had to be made. Will we put Baylor in the budget? By all means. [But there] will be an asterisk to show the escrow till the matter is concluded."

Naylor noted that four law firms had studied the Baylor-BGCT relationship. "If it took that many lawyers two years to make a conclusion" to amend the charter, "other lawyers are going to have other conclusions."

When the applause died again, Naylor declared, "I'm simply amazed to hear that a trustee is not responsible to the group that elected him. I don't understand that. . . . Trust to me, means trust."

Naylor made the motion, previously passed by the committee, that trustees elected to the Baylor Board "shall not assume the office of 'trustee' as defined under the amended Baylor charter unless and until they are directed to do so by formal action of the [BGCT]."[39]

Attorney Kenneth Stohner, Jr. one of the seven lawyers mentioned earlier who opposed the committee's action, offered an amendment: "That this convention elect no trustees as long as the amended charter of Baylor is in effect and [not] until the select [Naylor] committee has finalized its report and the [BGCT] has had the opportunity to vote on the relationship between Baylor and the [BGCT]."

After the amendment failed on a ballot vote, the Naylor motion passed. Naylor then came back briefly. "We've [walked]this rough road before. We're going to find a way to walk together. We can walk together in Texas."

The Committee on Nominations later presented their 16 nominees for the Baylor Board. The report could be amended only by nominating one substitute at a time. Calvin Pearson proposed Jay Gross, pastor of First Church, Texas City, for election instead of committee nominee Max Brown, pastor of First Church, Galveston. After Gross lost, the committee's entire slate was elected.

The large contingent of Baylor supporters vigorously applauded a motion to free the escrowed Baylor funds from the 1991 budget. The motion passed 2,164 to 1,991. However, a second ballot was called after an error was discovered in the printed version of the budget and several messengers complained that it had been reported by Baylor supporters that funds would be cut off to ministerial students when such was not the case. On the second vote, the motion failed by a 29-vote margin — 1,995 to 1,966.

Texas conservatives clearly opposed the Baylor breakaway. Moderates were divided. Moderates, who included the Baylor supporters, united on approving a motion — 2,432 to 1,487 — to encourage the BGCT administrative committee and executive board to "explore ways to provide financial support for Associated Baptist Press."[41] Moderates won easy approval of the report that called for the convention to start on Monday, with no pre-convention meetings recommended. And the moderate majority re-elected Phil Lineburger as president to the customary second term with no conservative opposition.

All while Reynolds was telling everyone within earshot that the trustees had acted to save Baylor from a fundamentalist takeover of the BGCT.

Reynolds Meets The Press

Reynolds held a press conference after Lineburger's reelection. Naylor, he said, had used his "opportunity as chair of the committee to editorialize in an unbelievable fashion. [If] Dr. Naylor really had the tremendous love for our institutions, that he seemed to want to convey today, he's had a perfect opportunity for the last 12 years to . . . show righteous indignation about what has happened to SBC institutions and agencies. . . . It seems to me that he's caught fire here in the last few weeks."

The personable Phil Lineberger came into the press room. "Dr. Lineberger is on a tight schedule," a press aide said. "Would you mind, Dr. Reynolds, if the press could ask him a few questions? Then he'll be going."

Reynolds stepped back. "Be glad to. He's one of my favorite people."

A reporter asked Lineberger how the SBC struggle might be affecting Baptist institutions in Texas.

"I don't think it's affected Texas adversely at this point," Lineburger replied. "Baylor has made a decision and perhaps that is an adverse effect. Texas Baptists," Lineberger declared, "have been a tremendous example" to other Southern Baptists. "It's been very difficult for anybody to say Texas has slid away from good, solid conservative theological education or aggressive evangelism and missions."

Asked how he saw the Baylor issue, Lineburger said, "That's a very difficult question. . . . I would say that the trustees went against the constitution of the [BGCT]."

Would the trustees elected by the BGCT operate under the constitution of the BGCT or [under the new Baylor plan]?

"I can't speak for Baylor," Lineberger replied. "I can only say that the trustees of the BGCT will operate under the constitution of the BGCT that says they are trustees of Baylor."

Did Lineberger favor continued financial support by the BGCT, "if the courts decide that Baylor can break free from the convention?" Lineburger declined to answer "that hypothetical question because we're involved now in a committee process."

The questions trailed off. It was obvious that Lineberger was not going to say anything to sharpen the differences between Baylor and the BGCT.

Reynolds came back to bemoan the "creedalism" which, he said, was being forced upon SBC institutions. "Southern Seminary," he mourned, "is now going to have to live according to the criteria of the Peace Committee. . . . Baptists have not been a creedal people. [We don't want] Baylor to become a creedal institution.

"You can join a Baptist Church by simply walking down the aisle and saying, 'I want to become a part of this church,' and you would be voted on right there. We do more than that at Baylor. We talk with our people and ask them to tell us about their Christian pilgrimage, but we don't ask them . . . to sign any articles or creed. . . . When they come with us, . . . we ascertain that they are Christians. . . . We interview them and take their word for . . . where they stand in . . . their commitment to Christ . . .

"We can discriminate on the basis of religion at the time of hiring, as a church-related institution. Once an individual is hired, [we] cannot discriminate. . . . We hired this Mormon man in good faith. He does not pose a threat to us and the well-being of our people. As long as I'm president, he's not going to be terminated."

A reporter asked, "If an Episcopalian gave Baylor a very generous gift, is there anything that would keep the Board of Regents from being able to say that the Board now constitutes 23 Baptists and one Episcopalian?"

"Yes, because the charter and bylaws calls for all the [regents] to be Southern Baptists?"

"Could you change the charter and bylaws?"

"The regents could amend the articles and change the bylaws, I think the likelihood of that coming to pass is exceedingly low."[40]

Baylor Clout

Reynolds and other Baylor people felt a response was a needed to Naylor's remarks. Outgoing Baylor trustee chair Winfred Moore asked to respond. Moore had been hired as a Baylor religion professor after his retirement as pastor of FBC, Amarillo, even though he held no earned doctorate. Messenger Richard Dugger called Moore's "point of personal privilege" out of order for five reasons, including the fact that "he has not been maligned before this body." The BGCT vice president who was moderating "refuse[d]" Dugger's point of order and asked those who wanted to hear Moore to raise their ballots. A majority did and Moore proceeded amidst loud applause.

Moore spoke for about 20 minutes, stressing some of the same points Reynolds had been making: The trustees had acted to save Baylor from the SBC "take-over" group. They began notifying BGCT leaders within an hour after adjournment. Baylor lawyers had met with the BGCT committee's counsel. Baylor had paid for booth space at the convention. Baylor's "commitment to the [BGCT] is the same now as it was before September 21. Nothing has changed. We are family and Baylor is still family."

Moore sat down and Presnall Wood was introduced to give the Baptist Standard report. Microphones had been flashing throughout Moore's speech. Finally Dr. Hal Boone, a retired medical missionary confined to a wheel chair, was recognized on a point of personal privilege. "I am a paid up member of the Baylor alumni association and presently a trustee of Baylor," he said. "I was at the meeting September 21, that day which shall live in infamy in Texas Baptist history. I would like a position on the platform . . . to answer my esteemed colleague Winfred Moore and to tell the truth, the whole truth that has not been told about that meeting. Or may I speak from here? I'll take no more time than my colleague Winfred Moore."

The moderator asked messengers to raise their ballots if they wanted to hear Boone. He ruled that Boone could not speak, because he did not get a two-thirds majority. Boone asked for a vote by marked ballots. The moderator asked for raised ballots to authorize a marked ballot vote. He ruled the response to mean no.

Boone's microphone remained on. "The truth must be told," he said. "I voted against the separation of Baylor from the BGCT on grounds that history repeats itself. If Baylor removes itself from its roots, [it will be taking] the first step on the slippery slope of secularism, as Harvard, Princeton, Yale, Chicago and Wake Forest have done. Wake Forest now has a bartending course. How long will it be before Baylor has a course in bartending?" The Baylor crowd answered with loud boos.

"History will repeat itself," Boone concluded. "Someone wiser than I has said that those who do not read history and learn from history are doomed to repeat it."

The moderator had kept his eye on his watch during the entire two minutes that Boone had been speaking. "Thank you, sir," he said. "Now, are there any questions or responses to Dr. Wood's Baptist Standard report?"

Minutes later, Herbert Reynolds was recognized at a floor mike and given time to reply to Boone's statements. Reynolds spoke twice as long as Boone and said he had heard "similar things from you and others of like mind over a number of years. . . . As you were making such statements, you were doing everything possible to drive us away. . . . Look at Jimmy Swaggart and Jim Bakker and people like them. You don't look at another individual and say that just because he also happens to be a minister, he's very definitely going to go down the same road as these fallen angels. Baylor University is no more likely to go down that path [toward secularism] with all the wonderful ministries that we have in Texas Baptist life." Reynolds received standing applause.

Two Trustees Debate the Issues

Boone had now rolled his wheel chair to the side of the crowd and was talking with the media. "Just read history, look at the universities that have been founded for the express purpose of training men for the ministry. What happened to them was they departed from their founding Christian bodies. History will repeat itself."

Boone recalled that "Dr. Reynolds reassured me in that board meeting, 'As long as I'm president of this institution, as long as I'm here, this institution will remain Baptist and Christian.' And I believe that. But I said, 'Dr. Reynolds, you're not going to be here long. That's my feeling as a physician. Since your heart bypass, you've had heart pain again. You've had angioplasty. You're going to continue to block up.'"

While Boone talked, trustee John Wood, pastor of FBC, Waco, who had voted for the charter plan, moved up. "Hal, as a Christian brother and I love you, you know that, we've known each other for

25 years. Let's just take one thing. You say we voted to separate ourselves from Texas Baptists."

Boone: "That's exactly what happened. Right?"

Wood: "No, we haven't separated ourselves from the [BGCT].That's your interpretation. We voted to separate ourselves from the fundamentalist takeover."

Boone: "What do you know about fundamentalist takeovers? . . . . Where did it come from?

Wood: "Where did it come from? From you and your cohorts."

Boone: "Oh, my."

Wood: "And Pressler."

Boone: "Come off of that, John. You're not telling the truth. I know my own heart. I was in the meeting and I voted. Do you have some divine revelation?"

Wood: "I voted to save Baylor from a fundamentalist takeover."

Boone: "There's no fundamentalist takeover. No plan."

Wood: "That is a lie, an absolute — "

Boone: "Name [those whom you say are going to take over Baylor]."

Wood: "You and Paul Pressler and Paige Patterson and W.A. Criswell and Adrian Rogers and how many do you want me to name?"

Boone: "John, the <u>Baptist Standard</u> even says there are problems in our theological seminaries and there are problems at Baylor. . . . They teach evolution as fact."

Wood: "You said we voted to separate ourselves from Texas Baptists. We did not do that."

Boone: "Baylor is no longer under the aegis of the [BGCT]. Now admit that. It's no longer responsible to the BGCT. Right? Am I right? That's true. That's the absolute truth. It is no longer responsible. The total governance of Baylor University [will] be by a self-perpetuating board of regents."

Wood: "That's correct, but the purpose of that was to prevent takeover, not to separate from Texas Baptists."

Boone: "Come on, John. That is not true."

Wood: "I have a sacred trust . . . to prevent Baylor from becoming a Harvard or Yale. But . . . the immediate concern is to keep it from becoming a Criswell Bible Institute or a Bob Jones. Now we deal with governance. And Hal, you're right on one side of it, but there are two sides to it, not one side. We have exercised our protection from becoming a Bob Jones or Criswell Bible Institute We've got to keep the faith."

Boone: "Have you ever studied history? Church history?"

Wood: "You're right, Hal. But that's a trust we've gotta keep."

Boone: "What's going to happen after Herb? Who's going to be the next president when Herb leaves."

Wood: "I don't know."

The dialogue-argument continued with Wood saying, "You're not going to see Baylor [become a purely academic institution] as long as I'm there."

Boone: "Well, how long are you going to be around?"

Wood: "We've got to work on it."

Boone: "You know very well that they teach evolution in the religion department. We've got atheists and agnostics teaching at Baylor. There's a Mormon on the faculty."

Wood: "You don't know [all] that."

Boone: "Well, you know _____ . He just retired. He said, 'I'm an agnostic.'. . . He's been teaching there for 40 years."

Wood: "That's over with. I do not know the man and I do not know that he's an agnostic."

The conversation came back to fundamentalism.

Boone: "John, you don't know what a fundamentalist is."

Wood: "Well, if it's believing in the fundamentals of the Bible, I'm one of them. . . . [But] I'm not a Presslerite."

Boone: "I'm not either. Don't you think I'm my own man?"

Wood: "I don't know, Hal, but I do know the Baylor University board of trustees did not separate from Texas Baptists."

Boone: "Oh, come on, John. It won't be one generation before Baylor is just like Wake Forest."

Wood: "I'm one of them that's gonna stand [against that]."

The dialogue ended with both agreeing that "there's more religion in the Baylor athletic department than there is in most universities."[42]

The spirited dialogue of Boone and Wood illustrated the division among Texas Baptists over Baylor. The convention ended with few minds having been changed.

Even though the BGCT funds for Baylor were still in escrow, Michael Bishop, Baylor's vice president of communications, saw the convention as "a big victory. We got their attention. They see the respect Baylor has among Texas Baptists."[43]

Paul Powell, a powerful figure among Texas Baptists, succeeded Winfred Moore as Baylor board chair. Powell also serves as president of the powerful SBC Annuity Board and as chairman of the BGCT budget's allocation committee. Early in December, Powell named six Baylor board members to the university's sub-committee to begin bilateral discussions with the BGCT special committee on the relationship of Baylor to the BGCT.

Baptist Standard editor Presnall Wood said, "[Texas Baptists] are evenly divided" on what should be done. ". . . The [BGCT special] committee faces the rather stern reality that any conclusion or recommendation will be both vigorously approved and opposed."[44]

A New Plan Proposed

On March 18, 1991, the study committee proposed a new way for the BGCT and Baylor to "walk together." The plan reportedly calls for Baylor to return to a single-tiered board in which the convention would be directly involved to some extent in election of 75 percent of the trustees. Paul Powell said he would present the proposal to the Baylor board of regents at their next meeting, May 2.[45]

As of April 5, no legal suit has been announced. Back in November, Attorney Carpenter expected that a legal test, if it comes, "would not go to trial for over two years." He worried that before that time, "the [special] committee might just talk itself to death."[46]

Carpenter says that "the conservative Baptist people of Texas have absolute trust in Dr. Naylor's capability and Christian transparency. We trust him implicitly. But we are very concerned that the majority of his committee may be working at cross purposes to him. There is a scenario that is worse than losing Baylor and that is losing it in such a manner that Texas Baptists feel that their historic interests in this institution were not adequately defended. If this happens it could bring the denominational dispute right into Texas with unpredictable, or serious consequences."[47]

While the talking — and praying — continues, Baptist academicians and denominational leaders in other state conventions will keep a watchful eye on what develops with Baylor. There is special concern in three other states.

Stetson, Furman and Meredith

Stetson University has asked Florida Baptists to reduce their funding of the university — to perhaps nothing by the year 2000 — in exchange for granting the school more autonomy in the election of its trustees. For years Stetson has been under fire from some Florida Baptists for what they see as diminishing Christian influence and a leftward drift in theology. The plan calls for the Florida convention to give up the right to approve the nomination of Stetson trustees, although it would still participate in the nomination process for the three-fourths of trustees who are Baptists. Stetson president Douglas Lee says his school intends "to preserve" its relationship with Florida Baptists. "We have no desire . . . to ever alter that relationship."[48]

Furman University in South Carolina, on October 15, 1990, and Meredith College in North Carolina, on February 22, 1991, followed Baylor in creating self-perpetuating governing boards, independent of their state conventions. The division in the Carolina conventions is just as deep as it is in Texas over Baylor.

Larry McCracken of Maiden, NC calls the Meredith action "unethical, immoral, unchristian and probably illegal."[49] Larry Penley says the Meredith break was necessary "to keep the fundamentalists out of our chicken-house. . . ."[50]

Furman trustees amended that university's charter just 24-days after Baylor acted. "It seems like a small group of people simply decided to rewrite the rules without even announcing it to the state convention," said Jim Oliver, a SC pastor. "The trustees think they're rescuing it. From what? I call it taking the school away from the Southern Baptists who began it, who paid for it and who sustain it."

Ray Rust, Executive Secretary-treasurer of the SC convention called the action "unprovoked, . . . a shock and . . . a tremendous disappointment to the vast majority of 700,000 South Carolina Baptists who . . . have supported Furman since 1826."[51]

As in Texas, the South Carolina state convention, with a record number of messengers, voted to escrow funds budgeted for Furman while committees hold discussions. SC editor John Roberts says "messengers [at the SC convention] were sharply and almost equally divided on this question, one side determinedly supporting the Furman move and fully convinced of its legality, the other calling for court action to solidify Convention control."[52]

Richmond, Mercer, Wake Forest, Jewell

Precedents have already been set for the Baylor, Furman and Meredith actions. The Virginia convention lost control of the University of Richmond several years ago and now elect only 20 percent of trustees. Mercer University's trustees nominate their successors, which are then approved by the Georgia convention. Wake Forest's board amended their charter in 1978 to say that the North Carolina state convention cannot elect or dismiss trustees.

William Jewell College in Missouri, listed by U.S. News and World Report "as one of the top 25 small comprehensive colleges" in the U.S. is dually aligned with both American Baptists and the Missouri Baptist Convention. Winfred Moore, at the Texas convention, argued that the new Baylor plan could work as William Jewell's had over the years.

According to President J. Gordon Kingsley, Jewell was founded by direct charter of the Missouri Legislature in 1849. The relationship with the two denominations dates from the time when the state convention was dually aligned with both Southern and Northern Baptists. The state convention later divided and today Jewell has a relationship with both affiliates. Kingsley says there is "no formula dividing trustees between the Missouri Baptist Convention and the American Baptist Convention," which has "less than 20 churches in Missouri, as compared to more than 1,600" SBC churches. ABC "financial support [for Jewell] is nominal, probably less than $10,000 last year."[53] The Missouri Baptist Convention contributes to Jewell about 100 times as much as ABC churches do.

"Unlike [three other Baptist colleges in Missouri], Jewell, according to MBC Executive Director Donald Wideman, "has a self-perpetuating board of trustees. However, like the others, [Jewell] submits the names of trustees to be elected — or approved — to the MBC Nominating Committee and thus on to the Missouri Baptist Convention in the annual meeting. The difference," Wideman says, "is that [Jewell's] trustees are submitted for approval, while the others are submitted for election. [Jewell] trustees are almost always approved as presented. There has been an occasion when the MBC Nominations Committee had questions or concerns and the name was withdrawn."[54]

Thus, relationships between Southern Baptist schools and state conventions differ and relationships in some instances are currently very unsettled. Baptist college and university administrators, understandably, seek to maintain good relations with their Baptist constituencies although disquieting news does sometimes leak out through the secular press.

A Jew Cries Discrimination

A huge flap resulted over a decade ago when the Richmond News Leader quoted Robert Alley, head of the religion department at the University of Richmond, as not "imagin[ing] for a moment that [Jesus] would have the audacity to claim the deity for himself."[55] More recently, the University of Richmond was troubled by a report in the same newspaper that a Catholic professor at the school, who belonged to a local religious group for Catholic and Episcopal gay men and lesbians, had died of AIDS.[56] Another Virginia paper reported allegations from a Jewish teacher, Derek Krueger, claiming that the University of Richmond Bible department had discriminated in refusing to hire him as a New Testament professor. According to the report, Robert Alley, now a humanities professor at Richmond, accused fellow Professor Robison B. James of making religion a test for the job in violation of university policy.[57] James is a leader in the SBC moderate camp.

The situations vary from one Baptist college and university to another. A few schools are considered very conservative. Others are strongly identified with the moderate camp., Some are divided among their own faculty. And some appear to be slipping from their Baptist roots and following a road already trodden by schools of other denominations. The question now troubling Southern Baptists in many states is: How far will Baylor, Furman, Meredith, Stetson and others who may follow, go?

References

1 Editorial, "Elect Messengers to Houston Convention," Baptist Standard, September 26, 1990, p. 6.

2 "Baylor President Denounces SBC 'College of Cardinals,' " Baptist and Reflector, December 17, 1984, p. 2.

3 Craig Bird: "Baylor Students Deliver 'Manifesto' to Reynolds,' Baptist and Reflector, December 26, 1984, pp. 1, 3.

4 Russell Kaemmerling: "In Conclusion," Southern Baptist Advocate, June, 1985, p. 39.

5 Roberts to Powell, May 13, 1986.

6 Taken from typed excerpts of Trustees' meeting, Baylor University, Waco, TX, July 18, 19, 1986.

7 December 2, 1987, p. 2.

8 "Conversation with President Reynolds," The Baylor Line, pp. 18, 19, 45.

9 Wilson to Hefley, March 17, 1988.

10 Paul Yowell: "Factions Struggle for Control of BGCT," The Baylor Lariat, October 27, 1989, p. 9B.

11 Toby Druin: "Joel Gregory: Texas Baptists Are 'Together,' " Baptist Standard, September 20, 1989, pp. 3, 4.

12 Paula Price Tanner and Sherry Boyd Castello: "Safe From the Storm," The Baylor Line, November, 1990, pp. 3-9.

13 Sherry Castello: "Conversation with the President," The Baylor Line, November, 1990, pp. 8, 9, 47.

14 Herbert Reynolds, Video sent to Texas Baptist pastors, September, 1990.

15 Toby Druin: "Threat of Takeover, Climate of Distrust Prompted Decision," Baptist Standard, October 3, 1990, pp. 3, 4.

16 June 14, 1990.

17 "Conservative Baptists Vow to Regain Control of Baylor," San Antonio Express-News, September 23, 1990, p. 1.

18 Figures from the BGCT 1990 Book of Reports.

19 Toby Druin: "Baylor Changes Charter; 'Regents' Will Govern," Baptist Standard, September 26, 1990, p. 3.

20 Quoted from Pinson's report to the BGCT, November 13, 1991.

21 Quoted from the Videotape.

22 Toby Druin: "104th Convention: 'Just a Spiritual Meeting," Baptist Standard, November 15, 1989, p. 7.

23 Toby Druin: "Executive Board to Consider Baylor Action," Baptist Standard, October 3, 1990, p. 3.

24 "Conservative Baptists Vow to Regain Control of Baylor," San Antonio Express-News, September 23, 1990, p. 1.

25 "Baylor Action," September 26, 1990, p. 6.

26 "Violated Trust," Baptist Standard, October 3, 1990, p. 2.

27 Tessie Borden: "Baylor Move Nets Protest on Both Sides," Waco Tribune-Herald, September 25, 1990, p. 1.

28 "Many at Baylor Glad Trustees Acted Against Fundamentalists," The Dallas Morning News, September 29, 1990, pp. 33, 38A.

29 Letter to Hefley.

30 Tessie Borden: "Students Look at Revisions in Confusion" and "BU Students, President Want Improved Academics for School," Waco Tribune-Herald, November 11, 1990.

31 "Toby Druin: "Executive Board to Consider Baylor Action," Baptist Standard, October 3, 1990, p. 3.

32 Toby Druin: "Committee Named to Study Baylor Issue," Baptist Standard, October 24, 1991, p. 3.

33 Toby Druin: "Panel Begins Search for Baylor/BGCT Remedy," Baptist Standard, November 7, 1990, p. 3.

34 Carpenter to Guenther, November 8, 1990.

35 Carpenter to Guenther, November 7, 1990.

36 Personal Interview, Houston, November, 1990.

37 "Baylor Politics," November 11, 1990, p. 2J.

38 Unless otherwise indicated, all quotations, citations of parliamentary actions and other information during the convention are taken from my tape of the proceedings.

39 Toby Druin: "Convention Denies Release of Baylor Funds," Baptist Standard, November 21, 1990, pp. 3, 4.

40 From my tape of Reynolds' and Lineburger's press conferences.

41 "Texas Baptists to Continue Escrowing Baylor Funds," Word & Way, November 22, 1990, p. 9.

42 From my tape of the conversation.

43 Daisy Teoh: "Close Vote Upholds BU Fund Freeze," The Baylor Lariat, November 15, 1990, pp. 1, 3.

44 "Questions Challenge BGCT Baylor Committee," Baptist Standard, December 12, 1990, p. 6.

45 Toby Druin: "Panel Proposes New BGCT/Baylor Relationship," Baptist Standard, March 27, 1991.

46 Personal Interview, Houston November, 1990.

47 Telephone Interview, April, 1991.

48 "Stetson Seeks Less Money, More Autonomy," Word & Way, September 13, 1990, p. 13.

49 Letters, Biblical Recorder, March 30, 1991, p. 2.

50 Ibid.

51 Pam Kelley: "Baptist Colleges Squirming," <u>Charlotte Observer,</u> November 8, 1990.

52 "Robert L. Slimp: "Furman University Trustees Vote School Out of S.C. Baptist," <u>Christian News,</u> October 29, 1990, p. 13.

53 "Convention Mainly Follows High Road," <u>Baptist Courier,</u> November 22, 1990, p. 3.

54 Kingsley to Hefley, March 25, 1991.

55 Wideman to Hefley, March 26, 1991.

56 The story was subsequently picked up by Baptist Press, December 14, 1977.

57 "Service Planned at UR for Assistant Professor," <u>Richmond News Leader,</u> November 20, 1990, p. 2.

58 "Richmond Professor Accused of Casting Anti-Semitic Vote," <u>The Virginia-Pilot,</u> March 15, 1991.

Chapter 17

"Future Directions"

The turnaround in the Southern Baptist Convention represents primarily a "resurgence" in conservative theology as applied to the doctrine of Biblical inspiration. The SBC reversal of a liberal drift is unique in American Christianity. Never before have conservatives in a major denomination overcome the opposition of the ecclesiastical establishment, including most of the denominational editors, and turned the body back to its theological roots to such a decided extent.

Reformers in the Lutheran Church Missouri attained a parliamentary victory in 1973 that brought major changes in Concordia Seminary of St. Louis. But in recent years, the conservative advance has been halted by bureaucratic compromise and control and toleration of non-traditional practices. The most notable evidence of this is the forced retirement of inerrantist Robert D. Preus from the presidency of Concordia Seminary in Fort Wayne, Indiana. LCMS President Ralph Bohlmann is reputed to be the power behind the blockage of large scale changes in the denomination. Herman Otten, editor of the independent [Lutheran] Christian News, says, "Bohlmann has allowed theological liberals, evolutionists, charismatics, religious unionists and unscripturally divorced pastors to remain on the LCMS clergy roster."[1]

The Depth of the Conservative Resurgance

The resurgence in the SBC has gone much further. Though the language may vary slightly, Convention officers, agency trustees and many denominational employees now affirm the SBC's historic position on Biblical inspiration. Denominational workers who cannot accept that position hold their tongues. Moderates who call this creedalism neglect to mention that (1) denominational employees have always had to hold to some doctrinal statement or "creed" and (2) that well into this century virtually all SBC leaders affirmed the Bible to be inerrant. Says Lewis Drummond: "[Southern] Baptists have always, historically up until the last 50 years, believed in the infallibility, inerrancy and total truthfulness of the Scriptures [although] they expressed it in different ways.[2] Drummond's assertion is amply demonstrated by quotations on Biblical inspiration from Baptist leaders of past generations, as cited in Volume 4 of The Truth in Crisis, Pp. 217-235.

For roughly the first 75 years of the SBC, Biblical inerrancy was taught in SBC institutions. "In general," said Glenn Hinson to the SBC Historical Society in 1984, "Southern Baptist colleges and seminaries insulated students from the impact of the liberal tradition.... Although professors at Southern [Seminary] studied abroad with eminent representatives of the liberal tradition, such as Adolf Harnack and Julius Wellhausen, they either did not communicate what they had learned to their students or else radically modified what they did pass on." Hinson said he was told by W.W. Adams, professor of New Testament at Southern Seminary, that A. T. Robertson who taught at Southern from 1888-1934, "never mentioned" higher critical studies to graduate students.[3] Robertson, who is still recognized as the SBC's greatest New Testament Greek scholar, studied under Basil Manly, Jr., John Broadus and James Boyce. All three were inerrantists.

The SBC resurgence has been accompanied by politics on both sides of the controversy. The Peace Committee plainly said: "When people of good intention became frustrated because they felt their convictions on Scripture were not seriously dealt with, they organized politically to make themselves heard. Soon, another group formed to counter the first and the political process intensified."

A Brief Review

The Bible "problem," as we saw in chapter one, first became apparent at Baylor University. Concern spread, leading to the adoption of the Baptist Faith and Message statement in 1925. The "heresy" came back, resulting in a reaffirmation of the BFM, with some revision, in 1963. However, some institutions did not require that employees subscribe to the BFM. Many individuals interpreted the BFM article on the Bible to mean that the Bible was only true in matters of faith and practice as interpreted by each reader.

The "muttering" by conservatives — in the form of state and SBC convention resolutions, sermons and letters to editors — became a roar in the 1970s. Pressler, Patterson, Powell, Rogers and other leaders came along at the opportune time to channel rank-and-file frustrations into the movement that would in a few years put conservative majorities on boards of institutions and agencies.

The 1979-1990 time of theological, ecclesiastical and political revolution in the SBC is now history. Conservatives have an undisputed majority on every board. This does not mean that every agency employee and church pastor are inerrantists. Lewis Drummond, president of Southeastern Seminary, said in 1988, "It's going to take another 25 years to see real substantive change throughout the convention."[1A]

The first stage in the resurgence, which brought control of boards, is now complete. The second — installation of agency executives who will incorporate the renewal into teaching, publications and programs — is well under way. The third stage — extending the renewal into state conventions, associations and local churches — is also in process and will accelerate as greater change comes to national agencies. This will take many years.

Conservative board policy in agencies and institutions, for the most part, has been not to fire, but to wait for resignations and retirements. The most notable firings to date have been at Baptist Press.

Executive Committee Hires Vice Presidents

Even as Baptist Press continued to operate, moderates and many state editors saw only a dismal future for the news service. Some editors took the lead in establishing the alternative Associated Baptist Press. Mississippi's Don McGregor and North Carolina's R.G. Puckett served on the ABP executive committee. Missouri's Bob Terry, who presided over the organization of ABP, declined to serve in an official capacity because of other commitments.[4]

The Virginia convention's budget committee allocated $50,000 as a line item in that state's proposed budget; North Carolina's budget committee proposed $30,000. State papers using the ABP service were asked to pay $1,200 per year. Bob Terry's Word & Way sent $4,000 for ABP services in advance.

Al Shackleford was elected a member of the ABP Board. Dan Martin was hired as interim news director. Floyd Craig, who once served on Foy Valentine's staff at the Christian Life Commission, was engaged as consultant to the directors. Don McGregor, retired from the Mississippi Baptist Record and was subsequently named executive director of ABP.

Baptist Press did not become the propaganda "tool" of the SBC Executive Committee some expected. During the interim period, press releases continued to be written by agency public relations employees.

In the fall of 1990, the SBC Executive Committee officers made good on their announced intention to separate Baptist Press from SBC public relations. They hired Mark Coppenger as vice president for public relations and California editor Herbert Hollinger as vice president for Baptist Press. The "conservative" Executive Committee did something which the denominational editors had never been able to persuade the EC to do when it was controlled by moderates.

Coppenger's vita showed a checkered, but impressive career. Holding a Ph.D. from Vanderbilt and an M. Div. from Southwestern Seminary, Coppenger had served as an Army officer, taught at Wheaton College, served as pastor of one of the largest SBC churches — which formerly had a moderate pastor — in Arkansas and as executive director of the Indiana convention and interim-editor of the Indiana paper before his election to the public relations job for the Executive Committee. Still, some denominational editors were "not impressed." Said Maryland/Delaware's Bob Allen: "Not much in that vita suggests the kind of public relations expertise Southern Baptists ought to expect at the level of a vice president of the Executive Committee." Allen suggested that Coppenger owed his job "to a spoils system in which loyalty to the cause is more important than qualifications for the particular job." Coppenger responded, "It really is an insulting and almost slanderous thing to say that one went to a job for carnal reasons. I had a very deep sense of conviction that God was leading in that way."[5]

Coppenger plans to publish the Southern Baptist Celebrator as a kind of "digest of the good things" that are happening in the SBC. Baptist Press "has its limitations," he says. BP news "must go through the state papers and [they] don't reach a large number of our people. And then of course, not every BP story is carried by every state paper. So the . . . Celebrator will be one more way to get the good news out. . . . A lot of folks haven't heard that there were 700 professions of faith in one day at the True Vine Church in Oakland or about 1,000 conversions in the Persian Gulf through a revival among our troops. Some haven't heard about the four-week crusade in Kenya where 53,000 people were baptized and 84 churches were started."[6A]

The EC officers interviewed "some of the finest men across the convention" for the Baptist Press vice presidency, "but God showed us that Herb Hollinger was the man we wanted."[6] Hollinger had been editor of the California Southern Baptist since 1983 and before that editor of the Northwest Baptist Witness for five years. EC Executive Director Harold Bennett said Hollinger was amply qualified by his work in mission areas of the SBC, service as a pastor before becoming a state editor and growing up in a journalism family.[7]

As a member of the SBC press fraternity, Hollinger's hiring was well accepted by denominational editors. Tennessee's Fletcher Allen called him "a bonafide journalist, . . . capable, reliable and cooperative." In welcoming Hollinger to the BP system, Allen said, "In your responsible new position, you will need — and get — cooperation."[8]

The changes in p.r. and Baptist Press apparently has not changed the minds of many moderates about the conservative Executive Committee. It is still excluded from funding by the alternate financial plan and by a number of churches as well.

Older moderates fondly remember the good times at EC meetings in Nashville, when THEY prepared recommendations which were almost always accepted by the convention. The changeover did not come in a single year. Moderates were nominated for second four-year terms by conservative Committees on Nomination. Not until 1987 did conservatives attain a working majority.

Another Look at the Seminaries

Let us now catch up with the seminaries. At Southeastern, moderate Randall Lolley resigned when he could not agree with trustees and was succeeded by conservative evangelism scholar Lewis Drummond. At Golden Gate, in a state where Baptists were far more conservative than in North Carolina, conservative Bill Crews was elected to fill the vacancy in the president's office. Conservatives will elect presidents of the other four seminaries when their presidents retire within a few years. .

The present climate at the six seminaries is mixed. Conservative presidents have kept Golden Gate and New Orleans relatively calm. Trustees have had no difficulties of consequence with faculty at Southwestern, notwithstanding President Dilday's penchant for tripping on his tongue. President Milton Ferguson's gift of diplomacy has helped forestall trustee-faculty confrontations at Midwestern.

The Situation at Southeastern

The confrontation phase has passed at Southeastern The moderate faculty majority is shrinking. Church history professor G. Thomas Halbrooks recently affiliated with the new Richmond Seminary. Two conservative teachers have been elected and another appointed at Southeastern.

Moderate faculty at Southeastern continue to be unhappy with the new policy that gives trustees more involvement in the hiring process. Southeastern's funding picture is clouded. Southeastern, like the other seminaries, is allocated funds from the SBC Cooperative Program on the basis of the number of Full Time Equivalent students. Faced with a sharp enrollment drop, Southeastern is presently benefiting from a funding freeze by the SBC Executive Committee, based on the enrollment in 1988-89. "This gives us a lot more per student," Drummond notes, "but one more full year after this and [the freeze] will begin to taper off." Unless the enrollment increases, "we'll have to make some [financial] adjustments." Drummond sees an upturn coming: "More prospective students are visiting the campus every day."

State denominational papers have given big play to Southeastern's accreditation problems. The seminary has been put on warning status with the Southern Association of Schools and Colleges. "SACCS," President Drummond says, "will give us probation or take away the warning status. That will come in December. We have to report to ATS" — Association of Theological Schools — "by May 1 and they will decide June 1 whether to put us on probation. I don't think they will drop us."[9]

The basic issue with the accrediting agencies appears to be the trustee-adopted procedure for hiring new faculty. The moderate majority claim their participation has been reduced. Former board chairman Bob Crowley blames the faculty for the situation.

A New Solution at Southern

Faculty responses to trustee actions at Southern have also attracted the attention of the accrediting agencies. An evaluation team from ATS paid a "focused visit" to the campus in February, 1991. The trustee executive committee is studying their report. In a letter to President Honeycutt, ATS said "sufficient evidence" had been found by the evaluators "for the need for further review" of the impact of recent trustee actions on the school.[10]

Following up on a motion in New Orleans, the SBC Executive Committee has asked its institutions workgroup "to study the procedures and impact of the accreditation of the six [SBC] seminaries."[11] James DeLoach, another former board chair at Southeastern, says that if accreditation is lost, Southeastern should withdraw all financial support from ATS and SACS and request other SBC seminaries to do the same.[12] President Dilday of Southwestern, currently president of ATS, says efforts to form a SBC accrediting agency to replace ATS and SACS could harm all the seminaries. Accreditation, he says, "ensures that our graduates are recognized. They can get jobs; their degrees are certified. Without that, their degrees are worthless. They can't get teaching positions or be hired as chaplains. Academic work at unaccredited schools cannot be transferred to credit at another institution. Financial support from foundations would be severely limited."[13]

The greatest concern has been at Southern Seminary in recent months. A confrontation and serious accreditation problems may now have been averted by recent trustee, administrative and faculty action.

Between December, 1990 and March 23, 1991, the seven-member Trustee Special Committee for Trustee-Faculty Relations and seven members of the Faculty Ad Hoc Committee met four times with President Honeycutt to study trustee actions of 1990, including the use of the Peace Committee statement on

Scripture as a guideline for granting faculty promotions and tenure. On the final day when the trustees were packed to return home President Honeycutt asked to meet with the committees separately one more time. Under Honeycutt's mediation, they reached an agreement. Larry Adams, Trustee Vice Chairman, gives Honeycutt the full credit: "We could never have done it without the president. He was the key figure."[13A]

The faculty voted 38 to 5 with three abstentions to accept the document titled, "Covenant Renewal Between Trustees, Faculty and Administration" of the Seminary. Honeycutt then mailed copies to all board members to study in preparation for their April 8, 9 meeting. In an accompanying letter, Honeycutt called the document "a dramatic step forward for Southern Seminary and the Southern Baptist Convention."[13B]

The "Covenant" encompasses six Articles:

1. GOVERNANCE: "As Trustees, Administration and Faculty we commit ourselves to a system of Seminary governance" in which "trustees make policy, the President serves as chief executive and academic officer and the Faculty fulfill "the implementing/teaching role."

2. COOPERATION: "We affirm our covenant obligation to cooperate with one another . . . in preserving the Christian heritage of Southern Seminary and in translating that heritage into an inclusive ministry to all Southern Baptists in a period of transition in denominational leadership and theological interpretation within the [SBC]. . . . Trustees, Administration and Faculty pledge respect for the convictions of all Southern Baptists and our intention to be sensitive to conservative viewpoints within the [SBC]."

3. INTENTION: "We . . . promise to continue our covenantal commitment to the Abstract of Principles as the confessional guideline for all teaching within the Seminary. As Trustees, we affirm the proper exercise of academic freedom and scholarship balanced with appropriate Faculty accountability and responsibility. Administration and Faculty affirm our common responsibility to implement Trustee policy by making specific educational decisions through established processes regarding the curriculum and the conduct of teaching within the classroom."

4. FACULTY SELECTION: "We pledge . . . fairness in selecting faculty across the theological spectrum of our Baptist constituency. In our effort to achieve a balanced representation through intentional employment of conservative evangelical scholars for future openings within the Faculty, we will seek new Faculty members who reflect a clear evangelical orientation in their view of the inspiration and authority of the Holy Scripture as clarified by [the] statement on Scripture" which follows.

The source reference indicates that the statement was drawn from the writings of Boyce, Manly, Broadus and Mullins. Salient points include:

* "Through the superintending influence of the Holy Spirit on the writers of Holy Scripture, the accounts and interpretations of God's revelation have been recorded as God intended so that the Bible is actually the written Word of God."

* "This work of the Spirit is plenary and totally trustworthy."

* "Having been given by inspiration, the Scripture is true and reliable in all the matters it addresses. Whatever the subject matter, Scripture is free from all falsehood, fraud, or deceit."

* "Ultimately, the Bible is to be interpreted in light of the centrality of Jesus Christ, who affirmed the complete veracity of the Bible and lived His life in fulfillment of Holy Scripture."

* The "acts of special revelation have been by God's prophets and apostles and under the providential hand of God, inspired persons have gathered them together to form the canon of Holy Scripture."

* "The Bible is the ultimate standard of authority for God's people, transcending temporal and cultural contexts."

The covenant further called for filling Faculty vacancies with persons who "will teach in accordance with and not contrary to the Abstract of Principles; affirm their experience of the spiritual rebirth through faith in Jesus Christ and demonstrate their active discipleship in a local congregation; understand and are committed to the distinctive doctrines of our Baptist heritage; embody the highest qualities of Christian character and church-related ministries; [commit themselves] to winning the lost and [advocating] the missionary imperative...; affirm the covenantal relationship between Southern Seminary and the [SBC] and its cooperating churches."

ACCOUNTABILITY: "Trustees are accountable to the [SBC], the President is accountable to the Trustees and the Seminary Faculty and Staff are accountable to the President.... Trustees covenant to function in accordance with and not contrary to seminary policies. ... Faculty covenants to function with acknowledged accountability for our actions.... We recognize that while freedom must ultimately be realized through the spirit and loyalties of persons, it must take form and be protected through regulations governing institutional practice."

AMENDMENT: "We acknowledge the right of Trustees to adopt formal policies and to amend seminary documents such as the Charter and By-laws and the Faculty Staff Manual; yet, any amendment of matters specifically addressed in this Covenant Renewal without concurrence of the Administration and Faculty nullifies its covenantal nature."[14]

The Trustee Special Committee, which worked with the Administration and Faculty in drawing up the proposed covenant, included both moderates and conservatives. It applies to the hiring of conservative evangelical scholars until a "balanced representation" is reached. Beyond that the covenant calls for "fairness in selecting faculty across the theological spectrum of our Baptist constituency," meaning that theological moderates could then be proposed to the trustees for hiring.

The "Covenant Renewal Document" was discussed for three hours on April 8. "Fourteen or 15 wanted to amend the document," says Vice Chairman Larry Adams. "We pointed out that the faculty could not amend it and the trustees had to vote it up or down."[15] The agreement was then accepted 49-7. "We had to do it," says trustee Gerald Primm. "It was this or see the struggle renewed."[16]

The mood on campus changed after it became known that the trustees had accepted the agreement and that President Honeycutt was "behind it one hundred percent." Trustees, faculty and students chatted cordially at an open-air luncheon.

The agreement, Adams says, covers seminary hirings until parity between "conservative scholars and others a little left of center is achieved. That will be several years from now. In the meantime, it will take us off the hook with the accrediting agency because it is a joint agreement. We've learned a lot from Southeastern Seminary and don't want to have the same problems here."

Adams calls the document "pretty much an inerrancy statement without using the term 'inerrancy.'" The statement on the Bible is "almost verbatim with the Chicago Statement on Inerrancy. Some conservatives are saying that it's much stronger than the Peace Committee statement [on Scripture]." Adams predicts that it will "be used widely throughout the SBC. Al Mohler, the Georgia editor, says it is 'an historic document,' and I agree."[17]

Back to the Boards

Let us now look at the big boards. Home Mission Board trustees and employed leadership are moving in the main stream of the resurgence. Baptisms, new churches, new missions, mission volunteers, chaplains and Annie Armstrong gifts all show increases. HMB president Larry Lewis notes that "Southern Baptists baptized 385,031 new believers" in 1990, "the largest increase in a decade." On average, Lewis says, the 139 elected HMB staff each led 19 people to Christ last year, a total of 1,000 more than was reported by the staff in 1989.[18]

Dissatisfaction with the HMB by moderates has abated to a considerable degree. Four of the top twelve contributing churches — 2,000 members or more — to the Board's last Annie Armstrong

Offering are viewed as moderates, five lean to the conservative side
and three can best be described as centrist.

The Picture at the Foriegn Mission Board

Funding for the Foreign Mission Board picture is less bright.
President Keith Parks prefers the Cooperative Program, but
understands why moderates set up an alternate funding
mechanism. For this and other reasons, Parks is highly respected
by moderates. Yet late returns from the Christmas, 1990 Lottie
Moon Christmas offering show a 1.4 percent downturn from 1990,
marking the first time in 53 years that the mission offering has
failed to surpass the previous year.

FMB trustees have amended their charter and bylaws to
eliminate by attrition the 12 "local" Virginia trustees. The board's
executive committee is studying the possibility of relocation from
Richmond. Virginia is to the left of other states along the
denominational spectrum. Both actions have made moderates
nervous.

The endorsement of Dan Vestal for president by 304 retired
foreign missionaries raised concern among conservatives that the
FMB family was not fully informed on issues in the controversy. A
report in SBC Today, in which Editor Jack Harwell quoted from a
letter from a missionary, did not lessen this concern. "Our
mission," the anonymous missionary wrote, "does not, as of this
date, have a single fundamentalist member. We are all, at least
politically, what the group which has taken over our convention
would call moderates. . . . I do not see how fundamentalists can go
on supporting indefinitely the large majority of 'moderate'
missionaries. Sooner or later the inquisition will reach us, probably
as soon as they feel they can safely get rid of Keith Parks. What
will we do then?

"Some will do what they have already done — compromise.
Some more recent appointees have said they have simply lied. They
have used words the fundamentalists wanted to hear and by which
they, themselves, meant something different, in order to follow
what they understood to be God's call. For example, one told me,
'Sure, I said God's word is infallible. But for me, God's word is
Jesus'. . . .

"I and many of my fellow missionaries, hope we will hear more
about some alternative before it is too late. . . . Please keep us in
your prayers. But also keep us in your plans."[19]

Leadership at the Sunday School Board is in transition. Some
speculate that the Search Committee for a new president may take
a year to complete their work. In the meantime, the Board operates
under a "lame duck" president.

A Look at the Annuity Board

Preachers sometimes say at conventions: "If the Convention splits, I'm going with the Annuity Board." The Annuity Board, with assets of almost $3 billion and growing at a rate exceeding $1 million a day, continues to be regarded as "neutral" by both sides in the controversy. Paul Powell, an opponent of the conservative movement and now also chairman of Baylor University trustees, was elected president of the Board in 1989.

J. Kirk Shrewsbury, Executive Director of Southern Baptists for Life, with the help of a few pro-life trustees, persuaded the Annuity Board to adopt pro-life policies. Then about the time the Board switched its insurance carrier to Prudential, broadcaster James Dobson announced that the company was giving money to Planned Parenthood. After a motion was offered in New Orleans calling for the Board to "exert positive pressure" on Prudential "to remove itself as a corporate sponsor of Planned Parenthood," the SBC Resolutions Committee drafted a resolution, which without naming the Annuity Board, called on all SBC entities and individuals "to carefully examine the charitable contributions of corporations they patronize."[20]

A bigger test of the Annuity Board could come if moderates organize into a new denomination and ask for continuance of their relationship with the Board. Presently, if an employee of a SBC entity takes a job outside the denomination, his participation is frozen.

A Survey of the Commissions

The SBC has seven agencies called "commissions." Three — American Baptist Seminary, Stewardship and Brotherhood commissions — have had easy sailing.

A motion at the New Orleans convention calling for a denominational accrediting agency for SBC colleges and seminaries was referred to the Education Commission. It was discussed, but no action taken. Baylor's Herbert Reynolds followed up with a letter to every college president warning that the idea could be destructive of Baptist education.

The Commission's <u>Southern Baptist Educator</u> ran a press release type story on the amending of Baylor's charter. The periodical quoted only Reynolds and Moore proclaiming the advantages.[21] In its published list of SBC colleges, the Commission makes no distinction between schools still controlled by their state conventions and those, such as Wake Forest, which have broken ties.

The Historical Commission was touched by the denominational controversy at the 1986 Atlanta convention when trustee chairman Marion Lark, after giving the Commission's report, said he "would not say that [the Bible] has scientific and historical facts where there is no diversity." Upset conservatives wanted to know if Lark "reflects the official position of the Historical Commission on the Bible?"[22] Lynn Mays, Executive Director-Treasurer of the Commission said Lark was speaking only for himself.

The Radio and Television Commission is on a more financially stable road with Jack Johnson, who succeeded the controversial Jimmy Allen as executive director. In January, 1991 the RTVC raised eyebrows when it announced the purchase of Jerry Falwell's FamilyNet cable network, with part of the purchase price to be paid by granting air time to Falwell. RTVC executive vice-president Dick McCartney said there was no board opposition to the arrangement, noting that the deal "gives us the potential for 10 to 12 million more viewers for less than the cost to get our present 10 million."[23]

Late Issues at the CLC

The high profile Christian Life Commission has experienced more conflict than all other commissions. CLC trustees approved in March, 1991 a charter change that would open the way for the SBC in June to merge the SBC Public Affairs Committee with the CLC. PAC trustees would complete their terms on the CLC's board, then their positions would be eliminated. Eleven CLC trustees would sit on the BJCPA board, where PAC members once served.

CLC Executive Director Richard Land has enjoyed generally good relations with his board. However, the March CLC meeting revealed differences on a constitutional amendment for school prayer which has been proposed in Congress. Land and CLC general counsel Michael Whitehead said that a Supreme Court ruling allowing "equal access" for student religious activities had eliminated the need for a school prayer amendment. A number of trustees disagreed, but the differences were more amicable than the headline over the story in one well-known Baptist paper indicated: "School-prayer Issue: Split Between CLC [and] Staff."[24]

The SBC passed a resolution in 1982, supporting a school prayer amendment which was opposed by the BJCPA's James Dunn. Some who support the legislation now in Congress want the SBC to pass a new school-prayer resolution at the June, 1991 convention.

The independent Southern Baptists for Life has worked for kindred interests with conservative trustees of the CLC. Having "accomplished . . . our major goals in Southern Baptist life," announced SBL executive director Kirk Shrewsbury, "we are closing our office in April [1991]."

SBL, under Shrewsbury's leadership, made numerous mass mailings, provided materials and channeled ideas on pro-life concerns to trustees on many agency boards. It was SBL, for example, that urged Sunday School Board trustees to push a reluctant BSSB administration to include a Sanctity of Life lesson in Sunday School quarterlies on the third Sunday of each January.

The Baptist Joint Committee for Public Affairs may be in for some hard financial times. To James Dunn's great disappointment, only three state conventions — Maryland/Delaware, Texas and Virginia — have come through with financial aid since the big slash in New Orleans. The BJCPA and the CLC are currently on opposite sides of a U.S. Justice Department petition requesting the Supreme Court to overturn lower court decisions holding that invocations and benedictions during public school commencement exercises in a Rhode Island school district violated the Establishment Clause of the First Amendment. The BJCPA supports the lower court rulings.

The CLC's position, according to spokesman Louis Moore, is that "such prayers are not unconstitutional because attendance at commencement is not required. If it was compulsory, then it would be a violation of the separation of church and state. We are concerned that the 'free exercise clause' of the First Amendment be upheld."[25]

Where Does the WMU Stand?

The WMU is listed under "Associated Organizations" in the SBC Annual. It was organized as an auxiliary to the SBC in 1883 by mission-concerned women who were not permitted to even speak on the floor of the SBC. The WMU's board is still not elected by the SBC, though the agency functions to promote mission endeavors at all levels of Baptist life.

In the minds of many conservatives, the WMU has in recent years identified too closely with moderates and with Women in Ministry, in particular. Former executive director Carolyn Weatherford Crumpler's runs for SBC office have not bettered WMU's image with conservatives.

In September, 1990 the WMU Executive Board invited Larry Lewis and Keith Parks to present their views on the so-called Atlanta funding plan of moderates. Afterwards the Board voted for the first time to speak out on the denominational controversy, affirming the CP and special mission offerings, while accepting the right of other Southern Baptists to choose other plans for cooperative giving.

In their statement, that, in effect, legitimatized the Atlanta Plan, the WMU leaders indicated no concern over theological problems which the Peace Committee discovered in its investigation of denominational institutions. The WMU Board virtually echoed the claims of moderates that the controversy was what was hurting missions, not a liberal drift.

The WMU is not likely to stop supporting the SBC Home and Foreign mission boards. However, the establishment of some kind of formal relationship with the Atlanta Fellowship could increase calls among conservatives for setting up an SBC women's missions organization, either apart from or in conjunction with the Brotherhood Commission. In the latter case, the name of the Brotherhood Commission would likely be changed.

Let us now give some attention to state conventions.

"Pioneer" conventions in the West, Northwest, East and Northeast have been much less touched by conflict than those in the old South for two reasons: (1) Pastors and church planters in mission territories, where there are fewer Southern Baptists, are more conservative in theology than comrades in the South. (2) Denominational leaders and editors in pioneer states tend to keep back or soften news which they think might unsettle churches in places where Southern Baptists are a small minority.

The situation in larger state conventions has been quite different, though it varies from state to state.

The Texas Scene

Baylor continues to be the top concern. The university must raise funds or increase tuition to make up for the almost $6 million frozen by the state convention for 1991. Opponents of the charter change are publishing an attractive paper, called The Baylor/BGCT Supporter, to counter the public relations blitz in favor of the charter change. The first issue quotes Lance Aldridge, a 1990 alumnus: "Throughout my years at Baylor, President Reynolds warned of a takeover of Baylor University. On September 21, President Reynolds took over. I went to Baylor because it was a unique Christian school. Now Baylor is losing that uniqueness."

March 22, the Baylor Board of Regents incorporated and elected trustees for the George W. Truett Theological Seminary. In doing so, Baylor Trustees re-elected at the 1991 BGCT convention, clearly disobeyed instructions of that convention.

President Reynolds said seminary operations could begin if Baylor regents determined the six SBC seminaries were "being led away from their historic mission by extremist elements. . . . If we put out a call to the faculties" of the six seminaries, "we would be overwhelmed by the applications of those poor people who have been under so much duress for so long." Reynolds didn't say where the money would come from to operate a new seminary. Jimmy Draper, chairman of the Southwestern Seminary board, called the incorporation move "totally unnecessary. I think we have an adequate seminary system and certainly don't think the kind of education they would give at Baylor would enhance the education system."[26]

In the meantime, the BGCT Executive Board demonstrated again that the majority were not aligned with the SBC conservative movement. The Board approved a resolution in support of Lloyd Elder and also voted to let state convention messengers determine the support they want to provide for the Baptist Joint Committee on Public Affairs. Since 1987 the BGCT Administrative Committee had been sending directly to the BJCPA the amount it would have received from Texas had its budget not been cut — $56,700 in 1990.[27]

The Baylor crisis is a common concern of Texas conservatives and many moderates. Differences continue on the operations of some SBC agencies. Conservatives continue to back the Cooperative Program. Twenty or so churches, among 4,236 churches in the state, have voted to divert funds or are considering diversion to the Atlanta Plan. These include South Main, Houston; FBC, Amarillo; FBC, Plano; FBC, Waco and four other churches in Waco; Broadway, Fort Worth; Park Cities, Dallas; FBC, San Angelo; Wilshire, Dallas; Trinity, San Antonio; FBC, Midland; and FBC, Richardson.

Oklahoma Takes Strong Stands

The 1990 state convention passed a strongly worded resolution supporting the Cooperative Program as the means of supporting missions and another calling for "necessary steps to be taken to ensure commitment to the historic relationship" between Oklahoma Baptist University and the state convention.

Among 1,491 churches, fewer than ten have voted to divert funds or are considering diversion. These include FBC, Norman, the leading CP contributor in the state; FBC, Muscogee; Northwest, Ardmore; Spring Creek, Oklahoma City; First, Ponca City; Main Street, Stigle; and FBC, Lawton.

Missouri Update

For several years the "show-me" state has had a strong conservative grassroots, with three out of the four state colleges among the most conservative in the SBC, supportive of an elected and employed state convention leadership with moderate leanings. Conservatives showed unexpected muscle at the 1990 convention, held in Kansas City — moderate territory. They defeated an effort to fund the BJCPA, forced postponement of action on a motion that would allow dual alignment of churches, raised a fuss about convention funding to Americans United, questioned Word & Way expenditures to Associated Baptist Press and provided enough votes to expand and make more inclusive a committee to "study the matter of handling designated monies."[28] State Executive

Director Don Wideman was already on record as "not encourag[ing] designations."[29]

Dick Wakefield, the winning presidential candidate, called himself "conservative in my theology," though "I've never felt myself in anybody's camp."[30] His opponent, Gerald Davidson — elected first vice president, "unapologetically identif[ied]" himself "as a conservative when it comes to the inerrancy of the Bible. I do not want to employ someone to teach . . . who believes that . . . the first 11 chapters of Genesis are a myth."[31]

Executive Director Don Wideman "anticipate[s] that very few churches in Missouri will choose to designate."[32] Fewer than 20 Missouri churches — most are in the Kansas City area — have voted to divert funds or are considering diversion. Among these are Kirkwood in the St. Louis area; Broadway, Kansas City; Second, Liberty; and Little Bonne Femme, Ashland.

Stirrings in Arkansas

After a raucous 1989, this state with strong conservative leadership was ready to settle down in 1990 when an unofficial group of 56 moderates from some 20 churches set up a committee to recommend responses to "recent tragic events" in the SBC. "No one suggested that we withhold funds," said Emil Williams, moderator of the group. "Everyone felt that there should be some redirecting of funds."[33]

Lakeshore Drive in Little Rock is the only church known to have voted to divert funds to the Atlanta Fellowship's program. Their association unanimously passed a resolution asking the church to reconsider.

Louisiana: A $200,000 "Parachute"

At the 1990 convention conservatives won all offices, except first vice president and approved the strongest pro-life resolution in the history of the convention.

Messengers clashed over an employment contract offered Lynn Clayton, the editor of the Baptist Message and an effort by Louisiana College President Robert Lynn to effectively remove the school from convention control.

The contract given by the Baptist Message board gave Clayton more independence from trustees and specified that "under no circumstances shall his salary be reduced" and that should he be fired, he would receive in damages three times his annual salary and benefits, a total of $200,000.

The proposed charter change called for, among other things, deletion of the statement under legal powers, ". . . consistent with the constitution, bylaws and business and financial plan of the Louisiana Baptist Convention." Opponents said this would open the door for the school to "operate without regard for the constitution and bylaws" of the convention.[34]

Opposition to both proposals mushroomed rapidly. Clayton and the paper's trustees agreed to restudy their contract and receive input from Louisiana Baptists. President Lynn postponed consideration of the charter revision for a year, to allow more time for discussion.

One church, St. Charles Avenue in New Orleans, has affiliated with American Baptists. One or two other churches could divert funds to the Atlanta alternate plan.

Moderates Are Weak in Mississippi

The fall, 1990 convention stayed relatively free of controversy. Few churches are interested in the Atlanta Plan. Northminister Church in Jackson, is known to receive into membership persons who have been sprinkled so long as they affirm that Jesus is Lord. The moderator of the local association has "admonished" all member churches to "discontinue this practice . . . " Northminister's pastor says there is a "possibility" the congregation will be dismissed from the association.[35]

Alabama: A Cooperative Program State

Charles Carter, outgoing president of the Alabama convention couldn't "conceive of" Baptist colleges in the state following the example set by Baylor and Furman. Carter saw "pockets of tension" among Alabama Baptists; the pockets hadn't "had cause to erupt," he said.[36]

Many conservatives worked hard for the election of Doug Sager as Carter's successor, but Rick Lance won with 54 percent of the vote. Lance called himself an "unaligned" person who "believe[s] in the fundamentals of the faith" and sees the Cooperative Program as the best way to support Baptist programs.[37] Bypassing the Cooperative Program "would most likely eliminate someone from being a mainline leader."[38] The convention passed a strongly worded resolution in support of the Cooperative Program as the "chief means" of missionary support.

Alabama editor Hudson Baggett called 1990 "a model convention" in which both presidential candidates pledged in advance to support whoever was elected.[39] A conservative pastor called it one "of the most beautifully managed (orchestrated?) conventions I've ever seen. . . . We went backward as far as election of trustee officers who might resist the secular drift" of colleges.[40]

In denominational loyalty, Alabama is much like Mississippi. Few churches have been talked seriously about diversion of funds.

Tennessee: Another Denominational State

The conservative presidential choice lost in the 1990 convention, but conservatives defeated an effort to put $28,000 into the convention budget for the BJCPA. A motion concerning the relationship of Tennessee colleges and other entities was referred to the executive board for study.

As go the SBC agencies in Nashville, so will go Tennessee. No more than six or eight at most of the 2808 churches are seriously interested in the Atlanta Plan. These include FBC, Jefferson City; Signal Mt., Signal Mt.; and Woodmont, Nashville.

A "Rooster Fight" in Kentucky

After the national convention in New Orleans, Kentucky moderates began talking about more autonomy for the state from the national body. In August they proposed that the state convention set up a funding mechanism where "any affiliated church . . . could provide direct or additional support to any national or international Baptist convention or agency included or not included in the [state] unified cooperative missions budget."[41] In contrast, Kentucky conservatives met to talk about increasing support for SBC causes. They also discussed possible candidates for the upcoming state convention.

Both sides bought newspaper ads and urged messenger attendance. Moderate backed candidates won the presidency, but a conservative was elected first vice president. Conservatives also blocked financial support of the BJCPA. Conservatives were unable to prevent creation of a special committee to study how the convention "receives and qualifies Cooperative Program gifts from the churches."[42]

Outgoing convention president Bill Messer said the situation reminded him of the time his grandfather planned to take roosters to a cockfight. Upon checking the coop, he found both birds with "bloody combs, missing feathers [and] exhausted from fighting." Messer said his grandfather eyed the birds and said, "You fools, didn't you know you were on the same team"?[43]

Conservatives, whom moderate Ken Chafin called "power-hungry preachers trying to control everything," haven't given up.[44] Conservative LaVern Butler denied that control was their motive. Moderates claimed to have been shut out of the SBC, Butler said, but Kentucky conservatives are suffering worse disenfranchisement on the state level. Butler noted that only four of 15 persons on a committee appointed to study the state's cooperative program were tuned in to the national conservative movement.[45]

A half dozen or so churches have voted to divert funds or are considering diversion. These include Crescent Hill, Deer Park and Buechel Park of Louisville.

Happenings in the Great Lake States

Illinois, Indiana, Ohio and Michigan all strongly support the Cooperative Program. No more than a half dozen churches are likely to opt for the Atlanta Plan. The fall Indiana convention adopted a resolution affirming the CP while expressing "profound disappointment in any attempts to decrease or withhold mission giving."[46] Seven or eight churches in Indiana have asked that none of their mission gifts go to support particular SBC entities.

Moderates Back in the "Saddle" in Georgia

Mercer University has been the focal point of controversy for several years. President Kirby Godsey is hanging on, despite campus demonstrations by students and professors calling for his ouster on grounds of financial and personnel mismanagement. Mercer's self-perpetuating board has sought to improve relationships with the state convention by approving an Advisory Committee to "enhance the communication between Mercer" and Georgia Baptists. Committee members are to be chosen by associations and approved by trustees who will remain in authority.[47]

At the November, 1990 convention, moderate Truett Gannon defeated conservative Bill Harrell by only 151 votes for president in what observers described as an amicable election. Gannon "desire[s] to see increasingly strong support for the Cooperative Program."[48] In another show of CP support, FBC, Atlanta led the state with $520,000.04 in CP gifts for 1990. Dunwoody BC, where Dan Vestal is pastor, gave $392,242.70. Dunwoody is considering diversion. Wieuca Road BC, formerly in the top 10 in CP giving, has voted to go with the alternate funding plan.[49] Several other churches in the Atlanta area could take the diversion route. A few churches are eying affiliations with another Baptist body.

Florida: Losing Control of Stetson

The relationship between the Florida convention and Stetson University has been rocky for years. At the November meeting, messengers first rejected a motion to cut all funding to Stetson immediately, then accepted a compromise that gives Stetson's trustees semi-autonomous status in exchange for cutting financial support from $950,000 in 1990 to zero in the year 2,000. The plan calls for the convention to participate in the nomination process for the three-fourths of trustees who must be Baptists.

The 1990 convention also refused to permit Patrick Anderson, an advocate of the alternate funding plan and a statewide director of Baptists Committed, to serve as a trustee of Florida Baptist Theological College.[50]

Were it not for Stetson, Florida could probably be counted as the most conservative state convention in the Old South.

South Carolina Responds to Furman Secession

Furman's secession from convention control brought out a record 5,050 messengers, more than twice the average attendance of any year since 1980. After heated discussion on the Furman action, the convention voted to escrow funds. A motion to take Furman to court was defeated. The convention also approved changing the name of Baptist College at Charleston to Charleston Southern University.

Conservatives kept the BJCPA out of the budget. The conservative candidate for president, W. Gregory Horton defeated Danny Gray by 2061 to 1928 votes. Conservatives also defeated a Task Force recommendation that would have permitted churches to designate out up to three SBC agencies and still receive credit for CP giving.

South Carolina is not North Carolina. Few churches — among them, FBC, Greenville — have diverted funds to the Atlanta Plan.

North Carolina: Conservatives Defeat a New Funding Plan

For many years the leadership of the Tar Heel state has been solidly in the moderate camp. A number of churches in the state are dually aligned with the ABC and SBC. Three white churches in Charlotte, expelled from the SBC Mecklenburg association because of baptism practices, have formed their own association. State editor R.G. Puckett and former Southeastern Seminary president Randall Lolley are notable opponents of the conservative movement. Hayes-Barton Church in Raleigh and FBC, Asheville stopped giving to the SBC Cooperative Program in 1988. After New Orleans, more churches began talking of dropping out. NC convention president Gene L. Watterson said, "The whole cooperative ministry" of the SBC "is unraveling." The SBC "as I have known it in my lifetime is dead," mourned L. Alan Sasser, pastor of Greystone Church in Raleigh. "For thousands of us, the 'fat lady' sang under the Superdome," declared Lolley.[51]

Perceiving a liberal drift beyond what was happening in other states, conservatives had been building strength during the 1980s. By 1990 they were ready to contest a proposed Cooperative Program change proposed by the state General Board, calling for gifts outside the state to be split between the traditional SBC channel and a designated budget which excluded some SBC agencies and included Associated Baptist Press and the BJCPA. The Conservative Carolina Baptist called this part of "a real and active movement to dismantle the historic form of the Cooperative Program. . . . Some conservatives," the paper said, "feel equally as repulsed by the idea of continuing to finance their state's current directions."[52]

With a record 6,500 messengers registered for the fall convention, conservative Mark Corts made a motion calling for all funds to be sent undesignated to the SBC, except that churches could exclude three recipients and still have their gifts counted as CP funds. Going up against the almost solid denominational establishment, Corts' motion passed by 122 votes. Conservatives did not contest the re-election of incumbent officers.

There will be a wide-open presidential election in 1991. The rumored candidates are conservative Billy Cline and moderate Randall Lolley. The Cooperative Program could come up for change again. Meredith College trustees have declared themselves a self-perpetuating body. Other college boards could follow. Chowan College president John Weems has said, "I will not sign a statement [of faith] or force my faculty and staff to sign a statement."[53] In a worst-case scenario, the convention could divide, with conservatives remaining loyal to the SBC and moderates linking up in some way with the Atlanta Fellowship, as a number of churches have already done.

Maryland/Delaware: Controlled By Moderates

This small convention, with only 281 churches, voted to allocate about $4,500 to the BJCPA. The allocation matches the amount of convention CP gifts that would have gone to the BJCPA during the year, had the SBC not voted to reduce the committee's funding. The conservative candidate for president, businesswoman Iris White, lost to moderate candidate Homer Carter.

Maryland/Delaware remains in the moderate camp, with an unknown number of churches interested in the Atlanta plan.

Dual Alignment in the District of Columbia

The DC convention is unique in that the 64 churches with 28,487 members are dually aligned with the SBC and American Baptists. Only 9,439 persons are enrolled in DC Sunday Schools. In 1989 the churches baptized 297 persons, one baptism for approximately every 95 members.

James A. Langley wears the "hats" of public relations, stewardship, promotion, editor of the Capital Baptist and executive director of the small convention. In a post-New Orleans editorial, Langley bemoaned the SBC's sharp funding reduction for the BJCPA and the Convention's movement from a "bond[ing in] missions and evangelism," to "creedalism." The decision of J. Frank Norris' church to "rejoin" the SBC, Langley said, "illumines" the denominational landscape "like banks of high-powered floodlamps light up a playing field."[54]

Question: If dissident SBC moderates form a new denomination, would some DC Convention churches become trilaterally aligned?

Division in Virginia

Virginia Baptists, in 1845, urged fellow Baptists to come to Augusta and "confer on the best means of promoting . . . . interests of the Baptist denomination in the South."[55] Virginia Baptists today are much more divided than in 1845. Moderates are stronger here than in any other state convention, but conservatives are a growing minority.

Virginia moderates tried and failed to have SBC bylaws changed so that members of the Committee of Committees would be chosen by state conventions. The state leadership finally decided to back a two-option plan for distribution of church gifts to the Cooperative Program. Under the plan, a church could choose to have its CP funds distributed according to the SBC budget formula voted on in the national convention, or do nothing and have its CP gifts allocated by the Virginia budget committee to selected SBC agencies and some non SBC causes, including the BJCPA and Associated Baptist Press.[56]

Conservatives lined up against the proposal. Kenneth Hemphill said it "may be a new approach but it is not the Cooperative Program." It would be "unfair," he said, to have a choice made for churches that do not decide to choose. Charles Fuller also opposed the plan, saying "the least we should do is to provide every Virginia Baptist congregation the privilege of making its own decision about what Cooperative Program budget it prefers to support, rather than presuming" that a "church's silence" would mean "consent."[57]

Conservative Howard Baldin said he could understand "those in Virginia who feel frustrated when they come home from a Southern Baptist Convention. I felt the same frustration at the Virginia state convention. Faithfully I have continued to support the Cooperative Program even when almost half a million dollars goes to the University of Richmond each year." Baldwin warned that "conservative churches in Virginia may even cut out the state completely and support only [SBC] causes. To every action there is a reaction."[58]

Conservatives passed out yellow stickers at the convention saying, "Save the CP." When the new plan was presented, Hemphill moved to make the Virginia Plan an option which a church could select with the option to reject the traditional formula. After much discussion the question was called. Conservatives understood that the vote to cut off debate applied only to the Hemphill motion and the question was approved overwhelmingly. Convention president Ray Spence then announced that the messengers had voted to stop debate and vote on the original budget proposal and that the convention would vote on that without chance for further amendment. Spence refused calls for a ballot vote and ordered a standing vote. He then ruled that the new plan had passed. Conservative T.C. Pinckney estimated that the margin of victory was about 60-40 percent in favor.

Virginia conservatives did not win a single vote. The "good news," according to Pinckney, is that "we had a much larger, more enthusiastic and more visible presence than in the last several years."[59]

Even with the new "Virginia plan" in place, a number of churches are considering the Atlanta funding plan. Grace Church in Richmond has gone further and deactivated its SBC affiliation to "become a member of the Southern Baptist Alliance and work within that organization to establish an inter-congregational relationship with other churches that feel they have been abandoned by the [SBC]."[60] The church has 570 members with Sunday School attendance reported to be around 100.

Virginia is in flux. The moderate majority could move further from the SBC. The conservative minority could send all their mission funds to the SBC Executive Committee, or even set up their own state structure.

Effects of the Conflict on Local Churches

It is impossible to chronicle what is going on in every one of the 37,785 SBC churches. Every congregation must at least be dimly aware of the denominational controversy. Many, though, still see it as a preacher fuss which they wish would stop. Pastors in Springfield, Missouri were asked how much the controversy had affected their churches. The great majority said, "Not at all."[61] The conflict has entered some churches, having a mix of conservatives and moderates and where the pastor or a leading layperson is promoting the Atlanta Plan.

Diversion of funds is more an issue in moderate-leaning churches than in other congregations, although a few conservative churches have chosen to negatively designate some or all their funds away from the state convention. Blue Valley Church in Stanley, KS and Immanuel Church of Wichita for example give separately to the Kansas Baptist Convention and the SBC Executive Committee. John Click, pastor of Immanuel, says his church was concerned about the proportion of funds being kept in the Kansas convention. Heartland Tabernacle of Belton, MO, until recently, bypassed the Missouri Baptist Convention because of doctrinal concerns with the state Executive Board over support of a missionary released by the FMB.[62]

Steps Toward Diversion

Moderate churches typically begin the diversion process by electing a Denominational Relations Committee to "study the current problems" in SBC institutions and their boards, "determine how to respond to the current SBC controversy" and "consider whether or not to use alternate funding of our Cooperative Program monies for dispensing to various denominational causes."[63]

The committee usually listens to taped sermons and reports of moderate messengers who attended the previous national convention and reviews printed materials from Baptists Committed, the Southern Baptist Alliance, SBC Today and denominational offices. The most popular study book is The Takeover in the Southern Baptist Convention, published by SBC Today. Some have used The Truth in Crisis series also. Committee members are urged to hear informative speakers coming to the church or area. Committee members of FBC, Muscogee, OK, for example, attended a conference, February 22 and 23, 1991 and heard a panel discuss, "What Does the Future Hold For Southern Baptists?" and Professor Leon McBeth speak on "Preserving Our Baptist Heritage." McBeth was identified by one program leader as "the author of the book on the 'History of the Sunday School Board' which the Sunday School [Board] trustees voted to have shredded last summer rather than allow people to read it. They did not like its truthfulness."

The committee then presents its findings and conclusions to the church. The committee at FBC, Richardson,Texas, reported: "Traditionally, Baptists have considered inerrancy to mean that God does not make mistakes and, therefore, His Word does not err. However, leaders of the ['fundamentalist'] movement made it clear that believing God's Word does not err, in and of itself, is not enough. Strings were attached in the form of additional requirements with interpretations added to the fundamentals of the faith."[64] The committee at Park Cities Church, Dallas, found that the Bible issue "has been used to create within the Convention fears which are in fact greatly unfounded and unwarranted, but useful to the fundamentalist movement" which has taken over the denomination and "exclude[d] all persons not openly committed to the movement." The committee recommended changes in the church's Cooperative Program budget of $550,000, to exclude the SBC Executive Committee, the Christian Life Commission, the Radio & TV Commission and Golden Gate and Southeastern seminaries.[65]

Differences in Diversion

If the majority so votes, some churches divert all their CP funds through the Atlanta Plan, while others send only a portion. Broadway Church, Fort Worth told members to check a box if they wanted their world mission money to through Atlanta. If they did not check the box, the money would go through the traditional Cooperative Program. Woodmont Church, Nashville divided their gifts according to the membership voting margin — 69 to 31 percent — in favor of the Atlanta Plan. Broadway Church, Kansas City, escrowed their CP money, $12,000, during the last quarter of 1990, then voted to release the funds to the Baptist Cooperative Missions Program and give their entire 1991 contribution of $40,000 directly to the BCMP.

The Fellowship Develops Further

The 70-member interim steering committee elected at the August, 1990 Consultation met in January and agreed that the name "The Baptist Fellowship" should continue to be used for the Atlanta group. They asked moderator Dan Vestal to appoint a task force to develop the legal framework for incorporation which attenders at the May, 1991 convocation will be asked to approve. Grady Cothen, president of BCMP reported that during the first quarter of operations — October-December 1990 — more than $258,000 had been received from 31 churches and nearly 100 individuals.[66]

A Proposed New Missions Center

The Fellowship steering committee met again in March and proposed a World Missions Center to serve as "a catalyst for cooperative missions' projects and ministry." The center would be a "think tank for world evangelization and strategic mission planning," and publish literature, sponsor conferences, crusades and mission partnerships, and be a center for "fostering renewal for missionaries, clergy and laity." Vestal reported the new funding plan had brought in about $1 million from 125 churches and a number of individuals to date. Vestal predicted that the Fellowship would receive $4 to $5 million during 1991.[67]

The committee invited the SBC WMU to participate with the missions center. WMU executive director Dellanna O'Brien didn't "know how to respond to this. We have had no contact with the Fellowship or with any individual" concerning the matter, she said. As to any possible WMU involvement, Mrs. O'Brien said it would have to be an "organizational decision."[68]

HMB Larry Lewis expressed profound disappointment with the Fellowship's proposed alternate missions center and said it would kindle additional distrust in the SBC. FMB president Keith Parks said the proposed missions center was the "inevitable result" of the SBC conflict, and "a calculated giant step away from mainstream Southern Baptists." SBC president Morris Chapman said it would be "in direct competition with the Southern Baptist Home and Foreign Mission Boards. . . The vast majority of Southern Baptists will lend no support to such a movement." Chapman also said he would be "extremely saddened" if the WMU ever considered "opening the door to participate with an organization such as The Baptist Fellowship." The Fellowship group, Chapman said, had not been "driven out" or "disenfranchised" in the SBC. They "are choosing to disassociate themselves from the majority of Southern Baptists."[69]

Name Confusion With Fundamental Baptist "Fellowships."

Two days after the committee's March meeting, James O. Combs, Editor of the Baptist Bible Fellowship's Baptist Bible Tribune wrote Vestal that he "was surprised to see that your moderate group within the [SBC] is selecting a name which . . . . seven or eight thousand independent Baptist churches in America . . . are now using . . . Are you fellows sure you want to use a name in which the public mind envisions an independent and fundamentalist stance? . . . People may get you confused with us. Do you really want this?"[70]

Baptists Committed to Disband; SBA Moves Closer to American Baptists

As plans further developed for the May 9-11 Convocation, SBC Today heard that Baptists Committed would officially disband as of June 1, if the Fellowship Convocation approves all the proposals being made by the interim steering committee.[71]

Meeting March 14-16 in Richmond, the Southern Baptist Alliance, voted to delete a constitutional provision dedicating the SBA to "the continuance of our ministry and mission within the [SBC]," and to "affirm cooperative ventures in ministry and missions" with American Baptists." However, the SBA voted to retain the word "Southern" in their name. Lynda Weaver-Williams of the group said, "We are no longer divided from our American Baptist brothers and sisters. . . . We have come to announce that the Civil War after all is over." Executive Director Stan Hastey said the SBA would continue as an organization and in cooperation with The Fellowship.[72]

Planning for the Convocation

The agenda of The Fellowship's Convocation, with John Hewett and Ken Chafin designated as chair and vice-chair respectively, was now set with talk that up to 10,000 could attend. Over 500 people were to be involved in a program following the theme, "Behold I Do a New Thing."[73]

A New Denomination Or Not?

The brochure promoting the upcoming Convocation quoted Dan Vestal: "Don't try to hold on to a past that will never return."[74] Fellowship leaders were constantly being asked, "Is this the beginning of a new denomination?"

Mercer University's Walter Shurden said The Fellowship was already functioning as a new denomination for some, but not for others. Cecil Sherman said that neither he nor his church had left the SBC "in the formal sense." Stan Hastey said the differences between The Fellowship and the current SBC leadership are "irreconcilable. The longer" we continue "battle in the SBC, the longer we will harm the SBC and also the cause of Christ. This is not something that can be talked out. There are some things worse than divorce." Daniel Vestal said The Fellowship was not yet a new denomination, but an "association and a fellowship of individuals, churches and institutions."[75]

"No one knows for sure," said SBC Today editor Jack Harwell, "but it is our opinion that out of the Fellowship convocation will come the basic structure for a new convention; that means a May visit could provide the chance to help make history."[76]

Secular publications anticipate division. U.S. News and World Report predicted in its 1991 New Year's outlook: "An official split in the nation's largest Protestant denomination could come as early as . . . spring . . . "[77]

What Kind of Denomination

If The Fellowship becomes a new denomination, what will it be like? Randall Lolley hopes that the new body would move "away from all creeds, confessions and statements . . . that would ensnare us."[78]

It will certainly be more diverse and allow greater doctrinal latitude in programs and publishing than the SBC, even the pre-1979 SBC. The new publishing house, Smyth & Helwys — not formally affiliated but closely associated with The Fellowship — announced in March publication of Apostasy: A Study in the

Epistle to the Hebrews and in Baptist History, by Dale Moody who was released from post-retirement teaching by Southern Seminary in 1986 because he did not believe in the eternal security of the believer. The March 22 SBC Today also carried an ad for its own publication, Clayton's Sullivan, Toward a Mature Faith: Does Biblical Inerrancy Make Sense? Sullivan says it does not. In another issue of SBC Today moderate David Reed commended the paper for carrying an ad for San Francisco Delores Street Baptist Church's support of lesbian and gay rights.[79]

A new denomination growing from The Fellowship will certainly be more in step with American Baptists and other mainline denominations. It will certainly involve more women in pastoral leadership. Broadway Church in Kansas City, with a pastoral team of four men and four women, is seeking to overcome "sexism." Paul Smith, the pastoral leader, uses "feminine names in my own worship privately and corporately to offset the male imagery so massively prevalent in our traditional hymns and liturgy. . . . At Broadway, we have refused to learn new hymns or contemporary worship songs that refer to God with masculine images or pronouns."[80] Other churches in The Fellowship would likely move in this direction.

The Homosexual Question

Mainline Episcopalians, United Methodists and Presbyterians are now debating the rightness of ordaining homosexuals. Mahan Siler, a former adjunct professor at Southeastern Seminary who does not condemn committed homosexual relationships, spoke at the March Convocation of the SBA. Question: Given the present gay scene in mainline denominations, how long would it be before The Fellowship begins debating homosexual ordination? Should this and other deviations from the present norm occur, how long could the right wing of the Fellowship typified by Baptists Committed and the left wing represented by the SBA — how long could they stay together? Could pastors with the theological convictions of Dan Vestal accept homosexual ordination?

Decline and Growth

A larger question is: Will The Fellowship ever attain a large membership, of say one million?

New Christian movements do tend to grow — at least for awhile — faster proportionally than older church bodies. However, the new denomination that split away from the Missouri Synod Lutherans did not. It subsequently merged with a larger and more liberal Lutheran body. Even the recent conservative offshoots off mainline denominations have not increased greatly in membership, although they have shown more vigor in missions and evangelism than their parent bodies.

Conservative or liberal, members who have family roots and life-long association with Southern Baptist churches and ministries, find it difficult to leave. First Presbyterian Church of Houston, a strong conservative congregation, voted 1,296 to 760 March 17 to remain in the Presbyterian Church U.S.A. and not affiliate with the conservative Evangelical Presbyterian Church. Hundreds, who voted in the minority, are expected to leave and establish their own congregation and affiliate with the smaller body.

Overall, conservative denominations and movements have grown, while church bodies entertaining greater theological diversity have declined. From 1965 to 1985, Presbyterians dropped 21%; Episcopals, 20%; United Methodists, 16%; Disciples of Christ, 42%. During this same period the Assemblies of God grew 116%; the Church of God, 147%; the Church of the Nazarene, 50%; and Southern Baptists, 34%.[81]

Anthony Campolo, a noted American (Northern) Baptist sociologist, who speaks often to both Southern and Northern Baptist groups, anticipates that a new alignment will affect Baptists both in the north and south. "There are significant numbers of American Baptist Churches in the North that would be much happier as Southern Baptist churches. There are churches all over the South that would be much happier as Northern Baptist churches."[82]

Whatever the future brings for SBC moderates by way of a new denomination or affiliation, it appears almost certain that some alternate structure and funding plan will remain in place for an indefinite time. However, The Fellowship's constitution includes a "sunset clause" which states that the constitution will expire at the conclusion of the General Assembly meeting in 1993 "unless reaffirmed by a majority vote of the members in attendance at the 1993 General Assembly." What then?

How many churches will the SBC lose to alternate funding and missions program and perhaps ultimately a new denomination? Paige Patterson thinks "not more than 500" will remove themselves "directly from Southern Baptist work. Another 200 or 300 may dually align? . . . . The Cooperative Program may be hurt by as much as ten percent or $14 million," though "I personally doubt that it will go that high. If it does, it will be momentary and, if the general economy rights itself somewhat, the Cooperative Program will also. If the Cooperative Program drops anywhere close to four or five percent, then I think . . . that conservative churches will begin giving around the state conventions and directly to the national convention."[83]

Of course, should the evangelistic and church planting goals set by the Home Mission Board be accomplished, then the losses of churches to a splinter group could be more than made up.

Looking Beyond the Sesquicentennial

The year 1995, marking the 150th year of the Southern Baptist Convention, will be soon be on us. The Convention will hold business sessions in Atlanta, then journey for a special sesquicentennial celebration in Augusta, where it was founded in 1845. The Forum and Women in Ministry have been invited to participate, but whether many from "The Fellowship" will join with SBC leaders on the occasion is yet to be known.

At the first convention, in 1845, William B. Johnson, the architect of the new structure, spoke both to the convention and the national body, from which it was separating. Johnson envisioned a field of service large enough for both bodies when he "hope[d] that our separation will be attended with no sharpness of contention, with no bitterness of spirit. We are all the servants of the same Master, 'desirous of doing the will of God from the heart.' Let us, then, in generous rivalry, 'provoke each other to love and good works.'"[84]

One hundred and forty-five years later, William Pinson spoke to the Baptist General Convention of Texas, divided over the action by Baylor University trustees. Pinson's words also apply to Baptists today and other Christians as well: "Remember, Satan is our enemy, not one another. Don't allow controversy to dominate. Let's stick to the main task the Lord has set before us. . . . Don't give up!"[85]

Stand for conviction, yes. Fulfill our stewardship, yes. Contend for the faith, yes. But let us do it all in love.

However we relate to one another in ministries and structures, may God help us to carry out entrusted priorities in the spirit of our Lord who said, "By this shall all men know that you are my disciples, if you have love one to another." (John 13:35, KJV.)

References

1 "LCMS Rules Against Preus," Christian News, March 18, 1991, pp. 1, 8.

1A Personal Interview, Wake Forest, NC, October, 1988.

2 Personal Interview, Wake Forest, NC, October, 1988.

3 "Southern Baptists and the Liberal Tradition," Baptist History and Heritage, July, 1984, pp. 16-19.

4 "Associated Baptist Press: An Urgent Need," Religious Herald, September 20, 1990, p. 4.

5 Tammi Ledbetter: "Coppenger Aims to Deliver Good News to People in the Pew," Indiana Baptist, April 9, 1991, p. 7. Ledbetter quoted Allen from his December 6, 1990 comments in the Baptist True Union.

6 "Hollinger Elected BP Vice President," Biblical Recorder, February 2, 1991, pp. 1, 10.

6A Ledbetter, op. cit.

7 "California Editor Elected Vice President for Baptist Press," Word & Way, January 31, 1991, p. 3.

8 "Picking Up the Challenge: Hollinger to Baptist Press," Baptist Reflector, January 30, 1991, p. 2.

9 Telephone Interview, March, 1991.

10 David R. Wilkinson: "Accrediting Team to Visit Southern Seminary," Religious Herald, February 4, 1991, pp. 3, 12.

11 Presnall Wood: "Accreditation," Baptist Standard, March 27, 1991.

12 R.G. Puckett: "Southeastern Trustees Deal With Accreditation," Religious Herald, March 21, 1991, p. 14.

13 Southwestern and Southeastern Trustees Hear Reports of Accrediting Alternatives," Indiana Baptist, March 26, 1991.

13A Telephone Interview with Adams, April 12, 1991.

13B Quoted from Honeycutt's letter, March 25, 1991.

14 Quoted from "Covenant Renewal Between Trustees, Faculty and Administration of the Southern Baptist Theological Seminary," March 25, 1991.

15 Telephone Interview, April 12, 1991. Trustee Wayne Allen had a heart attack after the meeting at Southern and was unavailable for comment.

16 Telephone Interview, April 12, 1991.

17 Telephone Interview with Adams, April 13, 1991.

18 Larry Lewis: "Annual Report to HMB Directors," March 13, 1991.

19 Jack U. Harwell: "Layman's Log," January 25, 1991, p. 7.

20 SBC Bulletin, June 14, 1990.

21 November, 1960, p. 7.

22 From a tape of the 1986 convention.

23 Toby Druin: "Bottom Line: Deal With Falwell More for Less," Baptist Standard, February 6, 1991, p. 3.

24 Word & Way, April 4, 1991, p. 17.

25 Telephone Interview, April 14, 1991.

26 Robert G. Wieland: "Baylor May Build Its Own Seminary," Tulsa World, March 29, 1991.

27 Toby Druin: "State Convention to Determine Amount in Annual Budget," Baptist Standard, March 20, 1991, p. 3.

28 "Messengers Vote to Expand Study Committee," Word & Way, November 1, 1990, p. 7.

29 "Wideman Pledges Ongoing Support for Cooperative Missions Program," September 13, 1990, p. 1.

30 Helen T. Gray: "Unity Pledged for Baptists," The Kansas City Star, October 25, 12990, p. C-5.

31 Pam Schaeffer: "Delicate Peace," St. Louis Post Dispatch, October 27, 1990,p. 6D.

32 "Wideman Pledges Ongoing Support for Cooperative Missions Program," op. cit.

33 "Arkansans Make Plans," Religious Herald, August 23, 1990.

34 Bill Ascol: "L.C. — Baylor Revisited," The Louisiana Baptist Trumpet, November 1, 1990, p. 2.

35 "Politics & Corridor Talk," SBC Today, March 22, 1991, p. 7.

36 Karen Estes Lowry: " 'You Can't Predict Baptists,' Says Carter," The Alabama Baptist, November 8, 1990, p. 1.

37 Karen Estes Lowry: "Lance: In Alabama, 'We Have a Family Agenda,'" Alabama Baptist, November 22, 1990, p. 3.

38 Garry Mitchell: "State Baptist President Supports Traditional Fund," Anniston Star, November 15, 1990, p. 17A.

39 The Alabama Baptist, November 22, 1990, p. 2.

40 Letter to Hefley, December 11, 1990.

41 Marv Knox: "Moderates Seek Greater Autonomy for KBC," Western Recorder, August 21, 1990, p. 1.

42 Annual Meetings, Word & Way, December 6, 1990, pp. 16, 17.

43 Bill Wolfe: "Kentucky Baptists May See More Fights Before Dust Settles," Louisville Courier-Journal, November 15, 1990.

44 Walnut Street Baptist Church Newsletter, November 27, 1990, p. 1.

45 Wolfe, op. cit.

46 "State Baptist Convention 1990," Word & Way, December 6, 1990, p. 16.

47 "William Neal: "Mercer Trustees Adopt Budget; Alter Committee," The Christian Index, April 26, 1990, pp1, 3.

48 Al Mohler Jr.: "Georgia Baptist Update," The Christian Index, October 11, 1990, p. 7.

49 James N. Griffith: "1990 Report of Receipts for Georgia Baptist Convention," The Christian Index, January 31, 1991, p. 12.

50 "Messengers Reinforce CP, Reject Alternative Plans," SBC Today, December 1, 1990, p. 1. "Stetson Seeks Less Money, More Autonomy," Word & Way, September 13, 1990, p. 13.

51 Erin Kelly: "Seeds of Rebellion Start to Sprout Among Moderate Baptists," Raleigh News and Observer, July 22, 1990, pp. 1, 9A.

52 "Editorials," September, 1990, p. 4.

53 Pam Kelley: "Baptist Colleges Squirming," Charlotte Observer, November 8, 1990.

54 "SBC Moves Further Into Exclusivism," September 19, 1990.

55 Robert A. Baker: The Southern Baptist Convention and Its People, 1607-1972, Broadman Press, Nashville, 1974, p. 159.

56 Letter to Pastors, October 26, 1990.

57 Letter to Pastors, November 6, 1990.

58 "Communicating Good News," Fall, 1990, p. 2.

59 Pinckney to Hefley, November 16, 1990.

60 Letter from the Committee, October 9, 1990.

61 Reported to me by Tom McClain, a pastor in Springfield.

23 Oikodomos, May 1, 1990, p. 5.

63 Quoted from instructions given to committees of FBC, Muscogee, OK and Park Cities Church, Dallas, TX.

64 Quoted from the Report, October 12, 1990.

65 Report to the church.

66 Stan Hastey: " 'Fellowship' to be Name of Group, Baptist Standard, January 30, 1991, p. 10.

67 " 'Baptist Fellowship' Leaders Endorse Formal Name," SBC Today, March 7, 1991, p. 6)

68 "Baptist Fellowship Leaders Solidify Organization," Word & Way, March 21, 1991, p. 3.

69 R. Albert Mohler Jr.: "Chapman: No One Being Forced Out," The Christian Index, March 7, 1991, p. 7.

70 Combs to Vestal, March 12, 1991.

71 "Baptists Committed Disbands?" March 22, 1991, p. 7.

72 Robert H. Dilday: "The End of the Civil War," Religious Herald, March 21, 1991, p. 8.

73 Jack U. Harwell: "The Fellowship Sets Agenda for Convocation," SBC Today, March 22, 1991, pp. 1, 3.

74 Quoted from the Brochure.

75 Reported by R. Albert Mohler Jr.: "Where Is The Fellowship Going?" The Christian Index, March 28, 1991, p. 6.

76 "When Do You Plan to Go to Atlanta?" SBC Today, March 8, 1991, p. 6.

77 Jeffrey L. Sheler: "A Rift Over the Book," December 31, 1990/January 7, 1991, p. 64.

78 R. Albert Mohler Jr.: "Where Is The Fellowship Going?" The Christian Index, March 28, 1991, p. 6.

79 "Advertisement Lauded," SBC Today, March 8, 1991, p. 11.

80 "The Most Sexist Hour," SBC Today, February 8, 1991, p. 10.

81 Les Parrott III and Robin D. Perrin: "The New Denominations," Christianity Today, March 11, 1991, pp. 29-33.

82 "Campolo Predicts New Alignments," <u>Word & Way</u>, November 15, 1990, p. 13.

83 Patterson to Hefley, November 20, 1990.

84 Quoted from Robert A. Baker: <u>The Southern Baptist Convention and Its People, 1607-1972</u>, Broadman Press, Nashville, p. 165.

85 From my tape of Pinson's address.

A Brief History

The Truth in Crisis

I am a "credentialed" Southern Baptist and a former pastor who became a religion writer of some repute. In 1985 I was serving as writer-in-residence at Hannibal-LaGrange College when Dr. Larry Lewis, then president of the college, called me into his office. "You've covered the Southern Baptist Convention for Christianity Today for several years," he noted. "You know more about our controversy than any other reporter I know. Why not write a little booklet to help us all better understand the issues in our denominational controversy." Larry never went beyond this. He never suggested that I take any particular angle. "Just write as you've seen it happen," he said.

Soon after I began work, it became obvious that the story called for a book where the theological, ecclesiastical and political issues and happenings could be adequately presented and documented.

I queried several publisher friends. One said, "I lived through the theological controversy in the old Northern Baptist Convention. Never again." Another said his company could "not afford to get involved in a fuss in a denomination as big as the Southern Baptist Convention. No matter what you wrote, we'd lose business." Another said, "I'll send you a contract." He later wrote his regret that the book had "been vetoed by the people upstairs. They're scared of it."

Russell Kaemmerling, the former editor of the Southern Baptist Advocate, then offered to publish the book under his imprint, Criterion Publications. Russell, as I learned later, happens to be the brother-in-law of Paige Patterson.

I feared that the book would be regarded as following the conservative party line. It was only after a good deal of discussion that I signed a royalty contract with the stipulation that I would write a report, not an interpretative history, and that I would have editorial control over all the contents.

Russell honored this agreement in every respect.

Volume 1 of The Truth in Crisis—the title came from Russell—was ignored by the press until Baptist Sunday School Board (BSSB) executives declined to sell it in the 1986 Atlanta convention book store. They expressed fear that the book might add to the disharmony in that convention. But it could be sold by Baptist book stores away from the convention, they said.

Russell, who had purchased large ads in several Baptist papers, was infuriated. I pled with Board officials to rescind the action, arguing that the exclusion of the book would result in even greater disharmony.

The media now jumped into the fray. The satirical SBC Enquirer announced "a public burning of The Truth in Crisis" during the time of the Sunday School Board report at the convention. Baptist Press director W.C. Fields denied me permission to hold a news conference in the press room, though he did finally agree to post an announcement of the conference that was held in a downtown hotel. The conference was well attended by secular media, including the religion editor of Time. The "banning" of The Truth in Crisis became one of the hottest topics at that convention.

Russell arranged for me to present a copy of the book to SBC president Charles Stanley at Sunday services in First Baptist Church, Atlanta just before the convention. After the services, books were sold under a tent on the church parking lot. More books were sold at Nelson Price's Roswell Street Baptist Church in Marietta, GA, and at Richard Lee's Rehoboth Baptist Church in Atlanta. Nelson, then president of the SBC Pastors Conference, also permitted me to "present" the book to Morris Chapman, the newly elected president of the PC, before 25,000 pastors.

When the convention book store opened, I assured the store managers that I held no hard feelings for the corporate decision not to sell the book there. Then I purchased a Baptist Book Store cap for $4.95. A customer stopped me going out of the store, thinking I was a clerk. "No," I said, "this cap is just to show I love the Baptist Book Stores."

The book became an issue at the August meeting of BSSB trustees in Nashville, where conservative trustees were seething over former Board president James Sullivan's characterization of conservatives in the Board's newsletter, as "Pharisaical legalists, extreme literalists, snake handlers, "and members of this extreme rightist group." ("James L. Sullivan Addresses Question of SBC Turbulence," Facts and Trends, July-August, 1986, pp. 10, 11.)

Trustee Joe Knott moved that BSSB president Lloyd Elder apologize in the newsletter for Sullivan's diatribe and to send copies of The Truth in Crisis to the 57,000 church staff members on the newsletter's mailing list. The motion was tabled by a vote of 40 to 33.

Russell encouraged me to begin work on Volume 2 and I did. Then in February he called to say he could not afford to print this second book. It was then that I learned that he had been operating on the proverbial shoe string and that three laymen had each invested $5,000 to insure the publication of Volume 1.

Without knowing how Volume 2 would be published, I went ahead with a planned research trip to Houston. A pastor friend there arranged for me to stay with one of his deacons.

The deacon, an attorney, asked how Volume 2 was coming along. "The publisher doesn't have the money to print and I don't either," I replied.

"The book needs to be published. What if I lend you the money and you publish the book yourself?"

"I don't know if we could sell it."

"You pay me only if you sell enough books to do so."

After returning home and talking to my wife, I agreed to the deal.

A $12,000 loan from this layman and his father paid for typesetting, cover art, a 5,000-copy printing of Volume 2 under our imprint of HANNIBAL BOOKS and the purchase of 1900 copies of Volume 1 which friend Russell had in stock. Russell also gave me a computer printout of the names and addresses of people who had bought books from Criterion by mail. I stored the books in our garage and used a back bedroom as the editorial and sales office.

We sold enough books to pay the loan in full with enough left over to finance the publication of Volume 3 in 1988. This was followed by Volume 4 in 1989 and Volume 5 in 1990. Along the way I was accused by a few people of making a profit on the SBC controversy. As a matter of record, I earned $6,000 in royalties from Volume 1 and another $6,000 in profit from Volume 2 and none from the last three volumes. From this I paid all my research and travel expenses.

In 1988, Marti and I published under our Hannibal Books' imprint, Where is God When a Child Suffers? by Penny Giesbrecht. We have since published several inspirational books by other authors, none of which are related to the Southern Baptist controversy. The most recent is Bernard Williams' The Rhyming Gospels. Lord willing, we are now in the publishing business for keeps.

I continue to serve as writer-in-residence at the college. The Conservative Resurgence in the Southern Baptist Convention is the wrap-up book, my "swan song," if you please, on the SBC controversy. Writing and publishing these books has, frankly, resulted in a tremendous drain on my time and energy and our household finances. If Marti had not been employed, the books could not have been published.

I seek no denominational office, although I have turned down three offers. Marti is serving her second year as a director of the Home Mission Board. Our hearts are in missions and ministry, not controversy. The greatest thrill this week came in leading a new employee to Christ.

My burden in writing The Truth in Crisis has been to inform, not pontificate on solutions to the crisis. My desire is to provide information that will enable the reader to understand all sides in every situation before forming an opinion. Although I am unashamedly a conservative in theology, I hold no ill will toward anyone in the denomination.

Some readers may think I have intruded too far into the inner sanctums of agency workings. My answer is that the agencies belong to all of us who are "citizens" of the Southern Baptist Convention. We have a right to know what our elected officers and their appointed staff and teachers are doing with the stewardship entrusted to them. Hang me if you will for inserting the conviction that many of the problems in the SBC, and in other fellowships too, come when denominational executives get "too big for their britches," conservative or liberal theology notwithstanding.

Enough. If you have corrections, questions, or comments, you may write me at 921 Center Street, Hannibal, MO, 63401. My telephone and fax number is 314-221-2462.

Finally, some appreciations:

To Marti, my loving, loyal and longsuffering wife of 38 years, for enduring through this final book. Marti is a member of the board of directors of the Home Mission Board. She keeps saying, "Tell more good things that are happening. Like the over 1,200 confessions of faith that were recorded by our 190-plus SBC chaplains in Saudi Arabia during the conflict with Iraq."

To Cyndi Allison, our oldest daughter, for designing the cover and the layout and doing the typesetting for this book.

To Dan Martin and Marv Knox and other denominational writers for their reports which appeared in BP and state papers.

To Dr. Lewis Drummond for writing the forward.

To the many, many who sent me a variety of news clips, tapes and documentation of important behind-the-scenes happenings.

To those who granted time for personal interviews.

To Dr. Lynn Mays and his staff at the Historical Commission Library in Nashville for all their help.

To my Lord and Savior, Jesus Christ, who called me into the ministry of journalism. I pray that this imperfect report of difficulties among God's people will in some way honor His name.

Finally, I join thousands of Southern Baptists in praying for an end to the controversy, so that all of us can give greater attention to our primary tasks.

Index

C

D

R

W

Y

Z

Please send me:

The Truth in Crisis

Volume 1, 1986   _____Copies at $7.95 = _____

Volume 2, 1987   _____Copies at $7.95 = _____

Volume 3, 1988   _____Copies at $7.95 = _____

Volume 4, 1989   _____Copies at $8.95 = _____

Volume 5, 1990   _____Copies at $8.95 = _____

Volume 6, 1991   _____Copies at $9.95 = _____

Guilty Until Proven Innocent by Keith Barnhart with Lila Shelburne. Dramatic true story of the prosecution of an innocent pastor charged with sexual child abuse. A must book for all who work with children.

   _____Copies at $9.95 = _____

Arabs, Christians & Jews, by James & Marti Hefley, for all who long for peace in the land where Judaism, Christianity and Islam were born.

   _____Copies at $10.95 = _____

Where Is God When a Child Suffers? by Penny Giesbrecht. How a Christian family copes with their child's pain in the light of God's love.

   _____Copies at $8.95 = _____

The Greatest Book Ever Written by Dr. Rochunga Pudaite with James C. Hefley, Ph.D. Praised by evangelical leaders as an outstanding apologetic on the Bible.

   _____Copies at $9.95 = _____

We Can Change America ... and Here's How by Darylann Whitemarsh. How to make things happen in the public arena. Especially helpful for pro-lifers to use in coming battles to save the unborn.

   _____Copies at $9.95 = _____

Please add $2.00 postage and handling for first book, plus .50 for each additional book.

MO residents add sales tax

TOTAL ENCLOSED (Check or money order) _____

Name _____

Address _____

City _____ State ___ Zip_____ Phone _____

MAIL TO HANNIBAL BOOKS, 921 Center, Hannibal, MO 63401. Satisfaction guaranteed. Call 314-221-2462 for quantity prices.

.